MAKING WORLDS

Making Worlds

*Affect and Collectivity in Contemporary
European Cinema*

Claudia Breger

Columbia University Press   New York

Columbia University Press
Publishers Since 1893
New York   Chichester, West Sussex
cup.columbia.edu
Copyright © 2020 Columbia University Press
All rights reserved

Library of Congress Cataloging-in-Publication Data
Names: Breger, Claudia, author.
Title: Making worlds : affect and collectivity in contemporary
    European cinema / Claudia Breger.
Description: New York : Columbia University Press, 2020. |
    Includes bibliographical references and index.
Identifiers: LCCN 2019035717 | ISBN 9780231194181 (cloth) |
    ISBN 9780231194198 (pbk.) | ISBN 9780231550697 (ebook)
Subjects: LCSH: Motion pictures—Social aspects—Europe—History—21st century. |
    Motion pictures—Political aspects—Europe—History—21st century.
Classification: LCC PN1995.9.P6 B74 2020 | DDC 791.43/658—dc23
LC record available at https://lccn.loc.gov/2019035717

Columbia University Press books are printed on
    permanent and durable acid-free paper.
Printed in the United States of America

Cover design by Julia Kushnirsky
Cover image: *Le Havre* (2011, Aki Kaurismäki),
    Photo Marja-Leena Hukkanen, c. Sputnik Oy.

Contents

MAKING WORLDS

Introduction

COLLECTIVE CLOSURES—CINEMATIC OPENINGS

On February 18, 2016, less than half a year after German chancellor Angela Merkel temporarily opened the country's borders to incoming refugees, a crowd of about one hundred protesters blocked a bus with recent arrivals on the way to their arranged accommodation in Clausnitz, Saxony, a small town in eastern Germany. For more than two hours, the crowd threatened and insulted the passengers, and in the end, when some of them were too frightened to exit the bus, the local police violently dragged them into the building where they were staying. The incident generated widespread shock and outrage after a brief video circulated through social media. Shot from within the group of protesters and apparently first posted on a Facebook page dedicated to the "defense" of a nearby town from immigration, the video documents the protesters' threatening hand gestures in the direction of the bus and their repeated shouting of the slogan "Wir sind das Volk" (We are the people).[1] In the German context, this slogan had been coined in progressive nineteenth-century literature leading up to the 1848 revolutions; more recently, it became associated with the Monday demonstrations that called for democratic reforms in East Germany and led to the fall of the Berlin Wall in 1989. Critics of the subsequent quick process of national unification—not initially a goal of most of the political activists—described a disturbing change in popular sentiment reflected in the increasing replacement of this slogan, "We are the people," with the nationalist "We are one people" during the winter of 1989–1990. In the 2016 Clausnitz incident, however, it is the first slogan, with its illustrious revolutionary history, that resurfaces, affectively charged with anger and hate, to assert a collective identity as anti-immigrant threat.[2]

Arguably, this local event is indicative of our larger, transnational cultural moment. Fueled by the precarity effects of neoliberal globalization, climate change, and contemporary wars, aggressive, openly hateful assertions of national, ethnic, and religious identities have increased across Europe, the United States, and many other parts of the world during the first two decades of the twenty-first century. I use the notion of *collective closures* as a general term for the political phenomena of bodily, verbal, legal, and material gestures that close discursive as well as physical borders and for the pretense at resolution they provide. The imbrication of such gestures of closure with negative affect clearly has a long history, including antiblack, anti-Semitic, anti-Slavic, and anti-immigrant racisms throughout the eras of colonialism, slavery, European nationalism, and fascism and their aftermath. The recent surges of political hate cannot be disentangled from these histories, warranting questions as to whether the current, unabashedly negative intensities in the public sphere confront us with feelings newly produced by globalization, digital media, and neoliberalism or whether they indicate the return of Euro-American modernity's repressed legacies of political hatred and violence. Yet however immense the weight of this past, if we want to imagine change, a closer look at historical shifts in articulations of political affect is crucial.[3] In this spirit, I begin by underscoring how the new mainstream presence of white supremacy, religious radicalism, aggressive nationalism, and Islamophobia in the age of ISIS, Viktor Orbán, Donald Trump, and the right-wing "Alternative for Germany" has been reshaping public spheres with intense charges of negativity: the new "normal" of European and North American political life feels and is different from that of the 1990s (or even the Obama years in the United States).[4]

In the scholarly realm, these shifts in political affect have been accompanied by renewed conversations on how to counter exclusion and hate with more positive notions of collective belonging on different scales, from the neighborhood or activist movement to the planet. Many of these conversations emerged from debates in the 1990s on multiculturalism, postmodernism, postcolonialism, and globalization. Since the 2000s, however, there has been an increasing focus on overcoming modernist and postmodernist conceptualizations that emphasize the violent dimensions of collectivity and the analytic primacy of difference over identity. Scholars have shown less agreement on *how* to rethink collectivity in more affirmative terms. Some have proposed a deliberate return to humanist conceptualizations of universalism and cosmopolitanism but have triggered controversy because these concepts are tainted by their entanglement with historical structures of domination and imperialism.[5] Competing posthumanist accounts have foregrounded the quintessentially collective nature of life and championed the political promise of renouncing human claims to rational organization. However, these contributions have provoked concerns about ethical orientation and political accountability within such a framework.[6] Humanist and posthumanist accounts alike have foregrounded the affective dimensions of collectivity, including the sense and sensations of belonging as an alternative to the critical framework of identity. These foci on, for example, joy, sympathy, and attachment along with hate and anger indicate how thoroughly the "affective turn" has shaped twenty-first-century investigations of collectivity.[7] Yet some scholars and public intellectuals have recently turned their backs on affect in response to the many political victories of populist and fascist parties and movements.[8] Returning to more traditional concepts of collective governance, these scholars have urged us to "think beyond the affect" or deploy "rational/sensible critique" against "impulsive feelings."[9] But this won't do: the negative intensities haunting contemporary public spheres will not be conquered by appeals to reason alone. Instead, the messy entanglements of affect and collectivity need to be addressed—and worked through—as such. The present book zooms in on these entanglements: the affective components of nationalism and racism as well as alternative identities and claims to belonging.

Just a few weeks before the Clausnitz incident, Firas Alshater, a Syrian actor, filmmaker, and activist who was granted political asylum in Germany in 2013, achieved instant celebrity with a short YouTube video entitled *Who Are Those Germans?* that went viral in January 2016.[10]

Announced as the first in a series of "sugar cubes" (*ZUKAR-Stückchen*, in the accented German spelling), the playfully satirical video dramatizes its title question with two documentary still shots of anti- and prorefugee activists and proceeds to answer the question with a street performance recorded on Berlin's Alexanderplatz. Blindfolded and equipped with a sign announcing his refugee status and "trust," Alshater invited hugs from passersby willing to reciprocate the sentiment.[11] After a long wait, people started to respond—more and more eagerly. Tongue in cheek, the video suggests Germans are just a bit slow to warm up. A few weeks later Alshater repurposed his third *ZUKAR-Stückchen*, originally announced as featuring beauty tips, to respond to the Clausnitz incident. Entitled *The Workshop*, the bitingly satirical video stages a "Clausnitz Training Camp," where locals with tattoos, combat outfits, and over-the-top Saxonian dialects can work through their reservations or fear of touch.[12] The exercise for beginners features "your first refugee," a toddler wearing cute cat ears. After several locals have mastered the challenge of touching the child and reported back to a TV crew, a volunteer proceeds to the advanced class, which reintroduces the adult, bearded Firas, once more blindfolded for hugs and now also with cat ears.[13] Performance, camera work, and soundtrack mockingly present the brave volunteer about to accomplish the hugging mission as a superhero bracing for action. Hauntingly, he is cheered on by a crowd of spectators in the door whose forceful hand gestures iconographically cite the Clausnitz hate video, emphasized by Alshater's temporary shift to black-and-white.

Strikingly dissonant in its fusion of the footage of hate with Alshater's earlier, tongue-in-cheek but heartwarming plea for affective openness, the short *Workshop* video in a small format presents the kind of (post)cinematic worldmaking I investigate in this book.[14] In the most general terms, I argue for the productiveness of artistic and critical engagements that directly or indirectly tackle the overwhelming presence of hate, fear, and aggression in the contemporary public sphere by unfolding intricate configurations of layered, diverging affects in complex, specific scenarios. My insistence on tonal layers and affective discrepancies is not to dismiss the significance of positive, empathy-inducing images and works, which many critics rejected for too long and which play a crucial role in many of the works I discuss.

(It was Alshater's initial hugging video that went viral with its dominantly warm tone.) But my wager is still that cinema—and by extension, the contemporary arts and humanities—can do more. The films I discuss neither provide merely heartwarming alternatives to political hate nor instead rely on the hope that critical thought will fix the affective mess of contemporary struggles. If the first of these gestures corresponds to clichés of mainstream cinema and the second to the reputation of much modernist avant-garde cinema, the arthouse-affiliated films I consider productively explore the creative spectrum between these alternatives.

Drawing on different conventions of contemporary transnational cinema, realism, and genre, Fatih Akın's *The Edge of Heaven* (2007) and *The Cut* (2014), Deniz Gamze Ergüven's *Mustang* (2015), Asghar Farhadi's *A Separation* (2011), Michael Haneke's *The White Ribbon* (2009), Alejandro González Iñárritu's *Biutiful* (2010), Aki Kaurismäki's *Le Havre* (2011) and *The Other Side of Hope* (2016), and Gianfranco Rosi's *Fire at Sea* (2016) present interventions reminiscent of Alshater's *Workshop* video in larger narrative formats, making time for more detailed, complex, and intricately engaging explorations. Set in different historical and contemporary contexts, they reimagine contemporary claims of collectivity by attending to and intertwining divergent feelings. Assembling gestures of hatred and violence with those of generosity and conviviality, these films make sense of people's attachments to violent collectives, unfold the conflicting commitments of complicated characters in impossible situations, or imagine transcultural connection, resistance, and solidarity in the face of persisting legacies of hate and inequality. Creating unexpected, unstable audience alignments, they shuffle and reconfigure "the sensible" (these are Jacques Rancière's words): they encourage us to see, hear, feel, and think again about present, past, and future forms of affective belonging.[15]

A SYNCRETIC MODEL OF CINEMATIC WORLDMAKING

I unfold this imaginative work conceptually by proposing a new model and interpretative methodology of affective cinematic worldmaking. This model facilitates a rich understanding of the processes of cinematic composition and reception. It is designed to support close readings of films but attends to aesthetic detail within larger circuits of production and spectatorship and orients us toward the cultural labor performed in these cinematic circuits. This methodological orientation does not come with strong political assumptions: insofar as the concept of affective world-making models cinematic processes in general, it can describe processes of hateful "closure" just as well as artistic openings onto alternative imaginations. However, the model does emphasize complexity and structural openness, and my readings pursue how these properties can be aesthetically activated to break apart hate and imagine political change.

Notions of worlds, worldings, and worldmaking have long circulated in humanities scholarship but have become a focus of attention in the past few years.[16] In film theory specifically, Daniel Yacavone's *Film Worlds* (2015) moved these concepts to center stage.[17] The notion of world(s) has multiple meanings in this current scholarship: it variously references "the earth" or "globe"; smaller (individual or group) "life-worlds" of experience circumscribed by culture, environment, or social or personal context; and the (fictional or nonfictional) worlds of films and other works of art or entertainment.[18] These semantic layers are part of what attracts me to concepts of worlds, worlding, and worldmaking: they link debates on collectivity and affect to aesthetic theory. Furthermore, I draw on the heterogeneous philosophical genealogies of these notions. The syncretic model of cinematic *world(mak)ing* I propose brings together concepts of *worlding* and *worldmaking* that have been associated with competing and in part seemingly incompatible traditions: worlding, in particular, with Deleuzian affect studies (going back to Spinozist philosophy) and worldmaking with symbolic and cognitive approaches.[19] Both notions circulate in phenomenological approaches, which help me mediate between Deleuzian and cognitive concepts in some respects.[20] Another anchor for my syncretic endeavor is the philosophy of Bruno Latour, whose impact on film studies has been limited to date.[21] However, rethinking cinematic world(mak)ing with Latour can bridge persistent divisions in the field: between cognitive and Deleuzian approaches as well as between "textual" and technological emphases on form versus production, exhibition, and spectatorship.

Cognitive models of worldmaking have been developed in the framework of narrative analysis. David Bordwell draws on narratological concepts of the *"story world,"* as constructed through plotting, narration, and audience comprehension.[22] Viewers "build up" cinematic worlds by ascribing "intentions to the things moving on the screen," assigning "agency," and tracing "causes and effects."[23] In cognitive theory, narrative worlds are made by individuals with intentions: characters on the plot level and filmmakers and audiences on the level of composition and spectatorship.[24] Affects are of interest primarily as developed into clear-cut emotions with an evaluative component and a "narrative character" in their own right: emotions emerge from ethical or other concerns (at the intersection of narrative events with cultural norms or human proclivities) and circulate between characters and audiences, ideally moving toward a morally satisfying resolution.[25] Primarily focused on mainstream movies, cognitive worldmaking concepts privilege the aesthetic values of coherence and closure.[26] Of course, such narrative closure does not necessarily produce the political closures with which I began; narrative closure can instead celebrate the opening up of national or other collective enclosures. With respect to Alshater's first video, for example, cognitive theorists might point to the way the sequence of the performer waiting for hugs elicits anxious sympathy as a "moral and ideological compass for the viewer" and diagnose our satisfaction with the film's hopeful outcome.[27]

Alshater's *Workshop* video, however, refuses an analogous clear-cut resolution. A title merely alerts us that workshops will soon be available in Bautzen, another German town with a racist reputation, before Firas returns to vaguely promise that the shelved beauty tips will follow "sometime." With its unresolved tonal dissonances, the video is not a good fit with cognitive analytic emphases. Arguably, the video's affective potential could be better theorized through Deleuzian concepts of affect as a force that, in Brian Massumi's words, disrupts "semantically and semiotically formed progressions" and "narrativizable action-reaction circuits."[28] Inverting the values of cognitive conceptualizations, Massumi champions the excessive force of affective intensity in contrast to emotion as the "subjective content, the sociolinguistic fixing of the quality of an experience."[29] Instead of emphasizing storyworlds populated and generated by individuals with intentions, Deleuzian critics foreground bodily processes—of "becoming" or "worlding"—in a field of "transindividual entanglement."[30] In the cinema, Steven Shaviro appreciates "tense and unstable" compositions that displace "linear, psychological causality" and "coherent" characters; the evoked sense that "subjectivity were an effect of atmosphere" makes the viewer feel "dispossessed" as well.[31] From my perspective, this emphasis that humans are embedded in cinematic and life worlds not governed by our intentions presents a crucial corrective to cognitive approaches, and the focus on tension and instability allows me to highlight the significance of, for example, the uncomfortable affective imbrications and tilting effects that Alshater's brief video elicits in me. While I want to greet the director's upbeat persona on screen with joy, the hyperbolic staging of neofascist gestures makes me respond with physical shudders (I don't find it very funny; am I supposed to?), and the unresolved visual melting of racist iconography and antiracist hugging therapy leaves me shocked.

To be sure, even this attempt at describing my sensations arguably disentangles them artificially and imposes too clear-cut categorizations. Massumi might object because he insists that "affect is unqualified" and "asignifying."[32] As a categorical maxim, however, I find this very unhelpful: it does little to help us understand the "fascist contagion" of affect in contemporary politics and even less to help us conceptualize how films mediate such contagion—or other affective assemblies.[33] In *The Forms of the Affects*, Eugenie Brinkema forcefully criticizes Deleuzian affect studies for a lack of specificity: championing affect's "*immediate*" nature against signification and ideology, they characteristically deploy it as a singular force of disruption rather than engaging the plural and layered affective transactions elicited by specific films.[34] Thus, we are left without much guidance toward a closer reading of Alshater's haunting satirical montage of tenderness and hate, documentary, action drama, and comedy. How do these genre elements contribute to the video's force? How is my experience of affective incongruity shaped by my familiarity with the cultural codes of German right-wing subcultures? And where do I go from the moment of shock elicited by the visual cheer-hate montage?

The concepts of worlds and worlding offer help at this juncture. As deployed by Deleuzian scholars, they provide starting points for a richer modeling of cinematic processes, which my syncretic proposal develops more fully. Namely, notions of world and worlding counteract otherwise prominent Deleuzian antinarrative and antisymbolic emphases with themes of composition and connection: Kathleen Stewart describes worlding as a process of "linking things" in "sensing them out"; for Massumi, worlding indexes how affect's "interrupting" force simultaneously induces a "rebeginning of the world."[35] Gregory J. Seig-worth and Melissa Gregg link such bodily becoming to symbolic medi-ation with their notion of "affectual composition," which designates both a body's "affectual composition of a world" and a "creative/writerly task."[36] Latour, whose philosophy has its Deleuzian influences, develops the imbrication of bodily and semiotic processes more forcefully. Medi-ation, he insists, is a necessary condition of becoming—or worlding—as well as scholarly and artistic worldmaking, or "world-building."[37] From a phenomenological angle, Sara Ahmed spells out that even in a direct physical encounter, the apparent " 'immediacy' of affective reaction is not itself a sign of a lack of mediation" but is instead "shaped by past histories of contact."[38] If "the work of emotion involves the 'sticking' of signs to bodies" in the processes of everyday "world making," cinema's technologies add multiple layers of mediation, from the scenario via cin-ematography and lighting to the exhibition screen.[39] As Vivian Sobchack has forcefully argued, this does not, however, evict people's "sensing, enworlded bodies" from cinema's loops of artistic worldmaking.[40] Some of the ways in which films enmesh affects and significations are indi-cated in Gilles Deleuze's description of how cinema "surrounds" images "with a world" in "circuits" that connect them to real-world references, memories, and fantasies.[41]

My syncretic notion of affective cinematic world(mak)ing develops these indications to unfold the entwinements of sensations and signs, ontology and semiotics in the cinematic process. In pursuing how affects compose worlds, I open up prevalent definitions of both affect and nar-rative. In my usage, *affect* spans a spectrum from nonconscious inten-sity and unconscious affectedness to more conscious and more definite emotional experience; this allows me to underline the socio-symbolic inflections even of less definite affective responses (for example, my shudders in watching Alshater's video) along with the instability of more clear-cut emotions.[42] In turn, I reconceptualize *narrative* vis-à-vis its typical uses in cinema studies by infusing narrative worldmaking with the unwieldy forces of affective worlding. In my model of world(mak)ing, narrative operates as a realm of affective encounters: a performative process that encompasses not just (more or less linear) plot and clo-sure but also the anticohesive and variously "vertical," "horizontal," and "orthogonal" vectors of affect and sensation along with—and attached to—form elements, fantasies, memories, and intertextual associations. The model thus includes modernist and experimental forms within the domain of narrative, and it allows me to locate the productiveness of the cinematic interventions at stake in the multiple and layered associations they facilitate. As indicated, the force of Alshater's *Workshop* video is neither in an emotionally gratifying narrative resolution nor primarily in individual moments of affective disruption but rather in the process of making and remaking connections between heterogeneous elements with diverging affective charges. This includes the video's gestural citation of the action genre and neo-Nazi subculture, its culturally charged tropes of cuteness, the antiseptic atmosphere of the German office building in which it is set, and the viewer's more specific intertextual memories of both the lighthearted hugging video and the documentary footage of hate.[43] My physical shudders—likely coinduced by subconscious memories associated with the racist normalcies of the postwar Germany in which I grew up—entangle me in these dynamic webs of associations. In confronting me with both the intricate brew of racism that bubbles so close to home and equally intricate questions about antiracist strategy, the video challenges me to see, hear, feel, and think along different lines.

To provide a fuller working definition, I conceptualize *cinematic world(mak)ing* as a process of *multidimensional and multivectoral affective assemblage*, configuring interwoven affects, associations, bodies, gestures, memories, objects, perceptions, sensations, topoi, and tropes through images, sounds, and words.[44] As I explain later, the process is collectively undertaken by embodied, *nonsovereign* actors (in an encompassing sense not limited to on-screen performers) in the communicative (or rhetorical) loops of composition, production, and spectatorship as a practice of *multisensorial reading*.[45] Deliberately "mixing up" heterogeneous categories and form-versus-content distinctions, this notion of worldmaking includes compositional elements as traditional as screenplay and dialogue, acting, mise-en-scène, cinematography, editing, and sound—along with the audience responses that reconfigure all of these building blocks in the processes of reception.

My conceptualization of cinematic worldmaking builds on but also diverges from recent discussions in cinema studies. Thus, I follow Brinkema's influential call to imbricate affect with form analysis and engage in "the slow, hard tussle of reading texts closely," but I depart from her "*radical formalism*," which tries to isolate affect and form from narrative, bodies, and spectatorship.[46] Instead, my interest in rich affective assemblages radically contextualizes formalism: the outlined goal of conceptualizing contemporary cinema's ethico-political contributions to reshuffling the sensible, I argue, requires bringing together form with all of these (bodily and narrative) forces. This layered approach to cinematic reconfigurations of affect in—diegetic and life-world—context has some common ground with that of Yacavone, who opens up cognitive theory's emphasis on storyworlds with the help of phenomenological aesthetics and hermeneutics.[47] Yacavone acknowledges that film worlds are made by transfiguring material from "ordinary reality" and traces how they are experienced and interpreted against the backdrop of "all the other worlds" of our cultural experience.[48] Even as he spells out these connections, however, Yacavone remains oriented toward standards of aesthetic wholeness and autonomy. Ultimately "event[s] of artistic and cinematic truth," his film worlds are "defined largely by their alterity" from surrounding life worlds, and they evoke a global affective atmosphere, or "composite but unitary and aesthetically unified feeling."[49] My worldmaking model emphasizes precisely the ways in which inescapably life-world-entangled artistic compositions do not align neatly to produce one unified affective or aesthetic effect. The force of unresolved tensions in cinematic worlds resists closure also vis-à-vis the extracinematic worlds surrounding them.

As rich assemblages rather than unified wholes, cinematic worlds in my definition are *open worlds with porous boundaries.* Cinematic worldmaking variously engages real-world sensations, spaces, and objects; affectively charged memories; fantasies; and discourse elements attached to the images and sounds it assembles or to the allusions it facilitates, be it to other artworks or real-world events. This emphasis not only diverges from Yacavone's model of artistic worlds but also entails a provocation to common conceptualizations of fiction insofar as they emphasize its boundaries vis-à-vis the real world.[50] My own interest in the traffic across these boundaries does not imply that I reject the distinction between fiction and documentary altogether.[51] However, I ground fiction's imaginative affordances less in its global contrast with outside worlds than in how it reframes "the 'real'" through indirect and piecemeal forms of reference.[52] Alshater's fictional reconfiguration of hate affects me through its nonliteral referentiality even at its least realistic: a workshop participant's hyperbolic articulation of surprise that the refugee toddler has five fingers satirically evokes the dehumanizing legacies of racism. The haunting assembly of this statement with the combat clothes, the bare German office setting, the documentary footage of hate, and the real-world memories I attach to all of them saturates the outlandish trope with enough reality to make me cringe rather than laugh.

NONSOVEREIGN ACTS: COLLECTIVE WORLDMAKING

But who is the agent of this worldmaking process? Is it I, as a viewer, or is it Alshater? It is both of us, along with and attached to many others. This is the second important difference between Yacavone's *Film Worlds* and mine. Providing auteurist film theory with a phenomenological spin, Yacavone argues that the audience experience of a unified film world ultimately reflects the filmmaker's "creative vision" and defends a notion of "single authorship in cinema" as most relevant to his project.[53] Although I grant that cinematic structures of production and exhibition endow directors with significant privilege and that an auteurist lens can shape audience experience, my worldmaking model is based on a notion of *collective* agency.

This notion unfolds on two levels. First, it gives significance to the empirical plurality of participants involved in a film's composition, production, and reception. For Alshater's *Workshop* video, this includes his producer and coauthor, his editor, his cameraman, his one-year-old nephew, the actors he hired as neo-Nazis along with himself, and the video's dispersed internet audiences.[54] Latour has urged us to further include "non-humans" in such actor collectives, by which he means less the infamous, ideologically charged "apparatus" of 1970s film theory than a plurality of concrete, materialized forces from light rays and microphones to cat-ear props and office settings.[55] The insistence on these nonhuman actors does not fetishize any technological or natural force; rather, Latour traces their mediating impact in complex actor networks in which humans, too, are constitutively *nonsovereign.* This is the second layer of the notion of collective agency.[56] In accord with a lineage of subject-critical interventions from psychoanalysis and modernist sociology to Deleuzian posthumanism, Latour asks, "When we act, who else is acting?"[57] Rather than being sovereign (understood as autonomous or free from external control), action is, in Latour's catchy wordings, always *"overtaken"* or *"other-taken."*[58] Asserting that we are "all held by forces that are not of our own making," he describes action as "shared with the masses" or "a node, a knot, and a conglomerate of many surprising sets of agencies."[59] In adapting these notions for the processes of cinematic worldmaking, I underline that even the most controlling cinematic auteur, who may strive to minimize the collaborative agency of team members and audiences, does not make filmic worlds primarily by his or her conscious artistic intentions. Instead, cinematic worldmaking is shaped by variously nonconscious or partially conscious assemblages of affects, memories, fantasies, and discourse elements circulating through the bodies and brains of directors, team members, and audiences—along with the constraints and affordances of production standards, locations, equipment, genre norms, exhibition contexts, and audience expectations.[60]

I do not take this emphasis on nonsovereignty in the radically posthumanist direction in which actor-network theory has sometimes been (mis)understood as orienting us, particularly by film and media studies scholars with pronounced interests in technology.[61] While the ethically and politically significant cinematic reshuffling of the sensible pursued in this book often operates below the level of full consciousness, it cannot, I argue, bypass the sensations, experiences, and active responses of individual human participants. Rather, I emphasize the importance of reconceptualizing these humans: as nodes of collective affective processes or perhaps "creaturely" humans, if this word can be understood nontheologically to index nonsovereign, affective beings.[62] Drawing on recent explorations of Latour's oeuvre across the humanities, I develop this modified humanist emphasis on the common ground that his philosophy shares with contemporary neophenomenological approaches.[63] Thus, Latour asks us to distribute agency by deploying "the actors' own world-making abilities"—for example, by "listening to what people are saying" about "why they are deeply *attached, moved, affected* by the works of arts which 'make them' feel things."[64]

In the phenomenological tradition, Hannah Arendt's critical development of Martin Heidegger's philosophy is worth foregrounding for its early exploration of such nonsovereign human worldmaking agency.[65] With Heidegger, Arendt underscores that we are not autonomous beings: in her words, the "disclosure" of any individual subject through action always falls "into an already existing web" of "human relationships."[66] Therefore, action "almost never achieves its purpose," and the "agent is not an author or producer"—or as I would reword, no empirical author, director, or producer is the master of their world.[67] Alshater the filmmaker, whose action-comedy genre montage simultaneously mocks and courts heroic notions of agency, is also Alshater the refugee and actor who, in asking for hugs, restages his existential vulnerability to his reception by majority Germans. The force of contemporary racisms crisscrosses his idealistic call for acceptance and shapes (not only my experience of) his *Workshop* video more than his optimistic authorial proclamations.[68] But our failure to control the outcome of our actions does not dissuade Arendt from pursuing her guiding interest in "what we are doing," or human agency in the processes of world(mak)ing.[69] In Lauren Berlant's words, the insight that sovereignty is "a fantasy misrecognized as an objective state" doesn't have to prevent us from talking about the "capacious range of activity" people undertake in ordinary life contexts.[70]

Contemporary scholarship has critically underlined that Arendt undercuts some of her own emphasis on nonsovereignty in delineating the spheres of human worldmaking and political action against the backdrop of earthly/animal/bodily nature.[71] From postcolonial or ecological perspectives, some critics have turned back to Heidegger for his emphasis on humans' radical lack of worldmaking mastery and "more primordial" belonging to earth—despite "the dark cloud of Nazism" hanging "over his politics."[72] However, I argue, there is no need for this return to Heidegger: Latour offers an analogous corrective without altogether abandoning agency and without Heidegger's vulnerability to fascism.[73] Rather than playing earth against world, Latour ontologically brings the "world" "down to earth," anchoring it in a "*multiplicity* of beings," both human and nonhuman, beyond the divide between the natural and the social.[74] Where Heidegger evokes the earth "as the 'native ground' for a people," Latour's model of ontologically networked collectivity forcefully counteracts old and new assertions of presumably homogeneous traditions as grounds for collective identity.[75] As each nonsovereign actor is attached to multiple, shifting objects and groupings, "'we,' like

'I,' is a wasp's nest," a metaphorical swarm that requires active alignment for it to function as a people or other collective actor in a more emphatic sense.[76]

Latour focuses his inquiry on the latter question of collective agency in ethical or political alignment by asking how we can *"live together"* or compose *"one common world"* that includes human and nonhuman actors.[77] In *Reassembling the Social*, he develops this question primarily as one of scholarly agency, while indicating parallels with cinematic and other artistic worldmaking practices.[78] Latour's proposed methodology for assembling "a *collective*" in the programmatic sense operates by deploying "controversies about the social world" with the goal of eventually stabilizing them.[79] The ethos of this process is not one of critical mastery but one of collective nonsovereign agency: proceeding with care and respectful caution, the scholar "follow[s] the actors themselves" by reconstructing and integrating diverging perspectives.[80] In tracing associations between heterogeneous forces, this "very practical world-building enterprise" aims to do justice to the complexity through which Latour characterizes the field of life.[81] My inquiry into the processes of cinematic worldmaking embraces this methodology, if with the caveat that complexity alone does not yet make a common world: the political workings of specific cinematic assemblages need to be fleshed out. In my readings, I do so in part by supplementing Latour's insistence on measured multiperspectivity with more activist models of assembling collectives, including Deleuzian interests in cinema as a mode of "collective emergence" and Rancière's emphasis on political dissent.[82] But, first, how do we flesh out the idea of "following the actors" for the circuits of cinema?

FOLLOWING THE ACTORS: MULTISENSORY READING AND RECONFIGURATIVE CRITIQUE

In a nutshell, the goal is to attend to the perspectives of the—diegetic, performing, narrating, producing, and perceiving—human and humanlike actors that populate the loops of film composition and spectatorship without underestimating their ties with nonhumans and the myriad ways in which each of their acts is shaped by other forces. I develop this Latourian idea in dialogue with resonant scholarship on cinema and other arts. In film theory, relevant reorientations have formed an integral part of the turns to affect, sensation, and perception since the early 1990s, long before the recent explosion of (in part explicitly Latourian) interests in "postcritical" methods in literary theory and the humanities at large.[83] Thus, Shaviro's *The Cinematic Body* (1993) challenged film scholars to displace the critical habits nourished by psychoanalytical and ideology-focused approaches and embrace "film viewing" as "pleasure and more than pleasure."[84] Simultaneously, Sobchack's *The Address of the Eye* (1992) set out to overcome these approaches' "paranoia" by rethinking vision as "embodied."[85] Sobchack argues for the medium's potential to facilitate actual communication (rather than ideological deception) by positioning both the audience and the film as nonsovereign "viewing" subjects.[86] Laura Marks follows up by foregrounding *The Skin of the Film*—concretely, the tactility involved in cinema's "multisensory" images.[87] My Latourian proposal pluralizes the embodied agency ascribed to film in these accounts by detailing the multiplicity of material bodies and things that contribute to any film's composite agency. I follow Sobchack and Marks in emphasizing that perception—viewing, listening, feeling, and sense making—happens on all sides of the loop of film composition and spectatorship: *making* films, too, is an activity that entails world viewing, hearing, and experiencing. In other words, it is an activity of *multisensory reading* if we can think of reading as not primarily a matter of cognitive understanding but an affective process potentially involving all of our senses.[88]

I develop the notion of "following the actors," then, as an umbrella term for multisensorial reading techniques or, more broadly, methods and styles of perceptive composition and active reception that unfold a spectrum of affective relations in the processes of cinematic world-making. For example, chapter 1 compares two different forms of narration, Akın's foregrounded storytelling in *The Edge of Heaven* and what I describe as *A Separation*'s poetics of phenomenological close-up. I discuss how each film elicits relations of empathy and sympathy, but I also modify these traditional concepts by foregrounding more "piecemeal" affective responses in unstable interactions between (networked) cinematographers, characters, and audiences.[89] Thus, I am particularly interested in bursts of audience affect within alienating scenarios or in relation to characters whose identity we may despise, along with more reserved relations of gradual understanding or reluctant recognition that emerge as we try to make sense of people's attachments to violent collectives. The latter, I argue, is at the center of Haneke's *The White Ribbon*, discussed in chapter 4. My reading challenges the dominant critical perception that this haunting film presents a distanced analysis of fascism. Instead, I detail how its camera, voice-over, and editing trace the complex affective orientations that inform the brutal nonsovereign worldmaking practices of the film's diegetic actors.

I gesture at the readings to come at this point because my introductory example of Alshater's *Workshop* video has reached its limit. With its bitingly satirical tone and three-minute format, this video does not make much of an effort to follow its problematic actors, initiate dialogue with neo-Nazi audiences, or invite me to relate to the complexity of their worldmaking.[90] However, to be clear, I am certainly not advocating for hugging Nazis without a satirical edge. Alshater's biting *Workshop* video complements his earlier viral plea for acceptance; together, the two short films can serve as a reminder to fine-tune the reading ethos I outlined with reference to postcritical methodologies. My readings and conceptualizations do not fully displace critique but probe different modes of (what I call) *reconfigurative* critique.[91] This alternative style of critique complies with Latour's methodological directives by "slowing down" and "patiently" incorporating a layer of phenomenological description.[92] Reconfigurative critique explores perceptual alignments (for example, with characters on screen) but modulates such approximation with analytical distance: it affords degrees of contextualization and historicization by assembling diverging perspectives into a multiperspectival or collective account.[93]

In the heated debates about whether, or how, to seek dialogue with right-wing perspectives, the concept of reconfigurative critique steers a path between naïve faith in the power of love or rational deliberation, on the one hand, and the refusal of all engagement, on the other. Dismantling the imagined coherence of fascist, racist, and fundamentalist worldviews requires engaging their affective underpinnings in detail. Perhaps, as Latour urges us, it even requires sharing some of "the experience of the values" that others "seem to hold," while modifying the stories they tell.[94] This reconfigurative practice is helpful also vis-à-vis critical accounts of how we—here the involuntary collective of unaligned humans—got into the current political mess. In the United States, the 2016 election triggered controversy about whether Trump's ascent uncovered the true face of the nation's continued foundation in white supremacy and unabated misogyny or whether the blame should rest with "the left's" abandonment of the (white) working class for an increasing focus on "identity politics."[95] Against the latter charge, I insist on the actuality of racist and sexist affects or, more precisely, negative affects assembled with racist and sexist topoi and on the more or less hegemonic force of the discourses and institutions supporting these affects, from colonialism and slavery to neoimperialism and neoliberal globalization. Simultaneously, my readings resist simple answers in breaking down global diagnoses of white supremacy and sexism by closely looking at affective inconsistencies, layers, and assemblages. In engaging and reconfiguring these assemblages, I show how the multisensorial worlds of contemporary cinema pursue openings for indirectly and directly imagining different presents and futures—for example, cosmopolitan connection within socio-symbolic controversy (see chapter 1), revolutionary solidarity (see chapter 3), or sensual resistance (see the epilogue).

With its affinity toward longer cinematic (rather than three-minute) formats, my worldmaking model and methodology reflect the belief that contemporary cinema is, to put it plainly, worth our time. In this sense, the proposal for multisensory reading and reconfigurative critique aims to reinvigorate ways of thinking and feeling associated with the humanities, which have been losing ground in an educational and intellectual climate of neoliberalism.[96] With their political orientation but theoretical and aesthetic format, my scholarly investigations embrace the much-discussed goal of public relevance with the caveat that we ought not to measure such relevance with standards of instant transparency or immediate applicability. Emphatically, my approach defends the values of reflexivity, aesthetic sensibility, conceptual thinking, and imagination: where other recent innovation proposals for the humanities have sought grounding in troubled times by way of alignment with scientific paradigms and methods, I develop new—and fine-tuned—ways of reading rather than measuring.[97] Following Latour, however, I do not position these values and methods *against* the "harder" sciences. Rather, I ultimately see multisensory reading and reconfigurative critique as crucial supports for a larger transdisciplinary project of serious engagement with the real world(s) in which we live—along with and by way of serious engagement with imagined worlds.[98]

LOCALIZED WORLDMAKING: TRANSNATIONAL EUROPEAN CINEMA

The current rise of collective closures is clearly a transnational and transcontinental phenomenon, in many ways more indicative of our contemporary moment than of the stability of local traditions. At the same time, renewed fortifications along national, racialized, and religious lines activate powerful local historical legacies. My readings untangle some of these localized articulations in (transnational) European cinema. Importantly, the Europe I am evoking through my choice of films has very porous borders. For example, *Biutiful*, which I discuss in chapter 4, is a Mexican-Spanish coproduction set in Barcelona and directed by Iñárritu, who is now working mostly in Hollywood, and Farhadi's *A Separation* presents an Iranian drama unfolding in the wake of possible emigration to Europe. *A Separation*'s transnational dimension remains mostly virtual on the diegetic level and is actualized in its prominent reception in the European festival circuit. Thus, my use of "European" reflects contemporary conditions of transnational production and reception along with contested political borders and the realities of migration in the aftermath of imperialism, which saturate Europe with histories and memories from other parts of the world.[99] Rather than creating a coherent corpus or filmmaking tradition, this European delineation circumscribes a rough geopolitical orientation at local along with translocal layers of worldmaking. In the case of *A Separation*, this requires a dual zoom-in: certainly not wanting to appropriate the film for a Europe of neocolonial proportions, I attend to the parallel and intertwined logics of both its Iranian and its transnational circulations.

Most of my other examples fit the European label more squarely. I refrain from enlisting the notion of world cinema to circumscribe the inquiry, despite its apparent resonance with my theoretical model, in part simply to avoid undue claims to scope. I know European cinemas better than those of other regions and don't want to pretend to full-fledged transcontinental coverage. But the notion of world cinema has also remained controversial in cinema studies because of its commercial uses, which tend to reinscribe asymmetrical oppositions between the "West" and the "rest," sometimes grouping together widely different cinemas in universalizing fashion and at other times ironically reinforcing national boundaries.[100] Although similarly contested, the concept of transnational cinema proves to be a better fit with my insistence on the significance of local scenarios and sociocultural contexts. Defined as "a condition of cultural interconnectedness and mobility across space," transnationality describes concrete "practices in the plural" that connect and transport people, films, affects, and significations across borders.[101] To varying degrees constitutive of cinema since its birth, these practices intensified in the post–Cold War moment of accelerated globalization, but even today they recontextualize rather than supersede the national.[102] Transnationalism is thus able to account for the force of national closures, although I understand the concept to emphasize the contingent genealogies and unstable contours of collective identifications more than notions of interculturality.[103] My choice of films emphasizes transnationality on the diegetic as well as extradiegetic levels of worldmaking: many of the works I discuss dramatize questions of diaspora and migration. But I embed this thematic focus in a broader investigation of different scenarios of collectivity, and I don't identify transnationality with migrant or minority cinema alone, which would risk reinforcing traditional conceptions of homogenous and stable national cultures.[104]

Rather, I read contemporary European cinema at large from the angle of the so-called migration crisis—that is, the crisis of majority Europe's enduring habits of ignoring the systemic emergencies unfolding at its southern and eastern borders. Contemporary migration flows have intensified long-standing debates on—and imaginative explorations of—identity, belonging, and (trans)local solidarity. European cinemas, I hope to show, are once more worth attending to today—if not primarily for their distinguished art traditions, then for how they engage questions of collectivity at the crossroads of transnational flows of art forms, ideas, and people. Of course, it would be rash to claim that these art cinema traditions, which have helped to secure Europe's privileged position on the cultural maps of the (post)colonial era for too long, are entirely irrelevant to my endeavor. To various degrees, echoes of modernist aesthetics continue to inflect contemporary cinema, and in chapter 2, I return to 1960s cinema to take a closer look at these resonances. However, the traditions of European art cinema are recontextualized through a transnational lens, reminding us of the transcontinental inspirations of European modernisms throughout their lifetime.[105]

As I situate European cinemas within a larger world, I ultimately do not discard the notion of world cinema as much as I mobilize and pluralize it through the insistence on worldmaking processes unfolding at different, often overlapping scales.[106] Nathalie Karagiannis and Peter Wagner have employed the notion of worldmaking as a way out of the "impasses of globalization theory": by foregrounding active negotiations of a "plurality of bonds, of their experience and their interpretation," the concept of worldmaking facilitates a thinking beyond culturalist "theories of conflicts between closed cultural communities," on the one hand, and the endless "flexibility" championed by postmodern approaches, on the other.[107] In my plural usage, the concept of *Making Worlds* targets overlaps as well as tensions between cinematic and life worlds at local, regional, national, European, transnational, and global—or, alternatively, planetary—scales.[108] In attending to cinematic imaginations that are of both *"the* world" and smaller collectives, my readings trace the (re-)creation of bonds that are significant, often contested, and sometimes fortified but that nonetheless are continuously changing and open to reconfiguration. Intertwining universalizing and localizing impulses, the films at the center of the following pages variously imagine open borders as they work through the actualities of collective closure.

A NOTE ON THE BOOK'S ORGANIZATION

Chapter 1 elaborates on key components of the book's worldmaking model from close readings of Fatih Akın's *The Edge of Heaven* and Asghar Farhadi's *A Separation.* I begin with these two films because both won awards for their complex, artfully constructed narratives and because both have been read in the context of twenty-first-century conceptual returns to the horizons of (affective) universalism, cosmopolitanism, and conviviality. Engaging these theoretical proposals for reassembling collectivity along with their critiques, I argue that both films gesture at larger horizons of human commonality only by carefully "following the actors" in sociopolitical controversies in localized contexts, thereby addressing concerns about universalism's and cosmopolitanism's entanglements in Eurocentric legacies and imperialist histories. The two films are quite different in form, and in reading them side by side, I detail two aesthetic paths for unfolding the model of affective worldmaking as complex cinematic assemblage.

Akın's multiprotagonist film intertwines its stories of religious hatred and affective alienation, immigration and exile, violence, leftist activism, and romantic and familial love that play out across northern Germany, Istanbul, and the Black Sea through a practice of foregrounded narration at a modulated distance that some critics have characterized as "post-Brechtian." In a continued dialogue with Latourian, cognitive, and Deleuzian approaches, I redescribe this practice as a method of forceful but nonsovereign storytelling. Exhibiting its imaginative intervention in a dialogic spirit, the film's narration invites layered audience engagements even with characters that are initially not very relatable. *A Separation* is narratively more reserved while employing a more unabashedly affective technique that I describe as a method of phenomenological close-up. In a fuller dialogue with phenomenological film theory, I argue that this poetics radicalizes a project of nonsovereign perception. I situate this worldmaking method as a contribution both to Iranian national cinema—against the backdrop of institutional censorship constraints—and to the transnational festival circuit, where in 2011 *A Separation* became the first Iranian film to win the Golden Bear at the Berlin International Film Festival, or Berlinale. Interweaving the politics of class, gender, secularism, and religion with the affective complexities of personal relationships, the film, as I will show, challenges Western audiences' culturalist readings not merely by affirming humanist connection but also by localizing planetary humanism.

While my focus is on contemporary conversations, chapter 2 takes a historical step back to anchor my argument in relation to the legacy of twentieth-century filmic modernisms. As demonstrated by the discussion on *The Edge of Heaven*'s post-Brechtian inflections, modernism's legacy continues to inform contemporary discourses, if often in a mode of negation and contrast. Thus, contemporary critics of all stripes (including both Deleuzians and cognitivists) tend to position Brechtian "distanciation"—arguably central to the avant-garde-affiliated European cinemas of the 1960s and 1970s—in a clear-cut opposition to affect.

In political terms, the aesthetic legacy of distanciation has been associated with leftist and modernist critiques of collectivity, as opposed to the more affirmative inquiries into collective belonging undertaken in the twenty-first century.[109] Chapter 2 reassesses these oppositions, detailing both unexpected continuities and smaller differences between 1960s political cinema and contemporary worldmaking practices. The historical genealogies traced in chapter 2 add depth (or layers) to my conceptualizations and demonstrate how the model of affective cinematic worldmaking allows us to rethink cinematic modernisms as well as contemporary cinema.

The chapter's argument for resituating modernist cinema proceeds conceptually by grounding the process of distanciation itself in the play of (negative and positive) affects and historically by returning to an early moment of Brecht reception in film theory and 1960s cinema. In this moment, I trace conceptualizations and practices of *defamiliarization* quite different from the later canonical notion of distanciation. These conceptualizations and practices emerged at the intersection with the phenomenological realism of André Bazin, who would become Brecht's film-historical counterpart in 1970s and 1980s film theory. Shunned by Brechtian film scholars at the time, Bazin has been rediscovered in the age of affect. My readings unfold conceptual imbrications of Brecht and Bazin through new takes on two films with a lasting Brechtian reputation: Jean-Luc Godard's *My Life to Live* (*Vivre sa vie*, 1962) and Rainer Werner Fassbinder's *Katzelmacher* (1969). In different ways, I argue, both films develop a poetics of intense defamiliarization, which facilitates reconfigurative rather than distance-based forms of sociopolitical critique. *My Life to Live* affectively follows the protagonist Nana in her sex work and nonsovereign "life living" in the Parisian world of capitalist patriarchy, the film's dominant collective. *Katzelmacher's* slow poetics raises the ethical stakes of such following by intimately intertwining affect with violence. The film traces its protagonists' everyday assemblages of money making, brutality, sex, tenderness, and inchoate longings for connectivity as they align to close off a provincial German neighborhood collective against a Greek "guest worker." In detailing these entanglements, the chapter also tackles affect's relations with sexuality as the dominant conceptual paradigm in 1960s and 1970s film as well as in social theory and political activism.

Chapter 3 returns to the twenty-first century to consider several films that do not quite seem to fit my model's focus on highly intricate worldmaking assemblages. Critics have variously described Akın's more recent *The Cut* (2014) and the first two films of Kaurismäki's unfinished refugee trilogy, *Le Havre* (2011) and *The Other Side of Hope* (2017), in terms of their apparent simplicity and a return to genre. In this chapter, I ask how the proposed model of worldmaking contributes to reading genre-affiliated films. My answer is twofold. On the one hand, I argue— perhaps unsurprisingly—that these films are anything but simple. While they present serious engagements with genre, these engagements proceed through intricate cinematic means of reflexivity and intertextuality. On the other hand, I show that genre does afford productive challenges to the carefully complex—and politically sometimes too cautious— assemblages of reconfigurative critique outlined in chapters 1 and 2. I develop this reading in dialogue with contemporary philosophies of revolutionary events—in particular, Deleuzian accounts of collective affect. Borrowing Massumi's words, I propose that *The Cut* and Kaurismäki's trilogy in progress use genre to assemble affective "cut[s]" of "decision" into hegemonic formations of collectivity.[110]

Akın's and Kaurismäki's films assemble these cuts in diverging ways. Starkly different from Akın's *The Edge of Heaven*, which was part of the same trilogy, *The Cut*'s adaptation of 1950s widescreen technology draws on the Western and melodrama to configure an unqualified, high-affect plea for mourning the Armenian genocide. However, this straightforward intervention into charged conversations on political memory proceeds through an intricate (and counterintuitive) aesthetics of intense affection-at-a-distance: *The Cut*'s widescreen exploration of existential vulnerability forcefully insists on the lasting rupture of collective identification brought about by genocide. In this sense, the film underwrites Deleuze's dictum that in "modern" (post-1945) political cinema, "the people," in the sense of an emphatic collective, "no longer exist."[111] But Deleuze also adds "or not yet."[112] Kaurismäki's refugee trilogy explores this opposite vector by indirectly probing Deleuze's speculation that a new basis for collective action would have to be sought "between the cracks" of established identity formations.[113] *Le Havre* and *The Other Side of Hope* reconfigure the sensible in such unabashedly optimistic ways that critics have described them as "fairytales." In assembling this antirealistic genre with comedy and musical, Kaurismäki's unfinished trilogy imagines affective events of unconditional solidarity with irregular immigrants. These collective events are not as immediate as imagined in Deleuzian theories of affect, but they are as forceful, as they boldly defy the apparent realist mandate that *"the people"* have to remain *"missing"* in twenty-first-century cinema.[114]

Both overlapping and competing with recent turns to genre, there have been various proclamations of new realisms in twenty-first-century cinema, philosophy, and theory. In chapter 4, I return to Latour's intertwining of rhetoric and ontology in the processes of worldmaking to conceptualize some of these new realisms in a way that overcomes old film-historiographical fault lines between indexical celebrations and postmodern critiques of realism. Latour does not anchor the project of developing better accounts of the world in the promises of immediacy on which both critical and celebratory accounts of filmic realisms have relied. Instead, he underlines the productive role of mediation and foregrounds the aesthetic criterion of "objectfullness" as achieved by the care and caution of complex assembly in following different actors' affective takes and social controversies.[115] My reading of Michael Haneke's *The White Ribbon* (2009) translates Latour's proposal into the realm of film aesthetics by detailing the film's complex shots, subtle modulation of a nonsovereign voice-over, and (what I describe as its) "local" editing regime. The objectfull assembly of the film's early twentieth-century world of religious authority challenges audiences to engage this seemingly distant cosmos much more closely and carefully than they would find comfortable in our own age of authoritarian returns.

The chapter's following two readings bring this Latourian model of realism in dialogue with Rancière's more forcefully political aesthetics as they explore the—open but significant—border between fictional and documentary realisms. Gianfranco Rosi's poetic documentary *Fire at Sea* (2016), filmed on the Mediterranean island of Lampedusa, powerfully dramatizes the European refugee crisis by configuring two starkly separated worlds: guided by his documentary ethics of tracing people's reality, Rosi contrasts the individualized lives of the island's long-term inhabitants with the refugees' collective state of emergency. However, the film's objectfull assembly of historical memories, human spatial practices, and nature's agency also indicates a shared world by collecting virtual links between these worlds. Enabled by fiction's different assembly protocols, Iñárritu's *Biutiful* (2010) provocatively goes further toward reconfiguring the sensible in Rancière's sense: through story details as well as cinematography and montage, the film develops unsettling links between its Barcelona-based family drama and the worlds of undocumented Chinese and African immigrants. Without pretending to resolve any controversy, *Biutiful*'s uncompromising dramatization of its flawed characters' ethical conflicts against the backdrop of neoliberal precarity, heteronormativity, and racism forcefully confronts viewers with a horizon of shared implication and responsibility.

Outside the fairy tale and the musical, collectives in the emphatic sense of coordinated political action in fact largely remain missing in contemporary European cinema: most of the works I highlight attain their political promise through scenarios of intricate realignment rather than straightforward revolution or collective resistance. In the epilogue, I therefore return to the question of such imagined resistance. Deleuzian and Latourian approaches to "a politics of affirmation" have encouraged us to attend to creative openings as afforded, perhaps, by filmic imaginations of collective joy—and energy—as bodily movement.[116] I explore this idea by reading Ergüven's *Mustang* against the backdrop of images of the 2013 Gezi Park protests in Istanbul. *Mustang* develops a—fictional but intertextually resonant—iconography of resistant collective physicality in the play of five adolescent sisters in rural Turkey as a cinematic counterpoint to a world of repression. The film's not entirely uncontroversial reception, however, underlines that it will not do to celebrate such creative openings out of context. With a concluding nod to the book's overall argument, I attend to *Mustang*'s gestures of resistant physicality as part of the multivectoral assembly of larger worlds. On the diegetic level, this includes tracing the sisters' diverging trajectories of adaptation, depression, and outright resistance. In the extradiegetic world of the film's making and reception, the approach facilitates a layered reading that critically acknowledges *Mustang*'s partial resonances with contemporary culturalist ideologies, while cherishing the narration's subtle invitations to make more specific political connections—including to the Gezi uprising. Contemporary cinema's contributions to reimagining our world may be precisely in balancing such moves of complication with more defiant, loudly resistant gestures of alternative possibility.[117]

CHAPTER ONE

Affects in Configuration

Controversy and Conviviality in Fatih Akın's The
Edge of Heaven *and Asghar Farhadi's* A Separation

COLLECTIVE OPENINGS?
COSMOPOLITANISM AGAINST HATE

In important respects, today's mainstreaming of political hate began
in the early 2000s—if not in the 1990s. As early as 1993, Samuel Huntington introduced his controversial trope of a "Clash of Civilizations,"
which would shape twenty-first-century discourses on "cultural" conflict between "Islam" and "the West."[1] But after 2001, such talk became
increasingly influential on both sides of the Atlantic. At the intersection
of "War on Terror" discourses and intensifying neoliberal globalization
crises with local legacies of racialization, European public discourses
on immigration and collective identity were redramatized in ways that
dampened the more hopeful bent of scholarly and political conversations around multiculturalism, postcolonialism, and globalization at the
end of the twentieth century.[2] A major facet of these twenty-first-century
collective closures was the return of religion to increasingly postsecular
public spheres, as indicated not only by Recep Tayyip Erdoğan's quest to
overturn Turkey's secular legacy but also by the broad relegitimization
of a rhetoric of Europe's "Christian" traditions.[3] The implied exclusion
even of the continent's Jewish histories has been activated in the resurgence of political anti-Semitism in the new populist governments and
movements, particularly in eastern Europe but also in western Europe.

Simultaneously, these postsecular affirmations of religious identity as (gendered and racialized) cultural identity have fueled the unabashed "politics of hatred" toward Muslim minorities that has taken center stage in the age of Brexit, Donald Trump, and the politicization of Europe's ongoing refugee crisis—but that had arguably become a dominant vector of political affect flows in Europe well before then.[4]

How do we counter such hate? Since the turn of the century, a range of scholars and public intellectuals has returned to concepts of universalism and cosmopolitanism as a promising basis for reimagining inclusive forms of collectivity on a larger scale. These conversations emerged in part out of discussions on right- as well as left-wing nationalisms in postcolonial studies but gained traction in response to post–September 11 collective closures.[5] Revising postmodern methodological foci on difference over commonality, Judith Butler answers the violence of oppositional culturalizations in "War on Terror" media coverage, which devalued "Muslim" lives, by emphasizing our "common human vulnerability."[6] With an analogous bent, Paul Gilroy counters the "noisy announcement" of multiculturalism's death—"itself a political gesture"—with an insistence on "fundamental commonality" and "an agonistic, planetary humanism."[7] "In the past," Gilroy adds, "western modernity described these utopian ambitions as cosmopolitan."[8] The scholarly return to these promises has remained controversial—and not only in competition with the alternative *post*humanist paradigms I engage throughout this study. Gilroy's own wording indicates that discourses on cosmopolitanism have dominantly been articulated in a European genealogy from the Greek stoics to Immanuel Kant and that they are deeply "entangled" in Europe's histories of colonial expansion.[9] As Aihwa Ong charges, cosmopolitanism's "values"—of "individualism, universality, and generality"—have functioned as "a vital part of the civilizing mission of imperialism"; the term remains associated with "elite Western subjects" formed by "European bourgeois culture" and its gendered ideals of sovereignty.[10]

Given these entanglements, Gilroy emphasizes the challenge implied in the goal of producing "a worldly vision that is not simply one more imperialistic particularism dressed up in seductive universal garb."[11] However, a range of contemporary proposals for "vernacular," "critical," or "discrepant" forms of cosmopolitanism has begun to tackle this challenge.[12] Inquiring into cosmopolitanism's multiple gene-alogies and present forms, the proponents of these proposals have questioned its individualist, rationalist implications and reconceptual-ized plural cosmopolitanisms as "located and embodied" practices of "(re)attachment, multiple attachment, or attachment at a distance" rather than seemingly sovereign detachment.[13] In other words, "cosmopoli-tics" might describe "contested" processes of worlding and cosmopol-itanism, the belonging to more than one overlapping world at different scales—"connected to the earth" or "solid materiality" but not one par-ticular "land" overcharged with the values of "ethnic homogeneity."[14] Perhaps it bears emphasizing that the latter values—of racial or cultural homogeneity—have fueled cosmopolitanism's use as a derogatory term, historically variously applied to Christians, aristocrats, Jews, homosexu-als, and intellectuals before it resurfaced in recent populist discourse to denounce the "globalized elites" or political "idealists."[15] In today's hard-ened discursive confrontations between the "politics of identity" and its no less politically charged critique in the name of a "unifying vision of the common good," cosmopolitanism's ability to facilitate alternative assemblies of collectivity might depend on how we work through all of this historical baggage.[16] Thus, Gilroy insists that developing nonimperi-alist cosmopolitanisms requires working through colonial legacies and "the enduring power of racism."[17] Only in foregrounding the actuality of these divisions can we approach togetherness in "the hard but scarcely mysterious work involved in translation, principled internationalism, and cosmopolitan conviviality."[18] As I argue in this chapter, Fatih Akın's *The Edge of Heaven* (*Auf der anderen Seite*, 2007) and Asghar Farhadi's *A Separation* (*Jodaí-e Nadér az Simín*, 2011) powerfully engage in this hard work—by way of two different methods of narrative worldmaking.

THE EDGE OF HEAVEN: FOLLOWING THE ACTORS THROUGH A PRACTICE OF FOREGROUNDED NARRATION

Akın's film—which won the 2007 Cannes and European film prizes for best screenplay, the 2007 Grand Jury Prize of the Antalya Film Festival, and the 2008 German film prizes in four categories—entwines stories of religious hatred and affective alienation, immigration and exile, violence, activism, and romantic and familial love that play out across northern Germany, Istanbul, and the Black Sea. While it has been widely praised for the complexity of its form and multiplot scenario, critics have articulated some hesitation about its ending, which (as I will detail) presents a strong affirmation of translocal solidarity and conviviality. Barbara Mennel, for example, worried that *The Edge of Heaven* "ultimately privileges humanist values over" the "radical politics" that it depicts in one of its plots—the story of Ayten, an Istanbul-based activist who unsuccessfully seeks refuge in Germany—and even the filmmaker wondered whether he might get in trouble "with leftists in Turkey."[19] Tim Bergfelder proposed a consonant reading with an affirmative charge. *The Edge of Heaven*, he claims, develops a plea for a "pragmatic, everyday cosmopolitanism grounded in concrete affective relations," a "vernacular cosmopolitanism" that counters the concept's Eurocentric affiliations at "the level of individual ethical choices and interpersonal interactions."[20] I agree that Akın's film presents a forceful antidote to the contemporary European politics of hatred, both by providing a complex commentary on collective identification at the intersection of multiple categories of belonging and by foregrounding a theme of affective connection through romantic and kinship bonds. I disagree, however, with how Bergfelder opposes this affective cosmopolitanism to more activist forms of politics. Refuting the charge that Akın's film is ultimately apolitical, my own reading shows how its rich configuration embeds the forceful affirmation of cosmopolitan affect in a cinematic tracing of (in Bruno Latour's terms) "controversies about the social world," which strengthens the claims of human togetherness by complicating them with reminders of division.[21] As I propose, *The Edge of Heaven* does so through a practice of foregrounded narration at a modulated distance, which exhibits its imaginative intervention even while inviting us to seriously engage in its rich world saturated with documentary elements. My reading conceptualizes this practice by seeking a fuller dialogue between Latour's philosophy and film-theoretical conceptualizations of foregrounding and affective audience engagement.

A striking feature of Akın's oeuvre to date is his exploration of markedly different elements of genre and form in individual films. *The Edge of Heaven* is the centerpiece of a trilogy, Love, Death, and the Devil, which also includes *Head On* (*Gegen die Wand*, 2004), a film that brought Akın broader national as well as international recognition, and *The Cut* (2014; see chapter 3).[22] However, *The Edge of Heaven* differs starkly from the "neorealism" of *Head On*, which partly resonates with contemporary forms of intensified continuity or the cinema of sensations, as well as from the high-affect widescreen aesthetics developed in *The Cut*, which participates in a wave of recent arthouse returns to genre by engaging the Western and period melodrama.[23] Instead, *The Edge of Heaven* draws on independent traditions to a greater extent—with Rainer Werner Fassbinder as an acknowledged reference point—and in some respects resonates with the films of the Berlin School, which gained prominence in the 2000s as Germany's new art cinema "wave."[24] But with its "will to form," *The Edge of Heaven* also presents a "counterpoint" to the Berlin School: where Berlin School directors Christian Petzold, Thomas Arslan, and Angela Schanelec explore techniques of phenomenological realism in privileging everyday spaces and bodily movements over tight plots, Akın integrates resonant documentary elements with a practice of storytelling that unabashedly emphasizes its own status as an act of narrative composition.[25] Thus, the filmmaker underlines the substantial research that was to ensure, for example, an accurate portrayal of the Turkish prison system, which he filmed with actual prisoners and staff, and his cinematographer, Rainer Klausmann, variously affords us views of the protagonists moving through the environments of Istanbul, Hamburg, and Bremen along with more rural locales.[26] But these views are framed by intertitles that announce each of the film's three parts as a story to be told, and the rapid cutting of the following establishing sequences, which introduce complex scenarios in Germany and Turkey, allows us to notice how they are arranged. Furthermore, the narration's nonlinear temporal structure, the repeated evocation of missed encounters among its protagonists, the pointed parallels in characterization that connect them, and the varying repetition of musical and other motifs, action moments, and entire sequences interweave the film's stories into a "fugue-like form," which at moments defies the demands of probability.[27]

In twenty-first-century transnational cinema, this complexity of narration has invited comparisons with the work of Atom Egoyan and Alejandro González Iñárritu, and in fact Akın had sought counseling from Guillermo Arriaga, Iñárritu's scriptwriter for *Babel* (2006).[28] The richness of narrative worldmaking at stake here is not exactly that of the "puzzle plots," which proliferated in turn-of-the-twenty-first-century cinema. Cognitive scholarship has explored the notion of complex narration for these plots.[29] The debate on puzzle films has focused on the degree to which they challenge "classical" protocols of narration through their antimimeticism and unreliable narration, including defiance of causality principles and the exploration of multiple levels of virtuality.[30] While I share the interest in nonclassical forms, my model of complex affective worldmaking assemblages does not primarily target postmodern practices of radical antimimeticism. *The Edge of Heaven* and the other films discussed here rather move beyond such playfulness: their multifaceted worlds are complicated, layered, and noticeably fictional but not impossible. More relevant is David Bordwell's use of the notion of "worldmaking" in *The Way Hollywood Tells It*: he (re)introduces the term here for a specific aesthetic trend in contemporary cinema—namely, the "massive detailing" of "rich," "layered worlds," which he observes particularly in science fiction and other genre cinema.[31] As outlined in the introduction, I deploy the concept of worldmaking more generally for the filmmaking process but emphasize cinema's virtual complexity, which is variously activated in contemporary aesthetic practices—including in transnational art cinema. Crucial to my proposal is, further, how the wealth of detail given in *The Edge of Heaven* and many of my other examples facilitates a corresponding wealth of—virtual but specific—connections, including similarities and contrasts. This draws my attention to the techniques of narration that establish these connections. In *The Edge of Heaven*, this includes the prominent cinematography and editing, the intertitles, and the music—in short, the unabashed rhetorical practice through which the film assembles its world.

For historical reasons I detail in chapter 2, film critics tend to associate such foregrounding of the narrative process with "Brechtian distanciation."[32] However, this association has become discrediting to many in the age of the affective turn. Indicatively, the first round of scholarship on *The Edge of Heaven* refuted it by relating the film's narrative form to viewing practices in the digital age: as Mennel proposes, the film does not create "a Brechtian alienation effect" because in the age of YouTube and DVD zapping, linear narrative and space-time continuity are no longer "the precondition for filmic illusion, fantasy, and identification."[33] Although I generally agree with this (with the qualification that illusion is also not necessary for affective engagement), I argue that the film invites a closer look at these issues. Akın suggested that *The Edge of Heaven* is made for the big screen—and thus the uninterrupted two-hour cinema experience.[34] The foregrounded act of composition forcefully develops a larger multivectoral but not radically discontinuous narrative: a complex configuration as a chronotope of intricate affective encounters that reshuffle both exclusive and all-too-facile inclusive collectivity claims. How this practice can be called "Brechtian" is a question that guides me toward a rethinking of the dominant film-historical dichotomy of affect versus distanciation. As I detail in chapter 2, the channeling of Bertolt Brecht's legacy through this dichotomy simplifies both Brecht's own theory and its reception in modernist film practice and theory. In this chapter, I begin to spell out my proposal for a new mapping of the intersection of film narration and audience engagement by showing that *The Edge of Heaven* does not critically distance audiences as much as it invites their (cognitive as well as affective) curiosity in and for the process of storytelling. Its foregrounded narration, I argue, creates a space for positive engagement along with cautious, at moments tongue-in-cheek deliberation.

When an interviewer suggested that Akın was not a "political filmmaker" in response to Akın's worries about getting in trouble with the Turkish left, the director defensively characterized himself as a "classical storyteller."[35] "Classical" clearly does not reference the film historians' normative model of more or less "invisible" Hollywood narration here.[36] Instead, the emphasis in Akın's self-characterization can be put on the notion of *teller* or the gesture of forceful world assembly.[37] In my usage here, "forceful"—or perhaps "assertive"—does not imply the presumptions to sovereignty that cinema scholars, along with literary narratologists, have often associated with rhetorically explicit narration, be it in the name of godlike omniscience or more worldly models of authority.[38] In line with the concept of nonsovereign agency spelled out in the introduction, I assume that sovereignty is not a useful concept for characterizing *any* kind of narration. This includes fictional narration, for which formalists have argued that the author, or narrator as endowed by the author, is epistemologically equipped with imaginative sovereignty over the created world, as opposed to its historical backdrop.[39] To reiterate, the first problem with this argument for the context at hand is that film worlds are assembled by an entire ensemble of human and nonhuman narrative agencies, such as the camera, the Dolby Digital sound technology, and the more conventional narrative elements of the intertitles, all deployed in *The Edge of Heaven* by different crew members.[40] In calling himself a storyteller, to be sure, Akın asserts the creative authority ascribed to him by auteurist conventions, but he also details his collaboration with Arriaga, editor Andrew Bird, and Klausmann (who creatively "translates" rather than just executes his ideas), and he describes the emergence of the project out of his desire to work with the film's two star actors, Hanna Schygulla and Tuncel Kurtiz.[41]

Second, the cooperation of multiple actors in this straightforward sense merely indicates one layer of the collective—networked—agency at stake. Like all other action, narration is not under the autonomous control of any empirical actor or group of actors: fictional as well as nonfictional filmmaking is shaped by production standards, financing opportunities, generic conventions, narrative techniques, and social controversies entwined with personal fantasies and memories. With Latour, I conceive of fictional narration as a nonsovereign "mediation" and "knot" of agencies also insofar as it rearranges real-world materials in an encompassing sense: including discourse elements with affective charges, entangled with conscious and unconscious desires, fears, hopes, and resentments.[42] Fictional worlds are never imaginatively closed and autonomous but remain bound to the intertextual and life worlds surrounding them through relations of piecemeal—unsystematic and fragmentary—reference. In the "actor-network" of nonhuman and human agents, the rhetorical practice of artistic world-building proceeds by "feeding off controversies."[43] This does not mean that all narration lacks authority. But claims to such authority—including fiction's persuasiveness and ability to engage—are based on the way the narration "follows" and arranges a plurality of perspectives rather than on anyone's pretensions to an autonomous, definite understanding of how the—or a—world is, could be, or should be.[44] On the level of aesthetic composition, such collective worldmaking can take different forms. I introduce Akın's assertive, rhetorically explicit practice of narration in *The Edge of Heaven* as a first mode of following the actors by way of deploying controversies.[45] The director comments on the film's dispersed origins in his encounters with different people, different life stories, and other films.[46] In creatively remaking and forcefully connecting all of them through the film's foregrounded act of narration, I argue, *The Edge of Heaven* is showcasing the implicit dialogicity of storytelling rather than pretending to authorial sovereignty: it presents an imaginative proposal of (possible, intriguing, relevant, powerful) connections for the audience's affective-cognitive engagement.[47]

As outlined in the introduction as well, I link Latour's plea for "following the actors" to ongoing debates on spectatorship and scholarly reading practices, including the methodological moves beyond distanciation and critical suspicion that have animated cinema scholarship since the early 1990s. In the processes of composition as well as spectatorship, cinematic practices of following the actors probe possibilities of spatial, affective, and ethical approximation through various combinations of empathy and fleeting affectedness, partial understanding, and reluctant respect. But *The Edge of Heaven* can serve as a first reminder not to categorically short-circuit such explorations of affective connection with an aesthetics of spatial and affective proximity. In following the actors, narration can modulate approximation and distance by zooming in and out both literally and metaphorically, detailing and comparing things, people, and events.[48] *The Edge of Heaven* navigates these possibilities to the overall effect of medium distance—notwithstanding a few moments of intensity, as we will see. In this way, the film departs from both a Brechtian modernism understood to curtail the play of affects and the naturalized narration of "classical" Hollywood, where the play of affects is maximized, in each case more or less effectively in the service of ideological control. The director motivates the increased camera distance (after *Head On*'s aesthetics of sensation) with the goal of creating "space" to "breathe" and allowing the audience *not* to "pull out" imaginatively.[49] Neither overwhelming us with affect nor analyzing at a cool remove, the film develops a practice of critically affirmative assembly through rich affective encounters: a form of reconfigurative critique as careful engagement.

MODULATING DISTANCE: CONSPICUOUS TOPOI, CAUTIOUS APPROXIMATIONS

The complexity of Akın's storytelling implies, first of all, that *The Edge of Heaven* does not simply cut all ties to the affective economies of fear and hate that have dominated European media representations of Muslim immigrants after September 11. In tackling these affective economies—along with the question of political resistance in Turkey—the 2007 film feels simultaneously distinctly historical and eerily up-to-date today. Although the so-called refugee crisis has radicalized political discourse on Islam and immigration all across Europe, the topoi of racialized culturalization that are dominant today were already in place in the early 2000s. At the time, German society saw heated debates around the hijab in public schools—characteristically framed as a sign of women's oppression—and around "honor killings" and "parallel societies."[50] In the Islamophobic climate of the "War on Terror," the "Clash of Civilizations" rhetoric introduced by Huntington in the 1990s acquired hegemony and became fused with long-standing stereotypes of female victimhood and male violence.[51] As *The Edge of Heaven* sets out to assemble discourse fragments, audience associations, and affects in this socio-symbolic context, the first part—critics have used the word *chapter*—introduces the viewer to an elderly Turkish man who pays a visit to a sex worker, Yeter, in the red-light district of Bremen in northern Germany.[52] The chapter title, "Yeter's death," gave us a hint up front that he will end up killing her, although unintentionally, after she moves in with him to serve his sexual needs exclusively. Yeter decides to accept this offer because, after his initial visit, she is threatened and asked to "repent" by two countrymen who overheard them speaking Turkish. The Islamists' "hate" has "unmade" Yeter's "world"—concretely, her livelihood as a sex worker.[53]

Cognitive critics have underlined how viewers build cinematic worlds by associating available cultural schemata and prototypes.[54] As we make such connections here,[55] the film's opening fits almost too neatly with dominant media discourses. Around the time of the film's production, 91 percent of Germans associated Islam per se with systematic gender discrimination.[56] Akın's worldmaking, however, is far from exhausted by these familiar connections. A second layer of links unfolds through the ways in which the film's foregrounded narration invites us to deliberate on the implications of narrative configuration. To audiences with some intertextual background, the elderly gentleman's self-introduction to the sex worker ("Please call me Ali") announces that he embodies the German labor-immigrant clichés associated with this fictional name. The protagonist of Fassbinder's *Ali—Fear Eats the*

Soul (*Angst essen Seele auf*, 1974) explained that everyone calls him thus because of their inability or unwillingness to remember his actual name.[57] And if names do indeed speak, that of the sex worker calls for an interruption: *Yeter* is Turkish for "enough."[58] Importantly, however, *The Edge of Heaven* does not invite us to arrest the process of worldmaking on this layer of (meta)reading attentive to the film's composition, which could consolidate its workings in a distanced modality of intertextual play, irony, or parody. As the film unfolds further, the foregrounded cliché plot opening and character portrait are developed into a more intricate configuration. Multiplying associations in an artful play with differences and similarities, the film's multivectoral assemblage makes room for the complexities of fictional experience in a world of overdetermined events and complicated actors. Played by one of Akın's two star collaborators, Tuncel Kurtiz, Ali develops unexpected gravity.

In theoretical terms, I conceptualize characters in analogy to authors and narrators, on a middle ground between cognitive humanism, Deleuzian posthumanism, and ideology-critical approaches. Variously modeled on extradiegetic humans, characters are neither "atomized" individuals with a set of stable motivations nor necessarily straightforward representations of cultural prototypes; rather, they are nonsovereign agents assembled from heterogeneous affects and associations, including the imago of the actor embodying them, other intertexts, and media representations.[59] But this radical overdetermination does not preclude us from endowing characters' subjectivities with experiential weight. Diverging from radically posthumanist takes, my conceptualization of distributed agency assumes that for (human) viewers, some of the affective richness and cultural productivity of cinematic worldmaking is in fact about humans—if nonsovereign and thoroughly complicated humans. And rather than treating viewers' affective enmeshments merely as symptoms of "ideology's damaging imprint," my readings attend to "the pleasure"—and hurt, anger, and more— "bound up in" characters' as well as audiences' nonsovereign "activity of worldmaking."[60]

In *The Edge of Heaven*, the narrative crafting of world details and layered connections complexifies Ali from the beginning. On his way to Yeter at the outset of the first chapter, Ali walks by a May 1 demonstration. A beret on his head, he signals joyful appreciation of the socialist songs intoned by the protesters, including communists along with moderate German union representatives. Subsequently, the interplay of dialogue, gesture, mise-en-scène, and editing carefully distinguishes the labor-immigrant Ali from the Islamists, developing contrast through linkage as a way of making more careful distinctions. In the process, Ali's violent behavior is motivated by residual patriarchy and capitalist fantasy rather than by religion and by affects of jealousy rather than by those of hate, in a formation of desire structured by the demands of hegemonic masculinity. With a series of mostly long shots, the camera embeds Ali in a world of modest domestic comfort that includes his kitchen and small vegetable garden. In many respects nontraditional, although conscious of gender codings, Ali raised his son after the early death of his wife as, he says, "both mother and father." Whereas the Islamists shame Yeter upon discovering her Turkishness, he responds to the same news by saying that now *he* is ashamed. However, Ali's apparent working-class sense of belonging is destabilized by a fantasy of owning more than his carefully cultivated tomatoes. Indicatively, his declaration that he can pay for exclusive access to Yeter's body follows a successful horse-racing bet that supplements his pension and modest income from property back in Turkey. When he is hospitalized with a heart attack caused by excessive drinking, the aging lover suspects that his son, who answers his father's curious questions about his sex life with tactful silence, could have started an affair with Yeter in his absence. Drunk yet again after his return home, Ali tries to coerce Yeter into sex, arguing that he, after all, has "paid" for her. When she snaps, "You don't own me," he claims, staggering, "Yes, I do." In response, she packs her bags, and as Ali tries to prevent her from leaving, she angrily pushes him several times before he slaps her face once in return, causing her to fall fatally against the edge of the bed. While the camera (operated by Klausmann) has kept the film audience at a spatial distance with continued long shots, Ali's drunk anger is now dramatized through the closest (thigh-up) shots of the sequence, with him frontally positioned in the center of the frame. From an increased distance again, we then observe how he bends down and bursts into tears next to Yeter on the floor after realizing that she is no longer moving.

What is the film audience invited to make of this configuration of (in Latour's words) "overtaken" action?[61] Although Yeter's death is afforded by alcohol, social fantasy, a hand, and a piece of furniture, most of us will nonetheless want to insist that Ali be held accountable. What guidance does form provide in this situation? As I will insist repeatedly, the spatial positioning of the camera does not equal affective proximity or distance, but it does constitute one element of relevant form assemblages. The relatively distant camera position throughout most of the sequence would seem to support emotional detachment, if not Brechtian judgments of the petit bourgeois fool. However, there are diverging vectors in play. Cognitive scholarship has been helpful in breaking down grand dichotomies of distanciation versus identification. Murray Smith distinguishes between "various levels" and components "of engagement," including *sympathy* (or "acentral" feeling for) versus *empathy* ("central" feeling with), as well as *recognition* (the construction of character), *alignment*, and (moral) *allegiance*.[62] Alignment is not limited to perceptual overlap (or to point of view, POV); Smith breaks it down further into *spatial attachment* in the sense of narration restricted "to the actions of a single character" and *subjective access* to this character.[63] In the scenario at hand, the camera's relative distance is counteracted by how the chapter's narration has mostly followed Ali, introducing other characters as they intersect with him. Ali's highly affective performance also gives us cognitive access to his feelings, even if we do not share them—and the actor's star credit may further encourage a positive engagement. Nonetheless, the offered acentral alignment would at best seem to stir pity in most audience members. Or could some of this pity be converted into compassion in the moment of Ali's more closely framed outburst into tears? (I am positioning compassion on the spectrum between acentral and central engagement here.)[64] In foregrounding the human weakness of this patriarchal fool, how does the film's worldmaking complicate our relationship to him?

My point here is to underline the piecemeal and shifting nature of audience engagements, or the layered cinematic processes of "following the actors." Smith's model is more flexible than those of other cognitive critics, who characteristically underline neat and stable engagement lineups in cinematic scenarios that produce allegiance with the hero and aversion to her enemy.[65] Nonetheless, my model of affective cinematic worldmaking goes further in breaking down audience engagements. Keeping in mind that categorical distinctions have only heuristic value in the fluid world of affect, I trace unstable, layered transactions at the intersection of specific formal configurations and audience responses. On the latter side, we need to account, for example, for conflicts between or confluences of any viewer's (affectively charged) values and (normatively costructured) affective memories. Audience responses to Ali will be inflected not only by whether we object to his patriarchal claim— I suspect that most arthouse audiences of this film will. More intricately, they will be shaped by the ways in which any individual viewer's feminist commitments are experientially charged and interact, for example, with conscious or unconscious associations triggered by the image of a pathetically violent, aging father.

On the diegetic level, Ali's son, Nejat (who has not seen the described scene unfold), harshly proclaims his father a "murderer." The configuration of Nejat's own story provides a counterpoint to the affective modulations invited by Ali and Yeter's encounter. While Nejat's story remains subordinated to that of his father throughout most of the film's first chapter, it becomes the film's focus after Yeter's death. The affective key of these sequences is very subdued. If Ali displays excessive emotion, his son shows too little. The generally soft-spoken, quiet Nejat is played by Baki Davrak, whom German audiences may remember as Murat, the shy high school student struggling with coming out as gay in Kutluğ Ataman's *Lola and Billy the Kid* (*Lola und Bilidikid*, 1999). While Nejat's sexuality remains undetermined, *The Edge of Heaven* activates the intertextual memory of Murat's educational orientation. Nejat is a literature professor at Hamburg University, where early on we see him lecture about the quintessentially German poet Johann Wolfgang von Goethe. Once more, the film conspicuously draws on discourses of immigration, here in reverse-stereotypical fashion: all too perfectly, Nejat's position and lecture topic fulfill majority-German demands for the "integration" of its Muslim community, whereby "integration" easily slips into calls for assimilation to models of secularized Christian tradition. Nejat's lecture style, however, is unaccented, almost casual, as if emotionally absent or bored. In a 1990s film (with its typically postcolonial interpretations at the time), such a withholding of affective participation might have been dramatized to the effect of "mimicry" in the sense of a superficial, subliminally mocking repetition of national culture with a difference—as, for example, in Murat's hilariously parodied German teacher in *Lola and Billy the Kid*.[66]

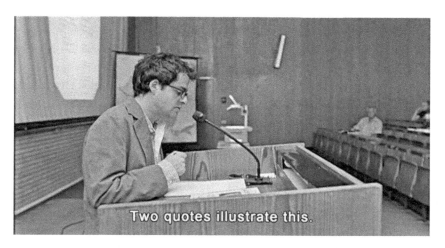

FIGURE 1.1 *The Edge of Heaven* (dir. Fatih Akın, 2007).

But the notion of parody is not appropriate to the mode of presentation in *The Edge of Heaven*. Whereas the earlier film employed techniques of hyperbolic acting to make its majority-German characters into an outrageous spectacle, Davrak's portrayal of Nejat's professorial behavior is low-key and inconspicuous. Instead, the film engages our curiosity for the narrative through the foregrounding work of the camera in this scene, which first captures Nejat's back and then slowly moves around him in a 180-degree tracking shot as he speaks (figure 1.1), before a cut to a student sleeping soundly through his lecture invites an audience chuckle. With its tongue-in-cheek accent, this presentation makes us wonder about the configuration it sets up. Its slight artificiality is underlined in a later scene in which Nejat decides to give up his prestigious university position and buy a German bookstore for sale in Istanbul. The majority-German bookstore owner, who presents a somewhat more caricatured, effeminate double of Nejat in body type, clothing, and acting style, comments: "That would be funny, if . . . [laughs] a Turkish professor of German from Germany ends up in a German bookshop in Turkey. . . . That fits!" Looking half amused, half irritated, Nejat hesitates before he answers with a note of impatience in his tone: "Yes, maybe." To audience members attuned to critical debates about immigration imaginaries, Nejat's subdued reaction might well signal irritation with such invocations of cultural hybridity, which remain bound to the idea of encounters between two relatively stable worlds.[67] While some German critics followed the bookstore owner in reading *The Edge of Heaven* as a film about people "between two cultures" and the "mixing of identities," its emphatically transnational narrative world no longer operates along such dichotomies.[68]

The attention to narrative configuration invited by the film's foregrounded narration does not, however, come at the expense of all affective engagement with Nejat. Before he cut his ties with Ali, the first chapter introduced him as a caring, if introverted son. And Nejat actually served as our very first human access point in the film: the (narratively unconnected) opening sequence preceding the first chapter followed him driving through rural Turkey. In the film's first moment of intensity, we were even briefly perceptually aligned with Nejat through a POV shot inviting us to coexperience his driving into a mountain tunnel, which seemed to motivate the screen going black before the intertitle "Yeter's death" announced the first chapter. In experiential rather than metacritical terms, we might now make sense of Nejat's understated professional performance as one of *disaffection*: an orientation of both "distance" and potential "disloyalty," implying "blockage" but also a "strategic emotional flow."[69] To be sure, this is a speculative approach fueled by audience curiosity. Nejat's demeanor, unlike his father's, does not provide much access to his feelings throughout this chapter of the film. As a counterpoint to the presentation of Ali's excess affects, this withholding of access presents a second facet of Akın's post-Brechtian modulations of distance and intimacy: following its actors via thoroughly acentral forms of alignment, the film creates space for exploring affective responses—including the negative response of withdrawal.

TRACING CONTROVERSY: RICH AFFECTSCAPES, COMPLICATED ALIGNMENTS

Nejat has come to Istanbul with the intent of finding Yeter's daughter and financing her university studies, presumably in atonement for his father's deed and in response to Yeter's expressed wish for her daughter to get an education, like Nejat. To his cousin, he now explains his decision to stay by saying "Maybe teaching isn't my calling." However, the bad impression we have of Nejat's teaching at this point of the film is

complicated in the second of its three chapters, entitled "Lotte's death."
As another, temporally parallel story unfolds, the audience learns that
the student sleeping during Nejat's lecture was Yeter's daughter, Ayten,
who has fled to Germany after getting in trouble with the police for her
affiliation with the Kurdish resistance movement in Turkey. The chapter
opens with documentary-style footage of an Istanbul May 1 demonstration. Unlike the Bremen march opening the first chapter, this one is
accompanied by a massive police presence; the masks worn by some
protesters and their angry chants contrast with the cheerful singing at
the German May 1 parade.[70] In the midst of the Istanbul agitation, Ayten
had picked up a gun on the street and hidden it, presumably for later use
in her group, which is described by the state as "terrorist."[71] In Germany,
Ayten has ended up homeless and hangs out at the university for shelter.
Diegetically, her sleeping through a lecture in a language she does not
speak merely indicates exhaustion. For the film audience, however, this
narrative reassembly enables a different reading: the activist's sleep now
also unfolds as a political commentary on Nejat's lecture, which discusses Goethe's stance against revolution. In the first chapter, we heard
the first of two fictional quotations Nejat announced as evidence for
Goethe's position against such—unnatural—upheaval: the revolutionary is like a "fool" who demands roses in the midst of winter.[72] As a
foreshadowing, the cut to Ayten positioned her as precisely that fool.
Now our perspective is reversed. Focused on Ayten through a medium
shot, we hear the repetition of Nejat's words as emanating from the
background of the lecture hall. Only afterward, a cut to him positions
the professor, waist-up behind his podium, as the established, if disaffected representative of Goethe's belief in seasonal circularity; his second quote suggests that revolution destroys as much as it creates.

In contrast to Goethe (and Nejat?), Ayten has an agenda for change.
Her politics is contoured further when she meets Lotte, a naïve but
spontaneously generous student of English who takes her home. Home
turns out to be the house of Lotte's mother, although she assures Ayten
that she lives there only temporarily after a stay abroad. Ayten, whose
at moments harsh demeanor presents a counterpoint to Nejat's gentle
politeness, soon gets into a fight with Lotte's mother, Susanne, who is
not pleased with having to host her. Through the interplay of tone of
voice, words, gestures, and audience associations, the sequence further

unfolds the film's rich reservoir of affects. Piece by piece, the film assembles a tense, layered configuration that cannot be easily mapped in clear-cut terms—and cannot be easily resolved by taking sides. With a noticeable ironic charge, Susanne comments on her daughter's "very generous" taking in of "a strange/foreign [*fremde*] woman." Her distant tone indicates hostility or anxiety under a surface of collected rationality, as she closes off her domestic space and herself. Countering with more definite hostility, Lotte aligns Susanne with a national "We," of which she refuses to be a part: "That's so German, mom."

In which ways can affective orientations toward closure versus openness and withdrawal versus reaching out thus be described as collective? Lotte's charge touches on an entire legacy of theorizing the alleged German coldness and lack of empathy in the wake of the Holocaust, which has recently come under postcritical scrutiny. Anna Parkinson has shown that the widespread inability, or unwillingness, of Germans to express the normative emotions demanded by postwar official culture does not equal the absence of complex, if mostly negative affects.[73] As indicated in the introduction, however, I hold that such nonnormative affects are also deeply historical, configured in the entanglements of fascist and postfascist discourse, violence, and bodily memory. In this sense, Susanne's affective orientation at closure—as a lid on underlying negativity—could in fact qualify for a national label, as long as we remember the contested and changeable nature of affects in the assemblages of specific institutional and discursive contexts. Short of consolidating into a homogenous habitus, mesh-ups and holdups of coolness, reserve, irony, anxiety, and hostility certainly circulated through everyday interactions as well as state discourse and artistic works in postwar Germany, a context that was in some respects more nationally circumscribed than twenty-first-century culture.

In Akın's 2007 film, a concrete reminder, and remainder, of this postwar culture is found in the circumstance that Susanne is played by Hanna Schygulla, the major female star of Fassbinder's New German Cinema. If we have recognized her, this association can substantiate Lotte's charge, insofar as Fassbinder's legacy has been associated with the pursuit of collective holdups of affect in postwar Germany. Simultaneously, the association adds star credit. Moreover, Schygulla played not only Maria Braun, Fassbinder's most explicitly allegorical representation of Germany's "icy" postwar culture, but also Marie in *Katzelmacher*, who, as I detail in chapter 2, defies her neighborhood collective in opening up to the Greek "guest worker" Yorgos.[74] On the diegetic level, configuration details such as Lotte's "spoiled daughter" reliance on her mother's domestic labor may facilitate some audience understanding for Susanne. Nonetheless, the overall assembly of Susanne's encounter with Ayten seems suited to stir disapproval of her condescending behavior toward the guest. Visually, she is positioned as literally unmoved in her chair in the center of the kitchen. Pitting cherries, she ignores Ayten's arguments, stubbornly repeating her own political recipe for Turkey, naïvely liberal even in 2007: "Maybe things will get better once you get into the European Union." Calm in tone, Susanne also attacks the refugee as a "person who just likes to fight." Faced with these poses of superiority, Ayten loses her calm: angrily, she declares that she doesn't "trust the European Union," a body of governance run by former colonial powers. "It's globalization, and we are fighting against it." This critique of political Europe notwithstanding, Ayten articulates her agenda through the universalized codes of the European Enlightenment.[75] In line with the left-wing reaffirmations of humanist paradigms in the 2000s cited earlier, she demands "100 percent of human rights, and 100 percent freedom of speech, and 100 percent of social education" for Turkey.

With Ayten's agenda, the film thus introduces an activist notion of universalism. In Gilroy's words, she claims an "agonistic, planetary humanism," which keeps the impact of power differentials in sight, and, in contrast to imperially universalist globalisms, reimagines the world as a "finite place . . . with strictly limited resources that are allocated unequally."[76] These sharp inequalities are dramatized in Ayten's spatial position as she nervously circles around Susanne, at the edges of the frame and for a moment beyond, before a series of close-ups highlights the encounter's affective charges. Mireille Rossello has targeted a European "crisis of hospitality" with respect to the construction of refugees as "objects of . . . public generosity," a construction in which the host is deemed to be sovereign, while the "guest" is stripped of any rights.[77] When Ayten, literally a guest in a German household, gets upset in response to Susanne's provocations, the host declares, still almost motionless in her chair, "You can talk like that in your house." Ayten's vulnerable position is confirmed when she later follows Susanne's advice to request political asylum in an unfortunate encounter with traffic police. Ayten is denied refugee status based on article 16a of the German Constitution, the article controversially reformed in 1993 so as to restrict the country's unconditional postwar commitment to granting political asylum.[78] Turkey's status as a candidate for European Union membership, the judge argues further, would make torture or mistreatment upon return unlikely.

In contrast to the heightened affective atmosphere in the German kitchen, this legal notice is neutral, even friendly in tone: the judge claims she understands Ayten's personal motivations and takes her political activism to be credible. But the notice is also definite, whereas Susanne's anxious hostility is narratively unfolded as part of an overdetermined and shifting affective configuration that is not easily decoded as symptomatic of one definite condition, even if it has national layers. From the courtroom, a cut takes us back to the house, while the judge's reading of the sentence continues as a voice-over, connecting the two scenarios. Her calm voice contrasts sharply with Lotte's visible agitation. Planning to follow the deported Ayten to Turkey, Lotte wrongly accuses her mother of having hidden her passport. Susanne, who, as we will learn later, has paid the court fees for Ayten, charges Lotte with being "blind" in her rage. Nonetheless, we may empathize with Lotte's intense affect. Despite all the outlined complications, this second chapter of the film has emotionally drawn the audience in more fully than the first by aligning us with the developing passionate love between Lotte and Ayten, both through closer shot framings than in the Nejat-Ali plot and through the narration's foregrounding of the emergence of these positive feelings. On the dance floor during their first night out, the camera traces the women's flirtation in an atmosphere of ecstasy via happy intoxication, which opens the boundaries of subjectivity in the flows of affect: in close-up and extreme close-up, we variously see their faces and parts of both heads as they share a joint between them. Foregrounding laughter, smoke, and flowing hair, the scene's cinematography brings the audience experientially close to the developing sensual intensity. After recording the first kiss in its full length, the camera underlines its impact on the two women's subjectivities with a close shot-countershot take that shows shock, or awe, on the intoxicated faces.

It is not the kind of shock that would lead to hungover regrets. The film portrays Lotte and Ayten's lesbian relationship without any coming-out drama unless we attribute some of Susanne's discomfort to this layer of the situation. Such a reading is not supported by explicit verbal statements: rather than confirming foregone conclusions, the cinematography and acting encourage the audience to attend to ambiguous clues such as Susanne's apparent subdued agitation as she observes the girls' giggly, newly intimate return from their night out. Akın explained that with a same-sex relationship, he intended to avoid the clichés that would have been transported by a "young, dark, hairy Turk" falling in love with an "innocent blonde"—and, of course, a muscular blond guy setting out to save the dark refugee woman would not have been any better.[79] Although the film underlines the continued impact of racialization on the Turkish-German imagination by holding onto the color code grounding these stereotypes, the lesbian reconfiguration of the romance narrative seems to enable imaginative explorations of a queer escape into potentially egalitarian space. In *The Cultural Politics of Emotion*, Sara Ahmed similarly solves her dilemma of wanting to affirm "love as 'towardness'" without ignoring the prevalence of love's exclusive political configurations: she champions the realm of queer pleasure as one that "opens . . . up" the body in "reach[ing] out to others."[80] In doing so, however, Ahmed implicitly juxtaposes the productive excess of sexuality with politically captured feelings, in a queer studies variation on the dominant affect-versus-emotion binary.[81] *The Edge of Heaven* displaces these categorical delineations in the way that it entangles sex(ual affect) and emotion. Imbricating pleasure with romantic and other emotional intensity, the camera dwells on the women's tenderly entangled limbs in bed, dramatizes Ayten's longing for her own mother after the fight with Lotte's, and shows her reaching out for Lotte across the bare, dominantly (cold) greenish-blue room she is assigned in the refugee hostel.

In this sense, *The Edge of Heaven* more fully unfolds an affirmative imagination of love than Ahmed's theoretical work. However, the film does not pretend to actually solve any dilemma by dissolving complex political configurations of power and affect into queer feelings. Instead, its practice of modulating distance and intimacy through foregrounded narration entangles this love in a web of affective complication. Artful variations of spatial distance contribute to this modulation. Even on the dance floor during the first night out, a cut to a very long shot reminds us of the camera's presence as a potentially distant observer and implicitly dramatizes its creation of intimacy as such. In the refugee hostel, Ayten's gesture of reaching out for Lotte on the opposite bed is also framed from a striking distance, following an extended close-up on each of their faces. While these contrastive imbrications of spatial distance and intimacy may dramatize the whirlwind of diegetic affects involved, they also offer different modes of audience engagement. The outlined invitations for affective involvement in this chapter of the film make the notion of empathy—or feeling *with*—more promising than in the first chapter. Simultaneously, the cinematography still underlines acentrality. Thus, it encourages us to explore imaginative alignments, and perhaps even experience affective intensity, without pretending that we can actually feel Ayten's pain or Lotte's anxious longing: we can be "affected by that which" we cannot fully know.[82]

Precisely how each audience member is affected depends, as indicated, also on "where they are": on their positionality, to use the notion coined by feminist scholars in an attempt to de-essentialize concepts of group identity along with more fluid configurations of conscious and unconscious memories and fantasies. Despite their overall affective engagement, my students have variously distanced themselves from Ayten's harshness or Lotte's naivety. The latter is explored more fully through Lotte's relationship with her mother in the course of the film. Not only is Lotte's generosity based on her privilege of maternal economic support, but also, as it turns out, her postadolescent rebellion repeats her mother's own story. Like Lotte, who says she just returned from a three-month-long trip to India, Susanne hitchhiked there decades ago because, as she tells Nejat in the film's third chapter, that "was the thing to do then." If Susanne, who thus fashioned her self along the lines of transnational rebellion once, has since lapsed back into the "German" mindset that her body language presented in her initial encounter with Ayten, can we assume that her wide-eyed daughter has escaped that mindset for good? Is her economically asymmetrical relationship with Ayten not impacted by the legacy condensed in the film's colonial topoi, including the choice of India as a travel location? Does Lotte's repeated announcement that she wants "to help" Ayten not reiterate the proverbial gesture of the benign colonizer?

Consequently perhaps, there is no happy ending.[83] As announced by the title of the film's second chapter, Lotte dies, too—just like Yeter—by a violent, narratively overdetermined accident. When Lotte renews her pledge to help her lover in the prison, Ayten, pressured by fellow activist inmates, asks her to retrieve the gun she had hidden earlier. As soon as Lotte does so, however, children on the street steal her purse containing the gun, and when she demands it back, one of them shoots her. Yet again, multiple associations on different levels offer themselves. Narrative composition is foregrounded insofar as the incident is conspicuously in line with Anton Chekhov's proverbial recipe for good storytelling, which requires a gun introduced early on to go off in a subsequent act.[84] Simultaneously, the circumstances of Lotte's death once more dramatize distributed agency in human-nonhuman networks.[85] But they also unfold yet another set of political complications. Namely, we may wonder whether these are some of the "illiterate Kurdish street children" about whom Nejat was alerted during his search for Ayten. When a police officer asked for his motivations for financing Ayten's studies, Nejat articulated a less explicitly political humanism than Ayten herself: "Because knowledge and education are human rights." "Well put," the casually dressed, apparently leftist police officer replied with a half-ironic smile, and then he asked whether Nejat would consider helping one of the street children instead. Nejat's facial expression suggested that he was unsettled by the question—and a cut ended the dialogue before he found an answer.

ON THE OTHER SIDE: TRANSLOCAL OPENINGS

Nejat's dilemma unfolds in analogy to that inscribed in Lotte's desire to help Ayten. Although easily overcoming the bounds of nation, culture, and gender, their love and openness are not actually universal—unconditional in the sense of Ahmed's analysis or "undifferentiated," as Gilroy characterizes the politics of "planetary humanism."[86] Rather, their affective engagements are delineated by two influential topoi of presumably universal connection that sustain much apolitical narrative in the worlds of Hollywood & Co.: those of romantic love—if revised toward queer inclusiveness—and the modern nuclear family—if opened up toward transnational "adoption." After all, Nejat has come to Istanbul to atone for his father's deed and in place of Ayten's mother. When the third chapter brings closure in affirming such substitute familial bonds, the tension between Nejat's abstractly humanist motivations and their underlying circumscription by personal relations arguably also allegorizes the film's overall political dilemma. However, its foregrounded practice of complex assemblage actively integrates this dilemma into its layered worldmaking rather than canceling its significance in a happy ending. In effect, I argue, the humanist resolution remains political.

This is indicated by how this resolution is premised on dramatic change. After Lotte's death, both Susanne and Ayten—and Nejat, with their help—open up. In a moment of rage, Susanne had cut her daughter off financially in the last phone conversation we saw before Lotte's death. Now Susanne travels to Istanbul. The film's perhaps most striking—noticeable as well as unsettling—scene records her initial mourning process in the hotel there. The camera is positioned conspicuously high up in a ceiling corner of the large, luxurious room, where it holds still for a long time. From the unusual angle and significant distance afforded by it, we see Susanne's arrival and the passing of time—indicated by several dissolves without camera repositioning—as she turns to the minibar and later, at night, falls apart in grief, wailing loudly and helplessly throwing herself onto the floor, a minuscule figure blending in with her surroundings in the dim light on the far side of the room (figure 1.2). While the film audience is thus invited to focus on

FIGURE 1.2 *The Edge of Heaven* (dir. Fatih Akın, 2007).

Susanne's emotional unraveling, the artificially foregrounded framing has elicited contrary readings: commonplace associations of empathy with spatial alignment suggest that the shot is designed to "create distance and minimize emotional excess."[87] Positioned like a surveillance camera (my students have underlined), the camera can even be suspected of operating as a voyeur here, cruelly exposing private suffering. Nonetheless, another reviewer describes the scene as exemplary for the film's "aesthetics of quiet empathy."[88]

The key to this scene's puzzle, I argue, is in the multilayered process of narrative assemblage, or the interplay of diverging form elements and affects. First, the configuration underlines the need to break down audience engagements beyond established categories: affective intensity charges do not equal full-fledged character empathy. While the sound of Susanne's wailing, in particular, can affect us strongly, this does not necessarily translate into a coherent response of feeling with her.[89] With its incongruous form elements, the scene probes how we can be affected at a distance (perhaps by way of unrelated memories of mourning?) and experience a spontaneous piecemeal connection with an actor whom the narration neither has invited us to like much nor pretends to bring us close to now. Second, narrative assemblage matters despite—or precisely in developing—such heterogeneity of form elements and affective vectors. Whereas Deleuzians have insisted on the nonnarrative rupture performed by affect, cognitive scholarship has privileged coherence and continuity—for example, through the notion of the "primacy effect," emphasizing the importance of first impressions in reading a character.[90] Fritz Breithaupt reverses the latter idea and integrates a moment of change into the cognitive paradigm by assigning paradigmatic significance to the genre of Aristotelian tragedy: empathy, he suggests, is both produced and cathartically released when an unexpected event undoes our construction of character.[91] Less genre-bound, my own proposal intertwines instability and connection in mapping a larger vector of engagement. Within the film's worldmaking assembly, the hotel scene of what is "not quite yet" empathy initiates a gradual shift toward closer audience engagement with Susanne; her affective undoing underlines the instability of nonsovereign actors, but it is not out of character as much as it develops a layer of her self that was indicated earlier in her apparent agitation behind the cool façade.

While the hotel room scene primarily dramatizes the "turn[ing] in" of the body "on itself," the narrative foregrounding makes us attend to the importance of the event, preparing us for full-fledged empathy as the film now continues to trace Susanne's opening up.[92] Nejat had sublet a room to Lotte, and when Susanne meets with him the next day, he recognizes her as "the saddest person here." Susanne requests to spend time in Lotte's room and tenderly evokes her presence while reading her diary, including Lotte's reflections on the similarity of their life paths. Now we are gradually aligned more closely with Susanne spatially and, arguably, encouraged to shift our allegiance in experiencing the affective reshaping of her subjectivity. When she then identifies with Lotte's mission to help Ayten, Ayten helps herself. In partial analogy to Susanne's change, Ayten's is motivated by a—less striking and shorter—representation of affective opening up through mourning: during Susanne's visit in the prison, a series of close shots and countershots shows Ayten crying. The barred glass wall across which they talk on the phone once more intertwines distance and intimacy. Afterward, when Ayten decides to use her legal "right to remorse"—obtaining her freedom in return for renouncing her ties to her resistance group[93]—this solution does not come at the expense of all of her political identity. Although the film clearly advocates against violence, the narrative emphasis on Susanne's more radical change as a precondition for Ayten's indirectly vindicates her political vision. And if revolution is delegitimized by its violent effects, the film's layered configuration simultaneously identifies this violence (in the nonsovereign agency of the children) as the effect of the poverty and exclusion that call for revolution in the first place. All in all, Goethe's insistence on stability is not validated: the change effected through narrative reconfiguration does matter.

More skeptical critics have cautioned that the film's ending seems to background political specificity in its focus on transcultural connection through familial affect.[94] Looking out of the window of Nejat's apartment, Susanne, who is becoming a substitute mother for Nejat, asks about the people going to the mosque on the morning of Bayram. Nejat explains that the religious holiday is based on the story of God asking for but then not demanding a human sacrifice. As Susanne explicates in response, the same story can be found in the Bible. Does this simple gesture of cross-cultural connection displace Ayten's insistence on positionality? Do racism, gender, and class still matter in this film's world when we are now invited to empathize more fully also with Nejat, whose coolness melts in the memory of his father once reassuring the scared child that he would rather risk trouble with God than sacrifice his son? I believe they do. The argument is not only about the experiential weight of the bulk of the film over that of closure; it is also about the configuration of this closure itself.

With trembling lips, Nejat asks Susanne to take over the bookstore for a few days, and he sets out for his father's home village on the Black Sea, where Ali has returned after his deportation from Germany. Nejat's travel there is shown through the film's most extended use of repetition and variation. We return to the introductory sequence, which featured Nejat's drive through the Turkish countryside, including his stop at a provincial gas station. But the point of this narrative arrangement is not circularity.[95] The foreshadowing introductory sequence and its briefer variation at the end of the first chapter have now found an unambiguous spatiotemporal location in the film's narrative, and instead of following Nejat into ominous darkness, we accompany him to his destination. The point may, however, be about investing the affective journey with socio-historical layers—or insisting once more on the significance of location in a transnational world.[96] At the gas station, Nejat becomes involved in a conversation about the (to him, unfamiliar) music playing, per-formed by the regionally famous Kazım Koyuncu, whose early cancer death the attendant connects to the Chernobyl catastrophe.[97] As Nejat moves on, the soundtrack continues at increased volume. As a means of foregrounded affective narration, it further attaches the audience to Nejat, with whom we instantly align in a POV shot this time around. Underlining the vulnerability of humans in a shared world in which "environmental and medical crises do not stop at national boundaries," the film's narration thus carries the quasi-documentary insistence on socio-geographic specificity into the affective closing sequence and "an oppositional mood" into its cosmopolitan closure.[98]

When Nejat arrives in the village, his father is out on a fishing trip. The film ends with a shot of Nejat looking out onto the water. The classical storyteller's narration resists classical demands for closure. We don't know how the encounter between father and son will go—if Ali even returns: Nejat heard that he ought to be back shortly because the sea is getting rough, but he is nowhere in sight. To be sure, we should also not rashly stipulate another tragic event based on the connotations of *The Edge of Heaven*, the English title of both the film and its last chapter. The German *Auf der anderen Seite* (literally, On the other side) is much more polysemic. Granted, Akın's initial title idea was *On the Other Side of Life*, but even this version, with its more spiritual undertones, could index the repeated transnational border crossings of the film's characters or the opening up of their identificatory enclosures along with the mythical river of death. The final German title further connotes "on the other hand."[99] As a gesture of narrative caution, it summarizes the film's struggle to suture an oppositional political agenda, or its sustained critique of socio-symbolic regimes of difference, with the affirmation of a horizon of transnational, transfaith connection that counters the politics of hatred in contemporary Europe.

As I have argued, Akın's complex, simultaneously tentative and affectively engaging mode of nonsovereign, imaginative worldmaking does present a forceful contribution to this timely task. The foregrounded act of storytelling is political also in that it invites audiences to consider the presented configurations with engaged curiosity rather than submitting to the force of naturalized evidence produced by classical form—or returning us to Brecht's cool analytic certainty of having gotten the story right. Nor does the narration assume a (clichéd postmodern) stance of disengaged resignation in the name of ambiguity or undecidability. Instead, Akın's complex worldmaking assemblage explores plural, contestable, yet experientially significant possibilities of affective reconfiguration. The film's procedure through doublings and repetitions with a difference, which unfolds narrative's potential for engaging specificity and contrast along with relation and similarity, thus attains its significance as a means of breaking the hold of, while not forgetting, the legacies of hatred and inequality that stand in the way of inclusive imaginations of collectivity.

A SEPARATION'S POETICS OF PERCEPTION: FOLLOWING THE ACTORS AS A PHENOMENOLOGICAL METHOD

Farhadi's *A Separation* achieves a resonant reshuffling of the sensible (in Jacques Rancière's sense) with different narrative means. It was the first Iranian feature to win the Golden Bear at the Berlin International

Film Festival, or Berlinale, where it had its international premiere in 2011, as well as the first Iranian feature to win the Academy Award for Best Foreign Language Film (2012). Like *The Edge of Heaven*, *A Separation* was almost unanimously praised by reviewers for its complexity and artful narrative construction.[100] Some critics credited the director's theater background for his ability to set his work apart from the "neorealist mode" of "postrevolutionary Iranian cinema" familiar to Western audiences: whereas Abbas Kirostami, Jafar Panahi, and Majid Majidi prefer nonprofessional actors and "loose, simple narratives," *A Separation* is based on professional acting and "a meticulously constructed screenplay."[101] Simultaneously, *A Separation*'s complex worldmaking differs markedly from *The Edge of Heaven*'s "classical" story*telling* method, allowing me to outline a second aesthetic path on which my model of affective cinematic worldmaking gains contours as a methodology of following the actors of social controversies. In a nutshell, I argue that *A Separation* facilitates a project of *nonsovereign perception* through its mode of *phenomenological close-up*. In detailing this method alongside Akın's, this chapter indicates the breadth of cinematic possibilities for reconfiguring affects and collectivity claims between diegetic actors as well as audiences.

A Separation's process of narration is much less foregrounded than that of *The Edge of Heaven*—or foregrounded primarily through the ways in which it dramatizes restriction. This does not quite mean that the film's camera style is "muted."[102] As I will detail, Mahmoud Kalari's cinematography contributes significantly to the film's formal design. But instead of fleshing out rich scenarios largely from a comfortable narrative distance, the film's "closed mise-en-scène and tight shot composition" elliptically present more or less fragmentary views.[103] Through both its management of diegetic information and the ways in which it explores space and perspective, *A Separation* creates, in a reviewer's words, a "real immediacy" effect "right up close to the characters."[104] Farhadi himself describes the intended outcome as that of making the audience feel that "they were there in the room with the actors."[105] Consequently, the audience feels the charge of having to actively participate in the worldmaking process: we treat every "view, every dialogue particle, every look" as a piece of "evidence" for what happened and try to "work out our feelings," a challenge that "grows ever more intricate" as "our perspective constantly shifts" in the "emotionally wrenching" assembly of the film's "seething tensions."[106]

As indicated by the notion of evidence, some critics have compared the role of the audience to that of a judge called on to adjudicate a diegetic conflict that involves an Iranian middle-class couple in crisis, their legal entanglements with a lower-class family, and, perhaps, "the situation of Iranian society overall."[107] This reading is facilitated by the film's opening scene, which spatially aligns the audience with a family court judge, whose voice we hear but whom we do not see. Looking directly at the camera in a long take of the courtroom, the protagonists, Nader and Simin, argue their case for a divorce. Simin wants to leave the country, whereas Nader insists on staying to care for his Alzheimer-stricken father. The cinematography of this introductory moment, however, differs starkly from that of the remainder of the film. If the opening makes us "expect a film of long fixed-angle takes," the camera afterward "roams around freely, framing and reframing tight groupings of people in confined spaces."[108] In exploring this cinematography as a crucial part of the film's worldmaking, I argue that the audience's participatory role in the film is overall not that of a judge—or not that of a judge in the classical juridical sense of an authority endowed with the sovereign force of legal rationality. More cautious comments, partly in the same reviews, suggest that *A Separation* may be about "aspects of hearing, appeal and mediation" more than reaching a verdict or even "any answers."[109] In this spirit, I situate the film as one about (multisensory) perception, which investigates the limits of mutual understanding in an "intricate web of social, ethical and religious dilemmas" but does so without abandoning the project of seeing, hearing, and sensing others.[110]

My primary theoretical interlocutors for this reading are Vivian Sobchack and Laura Marks. As outlined in the introduction, Sobchack's *The Address of the Eye* (1992) set out to counter the "paranoia," "suspicion," and "pessimism" of then influential semiotic, psychoanalytic, and Lacanian film theory.[111] Turning instead to Maurice Merleau-Ponty's existential phenomenology, Sobchack reconceptualizes cinematic vision in terms of possibilities for "communication and insight."[112] Whereas Lacanian theories position the spectator as "subjected" and film as a technology of "disembodied and godlike vision," Sobchack situates embodied perception as an "opening upon the world."[113] In the dialogic encounter between nonsovereign film and nonsovereign audience, vision is not primarily " 'deceptive' " but affords intersubjective relation in originating "the visual seer and the visible Other as co-emergent subjects."[114] In this sense, it can facilitate embodied—rather than detached—cosmopolitical openings, across transnational as well local divisions. With respect to *A Separation*, Sobchack's methodological challenge can be contoured against Rob White's short reading in *Film Quarterly*. In a nutshell, White positions *A Separation* as a political allegory of more or less totalitarian rule: the film's "pretenses of intimacy," he claims, trigger "our own empathy" to the effect of distracting from and risking to obscure the film's "sinister institutional dimension."[115] Following White for a moment, we might locate an initial nod to this sinister dimension in the introductory credit sequence. In close-up, we see the scanning of passports—presumably for the visa documents that Simin will waive around in the divorce court shortly—*from within* the copy machine, which could metaphorically stand in for the "evil eye" of either, or both, the state and the filmic apparatus. However, I don't think that these suspicious associations exhaust the workings of the striking shot, as its play of light fleetingly illuminates official photos and information. Presenting these identity objects in a haptic close-up along with the hands working the machine, the shot alternatively provides an initial hint at the film's poetics of nonsovereign perception. The institutional, in other words, is introduced from the angle of the emergence of vision in the very midst of things: an object-like rather than a godlike view.

My insistence on this poetics, and the film's intimate layers dismissed by White, does not preclude the possibility that a "healthy dose" of suspicion may be appropriate for reading *A Separation*, in particular against the backdrop of Iranian censorship constraints. In theoretical terms, this qualification to Sobchack's methodological call—and fine-tuning of layered modes of reading—can be developed by turning to Mark's oeuvre. Whereas Sobchack's focus in *The Address of the Eye* is on shared human embodiment, Marks has probed different possibilities for localizing phenomenological aesthetics and methodologies.[116] Thus, Marks's *The Skin of the Film* (2000) develops the notion of "multisensory images"—and, specifically, "haptic, or tactile visuality"—for contemporary "intercultural" (primarily diaspora) cinema, and her more recent

Hanan al-Cinema: Affections for the Moving Image (2015) focuses on "Arab" film and media art, with "Arab" explicitly understood as a politically constructed category.[117] While Farhadi's film is yet differently localized, I find elements of both of these categorizations useful. In *The Skin*, Marks insists that perception "is never a purely individual act but also an engagement with the social and with cultural memory" and that "cinematic spectatorship" is thus a process of "collective reception" in sociocultural context.[118] If *A Separation* has, as Hamid Naficy suggests, "helped globalize the Iranian cinema" more "than any other single film" but, unlike earlier transnational successes, has done so precisely with "themes, characters and [a] primary audience" that are "strikingly 'Iranian,'" we need to emphatically situate this process of collective reception on different—national and transnational—scales.[119] And perhaps its "intercultural" dimension unfolds not only on the international festival circuit but also locally insofar as the film explores different cultures (and social controversies) *within* Iran. In *A Separation*'s opening scene, Simin's loosely tied hijab and Nader's beard and hair quickly position the scenario in a Muslim context for a (stereo)typical Western viewer and may evoke a host of associations attached to that diagnosis, whereas Iranian or contextually more attuned audiences may be just as quick to place the couple as secular and likely upper middle class.

As Marks insists, cultural memory resembles "a minefield" more than a smoothly unified tradition.[120] *Hanan al-Cinema* reconnects these potentially explosive sedimentations to the question of reading through the notion of "enfolded"—more or less inaccessible virtual—meanings. Marks develops this concept at the intersection of Deleuzian thought and Shiite philosophy, which resonates for my context by way of Iran's majority-Shiite tradition. (Of course, Iran in general could be assimilated to *Hanan al-Cinema*'s "Arabophone" world only at the price of Orientalist generalization.)[121] Referencing, not least, the attitude of "deep suspicion" in the Shia tradition, Marks introduces the notion of "dissimulation," or "saying one thing and meaning another," under conditions of religious persecution as an example of enfoldment.[122] This links directly to Naficy's characterization of postrevolutionary Iranian cinema through its "hermeneutics" of "dissimulation," "indirection and negotiated meanings."[123] My reading of *A Separation* balances these localizing methodological impulses with Sobchack's encouragement not to let suspicion reign supreme. As a transnational viewer with a limited, uncertain grasp of contextual enfoldings myself, I aim to proceed carefully, grounding myself in a "thick description" of the film's fabric of experiential views.[124] With reference to White's concerns again, my reading thus situates the film as a layered worldmaking endeavor that intricately "folds" questions of public institutionality and private perception into one another, without annulling the distinctions in a totalitarian manner. Rather, *A Separation* reconfigures audience perceptions in dramatizing how the political and the personal are always multiply entangled.

LAYERED WORLDMAKING: POLITICAL INTIMACIES

Although the Iranian state is arguably better characterized as "authoritarian" than as "totalitarian," censorship and government control clearly provide relevant backdrops for Iranian postrevolutionary cinema—and, more specifically, for *A Separation*'s production and distribution in a historical moment of "escalating internal public diplomacy struggles between filmmakers and the government" after the protests around the contested 2009 presidential election.[125] When *A Separation* began its triumphal course through transnational cinema circuits with the Golden Bear at the 2011 Berlinale, the prevailing enthusiasm did not prevent critics from noting the "political" dimension of the award: Jafar Panahi should have been in Berlin as a jury member that year, but he was under house arrest in Iran.[126] Farhadi was even briefly banned from working on *A Separation* because he had publicly expressed support for Panahi along with the exiled Mohsen Makhmalbaf in fall 2010, and official Iranian reactions to *A Separation*'s international success remained mixed.[127] But unlike Panahi's *This Is Not a Film* (*In film nist*, with Mojtaba Mirtahmasb, 2011) or his more recent *Taxi Tehran* (*Taxi*, 2015), which also won the Golden Bear in Berlin, Farhadi's work does not explicate questions of censorship in an open battle with the regime. Instead, it navigates Ministry of Culture interferences and Islamic Guidance regulations in a way that has allowed Farhadi to remain a presence also in the national circuit.[128]

Read against this backdrop, the film's introductory scene in the family court "unfolds" more than one layer. Giving credit to White's reading, we might underline that the spatial alignment of camera and judge presents another virtual association of camera and state—and, by extension, of state and film audience. In the couple's heated dialogue, Simin argues that the plan to leave the country with their ten-year-old daughter was originally conceived by the parents together. When she references her daughter's "future" in explaining her wish to emigrate, the judge asks pointedly, "So the children living in this country don't have a future?" Simin bravely responds that as "a mother," she would rather not see her daughter "grow up in these circumstances," but his insistent follow-up question—"What circumstances?"—makes her fall silent and avert her gaze. Reviewers have variously highlighted this moment: Did the director refrain from having her say more for fear of censorship? Is the overall film made "to answer the judge's question," or is there no need for an answer because "everyone knows the social constraints that would make an educated, affluent woman want to leave Iran"?[129] In addition to the controversial topics of emigration and divorce, the latter of which was treated more scandalously in Farhadi's earlier *Fireworks Wednesday* (*Chaharshanbe Suri*, 2006), the provocation interrupted here arguably includes Simin's direct camera address. The modesty prescriptions originally put into place in 1982 demanded that women adopt "a demure attitude, and an averted gaze" toward strangers.[130] *A Separation* is not the first postrevolutionary film to challenge this rule, and the provocation is also diegetically attenuated by Simin's anger, which authorizes the momentary "breaking of modesty rules."[131] Nonetheless, I imagine local audiences noticed both that Simin looks down into her lap in response to the judge's insistence and that the aversion of her gaze does not last. When the judge then asks whether the child would be better off abroad with one parent or in Iran with both, Simin shoots back that she would prefer for Nader to come along and proceeds to argue her case. The unimpressed judge dismisses her "problem" as "small" and asks both partners to sign his refusal to finalize the divorce. Simin complies only after once more looking directly at him—and us—in silent defiance, now in close-up, as she has approached the judge's/camera's table.

What exactly is the audience supposed to make of this confrontation? As I question my own perception along with those of the judge and other audience members, the film's "sinister institutional dimension" is becoming ever more intricately entangled with other layers of the political and the personal. Exclusively referencing the gender-symmetrical aspects of Iranian divorce law, the judge cites the lack of "mutual consent" regarding the couple's daughter and underlines that the father "has rights, too." (Nader angrily consented to Simin leaving but refuses to let their daughter go; as he argues, and Simin confirms, the child does not even want to go.) Am I to conclude that Simin's request is in fact problematic in the given situation, or am I becoming complicit with the state employee with whom I am spatially aligned if I trust his reasoning? My own suspicion makes me wonder whether the judge is indirectly punishing Simin for her expressed emigration desire and whether the director and his team may want me to notice the gendered imbalance emerging in body language as a negotiated stand-in for legal and social asymmetries that remain unspoken. At the same time, I caution myself against localizing the judge's demeanor to the degree of taking Western superiority for granted: everyday protocols of gendered problem measurement notoriously characterize more or less residual informal patriarchal structures all across the world.

With perhaps too much trust in smooth transcultural perceptions, some Western critics have described all the judges' voices in this film as "fair and reasonable" or even "just."[132] Meanwhile, the reviewer for *Christian Century* indicates his culturalist lens in situating the film as almost exclusively about gender inequality, or "the many forms of separation between men and women" in the Muslim context.[133] In not wanting to settle for either of these straightforward alternatives, my best bet may be to slow down and start from a thicker description of the highly affective encounter framed by the judge's cool intervention. The actors' performances forcefully present Simin's angry agitation and Nader's even fiercer anger, which breaks through his initial disengagement—at one point, the judge asks him to calm down. However, this intensity does not entirely undo recognition and communication. Simin's and Nader's mutual exasperation with each other never tilts into hatred. "He is a good, decent person," Simin says in response to the judge's request for a more actionable divorce rationale, and their reciprocal insistences that they care for their daughter indicate an enmeshment that will not be sorted out easily. In opening to this challenge, I argue, the film's poetics of perception and affective intimacy do not just "distract us" from its institutional dimension (as White has it) and do not gradually shift its "center of gravity" from "the public to the private."[134] Rather, *A Separation*'s foregrounding of affect in the cinematic process of following nonsovereign actors constitutes both a basis and in some respects an end of its politically sensual and sensually political intervention.

In attending to the layers of these political intimacies with a range of readerly affects that includes suspicion but also a warmer curiosity, empathy, and respect, I aim to fine-tune the phenomenological method in a way that escapes the pitfalls of both culturalism and delocalized universalism. In "the 'humanist framework'" of "international festivals" and review circuits, *A Separation* has been described as a "parable about ethical behavior" and the "universality of human conflicts," or the ways in which "abstract ideas of justice or objective truth clash with human frailty and limits of understanding."[135] These responses seem to attest to the film's cosmopolitan force in facilitating (with Sobchack) recognition of the cultural, social, or cinematic Other as a human *"subject-for-itself,"* perhaps by virtue of how *A Separation*'s poetics allows us to imagine our bodies as present in "a world shared by other bodies."[136] But what exactly are the contours of that shared world and the limits of solidarity within it, in both a transnational context and the local one navigated by the film's diegetic actors? While forcefully supporting gestures of humanist connection, *A Separation* also examines how the challenge of "seeing the Other" is not yet met by this first layer of recognition. In part through its exploration of spatial divisions, the film's worldmaking investigates obstacles in the path of vision, or a host of intertwined separations, including that of the couple and the one "between father and daughter," along with "the division between classes, between secular and religious aspects of society, liberal and reactionary points of view, men and women, and so on."[137] In tracing the imprint of all of these (affective and structural, intimate and political) separations on the processes of perception, however, the film never falls back on a hypersuspicious diagnosis of perception as plain deception: as designed, the film's separations afford *some* openings.[138]

PARTIAL PERCEPTIONS: SEEING AND HEARING ACROSS SEPARATION

When the camera starts to move at the end of the opening scene, it follows Simin and Nader out of the courtroom before a cut takes us into the staircase of their apartment, where two men struggle with a

FIGURE 1.3 *A Separation* (dir. Ashgar Farhadi, 2011).

piano that Simin has apparently sold. The sequence begins to unfold the film's overall characteristic poetics of perception. In several subsequent shots, the look of the camera remains halfway blocked by the prominent obstacles of the staircase and the piano, seen from too close an angle, perhaps approximating the carriers' field of vision. As Simin meets the men in rushing home, she first comes into view as afforded by the materiality of the piece of furniture in the foreground; the viewer is not provided with any sense of stability or overview either (figure 1.3). In Latourian terms, mise-en-scène and cinematography thus reassemble the social not as a set of given power structures but as a complex assemblage of nonhuman along with human actors: the claustrophobic space of the stairway, which will play a significant role in the film, and the heaviness of the object at the center of the transaction impact the encounter between Simin and the men. Importantly, this phenomenological poetics does not "bracket" the social in the sense of Edmund Husserl's classical *epoché*, which would effectively sacrifice social specificity to a universalist focus.[139] Rather, the camera traces how the subject's "*embodied*" experience is also "*situated*" in the entanglements of gender with class.[140] Steep angles underscore Simin's vulnerability below the men who are blocking her way while arguing over the negotiated transport price in relation to the exact number of floors. If the spatial configuration thus gives force to gender asymmetries, Simin's class standing endows her with a means of ending the confrontation: curtly, she promises to pay extra and orders the men to let her go by.

Could she have responded differently? Later in the film, Nader will charge Simin with being a "coward" for her tactics of settlement and evasion—and, by extension, emigration. Instead, he teaches their daughter, Termeh, to assert her presence and demand respect in public space. At a gas station, he protectively, and perhaps a bit proudly, watches her through the car's side mirror as she fills up the tank in her school uniform. Afterward, Termeh complains that everyone is "staring," but Nader just says to "let them" and insists that she go back out to demand the proper change, which the gas station attendant has not volunteered. Reminiscent of her mother, Termeh was willing to write it off as his "tip." With Nader's support (he authoritatively signaled to the attendant to wait), Termeh retrieves the change and afterward races up the stairs at home with Nader in shared joy: he allowed her to keep the money she earned. While social structures of gender oppression are thus dramatized as a significant backdrop for the action, the film's focus is on the conflict between different response tactics and on the practices of nonsovereign worldmaking they afford.

Our first introduction to Termeh came at the end of the piano transport encounter on the staircase: a cut to a close-up of her looking up from her schoolwork as she seems to hear her mother approaching. Termeh's gaze shifts into another fairly direct camera address that is, however, softened by the effect of the glass panel through which we see her, with all sharpness resolved into a haptic play of layered reflection and texture, including her loosely draped hijab and a blurry obstacle on the left side in the foreground, possibly a curtain (figure 1.4). Between the stairway scene and this shot, we have been introduced to how we will see most of the film. Again and again, Kalari's cinematography makes use of the apartment's multiple glass partitions, as well as various types of windows (or, as indicated, car mirrors) in other spaces. And more or less prominent, blurry obstacles tend to occupy the foreground of the image: doors and walls along with the fabrics of scarves or men's shirts, characteristically out of focus but stubbornly there.

These shots do not all have the same effects: the type of glass, the lighting and positioning of the camera in relation to the glass, and the

FIGURE 1.4 *A Separation* (dir. Ashgar Farhadi, 2011).

placement and kind of obstacles make a significant difference. Nonetheless, several shared features stand out. First, the elements of blockage, combined with the lack of sufficient distance that would be needed for any sense of overview, underscore the nonsovereign nature of the look. The dominantly shallow depth of field further restrains the camera in a mode of vision that approximates, or arguably foregrounds, that of a non-technically enhanced human eye: as Sobchack underlines with reference to Merleau-Ponty, our "vision ends gently rather than geometrically"; " 'things dissociate' " as "we get very close to them."[141] The blurriness also adds to the affective charge of the image by encouraging haptic forms of (surface rather than depth) perception, or "the involvement of all the senses even in the audiovisual act of cinematic viewing."[142] Second, this exploration of nonsovereign, human rather than godlike vision does not equal the pretense of directly presenting a particular character's view. POV shots are part of the assembly—but not dominant. Some shots are bluntly unaligned (for all we can tell, Simin does not even notice Termeh as she rushes into the apartment) and seem to be motivated less by a realistic mapping of space than by affectively expressive considerations. For example, we get another glance at Termeh as her mother leaves later that night, once more made diffuse by reflection effects and squeezed in among window frames, wall, and blinds. Other shots do produce experiential intensity through spatial approximation to a character's perspective but remain noticeably acentral, including shot-countershot sequences that foreground the viewing character more prominently as an obstacle in the image than classical style would suggest.

In Sobchack's (and my Latourian) terms, the camera's "mobile engagement of embodied and enworlded subjects/objects" thus follows the film's actors rather than directly assimilating their vision.[143] Inviting the film audience into the room, it does not produce "identification" as much as probe acentral alignments in orientation, short of a pretense to occupying "the same *place* in the world," or "the same *body*."[144] Sobchack modifies her overall focus on intersubjective openings to acknowledge the persistence of separation: embodiment "both connects and separates our existence and address from that of others in the world we mutually share," and perception remains marked by *"partial opacity"* along with *"partial transparency."*[145] The third shared feature of *A Separation*'s characteristic shots is the way they dramatize this interplay by underlining that obstacles—or literal as well as metaphorical folds— in the field of vision inflect but do not prevent the act of perception altogether. Unlike plain "unreliability" or the characters' inability to "see or hear beyond their individual realities,"[146] the enfoldedness of vision thus dramatizes the *partial* nature of perception in Farhadi's film. I use "partial" here to indicate both the sense of onesidedness and the possibility of seeing the other side *to an extent*. The dominance of glass (over more opaque) partitions is crucial here: the film both depicts and affords its viewers acts of seeing others, though not transparently.

Exceptions include the opaque glass panel that shields the bathroom in Simin and Nader's apartment. Its ability to frustrate the look is dramatized in a scene set on the day after the initial court hearing. While Simin prepares to leave that night (for the time being to stay at her parents' house), Nader hires a housekeeper, Razieh, to help with his father. The next day Razieh promptly has to deal with the old man having peed his pants, while her daughter, who is significantly younger than Termeh, tries to get a glimpse of the action through that opaque panel. As a fairly explicit play on voyeurism checked by modesty standards, or modesty standards challenged by a child's curiosity, the scene functions as a boundary marker that puts into relief how perception is circumscribed by a body's position within a socially organized world—while not always as radically impeded by it. More characteristically, social separation in the film merely prevents sustained attention and immediate exchange. Another shot in the first apartment sequence, for example, features prominent reflective effects as Razieh tries to get Simin's attention through a glass partition. As we will learn, Simin does notice her but responds only indirectly—by asking Termeh to deal with the request. In this sense, the socio-symbolic layers of the film's spatial poetics operate visibly on the image surface: they do invite active acts of reading but do not (throughout) require the suspicious "depth approaches" of either Naficy's "Iranian hermeneutics" or Western cultural studies before the postcritical turn.[147] A further example is the way in which we repeatedly see Razieh and her daughter outside in the street: from a distance, halfway blocked by cars, and through the glass panels of bus stops. In tracing the strenuous commute Razieh has mentioned, the narration simultaneously indicates the cinema-going audience's presumed separation from that experience.

Step by step, the latent conflicts inscribed in these visual relations spin into the unfolding drama. Razieh, who, unlike Simin, wears a full chador on the street, called a religious hotline to inquire whether it would be a sin for her to change the old man, but her bright daughter's unsolicited promise not to tell her dad reveals that Razieh's concern is not about religious doctrine alone. In need of the pay, Razieh then convinces Nader to hire her husband, Hodjat, instead of her (we see the interview through the glass partitions shielding employees from customers at Nader's bank), without telling Hodjat that she tried to work the job herself. The next day, however, he is taken to prison by his creditors, and Razieh returns after all. Pregnant, she struggles with the physical labor in addition to her unsubdued daughter, who quickly discovers the toy potential of the grandfather's oxygen valve. Razieh later has to run after the grandfather when he escapes onto the street, and the panic on her face, traffic sounds, shots of cars, and hectic cutting trace the dangerous situation phenomenologically. The next day Nader and Termeh return to the apartment early and find the old man unconscious on the floor, tied to the bed by his wrist. Razieh is missing. Reviving the grandfather while trying to calm Termeh's hysterical crying, Nader angrily suspects Razieh has also stolen money from a drawer. (The attentive viewer may gather that it was actually used by Simin to pay the piano transporters.) Upon her return, Razieh defensively insists that she *had* to leave, while passionately refuting the theft charge. In the heated argument that develops, Termeh shouts at her father for touching Razieh as he tries to steer her out of their apartment. Nader backs off apologetically while Termeh herself rushes Razieh out. When Razieh returns, however, to insist on her pay for the day—doing precisely what Nader teaches his daughter—he roughly shuffles her out of the door to close it. Shortly thereafter we see Razieh getting up from a fall on the stairs. The child cries and asks "mommy" to "be careful"; a neighbor's question about what happened remains unanswered. Inside the apartment, Nader cries as well while he gives a shower to his father.

Much of the second half of *A Separation* revolves around piecing together the exact outlines of this incident and working through the resulting controversies of perception and interpretation. The challenge unfolds not only on the diegetic level but also for the film audience: we have seen things that individual characters have not seen but are not fully oriented either. Razieh has a miscarriage, and after her husband finds out what happened, they take Nader to court for having caused the loss of the child. While the characters repeatedly accuse each other of lying during court sessions and discussions at home, the film viewer's puzzle-solving activity may alert her not only to the ethical complexity of dissimulation but also to the unstable boundaries between intentional concealment and sincere-while-nonsovereign worldmaking. Where exactly does one draw the line in the midst of momentary lapses, well-intentioned omissions, partial reconstructions, and fragile but not characteristically downright illusionary truth claims? The controversies revolve around whether Nader just "pushed" or rather "threw" or even "hit" Razieh, whether the door and staircase angles would have allowed Razieh's fall to have been directly caused by Nader's violent gesture, and, most importantly, whether he knew about the pregnancy, which would result in a murder charge against him. (Only Simin's mother, old enough not to naturalize the legal realities of the postrevolutionary state, questions the implied equation of the embryo with a full-grown "child.") While the film audience had been unequivocally informed about the pregnancy, Nader disputes that he knew, and the accuracy of this claim seems to rest on whether he overheard a conversation between Razieh and Termeh's tutor, during which he was not visibly (to us) in the same room. When Termeh eventually catches

Nader in an inconsistency, giving away that he did overhear the conversation, he defends himself with the impact that his going to prison would have on Termeh, while explaining that in the moment of the angry confrontation with Razieh, he "didn't" know: "I had forgotten it. I wasn't paying attention." When Termeh suggests he say this in court, he adds, "The law doesn't care about this."

The binary legal framework won't do: the field of nonsovereign, socially embedded, affective perception is not exhausted by the polar alternatives of knowing versus not knowing and deception versus truthfulness as a path to ethical action. In exploring this field, the film dramatizes its characters as struggling and biased—but not plainly irresponsible coactors in the process of (as Latour might put it) stabilizing the controversy at hand.[148] As their interests and feelings collide with their moral standards and as their diverging moral imperatives collide with each other, they interrogate and correct their own perceptions— without heroically overcoming the separations in play by ethical force alone. Nader quickly admits that his theft charge was unwarranted, and after hearing Hodjat's backstory of unemployment and depression, he generously intervenes in court on Hodjat's behalf when the judge threatens Hodjat with jail for his heated demeanor. Unlike his family court colleague at the outset of the film, this judge is brought into view by the continued close and mobile cinematography, and he does strike me as a fair adjudicator within the legal framework at hand. He seems to earnestly try to find out what happened and is as willing to discipline Hodjat as he was unswayed by Nader's earlier plea on the grounds that the murder charge would ruin his (privileged) life. When Termeh now confronts Nader, he asks her to be his judge: "If you want me to, I'll tell them." She instead protects him in court (followed by tears in the car), but she may have told her tutor, who changes her earlier testimony and says Nader did overhear the conversation. Or did the tutor know all along that he had overheard it? When Hodjat asked her earlier to "swear on the Quran" that Nader didn't know about the pregnancy, she angrily obliged him, apparently without giving much thought to the gesture. The film audience may wonder about the tutor's earlier testimony because she had indicated the side she was taking: before her initial court appearance, she had asked Simin about how to protect Nader; Simin, however, had urged her to tell "the truth."

Meanwhile, Razieh acts on her own doubts. She meets with Simin at the latter's university and confesses that the embryo was not moving even before the confrontation with Nader. Perhaps its death was caused by an event that the film audience did not see, although the staging of how it came about, an abrupt cut, and subsequent indications of Razieh's distress had provided hints: she got hit by a car while rescuing the grandfather in the street. The mise-en-scène of the confession seems to imply a promise of virtual—feminine, if not feminist—solidarity: the similarity between the two women is underscored by Simin's more-modest-than-usual dress for her university class. However, the film does not deliver on this promise of gendered communication. Razieh no longer wants Simin to pay the "blood money" that she negotiated with Hodjat—without Nader's knowledge—as an out-of-court settlement of the conflict. (When Simin finally told Nader, he got upset about the apparent implication of accepting his guilt.) But Razieh also does not want to confess her doubts to Hodjat, who initially did not even want to accept the money but was coaxed by his creditors into embracing this solution for his severe debt crisis. And Simin fears for Termeh's safety in case she does not pay now; the unemployed Hodjat has been hanging out at her school.

The film audience does not see how Simin tells Nader about this conversation with Razieh; thus, the exact distribution of responsibility for the following showdown remains elliptically suspended. But the visual symmetry between the two women tilts into asymmetry as the editing links a distanced, through-the-window view of Simin as she changes into one of her regular loose scarves at the end of her university class with a closer view of Razieh through a glass partition as she dons a veil in her kitchen before serving guests in her living room. Nader and Simin have come to pay the negotiated sum after all, but before he hands over the checks, Nader asks Razieh to perform the gesture Hodjat had demanded from the tutor: to swear on the Quran that Nader caused her miscarriage. The pious Razieh cannot bring herself to do so. While in the kitchen with Hodjat, Razieh finally tells him about the car accident, and he tries to coax her into swearing nonetheless, offering to take the "sin" upon himself. With his creditors also present in the living room, Razieh's persistent refusal agitates him. When he tries to drag her along and she halfway attacks him in resisting, he starts beating her furiously in despair. The film audience may feel uncomfortably reminded of the stereotype that Hodjat powerfully countered earlier: when the tutor, who had seen their child draw scenes of family conflict, brought up the possibility that the miscarriage could have been caused by domestic abuse, he asked, "Why do you think we beat our wives and children like animals?"

In short, the diegetic actors' attempts to account for their uncertain perceptions and correct them in communication with each other have failed to resolve the conflict—and in some respects have aggravated it; the assemblages of affect and interest separating them remain too forceful. Hodjat storms outside, while Razieh asks the visitors in anguish, "Didn't I tell you not to come?" Visibly affected by her speech, Nader, Simin, and Termeh leave to find their windshield smashed. While they drive home in silence, the camera rests on Termeh's face for a long time. If the couple's separation still seemed reversible in the beginning of the film (both Nader and Simin reassured Termeh that it was only temporary), the external conflict has underscored their communication difficulties. Despite everyone's unmistakable sadness about this course of affairs, the film's final sequence returns us to court, where the divorce is now processed. The judge, whom we do see this time, asks Termeh with whom she wants to live. She claims to have made up her mind but seems unable to answer with her parents in the room. The judge sends them out, and the camera and film audience follow. During Nader's and Simin's silent wait on two different sides of a glass door in the corridor, the credits start to roll.

As Termeh's verdict remains suspended, the film's mood has shifted from an affective atmosphere of "fierce . . . energy" and fighting to one of sorrow: this is, perhaps, the major transition accomplished by the hard work of perception undertaken by diegetic actors and audiences alike.[149] Mutual recognition as nonsovereign humans positioned in complex webs of concerns is possible. Even if people can be driven to act "like animals" at moments, Farhadi's worldmaking has complexified this equation toward considerations of how creatureliness is imbricated with ethical agency. That the possibility of mutual recognition does not yet overcome the separations at stake indexes the affective challenge in the film's intense assemblage, whether we straightforwardly "sympathize deeply with both sides" or are rather unsettled by the ways in which "our emotions often disagree" with the insight into "the logic of everyone's position."[150] After my initial viewing of the film, I found that I was upset with Simin in the end for "betraying" Razieh's confidence and enabling Nader to exploit Razieh's faith. This moment of outrage both indicates and crisscrosses my dominant allegiance facilitated at the intersection of the film's formal cues with my own positionality: Simin is the film character relatively closest to my (educated, secular, feminist) self. All in all, I have come to share her sense that Nader is a decent man and, of course, want him cleared of the murder charge, whereas my ability to connect with Razieh's religious worldmaking has remained qualified. But the film's resolution has affectively unsettled this asymmetrical configuration, short of undoing it altogether.

Perhaps this personal response indicates both the limits of and the openings afforded by the film's work on perception. *A Separation*'s insistence that separations are not (socially) *given* as much as continuously reproduced in asymmetrical distributions of the sensible—of visibility, audibility, and mobility—does not yet cancel the orientational force of these separations. With the narrative's overall arrangement around Nader and Simin's divorce, the filmmaker and his team refrain from a pretense to symmetry in the class conflict they trace. In generating local orientation disturbances, however, the film's method of following the actors in unresolved controversies from the phenomenological angle of bodily perception creates affective openings that may continue to agitate us after the film's formal closure. In tracing the "bottom-up" configuration of politics from "interests and attitudes, ressentiments and religiosity, love and poverty" in the complex web of associations created by its puzzle poetics, *A Separation* makes me feel, as well as comprehend, that the task of creating cosmopolitical connections, or affective (and virtually activist) solidarity across national and transnational divisions, is not accomplished through easy gestures of transcultural or interclass understanding.[151] The film's forceful invitation to reorient—rather than merely distrust—my perceptions has left me with increased awareness also of the enfolded meanings that I may have missed and of the stories that have not been told. What might Termeh's future look like—either in "this country" or in the diaspora? In reaching out to transnational (along with national) audiences precisely by exploring Latour's metaphorical "wasp's nest" of collective articulation in a local context, *A Separation* loosens the hold of layered collectivity claims, thereby posing rather than answering questions.[152] What kind of (institutional, political, material, ethical) supports *could* dismantle the communication obstacles assembled by the force of intersectional inequalities, with the goal of a shared world that facilitates continued negotiations of overlapping attachments at different scales?

With its emphasis on the unresolved, *A Separation*'s phenomenological project presents a counterpoint to the more affirmative ways in which *The Edge of Heaven*'s forceful narration imagines virtual togetherness, even as both films intertwine their shared orientation at this ethical horizon with an interest in the controversies to be assembled first. The following chapters continue these explorations, some carried out via contemporary films that provide more clear-cut answers (see chapter 3). First, however, chapter 2 takes a historical step back to further develop the aesthetic concepts I deployed in characterizing Akın's and Farhadi's different methods of following the actors. In pursuing the modernist genealogies of Brechtian and phenomenological techniques of worldmaking, I continue to unravel the perceived oppositions between the associated "distancing" and "affecting" operations. By tracing their interplay in Godard's and Fassbinder's poetics of *intense defamiliarization*, I complicate the film-historical account according to which the counter-cinema of the 1960s coolly critiqued the hegemonic claims of (patriarchal, national, imperialist, racist, heteronormative) collectivity. In their differently modernist ways, *My Life to Live* and *Katzelmacher* affectively follow the actors of diegetic and historical controversies as well.

CHAPTER TWO

Critical Intensity

Jean-Luc Godard's and Rainer Werner Fassbinder's Defamiliarized Worldmaking Practices

In the previous chapter, I introduced the complex twenty-first-century interventions of Fatih Akın's *The Edge of Heaven* and Asghar Farhadi's *A Separation* against the backdrop of transnational new wave legacies. Specifically, I referenced the two competing modernist traditions of film philosophy and cinematic practice outlined by film historians: on the one hand, concepts of Brechtian cinema, as primarily associated with techniques of foregrounded narration and effects of critical distanciation, and, on the other hand, the legacy of neorealism, as affiliated with the production of affect and an aesthetics of immediacy—or as André Bazin had it, "style" turned into a "self-effacement before reality."[1] In this chapter, I develop a historical layer of this study's overall argument by returning to a moment in both film theory and filmmaking that precedes the solidification of these critical oppositions. In the emerging countercultural cinema and film theory of the 1960s, conceptualizations of Brechtian aesthetics were still in flux—and more entangled with the "phenomenological realism" of postwar film than today's conceptualizations seem to allow.[2] My readings in this chapter demonstrate how retrospective mappings of interventionist Brechtian narration and distanciation in opposition to affect and Bazinian realism fail to grasp the intricate workings of affect in two films from this moment. Jean-Luc Godard's *My Life to Live* (*Vivre sa vie*, 1962) entangles documentary techniques and references to fictional intertexts in following the (sex) work of a young woman struggling to live independently in contemporary society. With intertextual reference to *My Life to Live*, Rainer Werner Fassbinder's highly theatricalized *Katzelmacher* (1969) connects Godard's emphasis on gender, sexuality, and class to questions of national identity and xenophobia in tracing the genealogies of violence against a Greek "guest worker" (played by Fassbinder) in a small southern German community.

In unfolding Godard's and Fassbinder's cinematic practices of affective critique, I develop this study's guiding notion of complex affective assemblages into a rereading of modernism; in turn, this rereading will inflect my interpretations of twenty-first-century film in subsequent chapters. This chapter's argument has two main layers. On a systematic level, I disassemble the conceptual legacy of distanciation by tracing the (characteristically negative) affectivity that fuels the cinematic generation of distance and its theoretical conceptualization. Modernist "detachment," Rita Felski insists, was variously infused "with polemical energies."[3] In thus resituating distanciation, I suggest how even the most radical cinematic experiments in interrupting audience pleasure, empathy, or other positive affective relations—for example, in Godard's later work from the 1970s—can be read as affective worldmaking practices. On the level of aesthetics and historical practice, I simultaneously question the prevalence of distanciation in some instances of "Brechtian" cinema by describing alternative forms of Brechtian productivity in the selected early works by Godard and Fassbinder. As I argue, these alternative forms emerged at the intersection with the Bazinian phenomenology that would become Brechtianism's clear-cut cinematic opposite only in the 1970s, and they are more usefully characterized in terms of a *defamiliarization* with positive affective charges.[4] In describing them as practices of "intensity," this chapter deploys Brian Massumi's terminology to map complex assemblages of fluid affectivity exceeding the boundaries of presumably static subjecthood.[5] In line with the worldmaking model first spelled out in the introduction, however, this emphasis does not amount to treating affect as either asubjective or asignifying. Instead, my readings once again emphasize how these cinematic flows of intensity actively contribute to both diegetic and spectatorial processes of making subjects and worlds.

Furthermore, I claim Godard's and Fassbinder's acts of defamiliarization as practices of intensity with a critical dimension. In tracing the cinematic commentaries on collectivity unfolded through them, I unsettle the oppositional historical narrative according to which twenty-first-century attempts at imagining shared worlds in more affirmative terms reversed the critique of collectivity—as saturated with domination and violence—developed by modernist countercultural cinema. Unsettling, to be sure, does not equal undoing. Godard's *My Life to Live* and Fassbinder's *Katzelmacher* differ significantly from the more recent works discussed in this book, both in aesthetic terms and in the relative emphases of their commentary on collectivity. While Godard underlines his protagonist's mostly individualist struggle to "live her life" against a background collective of capitalist patriarchy, Fassbinder highlights the process in which collectivity as such is produced by way of sexual and xenophobic violence. At the same time, a fine-tuned account of their worldmaking assemblages also indicates how *Katzelmacher* takes seriously its characters' fraught attachments to their violent collective and how *My Life to Live* probes alternative forms of everyday collectivity. In short, their affective critiques of collective violence and subjugation do not imply a wholesale negation of needs for belonging.

As it is told from today's vantage point, the film-historiographic story of the modernist moment could not be more clear-cut. While Bazin's dominant rejection in 1970s film criticism has been countered by attempts at "opening Bazin" for the new century, authors with otherwise diverging affiliations in affect studies, phenomenology, and cognitive theory have unanimously profiled their approaches against the Brechtian legacy of the 1970s and beyond, targeting the "great modernist belief" in "self-reflexive distanciation" or plainly "the logic and legacy of Brechtianism."[6] In spelling out the latter charge, Murray Smith suggests that Roland Barthes, Louis Althusser, and others in and around the journal *Screen* in the 1970s developed Bertolt Brecht's critique of the emotion-ideology nexus into "an oversimplified account of the role and nature of emotional responses to fiction," marked by "dualistic oppositions" such as that between "feeling and reason."[7] As I argue, however, this oversimplification is largely one of Brecht *reception*, including Smith's own.[8] Smith's rejection of Brecht does not account for how his cognitive approach resonates with Brecht's writings in conceptualizing emotions—if less so regarding aesthetics and politics.[9] In the following, I return to Brecht's own discussions of emotion in theatrical performance and spectatorship along with his early reception in—largely Bazinian—French film theory around 1960. The ideas I trace in this context provide a historical lining for this study's syncretic model of affective worldmaking assemblages. As I should note, my reading does not aim to uncover a more authentic Brecht; rather, it indicates a differently Brechtian aesthetics also in order to address limitations of Brecht's historical theater theory, including the resonance with today's cognitive containments of affect. On the historical terrain mapped in this chapter, I submit, these limitations can be overcome by attending to Godard's and Fassbinder's critically intense practices of defamiliarization.

WITH ATTENTION AND AWE: GODARD'S "SEARING LOVE WITH A LENS"

The Brechtian dimension—or dogmatism—of Godard's work in the 1970s is a commonplace of his reputation as an "exemplary exponent" of radical " 'political modernism.' "[10] But even the early *My Life to Live* (1962) has been predominantly read through the lens of Brechtian "distanciation," disorientation, and disruption, backed by Godard's own characterization of the film as shot in twelve "tableaux," to the effect of accentuating "le côté théâtre, le côté Brecht."[11] And without doubt, the film's portrayal of the protagonist Nana's life and sex work does proceed in part through "classically Brechtian" techniques: the descriptive title cards introducing the tableaux, the use of documentary materials, and the foregrounded exploration of different camera angles, including sustained back shots in several tableaux.[12] Much less evident, however, is whether or how these observations can be translated into diagnoses of distance and distanciation.[13] The operations of reading at stake can be outlined through a closer look at Kaja Silverman's interpretation of the film (developed in a dialogue with Harun Farocki), which is in many ways highly perceptive but remains circumscribed by the analytical categories dominant in the 1970s. In particular, Silverman draws on the idea that filmic enunciation functions as a mode of aggressive subjection (of characters, actors, and audience) and Laura Mulvey's respective feminist critique of narrative as a means of investigating and punishing the female subject (positioned as image, or sexual spectacle).[14] Thus, Silverman suggests that *My Life to Live*'s anticipatory camera movements literalize the ways in which filmic "enunciation" undoes the "'free will'" of the characters, eagerly rushing toward the annihilation of the subject, which is signified by Nana's sex work and executed by her death at the end of the film.[15] Within this analytical framework, the ideological work of narrative can be challenged only by "*distanciation*" as the work of cutting through affect with (the equally negative) gestures of "interruption," "interrogation," "negation," or "deposition."[16] In Silverman's reading, Godard's film correspondingly gets credit for how it self-reflexively admits to its "complicity" with subjection and murder and interrupts its own attempts at dominating both Nana and the actor Anna Karina, Godard's wife at the time—to the effect that, as Silverman postulates, Karina survives Nana's death at the end of the film.[17] However, such credit remains limited. As Mulvey and Colin MacCabe suggest in a coauthored piece, the reductive conflation of "woman and sexuality" in almost all of Godard's films contradicts his otherwise "rigorous questioning of the film form."[18]

In a marked contrast with this secondary literature, the film reviews not only upon its initial release but even upon later reruns describe the relation between camera or director and actor as well as protagonist in the register of love: the film "admires" the "character," "falls for her," and thereby presents the director's "declaration of love" for his wife "with almost embarrassing directness": "Not since Stiller's camera turned to stare at Garbo has a man made such searing love with a lens."[19] The sexualized nature of this love is evident in these wordings, and the goal of my own rereading is not to displace the critical emphasis on sexuality that characterized the psychoanalytically inflected scholarship of the 1970s with a return to a more idealized notion of love. Rather, one of the tasks for this historical chapter is to detail the ways in which affect and sexuality are imbricated in Godard's and Fassbinder's films. The intense sexualization in play in this 1960s cinema is certainly different in degree, if not in quality, from what we see in most of the twenty-first-century films otherwise at the center of this study. In the spirit of Michel Foucault's historicizing analysis of the modern sexuality *dispositif*, this observation can be contextualized with how the modern deployments of sexuality as a (or *the*) source of human creativity, personal identity, and political struggle reached a culmination point in the 1960s and 1970s.[20] Arguably, recent scholarship has conceptually transferred some of the revolutionary potential then ascribed to sex toward affect, a shift that has provoked worries about unwilling scholarly complicity with a new era of sexual repression.[21] But perhaps we don't have to play the categories of affect and sex against one another. In the following, I investigate how we can read the emphasis on sex in 1960s cinema through a methodological lens informed more by affect studies than by (any dogmatic version of) Freudian or Lacanian psychoanalysis—but without desexualizing the films' intensity. With, if you will, a prosex twist, I also probe how this intensity can be unlinked from the affective negativity that infuses the critical frameworks of sexual subjection and critical distanciation. As I will demonstrate, this study's conceptualization of nonsovereign worldmaking agency is key to a reading of *My Life to Live* that escapes the pitfalls of both paranoia and naïveté. In the process, I am guided by the hypothesis that the emphasis on love in the cited film reviews indicates something more intriguing than merely their authors' precritical takes.

My contention is that *My Life to Live*'s affective-sexual assemblages critique patriarchal collectivity less through techniques of distanciation than through a phenomenological practice of close attention charged with awe and adoration. For the context of scholarly reading practices, Berlant describes her resonant interest in a phenomenological methodology that encounters its "objects of knowledge" as "scenes we can barely get our eyes around" and "from within a scene of contact."[22] *My Life to Live*'s cinematic practice, I propose, thus encounters its protagonist and lead actor as an object—and subject—of fascination and knowledge not contained by a framework of control and subjection. The mode of this encounter is introduced in the opening credit sequence, in the interplay between the performance of Karina and the gazes of the director, who coedited the film, and his cinematographer, Raoul Coutard. The sequence is composed of three long-held close-ups (two profile shots and one frontal one), which allow the camera—as endowed by the men holding and directing it—to stare with fascination and wonder at the actor who is to play Nana.[23] More specifically, they stare at her head and *face* (figure 2.1). Giving Mulvey her due, we can suspect that these stares are not free of sexual fetishism in that they entail a stylization and fragmentation of Karina's "body" by "close-ups."[24] Godard and Coutard's

FIGURE 2.1 *My Life to Live* (dir. Jean-Luc Godard, 1962).

particular choice of body parts, however, simultaneously foregrounds the traditional humanist sign of individuality—if in a defamiliarizing way. The spot-lighting on the back of Karina's neck in the two profile shots leaves her face mostly in the dark; the shots emphasize the texture of her hair above the neck and the silhouette of her face. Michel Legrand's repetitive lyrical soundtrack underlines the duration of our looking by setting in anew with each shot, only to end in the midst of it.[25] "An ode to facial beauty," the visual stillness of the sequence is punctured only by several little gestures of the actor, who licks her lips in an apparently seductive way.[26] In the frontal shot (positioned between the two side takes), more-distributed background lighting softly visibilizes Karina's (still shaded) face, with dark eyes and a misty, equivocally tender, apprehensive, perhaps even reproachful look, before she repeats the licking gesture after a—shameful? anxious?—glance down. The ambiguity of Karina's gestures underlines that the film audience does not have full access to her interior, but I do not think that we have evidence for translating this observation (as Silverman and Farocki do) into the claim that the sequence simultaneously sets up and seeks to "penetrate" her "mystery" by way of "police[-style] photographs."[27] With Mulvey, this would have the effect of sadistically "ascertaining guilt" and "asserting control."[28] I argue that, rather than penetrating, this intense introductory mise-en-scène performs a gesture of Brechtian *Verfremdung* that translates as *defamiliarization* more than *distanciation*.[29]

DEFAMILIARIZATION: A DIFFERENTLY
BRECHTIAN PRACTICE

As Brecht defines his signature technique in "On Experimental Theatre," *Verfremdung* "estranges an incident or character simply by taking from the incident or character what is self-evident, familiar, obvious in order to produce wonder and curiosity."[30] Can we think of curiosity as aligned not only, or necessarily, with suspicion here but also, more positively, with "strong desire" and "interest" (per the notion's lexical definition)—in short, with affective fuel for the social critique that the film will unfold? This phenomenological spin on Brechtian technique is inspired by the ways French film theorists read his theory when they first turned to it shortly before *My Life to Live* was made, in response to Brecht's growing influence in French theater in the wake of several guest performances of the *Berliner Ensemble* in Paris.[31] In 1960, *Cahiers du Cinéma*—the influential journal closely associated with the *Nouvelle Vague*, for which Godard was writing as well—ran a special issue on Brecht for the first time. Cofounded by Bazin, the journal was overall still primarily phenomenological in orientation; the editorial indicatively sounds a cinephilic note of caution, declaring that Brecht was not of interest for film theory if Brechtian critique "aims to destroy all the objects of our . . . adoration."[32]

Directly in the terms of Bazin's media ontology, Bernhard Dort's theoretical contribution to the issue begins by worrying that Brecht's efforts at "creating a *distance* between the different elements of the spectacle and between this spectacle and the spectator" appear "to be a direct denial of the cinema which is based" on character "identification" and "immediacy," or "the lived experience of all film viewers."[33] Dort then proceeds to rescue Brecht for the cinema by positioning "distanciation" as "simply a means to" an "end": it offers the audience "recreated images of social life," rendered "comprehensible" by way of a "constant movement between identification with the characters . . . and understanding of the historical situation which has made these characters what they are."[34] In other words, Dort approximates Brecht and Bazin in the name of a modified cinematic realism.[35] From my vantage point today, this modified realism resonates with Bruno Latour's onto-rhetorical methodology of *Reassembling the Social* by way of "following the actors" in an ongoing modulation of distance.[36] In its historical moment, Dort's Brecht-inspired rethinking of cinema as "an art of *mediated* reality" has parallels with how Godard navigated a partial departure from Bazin in his early essays—specifically, from Bazin's credo of nonintervention.[37] With reference to both Brecht and Bazin, Godard's early contributions to *Cahiers* imbricate "cinematic language" and "reality," the symbolic and the ontological.[38] In relation to *My Life to Live*, he speaks of a "theatrical realism."[39]

The "first requirement" for a Brechtian aesthetics, Dort proceeds, is therefore "that the viewer should be able to *look afresh* at what he is shown" and be astounded and disquieted by what is seemingly "'customary'" and "'usual.'"[40] This emphasis on the proximity of Brecht's *Verfremdung* to *ostranenie* (defamiliarization), coined by Russian formalist Viktor Shklovsky, receives a partial endorsement from the editors of the third edition of the authoritative English-language collection *Brecht on Theatre* (2015), who underline that Shklovsky's term has "stronger credentials" than the canonized English translations of *Verfremdung* as "alienation" and "distanciation."[41] In trying to counteract the cliché of a "cold and impersonal" Brechtian theater, they, to be sure, also caution against entirely assimilating Brecht to Shklovsky: for Shklovsky, defamiliarization aims to "intensify our sensations and perceptions," whereas Brecht ultimately intends to "reboot our cognitive apparatus" toward the goal of "understand[ing] the world better."[42] Dort's approximation of Brecht's technique to the phenomenological project of postwar neorealism by way of foregrounding "wonder and curiosity" (Brecht, as quoted earlier), or the moment of perception before critical diagnosis, thus arguably brackets Brecht's cognitivism. Precisely in doing so, however, it suggests a syncretic path on which Brecht's legacy can be imbricated with today's phenomenological and Deleuzian approaches to affect.

For *My Life to Live*, this connection can be developed through a closer look at tableau three, where Nana sees Carl Dreyer's silent *La passion de Jeanne d'Arc* (1928) in the cinema, a famous intertext featured extensively in the line of film theory extending from Bazin to

Gilles Deleuze.[43] With its emphasis on acting and human faces, Dreyer's film does not seem to fit Bazin's realist aesthetic preferences, but he defends Dreyer's classic against charges of theatricality by describing it as "a documentary of faces" and insisting that the director is "only concerned with the countenance as flesh," not "with the psychology but with the physiology of existence."[44] Extending this opposition between flesh and psychology, Deleuze reads Dreyer's *La Passion* as "the affective film *par excellence*," whereby "the affect is like the expressed of the state of things, but this expressed does not refer to the state of things, it only refers to the faces," as the close-up extracts "the face . . . from all spatio-temporal coordinates."[45] The *Jeanne d'Arc* shots included in *My Life to Live* show Antonin Artaud as Jean Massieu coming to prepare Maria Falconetti as Jeanne for her death. In the close-ups and extreme close-ups that largely characterize the film, we see the pigments of Falconetti's skin, her shaved head, the lines on her forehead, and the tears, which are visible on Jeanne's face throughout most of the film, here first caught in her eyelashes, later smearing her cheeks. The scene is intercut with two shots of Karina as Nana, whose carefully made-up face is more evenly beautiful: in the first shot, moisture shows in her eyes; in the second, after she blinks, tears stream on her face also (figures 2.2 and 2.3).

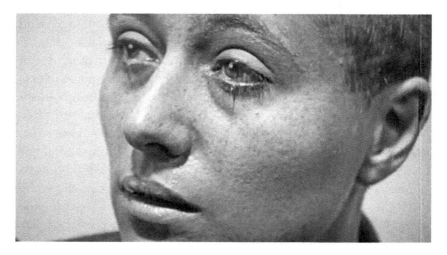

FIGURE 2.2 *My Life to Live* (dir. Jean-Luc Godard, 1962).

FIGURE 2.3 *My Life to Live* (dir. Jean-Luc Godard, 1962).

Just like *My Life to Live*'s introductory close-ups, the scene high-lights the physical (and wondrous and affecting) "reality of" the actor "playing" the character, folding "fiction" into "documentary."[46] Keeping Brecht in play along with Bazin and Deleuze, however, enables me to tilt their oppositional rhetoric into a more complex reading. Unlike the introductory sequence, Nana/Anna Karina's encounter with Jeanne d'Arc is clearly framed as part of the film's diegesis: physiology is layered with *gestus* and *fabula*.[47] Having just lost her apartment due to debts, Nana is with a suitor who hopes to claim her body in exchange for the movie ticket; we briefly see her irritation with his gesture of putting his arm around her in the dark cinema. Even as the film's aesthetics of defa-miliarization underscores the bodily presence of Karina as irreducible to Nana and makes its world, not least, from real-world affects circu-lating among director, crew, and actors, it thus also folds these affects into fiction, imbricating extradiegetic intensity with character emotion.

To complicate matters further, the tableau's staging of this layered actor-character emotion could even tempt us into the kind of psycho-logical reading that is shunned by Brecht, Bazin, and Deleuze alike. Does Nana/Karina's "mimetic" response to Jeanne/Falconetti not make for a classical scene of "identification" or empathy?[48] The reclamation of empathy in twenty-first-century cognitive and neuroscientific criticism indicates how Smith and others have sought to overcome Brecht's legacy. In particular, Brecht would have opposed the ways in which today's cognitive conceptualizations privilege evolved human motivations and stable group identities at the expense of socio-affective *processes* of subject formation. Where cognitive theory deploys empathy as a route to more or less universalist intersubjectivity against the backdrop of such clear-cut character and audience identities, Brecht's resistance against "introspective psychology" is precisely aimed at opening the "outworn, decrepit, subjective sphere of the emotions" toward collective flows.[49] Of course, this does not mean that we can assimilate Brecht to resonant Deleuzian interests: Brecht would have shuddered also at Massumi's celebration of sympathy as an immediate *"mode"* of "transindividual becoming," or animal affect in excess of human emotion.[50] As indicated, Brecht's critique of empathy does not reject all emotion; rather, it is directed at the dissolution of any sense of difference in the presumed synchronizing of spectator "perceptions, emotions, and insights" with those of the actors and characters in a mode of "direct transplantation."[51] In response to the fascist articulations of affective collectivity in his own day, along with their critical analysis in early twentieth-century crowd theory, Brecht underlines the mediating contribution of actively thinking and feeling individuals.[52]

Short of undercutting all audience feeling, Brecht's techniques of *Verfremdung* intervene to produce "emotions that need not correspond" with each other.[53] He insists on emphasizing the "distance"—or difference rather than complete identification—among copresent character, actor, and audience feelings and on not harmonizing contrasts, with the goal of creating "a rich and sometimes complicated emotional curve in the spectator, a fusion of feelings and even a conflict between them."[54] This emphasis on process, incongruity, overlap, and tension resonates with how I develop the notion of affect assemblages for this study. In Godard's film, the face of the spectator Nana/Karina shows intense sadness as she watches Jeanne—but not the utter despair playing out (again differently) on Jeanne's and Artaud's faces and not the glimpses of ecstasy on Jeanne's face. For Godard's audience, the rich emotional curve at stake may include sadness but likely also some combination of desire and pleasure, awe and curiosity about the configuration. The cognitive distinction of sympathy from empathy in terms of acentral vs.

central alignment (discussed more fully in chapter 1) may get at some of these differences, but it comes with too much emphasis on the moderation of feeling at a (safe) distance from an (intact) subject. Instead, there can be different, if partially overlapping *intensities* in play.[55]

The incongruence between these intensities is crucial for *My Life to Live*'s critical worldmaking project. In the scene at hand, it helps us to hold open the precise relationship between the different images and realities of women in play. Jeanne's ecstatic, self-sacrificial political resistance leads to her violent exclusion from the dominant religious collective portrayed in the film, but it also makes her into the heroic foundation of a new, national collective: according to the concluding titles of Dreyer's film, Jeanne's "heart has become the heart of France." Nana's modern resistance to the men trying to control her life is outwardly individualistic; implicitly, it thus opens up the national framework of Dreyer's pre–World War II film. Of course, Nana's individualism also relies on collective fantasies: as indicated in the dialogue with a colleague in tableau two, her desire for living intensely has been coinduced by romance novels. But keeping the outlined vectors of affective incongruity in play balances the linear, closure-oriented (Mulveyian) reading, according to which Nana's mimetic affective response to Jeanne confirms that death is also her own fate.[56] To be sure, Nana will die at the end of the film, but in Godard's layered or (in the terms I proposed in the introduction) *multivectoral* worldmaking, this outcome is neither natural nor necessary. In tableau three, the cinematic location of the dramatized production of affect adds layers of reflexivity, which impact the emotional curve experienced by Godard's spectator. As we activate whatever intertextual memory we may have of Dreyer's film or the aesthetics of cruelty associated with Artaud, whose face is so prominently included in the scene chosen by Godard, the feelings stirred by these associations may be accompanied by a more intellectual curiosity for the director's complex commentary. Notably, there is no reason to critically short-circuit such reflexivity with distanciation, understood as the interruption of all affective connection with the character, actor, or overall scenario unfolded through mise-en-scène, editing, and sound. Rather, the highly affective framing in the tableau at hand seems to solicit intensity for the film's social critique. Recalling Dort's syncretic conceptualization (quoted earlier), we might describe the process as a "movement between identification with the characters"—or in my categories, affective connection—and an "understanding of the historical situation which has made these characters what they are"—or complex contextualization.[57]

TRACING NANA'S NONSOVEREIGN LIFE MAKING

The sustained focus on its female protagonist and lead actor—and particularly, although not exclusively, on her face—characterizes *My Life to Live* well beyond the discussed scenes. Although Godard's film is not as radically shot from up close as Dreyer's, even its spatially more distanced takes contribute to *My Life to Live*'s curious approach to its human subject in the layered contexts of diegetic, intertextual, and life worlds. Thus, the distribution of perspectives—and, bluntly, face time—throughout the film is asymmetrical. To the degree that spatial positioning translates into affective orientation, we are far more distanced from the men surrounding Nana/Karina than from her. Even the sustained back shot featured in the first tableau following the introductory credit sequence continues the camera's probing, multiperspectival approach to the protagonist/actor by showing us the side of Nana/Karina that we have not yet seen.[58] The focus on her throughout most of the tableau underlines that it is she who matters, and not Paul, whom she wants to leave (as indicated by the descriptive titles) and who is left out of the image much of the time. The disorienting and potentially distancing effect of the back shot is also softened by the blurred reflection of Karina's face in the mirror on the wall behind her and the occasional glimpses of her soft cheek and eyelashes afforded by slight movements in the frame. The raised, slightly crumpled collar of Nana's coat doubles the line of her shiny black hairdo, thus foregrounding her sensual presence.

Simultaneously, this hairdo adds another intertextual layer: audiences with the respective film-historical background will decipher the iconographic reference to Louise Brooks as Lulu in G. W. Pabst's *Die Büchse der Pandora* (*Pandora's Box*, 1929). If we add the references to Émile Zola's and Jean Renoir's *Nana* in the protagonist's name (probably hard for French audiences to miss) and the quotation from Edgar Allen Poe's *The Oval Portrait* toward the end of the film, we certainly have to conclude that Nana is intertextually burdened with cultural images of femininity sentenced to death by a misogynist storytelling collective. (In some respects, it matters little whether this death comes about by way of political rebellion [Jeanne], illness [Nana], violence attracted through sex work [Lulu], or art [the bride in Poe's *Oval Portrait*].)[59] In folding these associations into its layered world, *My Life to Live* develops critical connections that anticipate second-wave feminisms. Resonant with feminist Marxism, the film situates sexual exploitation as a pervasive feature of capitalist society: in gesture and demeanor, Nana is shown to virtually serve as a sex worker even while she is still employed in the record shop at the outset of the film.[60] The opening encounter with Paul retrospectively evokes radical feminist tropes of the 1970s, suggesting that the personal is political, too: "You always want me to do what you want," Nana points out. But from within the network of such projections of control and subjection, the assembly of camera work and dialogue in this tableau also begins to contour Nana's claim to nonsovereign agency. When Paul heaps another classical femininity topos on Nana by charging her with theatrical acting, she flips the charge into an assertion of professional desire: "It won't be thanks to" him if she makes "it on the stage," which is "what [she] want[s]."

Although the film sets out to forcefully dramatize gender asymmetries, it is wrong to conclude (as even revisionist critical readings of the film have done) that Nana's femininity equals objectification.[61] In this logic, masculinity attains its contours in a quest for sovereignty, extradiegetically supported by the cinematic apparatus. As indicated above, Silverman suggests that the camera doubles the control pursued by Paul and later Nana's pimp, even as she cites Godard's own intention of not "spying on" or "trapping" but "simply following" her.[62] In contrast, a reviewer reads the film's "expressive use of a restless camera" and "varying camera/figure orientations" as indicative of the absence of a "secure perspective" and, thematically, the director's "self-questioning about patriarchy."[63] To be sure, this alternative form-ideology translation is as quick as Silverman's. In slowing down, my methodological proposal for cautiously tracing multiple links and associations in specific worldmaking assemblages aims to avoid such short-circuits between form and thematics—without, however, completely resigning from interpretation.[64] Here I note that *My Life to Live*'s panning camera does act in imprecise more than in consistently anticipatory ways. At moments too fast, at other moments trailing behind the character, this cinematography's as-if-nervous and out-of-sync feel is retrospectively reminiscent of postcontinuity cinema. We can ascribe this effect to self-reflexive intention or to authorial nonsovereignty (or some combination thereof); in any case, the lack of complete control projected by the camera work contours the agency of the filmmaker as one that is, in principle (and in line with the model outlined in the introduction), no less affectively networked than that of his female actor and character.

The patriarchy portrayed, critiqued, and arguably reinscribed in and through the film is, then, not the kind of totalizing system projected in some (stereotypically 1970s) feminist criticism: a stable, more or less transhistorical institution effecting binary relations of domination. Rather, *My Life to Live*'s patriarchal collective attains its contours in collective worldmaking processes undertaken by diegetic and extradiegetic actors with layered and shifting degrees of power, unevenly backed by hegemonic norms and socio-material relations that do not erase their shared lack of sovereignty. Even the director, with his socially and institutionally privileged position, remains entangled in the flows of desire, awe, and aggression that saturate the film's affective assemblages, composed from literary and cinematic intertexts, hegemonic gender codes, and, as the biographical literature has it, personal relationship drama.[65] In the words of a reviewer, only the film's final tableau actually projects an "'omnipotent author.'"[66] The showdown reassembles the film's diegetic patriarchal collective by aligning movements of male competition into solidarity: while she was supposed to be sold by her pimp, Nana ends up being shot by both factions when the deal goes astray. Despite all the intertextual foreshadowing of her death, the incongruous character of the film's worldmaking assemblage makes this narrative closure feel abrupt. Critics have described it as "somewhat unmotivated" and "not integrated": an unexpectedly comic tone comes into play when the first gun doesn't go off, and in contrast to the film-at-large, the ending relies almost exclusively on very long shots.[67] Even while I would not go as far as the reviewer who writes that up to that point, we could imagine that Nana herself made the film, his observations back the reading I propose: except for the ending, *My Life to Live* probes different degrees of closeness to its female subject.[68] Modulating the full-fledged perceptive alignment probed by point-of-view shots with varying third-person takes, the film, in short, also follows her embattled worldmaking in Latour's more emphatic sense of respectfully tracing actor perspectives as it assembles intertwined monetary, sexual, and romantic relations.

The film's project of following Nana's nonsovereign life living becomes legible as soon as we bracket the commonplace moves of distanciation-based interpretation, such as that of discarding the film title as straightforward contrastive Brechtian irony and entertain the possibility of different and at moments perhaps even literal reading strategies.[69] The film's motto, a quotation from Michel de Montaigne, situates sex work not as an erasure of the self but (in an opening gesture of probing Nana's perspective) as a worldmaking strategy of self-affirmation: "Il faut se prêter aux autres et se donner à soi-même" (Lend yourself to others but give yourself to yourself). Of course, action is (in Latour's words again) always "*other-taken*."[70] Nana expresses a resonant insight by quoting Arthur Rimbaud in a dialogue moment that critics *have* read literally because it seems to fit the diagnosis of her objectification: "Je est un autre," she says when questioned by a police officer about the 1,000 francs that she tried to pocket on the street instead of returning the bill to the woman who dropped it.[71] But if Nana speaks a truth here, why would we again discard as straightforwardly ironic her emphatic response to her friend Yvette's account of her turn to sex work in tableau six, according to which "we're always responsible for our actions"?[72] To be sure, Nana's tone is slightly playful here, and she concludes her monologue with a little laugh.[73] This introduces the possibility of character/actor *self*-irony, which (scripted or unscripted) does not equal the *author*'s ironic distanciation from the woman on screen. But even if the extradiegetic audience is encouraged to question Nana's existentialist proclamation that "We are free," Nana's speech overall does not signal a wishful denial of the constraints that circumscribe her agency.[74] Once more focusing on Nana throughout at the expense of Yvette, the camera seems to back her assertion of "ethical being" in the face of these constraints:[75] Nana encourages Yvette to take an interest in things, precisely because "things are what they are"—"Men are men, And life is life."

Rather than allowing herself to be reduced to an object, Nana develops her interests and assumes responsibility for orienting herself in the world over which she does not have control. While she accepts

Yvette's request to introduce Raoul, Nana's future pimp, Nana focuses her interest first on a shyly flirting couple at a different table and then on the guy at the jukebox (played by Jean Ferrat), who seems to have picked the (Ferrat) song playing, about a working-class romance that may be lacking Riviera vacations but not the greater-than-the-stars "light that shines in my baby's eyes."[76] All playful self-reflexivity notwithstanding, the film makes time to attend to Nana's longing gaze while she listens, before redirecting her, and our, attention to Raoul, whose disrespectful approach is cut short by gunshots on the street. On the extradiegetic level, this interruption is bolstered by one of the director's bolder moves of noncontinuous configuration.[77] It provides Nana with the time to further develop her own strategic agency by writing a job application letter to a (female) brothel owner in the following tableau.[78] In the process, to be sure, Raoul catches up with her again and now succeeds in seducing her with a more romantic approach. But when he later does not live up to the promises he made of treating her as a lover on her free days, Nana applies the skills she has refined through sex work to a nonwork relationship: in tableau nine, she asserts sexual agency in seducing the "young man" she meets while Raoul is neglecting her in a café. Critics have dramatized the incongruities inscribed in this sequence in terms of the romantic dichotomy of autonomy vs. subjection: Nana's flirtatious dance presents "her moment of greatest self-affirmation" and an "almost ecstatic moment of liberation," but its "gleeful release of energy" is "viciously undermined" by the "point-of-view shot" inserted in the sequence, which displaces her radiant smile with the bare "walls in which Nana is enclosed."[79] But do we really need to attribute viciousness here (as the affect apparently underlying distanciation)? Alternatively, we can follow the clue provided by the descriptive title of the tableau. It mediates the divergent affective vectors by tracing Nana's own perspective: "Nana wonders whether she is happy." If we conceptualize her bodily movement in terms of a nonsovereign, simultaneously affective and strategic worldmaking response to that question, we may be able to see layered performances between total liberation and "imprisonment," or between raw pleasure and critical distanciation: an everyday intermingling of pain, pleasure, and tactics in the "complexly articulated relations between pragmatic (life-making) and accretive (life-building) activity."[80]

My Life to Live explores such layered affectscapes not only in Nana's theatrical performance but also in the assemblage of her working life. In part, the mood configured in these sequences is quite gloomy: tableau five underscores her apprehension, fear, and vulnerability— heightened by her unfamiliarity with the rules of the trade—as she takes her first client to a room. Outdoor tracking shots of bare walls from (what seems to be) Nana's perspective are followed by the camera's exploration of her face, a close-up on the client's groin as he reaches for the money in his pants pocket, and a sustained shot of his violent attempt to kiss her on the mouth, perhaps encouraged by her blatant uncertainty even as to how much she can charge. While this shot iconographically recalls the encounter of Pabst's Lulu with Jack the Ripper, tableau eight ("Afternoons. Money. Sinks. Pleasure. Hotels.") provides a dedramatizing counterpoint.[81] Its focus is on Nana's acquisition of competence and the routines of the trade as Raoul answers her questions about rules, regulations, and practices. Both the voice-over dialogue and the visual montage accompanying it substantially draw on Marcel Sacotte's sociological account of prostitution and the TV documentary made from it.[82] However, they also provide an affectively layered counterpoint: Raoul's dominantly cool tone of voice and Nana's calm and professional inquiries are assembled with a range of more experiential image snapshots. In addition to fetishizing close-ups of Nana's shoes (quoting a recurring motif from the TV documentary), the montage includes close-ups of her variously bored or emotional face along with shots of her back or her hands as she performs sexual and other daily tasks—undressing or dressing, making the bed, exchanging money (now more assertively), and sharing a cigarette break with a colleague.

This exploration by no means romanticizes or downplays the debasing aspects of Nana's work life.[83] However, it is descandalizing with its emphasis on professional operations as well as Nana's emerging everyday sociality with the other sex workers. In fact, her brief but conversant interactions with these other women are the closest that the film provides to the imagination of an alternative collective. Steve Cannon intriguingly describes the film's cafés as "Nana's only access to some kind of collective, social life."[84] The cafés, however, remain hybrid spaces insofar as they are populated with former lovers and pimps as well as friends and strangers. In contrast, the sharing of pleasurable cigarette breaks and the women's interactions in hotel spaces during Nana's work routine provide glimpses at a female community not necessarily of ideal feminist solidarity but of respectful conviviality.[85] Engaging with her coworkers in ways not primarily based on dominance or subjection, Nana, in short, lives her life.

Simultaneously, the cafés *are* representative of *My Life to Live*'s exploration of Nana's, Karina's, and Godard's larger worlds precisely as hybrid spaces of agonistic and amorous socio-affective relations. A final look at one café scene I have not yet discussed will allow me to summarize the reading that I have proposed: of *My Life to Live* as a conflicted homage to (Karina as) Nana, an homage mixing desire and recognition of her struggle to live her life with the filmmaker's, and film team's, less generous affective agitations coshaped by hegemonic topoi of femininity. Tableau eleven is titled "Place du Châtelet—A Stranger—Nana, the Unwitting Philosopher" (Nana fait de la philosophie sans le savoir). In describing this café encounter, most critics have identified the voice of the stranger, Brice Parain, with that of the filmmaker.[86] It is in fact to be noted that the camera treats the philosopher significantly more generously than the other men in the film, with more face time even than Nana during their conversation. However, the shot–reverse shot pattern used here for the first time might also indicate that "communication and connection are actually happening" in an "exchange between two equals."[87] Rephrasing a bit more carefully, I read the tableau as an exchange between two humans with different kinds of power. The tableau title suggests that the event at stake is not Parain's philosophy of "detachment" as such but the competition of truths that arises as Nana—with or without the intention that the filmmaker denies her—challenges his talk of asceticism and renouncing life. Nana insists, "But one can't live everyday life with . . ." As she struggles to find her own word to complete this sentence, Parain fills in by repeating his concept, "detachment." Nana's objection, as part of her overall flirtatious approach to the stranger, nonetheless seems to leave an impression: Parain concedes that "the movement of life" is a matter of balance, of swinging back and forth between detachment and a more involved everyday. Transposed onto the poetological level, this concession, once more, resonates with Dort's alternative to Brechtian distanciation discussed earlier: the filmic movement between affective connection and contextualization.

More generally, the half playful, half agonistic encounter between Nana and Parain can be characterized as an exchange in which professional seduction and provocation meet more or less acknowledged desire layered with a professional habitus of lecturing. When Parain swerves back to the theme of renunciation, answering Nana's continued pointed questioning with learned philosophical discourse, we see Nana becoming momentarily distracted, perhaps even bored. A moment later she is clearly pleased when he affirms her insistence on the imbrication of truth and lies, as associated with the nondetached life of the everyday. Apparently encouraged, she proceeds to flirtatiously ask him about love. As the film's musical leitmotif sets in, his abstract response, with its continued recourse to the philosophical archive, acknowledges that "one thinks with the constraints and errors of life." Perhaps her radical follow-up postulating that love should be the *only* truth affectively loses the director along with the diegetic philosopher. The latter declares that this would be the case only if love were always true, and the director cuts off the tableau without giving Nana another chance to respond. In a gesture analogous to the abrupt ending of the overall film, Godard thus asserts his extradiegetic power against the affective challenge of Nana/Karina's bodily presence and speech—but not without first having indulged in his admiration, lust, and awe for the duration of the tableau, and for most of the film.

SLOW CONFIGURATION: FASSBINDER'S *KATZELMACHER*

Nana's death is utterly senseless: in contrast to Jeanne, she does not become the foundation of a new collective, hailed by the people as the heart of the nation. As indicated, we may be tempted to read this shift as an indirect critique: the national collective is displaced with an implicitly transnational focus on cosmopolitan Paris sociality and capitalist patriarchy. Godard's first film with Karina had explored the nation's imperialist entanglements (*The Little Soldier*, 1961). In *My Life to Live*, to be sure, the Algerian War of Independence is present as a vague allusion only: the gunshots in the street in tableau six were "political," Raoul tells Nana when he reencounters her later.[88] If Godard's film thus peripherally encourages audience associations between different contexts of domination and violence, these links take center stage in *Katzelmacher*

(1969), Fassbinder's first major success, which established his national reputation.[89] The title, a Bavarian hate-speech term, is sometimes awkwardly translated as *The Cock Artist*.[90] *Katzelmacher* investigates parallels and overlaps among sexual, gender(ed), and ethnically charged national violences, or the operations of exploitation and exclusion organized by attachments to patriarchal domination, heteronormativity, and the fiction of a closed community protected from the intrusion of "foreigners." Despite this different thematic emphasis, *Katzelmacher*'s resonances with *My Life to Live* are not limited to the explicit intertextual connection Fassbinder establishes—if in part facilitated through it.[91] As with *My Life to Live*, I propose, *Katzelmacher*'s aesthetics can be described in terms of a critical intensity that operates less through distanciation than defamiliarization in the outlined sense. What *Katzelmacher* adds to my investigation in poetological terms is, first, its particular rhythm, which allows me to expand my rethinking of Brecht at the intersection with phenomenology to questions of narrative and temporality. Second, there is a stronger emphasis not only on incongruity but also on active *conflict* in its worldmaking assemblages: the ways in which tenderness and violence are imbricated in *Katzelmacher* heighten the stakes of rethinking critique as a practice of affective following.

As with *My Life to Live*, my reading of *Katzelmacher* goes against the grain of existing interpretations, including in this case many of the nonacademic reviews.[92] To be sure, Fassbinder has not generally been included in the "'hardcore' of political modernist cinema" exemplified by Godard along with Alexander Kluge, Jean-Marie Straub, and Danièle Huillet.[93] Instead, Fassbinder's authorial signature has been located precisely in his interest in emotions: although he was influenced by Brecht, Godard, Straub, and Huillet, his films complicate the binaries of distanciation and affect, rupture and attachment through his uses of popular, specifically melodramatic forms.[94] However, critics have focused more one-sidedly on the impact of "Brechtian modernism"—understood as an equivalent of distanciation—when it comes to Fassbinder's early, heavily theater-inflected work, such as *Katzelmacher*.[95] In particular, the emphasis in these readings is on motifs of aesthetic stasis, which is straightforwardly translated into a technique of social critique. As Laura McMahon argues, for example, *Katzelmacher*'s static camera and frontal, in part tableau-like shots recall the "Brechtian use of form as critique" in Godard's *My Life to Live*, as they emphasize "the film's themes of social oppression and entrapment."[96] Fassbinder himself describes his camera use in *Katzelmacher* as part defiance in response to the mixed reviews of his first film, part solution to a practical problem: the camera they had secured for the project was very heavy.[97] In the secondary literature, however, the film's "frozen *tableaux vivants*" are read symptomatically: they "stand for the monotony and the social coldness," and the "petrified bodies" produced by the "deeply anti-naturalistic," "static acting" operate as a "sign of alienation."[98] With its endless repetitions of the "same" gestures and shots, the critics add, *Katzelmacher* transforms "the very idea of movement or narrative progression into its opposite: a regression."[99]

To make sense of the persistence of these topoi, it may be useful to recall the trajectory of the conceptualization of distanciation (along with resonant techniques of critical intervention) in antinarrative terms. This trajectory can be described as a psychoanalytic and more generally modernist legacy with an afterlife in contemporary queer and, ironically, even affect studies. Antinarrative motifs pervaded 1970s Brechtianism, including Barthes's insistence that in epic theater, "all the burden of meaning and pleasure" is "on each scene, not on the whole"; Stephen Heath's championing of Brechtian montage as an "interrupt[ing]" of "narrative totality"; and Mulvey's critique of classical Hollywood cinema's sadist battles "in a linear time with a beginning and an end."[100] These motifs resurface, for example, in Lee Edelman's contemporary psychoanalytic insistence on "rupture's 'no'" and the "relentless force" of sex as resisting the "movement" of "story" oriented at some "payoff . . ., comprehension or closure"—in short, "a future."[101] But as indicated in the introduction, antinarrative insistences are equally prominent in affect studies as a paradigm that has generally displaced psychoanalytic foci on negativity and unconscious interiority with the interest in surfaces, bodies, and transindividual intensities.[102] Playing event against structure, Massumi conceptualizes affect as a "static" state of "suspense, potentially of disruption," or a "hole in time" that is "disconnected from meaningful sequences, from narration."[103] Finally, programmatic emphases on "interruption," "pause," and "repetition"; "asynchronous, discontinuous," or "stopped" time; and frozen "movement" persist even among those queer and affect studies authors who have set out to reconceptualize critical temporalities.[104]

Elizabeth Freeman, whose work resonates with mine in its emphasis on the affective dimensions of rhetoric and on "close reading" as "a way into history," introduces her "longing for form" as a multivectoral one "that turns us backward to prior moments, forward to embarrassing utopias, [and] sideways" to seemingly "banal" forms of "being."[105] Still, her study ends up foregrounding the first of these temporal vectors—"the disruption of present by past"—perhaps due to the deliberatively antinarrative aesthetics of many of her sources.[106] Similarly, Berlant invites us to take the forward vector of "optimism" seriously as "an orientation toward the pleasure that is bound up in the activity of worldmaking" and replaces fictions of radically disruptive events with notions of "situation," "systemic crisis," and "scene."[107] Nonetheless, her imagination of political alternatives to the status quo keeps returning to figures of "detaching," "self-interruption," and the "glitch" as positioned against narrative continuity.[108] In this sense, the legacy of antinarrative distanciation continues to reverberate today.

While building on Freeman's and Berlant's rethinking of temporalities, my model of multivectoral affective worldmaking assemblages proposes a more full-fledged reconceptualization of narrative. As indicated in the introduction, I underline how narrative worlds are configured through the variously horizontal, vertical, and orthogonal vectors of affect, pleasure, spectacle, association, memory, and intertextuality that feed into (forward) action and (backward) analysis. The model thus opens the domain of narrative toward modernist forms, including montage, while locating modernism's productivity not primarily in the endless returns of interruption but in ongoing processes of productive reconfiguration.[109] This insistence does not annul the aesthetic difference made by modernism. As I detail in the following pages, part of *Katzelmacher*'s specific signature is in fact located in its temporal form, which can be characterized as Brechtian with a phenomenological difference. Key to describing *Katzelmacher*'s modernist narrativity is a closer look at Brecht's concept of fable, or fabula: it does in part precisely what 1970s Brechtianism ascribes only to montage in its presumed opposition with narrative. Devised as an "answer to the inadequacy of the traditional dramatic structure," the fable "develops in contradictions" and puts significant weight on "each individual gestus."[110] Furthermore, the fable is what I call a multivectoral assemblage in that it encompasses not only the plot but also the "acting, music," and "set design."[111] In configuring these elements, *Katzelmacher*'s fabula carefully crafts a rhythm of narrative worldmaking. Intercutting between scenarios, the montage multiplies associations—of contrast as well as similarity—between details, creating surprising complexity from its limited repertoire of visual elements. The phenomenological difference is in how the film does so slowly, contrasting movement with pause while assembling a plot from allusions and associations.[112] This poetics of deliberate deceleration dramatizes the multivectoral possibilities of narrative: as Berlant remarks, "To not rush into story while inhabiting action is to experiment with relation."[113]

MESSY AFFECTSCAPES

Katzelmacher's phenomenological experiments with relation invite a "queer attentiveness" to "affective mess," or the intricate entanglements of pleasure, desire, tenderness, longing, and violence.[114] The second part of my argument at first parallels that on *My Life to Live*: once more, acting and mise-en-scène—in the encompassing sense of shot composition—are doubtlessly Brechtian, in part because of their pronounced artificiality, but they do not add up to some sum of coldness or the disruption of all actor, character, and audience affect.[115] My own affective response to the film (much more so than to Fassbinder's later works) has been shaped by dimensions entirely missing in the distanciation-focused scholarship—namely, what I would describe as the striking beauty and intensity of the film's images, or its "hypnotic effect."[116] Analytically speaking, this effect is likely induced by *Katzelmacher*'s black-and-white aesthetics, the lighting (in particular, the use of overexposure), and the stylization and visual simplicity of the more tableaux-like shots: the bare walls often surrounding the actors accentuate their bodies in space.[117] This effect of intensity, I propose, provides an opening into the "messy" affective layers of the film: a world in which gestures, movements, and suspected character feelings as well as audience feelings do not line up neatly—perhaps even less neatly than in Fassbinder's later melodramas—although they are not therefore absent or present merely to be disrupted or disruptive.[118]

These defamiliarized filmic affectscapes are also messier than those in *My Life to Live* insofar as Fassbinder's film does not invite a comparable alignment distribution. In *My Life to Live*, we can affectively connect with Karina's striking performance and Nana's life-making struggle in condemning the violent patriarchal collective surrounding them. In contrast, collective violence is intimately woven into the intensity of *Katzelmacher*'s tableaux in ways that resist such easy side taking. Long before Jorgos, the Greek "guest worker" (played by Fassbinder), is beaten up, or even enters the film, violence recurs as entangled with a number of characters' everyday gestures of sex, love, and advancement.[119] The fact that everyone is implicated in that mess does not, however, necessarily mean that the film invites no empathy at all for its characters and reduces them to social types or "clichés."[120] Rather, the responses invited from its audiences may include "a troubling mix of sympathy and antipathy" or, in my own categories, piecemeal affections perhaps not canceling but complicating moral judgment.[121]

The film's slow assembly of such mess can be exemplarily traced in the exposition sequence, which intercuts three scenarios introducing us to three couples. They all seem to be involved in repetitive daily activities, although the situations turn out to be infused with forward orientations both diegetically and extradiegetically: as the characters plan or dream about the future, the film begins to unfold a plot from allusions. In the first scenario, Erich picks up Marie (Hanna Schygulla) from her work by car and then sits with her and increasingly more characters at the outdoor railing where many of the film's group scenes will be set; in the second one, Helga and Paul have sex; in the third one, Peter and Elisabeth (Irm Hermann) eat dinner.[122] Establishing connections, the intercutting (1-2-1-3-1-2-1-3) unfolds both the film's small social cosmos and its narrative rhythm of decelerated action as the multivectoral exploration of a *situation* in Berlant's sense, "a state of things in which something that will perhaps matter is unfolding amid the usual activity of life."[123] At Elisabeth and Peter's table, the atmosphere is decidedly frozen. Physical movement is limited to the gestures of eating, and initial silence is followed by a verbal exchange in which Elisabeth icily proclaims that the "thing" (*Sache*) Peter does not want to be involved in is none of his business anyway. Later the film audience will gather that this "thing" is her intention of renting a room to the Greek "guest worker" who is the ostensible focus of the film but who first appears in minute 37—in contrast to his immediate entrance in the play on which the film is based.

In centering our attention on the gestures of life making preceding Jorgos's arrival, the film's poetics of deceleration and allusion traces both differences and similarities among its characters' future orientations. In the car—arguably the quintessential fetish of German postwar economic progress—Marie worries about Erich's equally unspecified plans, which, as she implies, could get sent him to prison.[124] Indicative of the film's performative nuances that have been buried in the diagnosis of its presumed Brechtian coolness, Marie's habitus in this shot contrasts with Elisabeth's iciness: with her head on Erich's shoulder, Marie dreamily talks about the "loneliness" she anticipates.[125] When he coolly responds that things will not go wrong, and, besides, there are other guys, she resolutely—and more harshly—declares that there is "no one else like/ than" him (keinen anderen wie dich). The shift in her tone signals that Marie's performance of affect cannot be straightforwardly opposed to either Erich's strategic coolness or Elisabeth's intense coldness, which is noticeably charged with hate and at moments tilts into hysterical aggression. In the following shot at the railing, in which Rosy, Erich's former girlfriend, is present as well, Marie talks about the importance of "advancement" (*Weiterkommen*) in a voice that is soft, if not quite as dreamy, once more leaning against Erich.

As the audience learns in the pub sequence following the exposition, Paul and Helga have analogous negotiations. Paul is scheming with Erich in the bathroom. The location suggests sexual associations, but we still don't know of which kind; the focus of the almost dialogue-free shot is on Paul's hesitation. Helga objects to his hanging out with Erich, who has been to prison already (she says) and who (we will learn later) encourages Paul to squash Helga's insistences with violence. In the exposition sequence, we first see the outcomes of such teaching—or evidence of its redundancy—when Paul violently pushes Helga away from him. While shocking (and thus interruptive), the gesture emerges from a narrative rhythm of affective intensification: the first bedroom shot of Paul and Helga pursued the asymmetries of their intimate gestures in varying the dynamic between Marie and Erich. More sexualized than Erich, Paul slowly undressed in the foreground while Helga anxiously made the bed behind him with rapid movements, contrasting also with Marie's quiet self-assurance. The second shot intensifies these vectors: it fetishizes Paul's leg in sexy overexposure as he puts his pants back on, while Helga

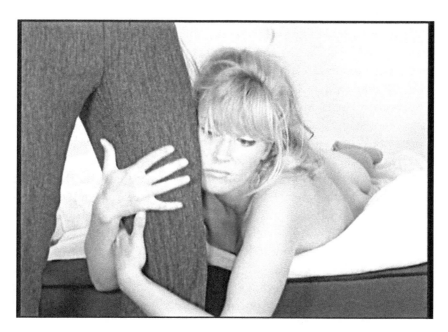

FIGURE 2.4 *Katzelmacher* (dir. Rainer Werner Fassbinder, 1969).

clings to him, leaning her head against the leg and stroking it, with an expression of resigned longing on her face (figure 2.4). Paul impatiently tries to free himself a couple of times and then violently accomplishes that goal, cruelly instructing Helga to put "it" (her feelings?) on "the bill."

Character speech in *Katzelmacher* overall deploys Bavarian dialect with a defamiliarizing spin: with largely high-German pronunciation but local syntax. In this way, Paul explicates later that "a love and those things, that always has to do with money."[126] As indicated, critics have followed his lead in discussing the "commodification of emotions" in Fassbinder's films, the reduction of attachment to monetary circulation or power.[127] A more careful critical rendering of Paul's statement, however, would be "all emotions are shot through with financial transaction." And the reverse is also true. Rather than just reducing emotion to money—or even to sex—*Katzelmacher* simultaneously insists that all financial and sexual transactions are shot through with feelings.[128] On the diegetic level, not only does Helga bill her relationship with Paul as romantic rather than merely transactional (her tender gestures persist even after repeated violent incidents), but the others who gossip about them do so as well. When Helga later gets pregnant and Paul's attempts to violently induce an abortion fail, he asks her to forgive him, and they plan on marriage, in line with her earlier hopes and reverting to the bourgeois formula for legitimately mixing money, sex, and romance. Less predictably, feelings enter even those relationships that *are* clearly portrayed as sex work in the film. Paul's client Klaus is at one point awkwardly introduced to the group of friends and later incidentally almost forgets to pay. More forcefully, *Katzelmacher* stages the imbrication of money, sex, and feeling—or sexual and romantic feeling—in the emerging relationship between Rosy and Franz.[129] Franz has no problem with paying for sex or even publicly boasting about his ability to pay (after all, he has a job), but he nonetheless articulates longings for something "more" that slowly invades the framing of their relationship despite Rosy's resistance against feelings.[130]

Rather than presenting only disenchantment, the film features a narrative play of conflicting affective vectors: more dramatically than *My Life to Live*, it stages both the "fusion of feelings" and the "conflict between them" that is aimed at in Brecht's theory of affective incongruity on the stage.[131] On the level of audience response, the emphasis on conflict is first driven home with Paul's violent gesture toward Helga in the introductory sequence discussed earlier. As indicated, its disruptive effect is contingent on the preceding affective intensification produced by acting, mise-en-scène, and editing: Paul and Helga's encounter replays and heightens the vectors of Marie's tenderness and Erich's coolness, Elisabeth's iciness and Peter's recalcitrant response. While the analytical vocabulary of distanciation cannot account for this affective shock effect, my description entails deliberate restraint in not quickly specifying its exact components. The beautifully stylized bed scene is arguably more blatantly sexually charged for the audience than the diegetic encounter itself, with the fetishization of Paul's foregrounded leg as well as Helga's face and hair. But how precisely is sexual desire layered with aesthetic appreciation and character relation in my response to this tableau? What combination of empathy, sympathy, desire, and irritation does Helga's stubborn devotion provoke in me? Or do none of these terms actually get at the intensity charge that fuels the shock produced by Paul's eruption?

The methodological caution indicated in these questions is more an attempt to trace the messiness of the film's aesthetic worldmaking assemblages than a categorical resistance against specification. This caution does not preclude me from slowly sorting through some of the entanglements as I go along, only from all too quickly decoding *Katzelmacher*'s noticeable insistence on sexual layers. Critics have variously read the film in straightforwardly psychoanalytic terms by postulating that "all" of the film's "serial chain[s] of signs . . . refer to sexual desire as the basis of social power relations" or that "the genital sphere is identified as the gamete of violence and xenophobia."[132] My attempt to open up these origin narratives in attending to multivectoral affect flows does not imply a full rejection of the psychoanalytical thought that shaped both criticism and cultural production in the 1960s and 1970s. Helpful specifications can be developed with André Green, who wrote *The Fabric of Affect in Psychoanalytic Discourse* (first published in 1973) in response to the "'forgetting' of the affect" in Lacanian psychoanalysis in the 1960s and 1970s.[133] Green emphasizes the revised topography of affect in Freud's later work, which, Green argues, came about in his confrontation with "the limit of interpretative power."[134] In other words, if the early Freud did blame the genital sphere in identifying affect with the sexual unconscious, he later questioned the linear analytic vectors of symptomatic reading.[135] Notwithstanding the dominant turn away from psychoanalysis in twenty-first-century theory, Freud's later work has indirectly shaped contemporary affect studies—for instance, through Eve Sedgwick's return to Melanie Klein's revisionist account.[136]

Katzelmacher's poetics of slow unfolding, I propose, resonates with the interpretative caution of the later Freud. A recurring motif in the 1969 film reviews is the observation that the film refrains from contouring the protagonists' backgrounds, as the director "does not want to explain, but only to show": *Katzelmacher* is a "didactic play" that "doesn't teach anything."[137] In phenomenologically foregrounding the disorderly, heterogeneous, and conflictual presences of affect, the film's assemblage brackets simple causalities and summary explanations.[138] Importantly, this applies not only to the sexual origin narratives of the early Freud but also to the biological explanations that would come to displace them in his own work and that of his competitors from Klein to contemporary affect studies and neuroscience: the belief in the primacy of "the destruction drives,"

Massumi's animal sympathy, or the cognitivists' evolutionary pressures.[139] Simultaneously, *Katzelmacher*'s bracketing of grand explanatory
narratives does not equal an abdication of all interpretative possibility.
Rather, the film's slow rhythm of multivectoral worldmaking invites me
to develop a thick reading of its messy associations of romantic intimacy,
financial advancement, lust, fantasy, and violence.[140] Temporarily letting
myself be hypnotized by the film's visual intensity, I do not surrender all
critical faculty. As I look more closely at the connections *Katzelmacher*
makes in exploring collective attachment and violence, I merely (with
Berlant) trade the habitus of diagnostic "pathology" at a distance for an
orientation "toward the pleasure," pain, and aggression "bound up in the"
diegetic as well as filmic "activity of worldmaking."[141]

COLLECTIVE ASSEMBLIES: GESTURES OF ATTACHMENT, DETACHMENT, AND CLOSURE

Helga's arguing with Paul in the pub about his association with Erich
is followed by one of the film's virtually frozen, unmoving images as
Marie and Erich pose on a staircase. The shot's pronounced stillness
foregrounds their dialogue, which is slowed through pauses between
individual sentences but is not as radically denaturalized as some of the
other—delayed or tonally defamiliarized—speaking in the film. Marie
once more articulates her hesitation toward Erich's scheme—now with
an emphasis on her own resistance and thus a stronger suggestion that
they are talking about (sex) work he wants *her* to do. Erich reminds her
of their shared goal of leading "a better life," and when she responds
tangentially by underlining her feelings for him ("Ich hab dich so lieb"),
he tries to turn her intimacy discourse to his advantage by insisting that
she consequently has to listen to him. The foregrounding of this verbal
exchange makes it easy to comprehend the cruelty in Marie's optimism:
her attachment to Erich will likely hurt her.[142] But her soft voice, the
lighting (in particular, on Marie's face and legs) that relies on Hollywood
codes of romantic love as well as sex, and the theatrically heightened
contrastive black-and-white arrangement of their clothes against the
background of the light distribution in the shot's four-part spatial division by the staircase create an "intensity of expression" that, I propose,
invites us to bracket distanced judgment (figure 2.5).[143]

FIGURE 2.5 *Katzelmacher* (dir. Rainer Werner Fassbinder, 1969).

Short of creating straightforward character empathy, the tableau's affective defamiliarization heightens my sensual as well as cognitive attention in a way that instead allows me to listen closely to Marie's words in the rhythms of decelerated configuration. Her next line, "and the fear I have of the others," provides a counterpoint to Helga's conclusion in the previous scene. When Helga warned Paul against associating with Erich and received another slap in response, she generalized her disapproval into a critique of the dangerous power of collectivity: one ought "to free onself" (sich lösen) from "the others." In contrast, Marie insists on the reality of her attachment to the collective and her corresponding vulnerability. In yet another counterpointal twist, Erich's answer varies Helga's discourse of intimacy for his purposes: "I am important in your life and no one else." A cut lets Erich have the last word for now; a less artificially stylized but also visually striking shot on another staircase links the exchange to the way Rosy urges Franz to keep their relationship from the others. But when we next join Marie and Erich in an intimate space (where he strokes her neck half tenderly, half distractedly), she responds that she has thought things over and that "this" is not for her: "Was die anderen denken, das stört einen Mensch[en]." The English subtitle, "It bothers me what others think," does not capture the generalizing implication of her words: a human, Marie insists, is affected by the verdict of the collective.

Realizing that his attempts to persuade her are failing, Erich now uses the technique he recommended to Paul: approaching Marie in a seemingly tender way, he suddenly hits her several times. Marie's response is less subdued than Helga's: she cries out dramatically. Shortly afterward, she starts making excuses to protect herself from his continued intimacy and eventually leaves him for Jorgos. Unlike Helga, Marie does not seem willing to accept Erich's conceit that "a pain"—or in any case Erich's violent practice of strategic pain infliction—is a necessary part of "a love."[144] Like Rosy, who wants to be different from the others, Marie does assume agency in sorting through her conflicting attachments. The emerging similarities and differences do not line up to create a global contrast between these two and the rest, but they indicate a spectrum of resistances. While not pretending Marie or Rosy has achieved full-fledged liberation, the film does endorse their different orientations by endowing them with some of Nana's force.

The intertextual connection between the two films is made explicit in an exchange between Rosy and Gunda about romance novels. With some feeling in her voice, Rosy cites a passage that she particularly liked, a German translation of the exact quotation used in tableau two of *My Life to Live*: when a male lover credits the first-person narrator with living an "intense life," she interrupts him to protest the "logical" conclusions he draws from his observation and locates a moment of "bitter triumph" in that gesture of interruption. "No more anxieties about starting a new life," Rosy keeps quoting, "an elegant way to escape from this dead end"—or from this impasse, as Berlant might put it?[145] Unlike Godard's tableau, Fassbinder's simple mise-en-scène endows Rosy's slow reading with our undivided attention and thus underlines her fantasy of making a different life for herself in resisting collective pressure. A few minutes later this emphasis on resistant fantasy is developed through another allusion to *My Life to Live*: in one of *Katzelmacher*'s most pronounced scenes of physical movement, Rosy dances in her apartment to her own intonation of The Who's *Young Man Blues*, with no music other than her voice and finger clicking. Reminiscent of Nana's dance for the young man, the scene has been analogously acknowledged by critics as a moment of pleasure in Fassbinder's film.[146] However, Rosy's dance is just for herself. (Or just for the camera in the frontal shot, which would correspond to her professional ambitions on the diegetic level, although she is not looking at us in an overtly exhibitionistic manner.)

If Fassbinder's version thus facilitates more of an escape into personal pleasure and fantasy, the flip side to this shift in accent is that Rosy cannot find a collective space for her desires. In the earlier conversation about the romance novels, even Gunda, who is also isolated as apparently single,[147] fails to share Rosy's fantasy. After a prolonged silence, Gunda switches the topic to gossip about Elisabeth's fights with Peter; her pronouncedly disaffected tone presents a less intense variation on Elisabeth's aggressive iciness. The fact that Rosy joins into that gossip indicates that her private fantasy world does not shield her from the aggressive sociality of her everyday surroundings.[148] In other words, *Katzelmacher*'s worldmaking assemblage keeps reminding the audience of the oppressive force of violent collectivity, even as it simultaneously emphasizes two alternative vectors of character orientation: the experiential weight of collective attachments, on the one hand, and the promise of detachment fantasies, on the other.

In its oppressive force, *Katzelmacher*'s collective resonates with Brecht's "fascist collective"—or "crowd," in which "the interests of *all* [are] equally harmed."[149] The affective process of its assembly, however, is not usefully conceptualized through Brecht's opposition between this "mob" governed by "emotions" and "a collection of individuals, capable of thinking."[150] Evocative of a Latourian network more than the crowd of early twentieth-century German theory, *Katzelmacher*'s collective is a moving figuration constantly remade by the often strategically affective gestures of nonsovereign actors, whose subjectivity is assembled in this very process. When Marie starts to defy the overall group in embracing her emerging relationship with Jorgos, she publicly moves into the position Rosy occupied in more closeted fashion. First, Gunda and Helga call her a "slut" to her face; later the jealous Erich repeats the charge, and when Marie's talking back prompts a threat of violence, Gunda admonishes her rather than him: "You may not talk like that with anyone because it upsets everyone."

Fassbinder's tracing of these gestures of closure strongly resonates with Sara Ahmed's phenomenological account of how "emotions work to" materialize collectives in aligning "some subjects with some others and against other others."[151] They do so by moving "sideways" (e.g., from Rosy to Marie) through "'sticky' associations between signs, figures and objects," accumulating "affective value" in this very process of circulation.[152] Jorgos's exclusion operates as such a hateful gesture of closure as well. Although it is performed as the seemingly self-evident result of the collective's existence, the gesture itself creates "the very effect of . . . boundaries of bodies and worlds," as it contours the everyday group making in new terms.[153] When Jorgos approaches the outdoor railing for the first time, the conversation shifts from Rosy's sex work to his appearance: "Ein Ausländer!" (A foreigner!) The sticky rumors circulating in the flows of conversation from here on will charge this gesture of exclusion with narratives of sexual as well as political legitimation: the foreigner supposedly has a larger dick (Peter reports) and an uncontrolled sexual appetite (Gunda concocts an assault fantasy), and he is a communist, too, because there are plenty of those in Greece (according to the newspapers Franz has read). But these topoi are retrospectively grafted onto the initial gesture of aligning "bodily space with social space": "'Ein Ausländer.' 'Jetzt kommt er schon her.'"[154] The subtitle translation, "He is coming our way," might not carry the affective charge of the German wording, with its imagined threat of "proximity" and provocation of spatial transgression in the move "here."[155] Later the four men beat up Jorgos when he again arrives at the railing in a moment in which Erich "has an anger" (einen Zorn hab ich), shortly after his confrontation with Marie. Unlike standard German, the deployed Bavarian dialect makes this feeling into "a property," but *Katzelmacher*'s cinematic assembly underlines how "'the subject' is simply one nodal point in the economy" of affective circulation that accumulates intensity in the group members' repeated affirmations of the gesture of violent closure.[156] "He was walking around as if he belonged here," Gunda asserts. Helga echoes that "an order has to be reestablished," and Paul claims that "a revenge has to be": "We belong here and nothing else."[157]

Of course, the opposition of "we" vs. "the foreigner" is not invented by the first gesture of exclusion: the affective economy of aligning the collective against Jorgos "depends on past histories of association."[158]

But the backward temporal vector of historical analysis is astonishingly undeveloped in *Katzelmacher*, in notable contrast to Fassbinder's later historical melodramas. A mere hint is provided by one exceptional comment on Elisabeth's past: "When a person's had as much misfortune in life as she has," Gunda interjects in the midst of gossiping about her, momentarily even softening her voice with a touch of sympathy. Apparently, there *is* a backstory to Elisabeth's particularly pronounced coldness and cruelty, and as the film audience, we are free to project connections with "multiple histories."[159] In line with chapter 1's reflections on the question of "national" affect assemblages, my own associations certainly include suspicions about affective stoppages in the wake of fascism. The film, however, does little to support these desires for symptomatic anchoring. Elisabeth's life story remains as unspecified as the background of the others. Instead, *Katzelmacher*'s slow rhythm of narrative configuration insistently attends to the unfolding of violence in its dynamic, layered present, including Elisabeth's daily abuse of Peter and his delayed response, which presents variations on the other group members' violent gestures.[160]

To (begin to) conclude, Fassbinder's critique of violence operates through a close-up on the emergence of gestures rather than their full-fledged contextualization in character histories. It still deserves to be called critical insofar as it does not condone the acts or downplay their horror in any moment. In tracing their daily occurrence, this critique merely slows the moves of generalizing explanation that encourage summary condemnations of people and summary diagnoses of the forces driving them. Instead of "interrogating" or "demystifying" behaviors, *Katzelmacher* defamiliarizes them.[161] At the intersection of Brecht and phenomenology explored in this chapter, this "making strange" reboots our senses along with our cognitive apparatus; it is effected by, and effects, intensity more than distance. As we follow the film's messy entanglements of longing, strategizing, desire, tenderness, and violence, the critical habitus of "judicious and knowledgeable detachment" that has been associated with modernism's practices of distanciation is displaced with unstable audience affections variously composed from flashes of sympathy, desire, longing, discomfort, complicity concerns, and visual fascination.[162]

In making time for such affective mess, the film's multivectoral, slow worldmaking thwarts linear teleologies—but not simply by freezing movement. Rather, it does give significant weight also to *forward* orientations. The film's motto, a quote from Fassbinder's friend Yaak Karsunke, states: "It is better to make new mistakes than to perpetuate the old ones to the point of general unconsciousness."[163] Read affirmatively rather than through the lens of oppositional irony, this suggestion corresponds to the productive irritation that, I believe, is offered by Fassbinder's conflictual worldmaking assemblage: in the end, the film holds onto the feelings that it insistently shows are compromised with violence and self-interest. The openness toward a different future indicated in Marie's emerging relationship with Jorgos is visualized in a motif of green space. The park setting that provides the background for this plot development contrasts with the film's signature shots at the railing: leaves rustle in the wind and glitter in the sun as Marie seduces Jorgos and also in a subsequent scene in which she confidently refutes Gunda's and Helga's judgments by declaring that she knows "where to put [her] love." To be sure, this park setting is as minimalist as the film's overall mise-en-scène, and its uses deconstruct any fantasy of a pure, idyllic outside: the green space motif does not escape the film's poetics of affective conflict but contributes to unfolding it.[164] Jorgos's rough gestures of desire halfway resonate with Gunda's assault fantasy (he grabs Marie's breast to indicate his "love"), and he deploys his presumed linguistic incompetence to evade Marie's discourse of monogamy (is he married in Greece? "nix verstehen" [no understand]). In turn, Marie fails to demonstrate real empathy when Jorgos later articulates his distress about the beating; instead, she pressures him to kiss her "because I want you to." But do these messy entanglements of love, self-interest, and brutality cancel the reality of longing?

Insistently, this question is posed also by the film's series of walking scenes, which have puzzled critics—and to which I want to turn in ending this chapter. These scenes are set apart from the remainder of the film both aurally and visually. Accompanied by Peter Raben's variations on Franz Schubert's *Sehnsuchtswalzer* (Waltz of longing), they feature *Katzelmacher*'s only instances of pronounced camera movement: lateral reverse tracking shots trace the outdoor walking of different (friendly as well as romantic) couples. The walking is so "measured" and "rhythmic" that critics have associated Schygulla's retrospective description of Fassbinder's early characters as "'intelligent sleepwalkers.'"[165] Cued by the difference in staging, even I initially wanted to read these walking inserts in terms of a global contrast with the overall film, as a portrayal of romantic illusions or the public façades created by the characters, which would then be ironized through the pronounced stylization.[166] But this hypothesis does not bear out on the level of dialogue. The competitive talk about what they feel for and with their lovers (Marie and Helga), the bickering about posture and the envy of the others (Elisabeth and Peter), the fantasies of marriage and faraway lovers (Helga and Gunda), and the rumors of rape (to which Marie objects as she walks with Helga) make for the same kind of messy assemblages of optimism, tenderness, and aggression featured in the overall film. Accompanied by the waltz of longing, the walking scenes just *present* these messy affects-capes in a more dramatized, radically defamiliarized way. They visualize movements of fantasy deeply entangled with reality even in their disappointment: active worldmaking forces, for better or worse.

The music resurfaces at the very end of the film, after Marie has the last word. As noted earlier, Marie is played by Hanna Schygulla, whose radiating presence and (at the time) emerging star appeal have both bolstered, and been bolstered by, the character's impurely affective performance throughout the film. All around her, the future orientations of optimistic and brutal scheming are subject to pragmatic adjustments: the group articulates their respect for Elisabeth's economic rationale for encouraging the immigrant to stay (she knows business); Rosy suspects she might be too old for an acting career after all; Erich and Paul plan on doing their compulsory military service. Against this backdrop of accommodation, Marie declares dreamily that Jorgos will take her to Greece in the summer. "What about his wife?" Helga asks skeptically. "That doesn't matter," Marie insists. "Everything is different in Greece." Of course, we may suspect that Jorgos's earlier defensiveness about his wife belies this optimism and that it will end up hurting Marie once more. But the music, which sets in as the screen goes black and transitions us out of the diegetic world, arguably invites us to nonetheless follow Marie/Schygulla's dreaming at a tangent. Minimally, we might acknowledge the difference that the character's affective opening up has made in the diegesis. If we let ourselves be affected by imaginative translations or piecemeal reconfigurations of the fantasy at hand, we might more fully align with its utopian orientation. In many of Fassbinder's later films, affective cruelty toward both characters and audience triumphs in excessively bleak, more or less realist closure. In *Katzelmacher*, however, Marie's concluding fantasy expresses longing for a world in which things would in fact be all different, resonant with the filmmaker's own "concrete utopia of anarchy."[167]

To be sure, this longing unfolds but as a counterpoint to the film's modernist critique of collectivity. In the following chapter, I introduce Aki Kaurismäki's refugee trilogy films as more full-fledged twenty-first-century reenvisionings of such utopian vectors. But first I develop the opposite emphasis by turning to Fatih Akın's bleak *The Cut*. As I argue, *The Cut* in some respects can be situated in the tradition of Fassbinder's experiential critique of collective violence, even as it seemingly turns away from art cinema legacies by embracing genre. Ironically, I further submit, it is precisely this turn to the high-affect forms of genre that produces more of an aesthetic of distance than this chapter was able to locate in Godard's and Fassbinder's early films.

CHAPTER THREE

Genre Assemblages

Affective Incisions in Fatih Akın's The Cut *and Aki Kaurismäki's Refugee Trilogy*

In many ways, the legacy of the European art cinemas discussed in chapter 2 is still very much alive in contemporary European cinema. Some of the auteurs—including Jean-Luc Godard—have remained active, and a new generation of filmmakers grew up influenced by them, as indicated by Fatih Akın's interest in Rainer Werner Fassbinder discussed in chapter 1. Furthermore, several "new" new waves have been celebrated for probing different forms of phenomenological realism, austerity, and minimalism, from Dogme 95 to the Romanian "new wave" and the so-called Berlin School—or *nouvelle vague Allemande*—of the 2000s.[1] Over the course of the past decade, however, these contemporary art cinemas have been increasingly affected by turns to "genre," a form of cinema explicitly outlawed in the purist Dogme 95 manifesto.[2] Of particular interest to my investigations here is a transnational resurgence of forms associated with the Western. In addition to Akın's *The Cut* (2014), which I discuss in the first half of this chapter, this resurgence includes, for example, *Gold* (2013) and *Western* (2017) by Berlin School directors Thomas Arslan and Valeska Grisebach, Jadu Rude's Romanian new wave–affiliated *Bravo! (Aferim!*, 2015), Nuri Bilge Ceylan's *Once Upon a Time in Anatolia* (2011), and Alejandro González Iñárritu's *The Revenant* (2015). Beyond (or before) these turns to genre, individual European auteurs carved out their eclectic styles by incorporating genre elements from the beginning. Thus, the comedy and crime elements in Aki Kaurismäki's incomplete "refugee trilogy," which I discuss in the second half of this chapter, resonate as a familiar feature of his unique auteurist brand.[3] A new twist in Kaurismäki's aesthetic is nonetheless indicated by the circumstance that critics have also widely described *Le Havre* (2011) and *The Other Side of Hope* (*Toivon tuolla puolen*, 2017) as "fairytale[s]."[4]

European critics often express ambivalence, skepticism, or disappointment in response to auteurist genre experiments. Perhaps due to his established oddball reputation, Kaurismäki got off lightly: notwithstanding some skeptical undertones implied in the fairy-tale labeling, *Le Havre* and *The Other Side of Hope* overall found a very warm reception. In contrast, Akın's *The Cut* was hit hard by critical ambivalence and disappointment.[5] The film fuses elements of the Western, historical epos, and melodrama to address the Armenian genocide and its aftermath. Critics compared *The Cut* to the earlier *The Edge of Heaven*, to which Akın himself had linked *The Cut* as the final part of his Love, Death, and the Devil trilogy, and characterized *The Cut* as "a narrative of almost archaic simplicity" against that backdrop: "a quaffable epic, for better or for worse"; "big, ambitious" but "a little simplistic emotionally."[6] One reviewer felt reminded of David Lean's widescreen melodramas: with its "majestic extreme long landscape shots" and the "measured, old-fashioned narrative mode" of the script by long-time Scorsese collaborator Mardik Martin, *The Cut* draws on "a form of now historical narrative cinema."[7]

Given this study's aesthetic affinities, I should be expected to join this chorus. We (stereo)typically associate genre cinema with clear-cut narrative patterns, definite character types and emotions, none of which sits well with my focus on highly intricate worldmaking assemblages. But how does the proposed model of affective worldmaking then allow me to attend to genre-affiliated productions? Part of my answer to this question—perhaps unsurprisingly—is that complexity is not absent here either. As I have emphasized, cinematic worldmaking in general can be characterized as a multivectoral, at least virtually highly complex process. The following readings detail some of the ways in which this complexity potential is activated also in the worldmaking configurations of specific genre-affiliated works. As ensembles of conventions and expectations circulating in the loops of cinematic production and reception, genres themselves are mutable constructs rather than homogeneous entities.

In turn, chapter 2's discussion of *Katzelmacher*'s aesthetics of visual reduction has indicated that art cinema legacies do not equal a straight-forward emphasis on complexity. In this chapter, I qualify the opposition between art and (popular) genre cinema more fully. More precisely, my first argument is that Akın's and Kaurismäki's films generate complexity both despite and—somewhat more surprisingly—*by way of* their genre affiliations. As I will detail, both of them hybridize genre with documentary elements, and they invite layered associations by foregrounding cinematic intertextuality. This emphasized intertextuality contributes to generic hybridity and mixes genre with modernist art. For example, *Le Havre* draws on Robert Bresson's minimalism, while references to Marcel Carné add film noir and poetic realism to its genre combination. In *The Cut*, explicit intertextuality induces a dimension of self-reflexivity reminiscent of cinematic modernism: the film dramatizes cinema itself as the trilogy's "devil," and Akın describes *The Cut* as in part "about my personal journey through cinema."[8] However, none of this amounts to a deconstructive take on genre. Rather, I argue that Akın's "bow to the look-and-feel of the great cinemas of the past" creates richly textured audiovisual worlds.[9] In this sense, the forces of genre themselves generate the complexity of association.

All these intricacies notwithstanding, my second argument in this chapter is about the productive ways in which Akın's and Kaurismäki's uses of genre strategically curtail complexity. Akın describes his motivation for delving so deeply into genre in *The Cut* in terms of the project's political intervention into the Turkish public sphere, where the Armenian genocide, unacknowledged by the government, long remained a largely taboo subject.[10] His primary aim, the director emphasizes, was "that Turkish viewers watching the film can identify fully with the main character."[11] He underlines that the political columnists in Turkey in fact discussed the film much more positively than the transnational film critics and reports that the "rhetorical trick" worked with his own parents: conservative Turks who could not relate to the first part of the trilogy, *Head On* (2004), they quickly developed full-fledged empathy for the Armenian protagonist of *The Cut*.[12] With respect to audience alignment, *The Cut*'s exploration of genre thus in fact constitutes a deliberate embrace of simplicity: a cinematic "cut" into social controversy, or into the complexity of plural nonsovereign worldmaking processes traced in

The Edge of Heaven. With no attempt at understanding the perpetrators, *The Cut* aims to facilitate a public process of unqualified mourning for and with a political "Other."

The film's high-affect aesthetics is, however, not sufficiently characterized as a sacrifice in cinematic art for a good political cause. As I argue, *The Cut* creatively adopts genre aesthetics in a way that provides an intriguing twist to my larger investigations in this study: against standard expectations, *The Cut's* political project of facilitating affective allegiance works through more of an aesthetics of distance than the modernist films discussed in the last chapter. Of course, the notion of distance has been used in very different ways by film historians and practitioners, and the distance at stake here is not entirely that championed by advocates of Brechtian modernism. *The Cut* draws more on the widescreen technology historically appreciated by Bazin and associated with 1950s popular cinema than on techniques of commentary and montage: it deploys CinemaScope for a radical experiment with spatial distance in the service of affective connection. In a different cinematic and thematic context, Akın and his team thus expand the haunting distance aesthetics of Susanne's hotel mourning scene in *The Edge of Heaven* (see chapter 1) to major parts of the trilogy's closing film. This experiment may have been too bold in its challenge to established critical categorizations and perceptive habits, and I concede to its loudest critics that it came together unevenly.[13] The film's strength, I argue, is not in plotting and dialogue but in how it probes intense affectedness-at-a-distance through the visual and aural mise-en-scène of the protagonist's wanderings. This mise-en-scène contours an ethical and aesthetic intervention lost in the discussion of the film to date: by contrasting a variety of collectives with the protagonist's minuscule figure in different desert landscapes, I argue, the film's creative adaptation of widescreen technology forcefully mediates the foreclosure of collectivity through genocide as an experience of radical isolation. While the film presents a strong, unequivocal critique of collective violence, its focus is thus less on the genocide as such than (in Jacques Rancière's words) on the "rupture" it effects with the hegemonic "'distribution of the sensible'" or the "dividing-up of the world" into national and religious collectives.[14] The film's uncompromising focus on isolation indirectly emphasizes creaturely human dependence on the collective, but it does so, I suggest further, in a way more resonant with Giorgio Agamben's reflections on the loss of political collectivity in the age of biopolitics than with Deleuzian ontologies of affective fullness and collective potential.

Whereas *The Cut* dramatizes the impossibility of reclaiming community in the aftermath of genocide, Kaurismäki's refugee "fairy tales" perform strikingly different cinematic cuts into social controversy. Their creative play with genre unfolds a counterpoint to Akın's insistence on mourning in that they probe imaginative possibilities of assembling a collective of solidarity in the face of current political realities. In detailing these imaginative solutions, I focus on the political potential of cutting through complexity. As I have argued in this study, the proposed model and methodology for cautiously tracing layered processes of nonsovereign, distributed worldmaking and evaluating diverging truth claims present a promising answer to the kinds of nationalist, religious, and fascist closures that have become increasingly hegemonic across contemporary societies. However, the model may not as easily lend itself to imaginations of radical change. While it is radically democratic—or egalitarian—in the spirit of Bruno Latour's call for listening to a broader range of actors, it links less smoothly to Rancière's notion of democracy as "a break with the axiom of domination."[15] Latour is skeptical about the possibility of radical ruptures in the first place: he cautions that liberation from the multiple attachments that sustain us is impossible.[16] But how can we then even imagine ways of (individually or collectively) cutting ties with the existing structures of oppression? My reading of Kaurismäki's "fairy tales" answers this question in a dialogue with theoretical imaginations of radical events in twenty-first-century philosophy. With reference to Brian Massumi's politics of affect and Alain Badiou's model of revolution, I show how the films stage a radical affective "cut" of "decision."[17] As I will detail, Kaurismäki's reclamations of collective affect do entail (if you will, Latourian) complications to Massumi's and Badiou's (in some respects fabulous) narratives of revolution. Nonetheless, genre becomes a way of imagining otherwise here. Defying the laws of realism, the refugee trilogy films envision that, as Bertolt Brecht hoped, "cooperativeness" or solidarity can be substituted for "pity."[18] In doing so, they counter Gilles Deleuze's verdict that "*the people*" as an agent of collective change "*are missing*" in political cinema after Hitler and Stalin.[19]

EPIC DISTANCE: THE AESTHETICS OF RUPTURED COLLECTIVITY IN *THE CUT*

Akın relates that he and his cinematographer, Rainer Klausmann, explicitly conceptualized the film's visual dimension "with the word 'distance,'" in a spirit of "classical storytelling."[20] For *The Edge of Heaven*, for which he also used the latter term, I suggested unpacking it by emphasizing the act of telling, or the film's techniques of foregrounding narration, in an art cinema lineage. To a degree, this still works for *The Cut* despite its turn to genre—as indicated, my readings in this chapter emphasize productive imbrications of popular and "high-brow" traditions and forms. But it is not the full story. To begin, *The Cut*'s opening titles evoke a classical fairy-tale framework: "Es war einmal" (Once upon a time).[21] There are different kinds of aesthetic distance in play in this verbal gesture: a technique of foregrounding and potential self-reflexivity meets the distance that enables traditional forms of narrative—namely, the temporal, spatial, and/or epistemological separation that facilitates contextualization, narrative connection, and analysis. To the dismay of (antinarrative) 1970s Brechtians, this latter kind of distance is a feature that Brecht's epic mode shares with "classical," normatively covert Hollywood narration. Akın's "classical" storytelling in *The Cut*, I propose, can correspondingly be characterized as "epic" in a twofold sense: on the one hand, the film does highlight cinematic mediation in line with Brecht's concept of epic theater, albeit not with any goal of distanciation; on the other hand, it develops narrative practices associated with the spectacular, high-budget genre of the film epos, although in a thoroughly deheroizing way. Perhaps we can begin to recover the common ground between these seemingly diverging notions of the epic by recalling their common origin in ancient Greek poetics: Brecht explicitly references Aristotle.[22]

The interplay of classical storytelling and reflexivity vectors is intensified by the second part of the fairy-tale opening: "Es war keinmal" (never). Although this double gesture constitutes a traditional Armenian as well as Turkish fairytale opening formula, transnational audiences unfamiliar with the convention may read the "never" as a gesture of derealization, further underlining the fictional status of the story about to unfold.[23] Simultaneously, the second clause undoes the potentially reassuring effect of the fairytale framing insofar as it facilitates a transition into the film's narrative account of historical disappearance. The titles continue: "After centuries of domination, the Ottoman Empire was in decline"; when the desperate Ottoman rulers allied themselves with the Germans in World War I, "minorities in the Empire were declared to be enemies overnight." While critical habit posits a tension between the interpretative vectors of self-reflexivity and historical representation, Akın's poetics intertwines them: he is interested in the process of storytelling as a fictional mediation of actual events and historical traumas. Unlike in much avant-garde criticism, reflexivity is intended not to displace other layers of meaning but to mediate their unfolding. This applies also to Akın's explicit embrace of cinematic intertextuality. In detailing his debt to directors and films ranging from John Ford's *The Searchers* (1956) and Elia Kazan's *America America* (1963) to Sergio Leone, Martin Scorcese (who is highlighted in the credits), Terrence Malick's *Days of Heaven* (1978), and Yilmaz Güney's banned *Yol* (Turkey 1982), Akın suggests that *The Cut* is "a film about a passion for cinema" as much as about "genocide."[24] And, of course, the title of the film itself alludes to the medium of cinema along with the event it designates on the plot level: the cut to the throat that renders the protagonist mute while saving his life in the genocide, as the Turkish prisoner tasked with killing him during a mass execution hesitates. But Akın forcefully vetoes any deconstructive reading of such foregrounded mediation: "Under no circumstances was the film to be playful or overly aesthetic."[25] Like *The Edge of Heaven*, *The Cut* unfolds documentary layers in how it incorporates meticulously researched historical details—for example, in configuring the protagonist's travel route via Cuba and alluding to the (at the time rarely discussed) German role in the Armenian genocide.[26] Also like *The Edge of Heaven*, but with higher ethical stakes due to its topic, *The Cut* thus foregrounds the process of telling as an integral, productive dimension of layered worldmaking.

This layered worldmaking function of reflexivity can be detailed for the central sequence in which the protagonist, Nazaret, attends a showing of Charlie Chaplin's *The Kid* (1921) in a refugee camp after the war. At this occasion, Nazaret encounters his former apprentice, who tells him that Nazaret's two daughters may have survived the death march. In this sense, the origin of the film's epic quest to find them, which structures the plot from here on, is explicitly located in the cinema.

But, simultaneously, much more is happening in this sequence, which weaves Chaplin's story of the tramp's love for his adopted child into *The Cut*'s drama of birth family separation. Most importantly for my argument, Akın deploys the early cinema classic known for its innovative "blend of comedy and pathos" for a multifaceted exploration of how cinema generates affect in relation to collectivity.[27] The sequence begins with character comments that allude to early twentieth-century debates about the powers of the new medium: a shocked woman rushing out of the projection room calls cinema "the work of the devil," while Nazaret's buddy would rather visit the whorehouse than see the film. The sexual analogy implied here accompanied cultural criticism of the cinema from the early days to psychoanalytic film theory of the 1970s: Laura Mulvey's key Freudian concept of "visual pleasure" was associated with the medium as early as Walter Serner's 1913 essay titled "Kino und Schaulust" (Cinema and visual pleasure).[28] But cinema's sexual powers are not the only potentially devilish force that worried the medium's early critics. In Serner's diagnosis, the cinematic "surplus of intensity" also satisfies the "terrible lust" that "surrounded the public executions and witches' pyre of the Middle Ages."[29] Others explicitly connected the new medium to early twentieth-century "crowd psychology," with its emphasis on unconscious motivations, "*contagious*" feelings, and a degree of "*suggestibility*, which individuals evince only in a state of hypnosis."[30] Such worries about the collective experience facilitated by the cinema would later resonate in André Bazin's concerns about the medium's capacity to facilitate identification with both the hero on screen and other audience members, which could turn "the audience into a 'mass' and . . . render emotion uniform."[31]

The Cut's assembly of the experience facilitated by Chaplin's film takes up these questions but ultimately develops them in a different direction: it highlights that the experience of collective affect facilitated by cinema is not actually a supernatural affair—or, for that matter, a "natural" one in the sense of a "given." First, Nazaret has to respond to his mundane, unfriendly interpellation into the audience collective.[32] As he enters the projection room and stands in wonder at the center of the crowd captured by the camera (figure 3.1), he is scolded: "Hey, asshole, sit down." Having listened to that call, Nazaret does affectively become part of the situational collective for a while: he joins in the shared laughter and joy

FIGURE 3.1 *The Cut* (dir. Fatih Akın, 2014).

facilitated by Chaplin's comic performance. Akın's choice of clips emphasizes the triumph of wit over brute violence by lingering on how Chaplin's character outsmarts his muscular antagonist. The intercut audience shots first show Nazaret's happy face in the midst of the crowd and then more fully explore the collective of joyful laughter in panning through the room. However, this experience of collective affect turns out to be unstable. As the diegetic on-screen scenario unfolds further, it seems that the action triggers Nazaret's memories of losing his own family in the genocide in a way that separates him from the experiences of the other refugees around him. When the authorities take the adopted boy from Chaplin's character, Nazaret can no longer laugh with the others, and he tears up when the boy, crying for his father, stands alone on the wagon driving him away. Even Chaplin's acrobatic rooftop rescue operation and his emotional reunification with the boy, which marks the end of the film in Akın's clip montage, do not bring relief. Nazaret's renewed separation from the happy crowd around him is first traced in an individualizing close-up, a device that *The Cut* uses sparingly—in particular in relation to twenty-first-century postcontinuity standards.[33] While we focus on his face, the enthusiastic clapping of the others around him recedes into a background contrast. From a distance again, the camera then captures Nazaret's spatial desertion on the floor of the projection room, where he stays put as the others exit around him.

This scenario of cinematic self-reflexivity can be described as a mise-en-abyme of the overall film insofar as *The Cut*'s larger explorations trace precisely the situational and highly unstable ontology of collective affect dramatized here. As indicated, *The Cut*'s focus is on how the experience of collective violence cuts through, and effectively undoes, collective identification. In the beginning of the film, such identification is still in place for Nazaret. In the introductory sequence, he attends confession in his orthodox church. The performance of Christian faith establishes his belonging to the Armenian community in the majority-Muslim environment of the Ottoman Empire. To be sure, the sin Nazaret confesses is his class envy: "I am angry at people richer than me." Rather than presenting us with any fiction of harmonious original community, the film thus marks the fraught (and ideological) dimension of religious collectivity from its outset, even in showing the protagonist's willingness to belong. The physical and figurative cut of genocide then radically undoes that willingness—or ability. In rendering Nazaret mute, the throat cut separates him from the realm of (presumably unmediated) oral communication that otherwise facilitates everyday conviviality in the film, not only among Armenians but also between the Ottoman Empire's ethnic groups.[34] When Nazaret now tries to communicate through writing, class interferes once more: the fellow worker in the soap factory where the protagonist found temporary refuge cannot read. Along with Nazaret's physical ability to speak, however, the cut of genocide undoes his identification with the symbolic order secured by heavenly authority, which constituted his life world at the outset of the film. Most strikingly, this erasure of collective identification is dramatized in a brief scene following Nazaret's encounter with a death camp during his escape through the desert (see the following section on this sequence).[35] Mostly in long and extreme long shots, we see him throwing stones at the sky; a close-up then highlights how he vehemently tries to erase the cross tattooed on his arm, the marker of cultural belonging turned into stigma.

The mise-en-scène of this decisive moment in the desert is indicative of *The Cut*'s overall cinematography of the genocidal "cut" into collective identification. In terms of historical contextualization, the film deploys iconographic detail to facilitate Holocaust associations: the cross tattoo will make most of us think of Nazi concentration camp

numbers and so will the images of Baghdad Railway trains in the immediate vicinity of the death camp.[36] The weight of these associations, however, bolsters *The Cut*'s more unusual imaginative contribution: the way
in which its cinematography dramatizes the experience of collectivity vs.
its absence. In the first part of the film, widescreen cinematography is
generally deployed for the kind of "ensemble staging" for which its early
practitioners found it most suited.[37] For example, a series of alternating extreme long, long, and medium long shots situates Nazaret in the
collective of forced laborers in the desert. The series shows their march
there, a labor site where the workers are brought into view through a
slow camera pan from an initial view of empty desert, an incident in
which a coworker gets punished by an officer, a group prayer and meal
in a tent in the evening, and an encounter with another collective of
women, children, and old men walking by on a subsequent workday. A
more individualizing two-shot captures how Nazaret helps a young girl
who stumbles, after which his labor collective watches a rape (of her?)
unfolding at a distance, with extreme long and long shots alternating
once more. The collective experience thus traced comes to an end with
the cut through Nazaret's throat.[38] In the second half of the film, the camera traces Nazaret's solitary flight through various desert and desert-like
landscapes. But this shift from the collective to the individual does not
come with the degree of increased spatial closeness that classical and
postclassical staging practices have trained us to expect.[39] The director
and his cinematographer continue to use close framings sparingly and
instead radicalize CinemaScope's potential for "*spacious* horizontality"
and (in its technically more advanced versions) depth.[40] Tracking the
protagonist's minuscule figure in different desert landscapes, the film's
aesthetic of epic distance now traces the foreclosure of collectivity.

Arguably, the most direct intertextual inspiration for this cinematography is two scenes from Kazan's "epic," yet new wave–inflected
Hollywood drama *America America*.[41] Kazan's film deploys space in relation to collectivity in a very similar way. Early on in *America America*,
an extreme long shot shows a minuscule figure stumbling through the
desert. It is that of Hohannes, the Armenian beggar who will become
friends with the Greek protagonist, Stavros, and eventually sacrifice
himself for Stavros. Hohannes's utter lostness in the world also fore-
shadows the temporary fate of Stavros, whom we see in an analogous,

extreme long desert shot after he kills the Turk who had promised him brotherhood on his journey through Anatolia, only to rob him of his family's wealth. With this act of violence, Stavros loses not only his civic standing but also his collective identity in Kazan's film insofar as *America America* ambiguously holds onto the ethnic stereotypes—of Greek meekness vs. Turkish cunning and brutality—governing its world of pregenocidal oppression and violence.[42] In Hannah Arendt's terms (with their focus on human relations), we might say that the extreme long shot of the protagonist in the desert dramatizes the "worldlessness of isolation" resulting from Stavros's fall out of collective belonging.[43] In *America America*, however, this shot remains a visual exception: Kazan's drama relies more on close and medium shots, and proportionally more of the film is set in city, indoor, and ship spaces. In contrast, Akın develops the extreme long shot of the individual in the desert into a prominent feature of *The Cut*'s cinematography (figure 3.2).

As indicated, *The Cut*'s use of vast desert and desert-like landscapes also significantly draws on the Western. Akın's acknowledged references to Ford's *The Searchers* and Leone's work cannot be described as primarily deconstructive: classical Western cinematography itself produced effects of "de-emphasizing humanity" in foregrounding the liberating but also "isolating immensity of the western landscape."[44] But *The*

FIGURE 3.2 *The Cut* (dir. Fatih Akın, 2014).

Cut's cinematography does perform an intervention into the ideologies associated with the Western by radicalizing the genre's deployments of space within the film's contexts of genocide and migration. It presents the "human's 'being in the world'"—here in the sense of our constitutive embedding in an environment—in terms that undercut any norm of freedom or heroism.[45] Nazaret is obviously not *The Searchers*' "invulnerable" hero in search of "autonomy," and he is not part of a "whole of organic representation," where the "milieu" (as Deleuze summarizes the narrative formula of the Western), encompassed "by the sky, . . . in turn encompasses the collectivity."[46] In *The Cut*, the "milieu" is emptied into a vast desertscape that is significantly less structured than Ford's western American landscapes and lacks both the promise and the purity associated with nature in classical Westerns.[47] The dramatic scene in which Nazaret finds corpses in a well that he approaches in the desperate hope for water underlines the simultaneous dependence on and contamination of this landscape by civilization. Indirectly, this infiltration was established early on: the film's very first landscape shot is the first extreme long view of the marching forced laborers discussed earlier.

FOLLOWING THE DESERT(IFI)ED INDIVIDUAL: INTENSITY AT A DISTANCE

As he wanders through this environment, the deheroized, minuscule individual is quite literally both *deserted* and *desertified*. The latter notion has been prominent in the Heideggerian tradition. I use it syncretically for how the film stages the protagonist's creaturely "embeddedness in a larger field of life" and exposure within an environment radically "unworlded" by genocide.[48] The film presents us with a human-desert assemblage devoid of any of the promises of ontological fullness, creativity, and collective worlding that contemporary posthumanisms have associated with the move beyond presumed human autonomy.[49] In particularly dramatic ways, this assemblage of human and desert is evoked by the film's presentation of the death camp. A title identifies the camp as the historical site of Ras al-Ayn along the Baghdad Railway line, a camp where an estimated 300,000 Armenians, mostly women and children, were killed—in part through massacres, in part by being left to die in the desert.[50] *The Cut*'s presentation of the camp emphasizes the

FIGURE 3.3 *The Cut* (dir. Fatih Akın, 2014).

latter aspect. The sequence begins in extreme long shot. The camera slowly pans from the city to a barely distinguishable configuration of tents and people in the sand as a group of inmates—captured as tiny figures—obeys an officer's order to get back to the camp. An extended long shot then presents the camp collective in more detail: a haunting monochrome assemblage of emaciated bodies, linens, dirt, and sand (figure 3.3).[51] As Nazaret walks through the assembled bodies, he is increasingly harassed by desperate requests for food, water, and help with burying the dead. A more pronounced camera pan foregrounds a few of these dead or dying bodies, among whom Nazaret finds his sister-in-law.

From here on, the sequence intertwines a collectivizing of individual suffering with an individualizing of collective death. While Nazaret sits with his sister-in-law, holding her, medium and long shots alternate with close-ups and very long, contextualizing shots of the camp. Lighting and camera work alternatingly melt Nazaret into and momentarily set his comparatively strong physique apart from the surrounding desert-human assemblage. In terms of theoretical resonances, the sequence's emphasis on the threshold between human and nonhuman and the policies of "letting die" evokes Agamben's discussion of the camp as "the hidden matrix and *nomos* of" Europe's biopolitical modernity.[52] "Stripped of every political status," the camp's inhabitants are "wholly reduced to bare life."[53] Agamben reminds us that this bare life is not "an extrapolitical, natural fact"; the human as produced by the modern radicalization of biopolitics is "situated at the point" where "nature and politics" become indistinct.[54] While *The Cut* underwrites this emphasis, the sequence also develops a counterpoint to Agamben by holding onto the individual as a node of nonsovereign agency. Agamben's (re)use of the racialized notion of the "Muslim" (*Muselmann*) as the most extreme figure of bare life is fraught—and rather obviously so with respect to the film at hand. But even apart from terminologies, the film diverges from Agamben's account insofar as Nazaret's sister-in-law does not appear to be robbed of "all consciousness," "memory," and "grief": she recognizes him, laments the death of other family members, and exercises agency in asking Nazaret repeatedly to put an end to her suffering.[55] To be sure, the limit of this agency is highlighted when the camera captures her resistance to dying: after much hesitation, Nazaret complies with her plea. As suicide assistance threatens to tilt into murder, the scene's ghastly staging nonetheless emphasizes the nonsovereignly human over the posthuman or antihumanist.

With two extended medium shots interrupted by a close-up on Nazaret's face, the choking scene is framed more closely than the overall sequence (and film). Its audience address complexly imbricates tenderness and violence. In terms of genre, we might describe it as evidence of how *The Cut* intertwines the affective economies of two different melodramatic traditions: the "sensational melodrama . . . of spectacular diegetic realism" meets the family melodrama associated with femininity and a personalizing of social conflict.[56] Even with its relative intimacy, however, the choking scene still operates on *The Cut*'s overall aesthetic spectrum of affecting audiences at a distance. The close-up on Nazaret's face during the moment of his sister-in-law's death encourages affective connection with him but also affords her symbolic privacy, and their ongoing visual embedding in the camp's undone world balances affective intensity with reminders of the extreme diegetic situation that the average audience member cannot possibly pretend to share experientially. In discouraging a facile empathy that would come at the expense of respect for the genocide victims and their descendants, *The Cut*'s aesthetics of nondistanciating distance operates as an ethical tool. We are invited not to claim that we fully understand (emotionally or even cognitively) but to let ourselves be affected toward a process of mourning, with respect for creaturely humanity at its limits.[57]

In Akın's own words, the goal of the film's widescreen concept was to respect the "dignity" of the victims and their families in the depiction of "violence."[58] Beyond the camp sequence, *The Cut*'s aesthetics of intensity-at-a-distance carefully refrains from any voyeuristic exploitation of violence. Even most of the execution sequence resulting in Nazaret's cut throat, which contains the film's only brief moment of bloody gore, is shot from far away. In this sense, *The Cut* presents a nonsensational variation on the spectacular melodrama, in contrast to the two most commercially successful mid-decade returns to the Western: Iñárritu's authenticity-hungry *The Revenant* (2015) and Quentin Tarantino's belatedly postmodern splatter flick *The Hateful Eight* (2015). Where these films emphasize their (anti)heroes' cannibalistic reunion with nature and theatricalized bloodshed, respectively, *The Cut* personalizes the genocide victims to facilitate mourning. Except for the Turkish deserter turned ally, the murderers remain anonymous: genocidal violence is committed by nameless state officials whose subsequent fate remains unknown and is later echoed by fleetingly introduced Klan members in the United States. The film's restraint vis-à-vis images of savagery does not negate the brutalizing effects of genocide. One of the film's momentary returns to an iconography of collectivity in its second half presents a crowd eager for revenge: at the end of the war, Armenians throw stones at Turkish soldiers and refugees in a narrow city street. Nazaret ends up resisting his interpellation into this street collective: about to throw the stone given to him by his friend, he sees a child get hit in the face and interrupts his gesture. The sequence is crucial for how it reconfigures the perpetrator-victim divide through role reversal. *The Cut*'s relative emotional simplicity—or polarized distribution of audience alignment—thus does not facilitate the full-fledged affective-moral polarization ascribed to classical melodrama. Rather than validating the "bloodlust" aroused by a despicable "villain," the film displaces the villain target with another creaturely human collective.[59]

Where the collective reassembles as a revenge crowd, the protagonist's refusal, or failure, to sustain affective belonging attains an ethical dimension. Nazaret's repeated flight into the desert and lone travel through a range of vast landscapes contour the radically exposed,

minuscule individual as a bare counterpoint to slaughter, an alternative to both collective violence and any more "classical" resurrection of
heroic Western subjectivity. In the words of a reviewer, the individual,
or separate (*einzelner*), human is shown simultaneously as "the sacred
and the abject."[60] In making the audience follow this protagonist over
the extended duration of the film's second half, often at a significant to
an extreme spatial distance, *The Cut* probes how we can let ourselves
be affected by such a liminal figure of radical human exposure. Despite
brief moments of subjective realism (we share Nazaret's vision of his wife
while he almost dies in the desert), the film's phenomenological dimension overall unfolds less by approximating first-person character per-
spective(s) than by using the protagonist's movement through space to
guide our attention and affectively orient us *toward* him.[61] The intensity
facilitated by these walking sequences unfolds at an angle from standard models of audience involvement: it is not straightforwardly about
empathy—or feeling with—or about sympathy—or feeling (pity) for—
from the safe distance projected in cognitive accounts. Rather, we are
challenged to endure a coexperience of radical isolation precisely by
remaining far from the human focal point of our attention in the projected
immensity of the desert. In immersing us in these extreme landscapes,
the film's spectacular vistas invite an intense affective response exceeding
character relation, if short of melting into an altogether transindividual
sphere. In part by (appropriately or inappropriately) associating their own
affective experiences of isolation, the audience members virtually become
part of a network of radically exposed creatures.

In conjunction with the widescreen cinematography, the soundtrack
operates as the second major contributor to this intensity in the desert
sequences. Composed by Alexander Hacke, who is known to German
audiences as a member of the industrial band *Einstürzende Neubauten*,
the music is *The Cut*'s one compositional feature that actually triggered critical enthusiasm precisely for its "bold" incongruity, as Hacke
"audibly bows to Ennio Morricone while incorporating an Armenian
folk song."[62] Mixing "distorted electric guitars with tender choruses"
or "pop-dynamics and folkloristic tenderness," the music in part works
to modulate epic narrative distance with high affect by way of tonal
switches from one moment to the next.[63] For example, Nazaret's initial
takeoff into the desert is accompanied by a seemingly harmless, melodic

rendition of the folk-song motif contributing to the telling of a historical tale. Then we briefly hear only the sound of a sandstorm, followed by dissonant electronic music when Nazaret finds the well full of corpses. But the film music also more radically *fuses* distance with high affect in superimposing these diverging moods.[64] When Nazaret throws stones at the sky after the death camp sequence, for example, the soundtrack builds the folk-song leitmotif directly into the electronic tune expressing Nazaret's anguish and anger. Perhaps less impeded by critical prejudice than the film's analogously incongruous visual design, this musical assembly successfully cofacilitates the film's project of affecting audiences at a distance.

With a more monotonous rhythm, the musical superimposition of diverging moods continues into the last part of the film. By now, Nazaret is walking through the bare snowy plains of North Dakota, where he will eventually find one of his daughters. The film's family drama attains a larger thematic significance insofar as Nazaret's focus on his daughters indicates the radical reduction of collective belonging and solidarity in the wake of genocide. Thus, Nazaret fails the girl who asks for his help in a Bedouin tent during his initial desert travels, while his empathy is activated when the North Dakota railroad workers assault a woman who is limping, just like (he has heard) his daughter. Importantly, the film does not melodramatically *resolve* this radical shrinking of collective orientation in the wake of genocide on the level of family. Closure remains suspended not only in that one of Nazaret's daughters dies before he finds the other one but also in that their reunion does not significantly change the film's iconography of desertion. In *The Cut*'s very last shot, the camera slowly pans sideways to trace Nazaret and his remaining daughter walking out of the graveyard and into the bare steppe, farther and farther away from us. As they become a minuscule double figure, the credits start rolling.

This visual permanence of isolation counteracts any temptation to read *The Cut*'s epic quest in terms of an ideology of family. Such a reading would be all too resonant with the neoliberal normativity governing the twenty-first-century world of the film's production and reception: in Wendy Brown's words, "only familialism . . . remains an acceptable social harbor" in our extrafilmic lives because the disintegration of the social has radically dismantled solidarity structures and "umbrellas of protection provided by belonging."[65] *The Cut*'s affective insistence on ruptured collectivity resists this neoliberal ideology in two ways: it does not find closure in family reunification, and it imagines minimal resurgences of collective solidarity in the form of situational everyday conviviality.[66] Thus, on the Dakota plains, Nazaret encounters the hospitality of other Armenian refugees who take him in for the night and share hot soup. At daybreak, to be sure, he leaves again, not interested in establishing any more permanent belonging on ethnic grounds. Earlier we saw Nazaret traveling north and sharing bread with a group of itinerant workers with different ethnic and racial backgrounds. These small gestures of solidarity in a bare world affirm the life-sustaining potential of collectivity negatively dramatized by the iconography of individual desertification. More permanent forms of togetherness, however, remain unattainable in *The Cut*'s postgenocide world. Its overall mode of mourning and its objection to old and new fictions of permanent collectivity contrast sharply with Kaurismäki's refugee trilogy, which activates a different combination of genres to develop an alternative political imagination.

ASSEMBLING COLLECTIVES OF SOLIDARITY: CONTEMPORARY FAIRY TALES (AND A MUSICAL)

> I have always preferred the version of the fairy tale, where Little Red Riding Hood eats the wolf and not the opposite, but in real life I prefer wolves to the pale men of Wall Street.[67]

Upon its premiere at the 2011 Cannes Film Festival and subsequent cinematic run in Europe and the United States, Kaurismäki's Finnish-French-German coproduction *Le Havre* (2011) was greeted warmly by critics as "a modern-day fairy story" that "unites two people as low in the social hierarchy as it gets" and has them "prevail, with a little help from the good folk of Le Havre."[68] "I didn't choose a genre," the director qualifies, only to confirm: "I just started to write and it turned out as an unashamedly optimistic fairy tale."[69] More specifically, *Le Havre* is a tale of solidarity against the neoimperialist regime of contemporary European border control. Along with 99 percent of his neighborhood (excepting one traitor), the aging bohemian-turned-shoe-shiner Marcel

Marx rises to the occasion by saving an immigrant boy who escapes when the police open the container in which he has traveled from Gabon to Le Havre. In a heartwarming community effort, they hide the boy and raise money for his eventual travel to his mother in London. Critics acknowledged a combination of continuity and departure vis-à-vis Kaurismäki's oeuvre to date: "No one else has made the deadpan so life-affirming" as his series of "dry comedies" since the eighties, and yet this is "his most exuberantly optimistic," "sunniest film," "a fable whose tone remains cheery and optimistic throughout."[70] While the director often experimented with alternative happy and unhappy endings in previous films, this one "radically place[s] two happy endings one after the other."[71] Thus, Marcel's wife, Arletty, who was diagnosed with a purportedly lethal illness at the outset of the film, also rises from the almost-dead in the end, even while Marcel has somewhat neglected her in his quest to save the boy. If the plotline seems set up for the very purpose of presenting difficult choices between private love and political empathy, the film ultimately rejects such a choice in going "full throttle with the fairy-tale aspect. Not even medical science means anything."[72]

In disempowering all forces of negativity, the fairy-tale format radicalizes the director's long-standing aesthetic minimalism, or penchant for "simplicity," as achieved by "progressively" reducing "an initial idea or narrative . . . until it is sufficiently bare enough to be true."[73] In even starker contrast with the complex forms at the center of this study than Akın's epic Western, the fairy tale represents a—if not *the*—paradigmatically simple narrative genre. In the age of structuralism, scholars such as Vladimir Propp used it to map archetypical components of narrative in general.[74] In some respects, Kaurismäki's film in fact lends itself to a Proppian plot analysis demonstrating the straightforward ideological or moralizing functions of storytelling: we can identify villains, helpers, donors, a hero, and two variations on a princess figure as they engage in acts of absentation, interdiction, or villainy and navigate a situation of lack and prohibition through counteraction, donorship, victory, return, and reward.[75] More interestingly, *Le Havre* in part also resonates with twenty-first-century contributions to neuroscientific narratology that have revitalized structuralist interests in systematizing narrative forms and functions by using simple generic formulas. In *Affective Narratology*, Patrick Hogan adapts structuralist narratology's three-step plot model for his project of showing that human beings' "passion for plot" is a function of our "emotion systems": a plot attains its emotional significance in guiding us on the journey from "an initial condition" of *"fragile"* to a more "permanent" form of "normalcy."[76] In some respects, *Le Havre* fits this model perfectly. Initially situated at the margins of his neighborhood, the film's penniless bohemian hero is shunned by the local grocer and (more gently) admonished by the baker for stealing a baguette, which he does with the intention of pleasing his frugal wife with extra earnings from the day's shoe-shining endeavors. At the end, Marcel's full-fledged neighborhood integration and the renewal of his personal life in health and happiness certainly suggest more stability.

The story of the boy, Idrissa, however, does not fit this model as smoothly: Idrissa is sent off onto the sea rather than reaching an (old or new) home, which Hogan closely associates with normalcy; the last shot of the boy shows him looking out at the water. Although this emphasis on spatial nonclosure is modulated by the fact that Idrissa is on his way to his mother, it indicates that Kaurismäki's enthusiastic imagination of how things could be different remains in tension with Hogan's orientation to stability and normalcy.[77] In search of theoretical resonance, I therefore turn to a different group of twenty-first-century accounts— or, as I provocatively suggest, theoretical *fairy tales*: the modeling of revolutionary events in Massumi's politics of collective affect and Badiou's Marxist philosophy. To avoid misunderstandings, my fairy-tale designation for these theoretical narratives has a playful touch. While asking how their imagination of radical political change is too seductively easy, it is not to brush aside that Massumi's and Badiou's (part analogous, part diverging) conceptualizations also provide theoretical resistance to genre. Their antinarrative inflections fit Lauren Berlant's diagnosis about the "waning of genre" in contemporary culture—particularly of "older realist genres" that promote fantasies and hopeful expectations not matched by current sociopolitical realities.[78] More precisely then, I draw on Massumi and Badiou toward a twofold goal in this chapter. To the degree that their theoretical notions of revolutionary events complicate "conventional genres of event" such as Hogan's, they directly and indirectly guide me in detailing how Kaurismäki's films, just like Akın's *The Cut*, open up generic forms in mixing them with other genres as well as art cinema traditions.[79] At the same time, Berlant underlines that Badiou's (and to a lesser degree Massumi's) events do constitute more classical narrative forms than, for example, her open-ended "situation" genre.[80] Along these lines, I explore the resonances between Badiou's and Massumi's theoretical fairy tales and Kaurismäki's films to detail how the refugee trilogy, again just like *The Cut*, reconstructs genre rather than merely deconstructing it.

Massumi describes "the *event* of decision" as a "cut" into complexity, an "orderer out of quasi-chaotic intensity."[81] In contrast to neuroscientific emphases on the purposeful action of individuals, Massumi's event unfolds as "a doing done through me."[82] Short of altogether erasing the irreducible complexity that characterizes this trans- and infrasubjective process without an "autonomous agent," the event unfolds its political potential in structuring chaos: it shapes practices whose " 'subject' " is "collective" insofar as "a number of bodies" are "indexed to the same cut, . . . attuned—differentially—to the same interruptive commotion."[83] In Massumi's ontological field of life, such a potentially revolutionary event comes about not by deliberating rationally but by mobilizing the "creative" worlding powers of "intuition" and "fabulation."[84] The event operates in the "unquantifiable currency" of "intensity," or in Spinoza's terms, "joy," through the existential force of "the immediate communication of affections between individuals" that Massumi describes as "sympathy" (with reference to David Hume and diverging from widespread cognitive usages of the term).[85] Massumi's political wager, if you will, is that the ontologically powered forces of good (affect) will prevail. His theory of the collective event thus restages the promise of Michael Hardt and Antonio Negri's "multitude."[86] In both of these contemporary Deleuzian philosophies, the crowd, which early twentieth-century theory dominantly assumed to be dangerous, has turned into a force of liberation. The "feral potential" of feeling with others, Massumi specifies, is at least potentially unleashed in contemporary society because neoliberalism's withdrawal "from the normative-disciplinary regime of power" undoes sympathy's dominant hierarchical organization through "established patterns of belonging" such as "family, community, nation."[87]

Badiou's conceptualization of the event diverges from Massumi's in key respects: eschewing the posthumanist celebration of "animal affect" (and sympathy), Badiou holds onto centrality of thought and—as we will see—a more heroic notion of the (hu)man instantiated by the event.[88] Nevertheless, the poststructuralist inflections of his account also make for significant resonance. Like Massumi's, Badiou's subject of the event is not a sovereign individual but a collective "subject of a revolutionary politics."[89] His description of the process introduces a quasi-Althusserian figure of reverse interpellation: the (pre-evental) "human animal" is "called upon to enable passing of a truth" and "enters into the composition of a subject" by "exposing himself 'entirely' to a post-evental fidelity."[90] Like Massumi, Badiou imagines our "seizure" by the event to be both immediate and affective insofar as it manifests itself "by unequalled intensities of existence," or "'affects of truth.'"[91] To even more dramatic narrative effect than Massumi's cut of decision, Badiou's revolutionary event induces "a real break" in the "specific order" in which it "took place": it creates radical change by cutting through socio-symbolic structures, instituting a truth process "heterogeneous to the instituted knowledges of the situation."[92]

The potential radical power in such gestures of aligning a collective subject from the Latourian "wasp's nest" of complex environments and social controversies is indicated by declarations such as "No human being is illegal" and "We are the 99 percent."[93] Upon its release, *Le Havre* was described as a cinematic equivalent to the Occupy movement, then in full swing, and an encouragement to the protesters in that "collective action in the movie, however implausible in its method of organization, is followed by nothing less than a miracle."[94] Candidly named Marcel Marx, Kaurismäki's protagonist subscribes to a version of left-wing anti-capitalism that recalls the romanticism of Zuccotti Park: "Money moves in the shadows." The cinematic solidarity event unfolded in the film resonates with Massumi's and Badiou's revolutionary events in how it cuts through hegemonic narratives, as pointedly introduced by a newspaper headline Marcel notices before first seeing Idrissa, which casts the runaway boy as armed and with connections to Al-Qaeda. Displacing discourse with action, *Le Havre*'s plot arguably supports the claims to immediacy made by both Massumi and Badiou insofar as Marcel and his neighborhood respond spontaneously and without any lengthy deliberations to the "*encounter*" with Idrissa, apparently "*directly* seized" by it.[95] Marcel first meets him at the pier, where the boy, standing below him waist-deep in water, addresses him with a request for orientation: Is this London? Just like the grocer and the bar owner later, Marcel responds with the simple gesture of offering food, perhaps (in Massumi's words) "affectively touched by the pleasure and pain of others" at "a level of immediate experience."[96]

Later Marcel explains that he chose the shoe-shining profession because it is closest to "the people." The film's introduction of this notion resonates with Badiou more than with Massumi, whose ontology of becoming in common does not sit well with such classical political terminology.[97] Badiou, in contrast, has no problem with the concept as long as it is not "accompanied by . . . an adjective of identity or nationality" or used to confer "the fiction of legitimacy" on existing states but instead materializes "in the dynamic form of a vast political movement."[98] Such a dynamic people would form around the "nonexistent mass" precisely of those excluded from the "official people"—today, in particular, the "newly arrived workers" described as " 'immigrants.' "[99] Le Havre unfolds its event of political solidarity by assembling such a collective subject of political action. In Laura Rascaroli's words, the film's "neighborhood community" is "strongly symbolic of a multinational and multicultural people that is yet to come," held "together by solidarity and by their rejection of majoritarian values, while still acknowledging their profound differences."[100] Latent at the outset, this community is more or less miraculously assembled in the generic frame of the fairy tale. As I detail in the following section, this miracle cannot be explained in Badiou's and Massumi's categories alone, but to a degree, it does seem powered by their fairy forces: in connecting "a number of bodies . . . to" the "cut" of the boy's appearance, Le Havre's "boundary-breaking treatment of possibilities" unfolds "intuition as a political art," releasing collective joy in the film's diegetic world as well as in that of the audience.[101]

The second part of the trilogy, *The Other Side of Hope* (*Toivon tuolla puolen*, 2017)—which had its international premiere at the 2017 Berlin International Film Festival, or Berlinale, to significant critical acclaim[102]—repeats the process with variations, some of which, however, are significant. The Syrian refugee Khaled arrives in Finland and is taken in by an odd restaurant crew after being denied asylum; they procure Khaled new papers, and although he had been separated from his sister on the European refugee track, they eventually manage to bring her into the country. Equally miraculous at moments (the police conveniently forego searching the restroom where Khaled hides during a raid),

The Other Side of Hope has been described as a fairy tale as insistently as *Le Havre*.[103] At the same time, reviewers have indicated that this second part of the trilogy also brings "reality" in differently—for example, specifically in a scene in which Khaled tells his life story (see "To Hell with Realism" later in this chapter for detail) and more generally in how the film does not "conceal" anything, "from the power of the police and despotic state authorities to the murderous Nazis."[104] The emerging solidarity collective is led by a businessman, Wikström, whose generosity is more limited and less spontaneous than that of *Le Havre*'s carefree bohemian—or in Badiou's and Massumi's theoretical narratives. The presumed immediacy of revolutionary affect is complicated with interfering negative vectors as well as deliberation when Wikström initially defends his garbage area against Khaled's defiant claim to a living space. As a result, they hit each other on the nose before Wikström grudgingly takes Khaled in as an employee with a small advance (minus "tax").[105] Later one of Wikström's employees needs to be actively convinced of the emerging plan to help. Due to the neo-Nazis, one of whom eventually stabs Khaled's belly, the happy end is also less clear-cut. The last shot of Khaled shows him wounded at the river, clearly hurting, if at peace—his sister made it—and comforted by a stray dog. The second happy ending is treated so reductively that it seems unmotivated except as a deliberate gesture of repeating *Le Havre*'s formula: a brief scene indicates that Wikström, who had left his wife in the beginning of the film, apparently due to her alcoholism, reunites with her; she simply indicates that she quit drinking when he left. Short of the full-fledged joy projected in *Le Havre*, this second installment of the trilogy thus assembles its world in a mixed mood.

In an interview about *The Other Side of Hope*, Kaurismäki discusses his own loss of political hope under the moderate-right coalition governing Finland since 2015 and distances himself from the unabashed optimism of *Le Havre*, but he still insists that "cinema is fiction."[106] The genres of fiction explored in *The Other Side of Hope*, I propose, include the musical along with—and as a mediating node for—the revolutionary fairy tale.[107] Reviewers have mentioned *The Other Side of Hope*'s "interweaving of music and action," including the repeated use of street musicians and bands.[108] The coincidence that these bands keep showing up with "their mixture of Blues, Country and Rock 'n' Roll whenever the man from Aleppo is in difficulties" corresponds to one of the typical ways in which musicals, in Richard Dyer's classical analysis, combine live performance with plot: the "division between narrative as problems and numbers of escape."[109] Just like the fairy tale, the musical has been associated with "'wish fulfillment'" and "utopianism," especially "in the feelings it embodies," as Dyer writes long before the affective turn, and it works through narrative tensions such as those of "scarcity" and "abundance," "fragmentation" (including displacement) and "community."[110] Unlike the fairy tale, however, the musical is hardly suited to exemplify simple narrative form. For Jane Feuer, its reflexive audience address and regular interruption of plot with the "lyricism of numbers" not only contrasts the "verisimilitudinous" with the "'unreal'" but also resonates with Godard's prototypically modernist "method," albeit not "goal."[111] In short, the musical has provided occasion to complicate critical dichotomies between modernism and Hollywood genre, reflexivity and high-affect aesthetics.

My reading deploys the genre label to underline how *The Other Side of Hope*'s intricate worldmaking opens up the fairy tale—without abandoning its promises. As indicated earlier, even *Le Havre*'s more straightforward revolutionary fairy-tale form is complicated through both its saturation with auteurist traditions and its combination with elements of other genres, including film noir, melodrama, and Kaurismäki's signature deployment of comedy.[112] Simultaneously, Kaurismäki's very commitment to simplicity, or reductive minimalism, cannot be associated with genre alone: it adapts elements of European postwar art cinema and American aesthetic modernism, including performance culture.[113] As I detail in the next section, the refugee trilogy's intricate assembly of these diverging, while entangled traditions and techniques undoes the pretensions to affective immediacy entertained in Massumi's and Badiou's theoretical fairy tales without thereby taking down their insistence on affective force.

RESHUFFLING ARCHIVES AND AFFECTS: INTENSITY IN MEDIATION

A fuller account of the aesthetic layers of Kaurismäki's cinematic assembly of solidarity collectives can begin by underlining how his films, just like *The Cut*, facilitate a wealth of associations through overt intertextuality. *Le Havre* showcases the stylistic influence of Robert Bresson's minimalism and alludes to Marcel Carné's poetic realism via character names, plot, and location, but the director's eclectic "engagement with 'the archive'" also encompasses Jean-Pierre Melville, Jacques Tati, Jacques Becker, Vittorio De Sica, Cesare Zavattini, and Yasujiro Ozu.[114] Furthermore, Kaurismäki deftly references his own earlier films—most specifically, *La vie de bohème* (1992), where Marcel Marx made his first entrance, played by the same actor (André Wilms). In the Finnish setting of *The Other Side of Hope*, such playful evocation of the director's own oeuvre at first glance trumps the overt recourse to transnational film histories. In addition to the *Le Havre* connection, there are substantial plot and mise-en-scène citations in particular of *The Man Without a Past* (*Mies vailla menneisyyttä*, 2002), with Sakari Kuosmanen, initially one of the "Leningrad cowboys," playing Wikström.[115] But, of course, such references to the Kaurismäki universe itself activate further associative vectors, including to the Marx Brothers and the genre of gangster films.[116] As usual in Kaurismäki's work, intertextuality extends beyond specific films to the worlds of popular culture, including music.[117] In *Le Havre*, the character of Inspector Monet recalls an entire literary and cinematic tradition: with his signature black hat, trench coat, and inscrutable behavior, he evokes the generic figure of the detective in genre fiction, film noir, and beyond.[118] Kaurismäki activates this figure's status as a morally ambiguous agent navigating the divergent realms of law and justice: the inspector's support is initially questionable but ultimately decisive for getting Idrissa on his way to London.

The indeterminacy of historical location suggested by Inspector Monet's generic appearance points to one of the most striking features that both films share with much of Kaurismäki's oeuvre: the intricate play with historical period and temporality facilitated by the indicated wealth of allusions to 1950s and 1960s cinema, along with Kaurismäki's fondness for mid-twentieth-century props.[119] Despite their "retro aesthetic," *Le Havre* and *The Other Side of Hope* are set not in the 1950s or 1970s but in a present moment in which militarized police units in twenty-first-century uniforms try to keep African immigrants out of France and the Finnish authorities make use of digital fingerprint devices.[120] The visual layering of such present actualities with earlier historical moments has been read in terms of political allegory. One reviewer suggests that *The Other Side of Hope* reminds us of a time when "we were not yet ruled by materialism" by staging a "clash of time periods" instead of a "clash of cultures," with Khaled as a contemporary figure and Wikström as one from the past.[121] In *Le Havre*, Idrissa is the "fully contemporary figure."[122] The film's community of solidarity is housed in the city's only neighborhood not destroyed in World War II. It was about to be sacrificed to twenty-first-century urban planning at the time of shooting, and the film crew actually paid for a demolition delay so that they could reconstruct this neighborhood with its small bakery, grocery, and bar, La Moderne.[123] But not everything lines up toward a straightforward temporal allegory that would deploy the humanist resources of an imagined better past. *Le Havre*'s traitor figure is "straight out of the world of Clouzot's *The Raven*" (or the Vichy era); here the film layers the present with the murderous rather than the utopian ghosts of the past.[124] The films' superimposition of historical moments also cannot be fully distributed along character or group lines: the Finnish police in *The Other Side of Hope* use typewriters along with digital technology (even in the same shot), and in Arletty and Marcel's apartment, with its midcentury furniture and vinyl record player, the "Reality Radio" channel accompanies dinner. Thus, the trilogy's "diverse temporal registers" stage the "conflicting claims of past and present."[125]

All operations of historical reference are further complicated by the pronounced artificiality of mise-en-scène in both films. With their "vividly theatrical lighting"; the "freshly painted" look of the meticulously color-coded sets in "primary colors, dominated by deep reds and blues, closer to a Miró painting than a Jean-Pierre Melville noir"; and, of course, their "wonderful/marvelous" (*wunderbar*) 35-millimeter glow, they present a "distinct Kaurismäki world," "Cinema-Finland," or "cinematic universe."[126] Even in *Le Havre*, however, this emphasis on theatricality does not straightforwardly come at the expense of all realism or documentary claims. As indicated in the introduction, my worldmaking model generally emphasizes fiction's openness to surrounding life worlds. Kaurismäki's aesthetic activates this vector in its own ways. In partial analogy to Akın with his meticulous research, he anchors his fictional worlds with real-world reminders, or (explicitly mediated) reality checks, including both films' documentary TV sequences. The refugee trilogy, however, differs from *The Cut* in its aesthetic flamboyance.

Rather than unobtrusively blending the documentary into the fictional, it arranges them contrastively, just like the primary colors in its painted sets, flashily enmeshing pronounced artificiality with bits of reality, and vice versa. In these folds of theatrical real-world reference, the films' retro objects "become things again" in the sense in which Latour uses this notion: "rich and complicated," they do not assemble straightforward allegories or authentic identities as much as affectively charged controversies in the worldmaking networks of citation, circulation, and reappropriation.[127] Framed and facilitated by the trilogy's explicitly intertextual, theatrical, eclectic mise-en-scènes, its revolutionary events lose some of their miraculous simplicity. If Marcel and his neighborhood seem to be spontaneously seized by sympathy on the diegetic level of Le Havre, there is certainly no such immediate, or even apparently immediate, seizure for the film audience. But how then does revolutionary affect come about to project—in the words of a reviewer, "an overwhelming feel for a better world"?[128]

In flamboyantly foregrounding mediation, Le Havre and The Other Side of Hope invite a closer look at the intricate "alchemy" of affective "fermentation"[129] that aligns on-screen as well as off-screen collectives of solidarity. Let me begin to unpack this affective alchemy from its perhaps most puzzling node, which is key also to the trilogy's comedic form: the "affectless," "radically dispassionate," "deadpan" acting style well known to longer-term Kaurismäki audiences.[130] In Le Havre, the effects of an often stilted and proclamatory spoken delivery are heightened by the decision to have Kati Outinen perform in French, a language that is, in her own words, not her "emotional language."[131] And as the actors "pose in unsmiling thought, for just slightly longer than necessary," the defamiliarizing performance style aligns with a relatively static camera to effect an aesthetics of slowness reminiscent of Fassbinder.[132] To be sure, the freezing of performances and images is far less extreme than in Katzelmacher (see chapter 2), but it has nonetheless evoked comparable responses of irritation in some of my students. Critics have acknowledged both Fassbinder and Godard as part of Kaurismäki's larger intertextual horizon, notably without jumping to conclusions about distanciation.[133] The coolness dominantly associated with Brechtian form is certainly an unlikely candidate for the dominant affect of Kaurismäki's cinema. However, scholars have deployed notions of paradox, irony, and parody to account for his films' "understated yet intense" or "minimalist yet melodramatic" ways.[134] Jaakko Seppälä speaks of Kaurismäki's "ironic minimalism" and of how the camera's "distance—both epistemic and spatio-temporal" makes the audience "paradoxically feel that it is with the characters and not with them at the same time."[135] Kaurismäki's films, he concludes, characteristically create sympathy rather than empathy (here in the cognitive sense); their use of humor invites audiences to look down on the characters "from a superior position."[136] This assessment of the filmmaker's oeuvre contrasts with Rascaroli's reading of Le Havre's "intense, emphatic closeups": reminiscent of a Dreyer film in their often "static and frontal" framings, these shots attract "attention to the human face in an . . . almost sacred manner."[137] But even Rascaroli's reading of Le Havre ambiguously holds onto the "concept of parody" for disentangling the film's humorous, dissonant form.[138]

My reading disentangles these apparent paradoxes in developing a fuller conceptual basis for Rascaroli's emphasis on Le Havre's affirmative vectors, or its bent toward homage rather than critique. Namely, I describe the aesthetics of the refugee trilogy in terms of intensity in theatrical mediation—including via moments of affective reduction. Resonant with the films discussed in chapter 2, Kaurismäki's refugee trilogy creates intensity in part by way of defamiliarization and formal emotional minimalism.[139] His uses of humor, I suggest, are better characterized as reparative play (in Sedgwick's sense) than as distanced parody or "'conspiratorial irony'" between creator and viewer.[140] "Free play" and techniques of "making strange" create "open" worlds from which "nothing is excluded."[141] (Or, more precisely, from which few human weaknesses are excluded; we are not invited to appreciate neo-Nazis, state apparatuses, and ruthless capitalists.) If we want to hold onto the notion of irony, it might be useful to think of it less as oppositional and more along the lines of its conceptualization in early German Romanticism: as a play of multiple perspectives—and small distances—in a process of reflexivity.[142] In this sense, humor characteristically operates as a tonally warm, "smiling conversation" here if conversation can be understood to connote less a "critical reflection" than a multisensory process assembling complex affects.[143] While not entirely devoid of aggression, the complex affective assemblies performed by Kaurismäki's feasts of cinematic mediation activate a range of pleasures—from the cinephilic joy that can accompany the recognition of intertextual references to the sensory delight in colors, objects, and human and nonhuman actors (such as Marcel's dog) foregrounded in close-up.

Sympathy may still come into play as an element of some of these transactions, perhaps particularly in the beginning of *Le Havre*, where the setup of Marcel's precarious social position recalls the outsiders and "losers" of Kaurismäki's earlier films.[144] In a scene framed at a spatial distance during the exposition sequence, Marcel is polishing the shoes of a customer in front of a posh footwear store, and the store's manager intervenes to chase away the socially marginal representative of an alternative economy of care instead of consumerism. Laughs, or at least audience chuckles, are invited by Marcel's witty defense, "But we are colleagues," and the manager's hyperbolic response: violently pushing Marcel and kicking his equipment, he calls him a "terrorist," which connects Marcel to Idrissa. Comically linking the incongruous, neither of these expressions is to be taken literally. The terrorism charge is as absurd (and thus funny) in Marcel's case as in Idrissa's, if nonetheless indicative of hegemonic contemporary real-world structures of exclusion.[145] Understood as figurative play and defamiliarizing cinematic mediation, however, these reductive associations contribute to the making of a world of unexpected connections and smaller differences. Simultaneously, this world is affectively polar insofar as it is a world of antiestablishment opposition: the configuration invites zero sympathy or respect for the manager and unlimited amounts of either, or both, for Marcel. To the onset of half melancholic, half surprisingly upbeat music, he quickly reassembles his gear and restores his spirits in a bar with a drink and some olives, highlighted in close-up for our vicarious enjoyment.

"TO HELL WITH REALISM": IMAGINING DIFFERENTLY IN THE FOLDS OF GENRE AND DOCUMENTARY

If Marcel's initial presentation ambiguously elicits sympathy, Idrissa's does not. The significance of the container scene introducing him attains its contours precisely against the background of hegemonic structures of sympathy in the modern "narrative grammar" of " 'humanitarianism.' "[146] Badiou references this asymmetrical structure of sympathy as a neocolonial legacy, which continues to shape contemporary human rights discourses. The hegemonic scene of perception, he summarizes polemically, is split to always assign "the same roles to the same sides," with "the good-Man, the white-Man" emerging as the active witness and "benefactor" of the passive victim.[147] In terms of character configuration, *Le Havre*'s fairy tale risks reinscribing precisely these asymmetrical roles via the topoi of the immigrant child and his white bohemian helper. The mise-en-scène of Idrissa's arrival and later relationship with Marcel, however, confound them.[148] In the arrival sequence, theatricality is deployed to foreground—or make strange—the relations of spectacle that Badiou locates at the heart of the human rights doctrine. In two medium close-ups momentarily aligning our spatial orientation with that of the immigrants, we see a diegetic press camera in action before and while the container is being opened as the extradiegetic camera frontally frames the interior of the container like a half-lit theater stage (figure 3.4).

But this mise-en-scène does not stop at exposing hegemonic relations of spectacle. Through its nodes of reflexivity, it rather reconfigures the scene of perception. As a series of sustained close-ups and medium close-ups introduces us to the individual people in the container (figure 3.5), they are lit by spotlights in a way "worthy of the first, sublime appearance of the star in a classical film."[149] And while the harbor

FIGURE 3.4 *Le Havre* (dir. Aki Kaurismäki, 2011).

FIGURE 3.5 *Le Havre* (dir. Aki Kaurismäki, 2011).

workers expected "more living dead," these shots show that the people in the container look just fine; they return the intra- and extradiegetic gaze with skeptical and wary but composed and dignified expressions. The script, Kaurismäki explains, called for filth and death, but he "could not go through with that" and decided "to hell with realism."[150] The strong defamiliarization effect created here carries through the further unfolding of the sequence. Encouraged by a silent exchange with an older immigrant in the container, Idrissa takes off to escape the approaching paramedics and police. His hesitant, agonizingly slow movements and the shift in his facial expression from calm determination to distress are suited to create audience anxiety, balanced by an acute awareness of the unlikelihood of the scenario. In my own initial viewing experience, this awareness—and the accompanying trust in fiction's ability to make things right—helped to keep my sense of humor activated. When the inspector, whose figure is also introduced in this sequence as perhaps the most "alien" element in the mostly contemporary mise-en-scène, prevents one of the police officers in his military outfit from shooting the boy on the run, the hesitant chuckles invited by the scenario assemble with relief and happiness—or the joy of cinematic defiance.

Defying the claims of realism, or the regime of death operating at the borders of contemporary Europe, *Le Havre*'s imaginative intervention displaces the neocolonial regime of sympathy with a different assembly of humanist affects. In some respects, the defamiliarized initial presentation of the immigrants resonates with Badiou's own programmatic counterfiguration: whereas the hegemonic grammar of sympathy "equates man with his animal substructure" by showing the "suffering beast" and "emaciated, dying body," Kaurismäki's camera seems to heroicize these people as virtually "immortal."[151] (Idrissa's name is also commonly translated as "immortal.")[152] For Badiou, immortality is associated with the human capacity for thought and liberated by the revolutionary event: the latter convokes (the collective subject of) "Man" as someone who "distinguishes himself within the varied and rapacious flux of life."[153] Badiou thus reaffirms a heroic notion of political humanism, resonant with the dominant gendered models of European modernity. In this respect, his tale starkly contrasts with Massumi's politics of affect as well as the emphasis on human vulnerability in other critiques of neocolonial asymmetries of perception.[154] The container sequence audaciously brackets vulnerability, and its artistic presentation resonates as a small Badiouvian event in its own right. All too heroic readings, however, are counteracted by the trilogy's overall emphasis on precisely the creaturely needs and pleasures (including food and drink) sidelined in the arrival sequence. In contrast to Badiou, the trilogy emphatically does not sacrifice creaturely happiness to the revolution.[155] Instead, its poetics of reduction keeps foregrounding the pleasures of simple sustenance: close-ups highlight the colorful vegetable stew prepared in the immigrant camp, Marcel's sandwich gift to the boy, and the one-egg omelet with a small glass of wine he can afford outside his neighborhood. Finally, *The Other Side of Hope* supplements a return to vulnerability, with its concluding focus on the injury Khaled suffers at the hand of the neo-Nazis.

If it is not ultimately heroic, might we be invited to read immortality in religious terms here? To Rascaroli, the initial presentation of the immigrants' miraculously composed looks is "reminiscent of religious *tableaux vivants*."[156] Importantly, the accompanying invitation "to consider" their "face[s]" does not project radical alterity along the lines of Emmanuel Lévinas's ethics.[157] Rather, the shots evoke a combination of individuality and human resemblance, or recognition as the ground for some combination of awe, curiosity, respect, and empathy in the sense of feeling "with" more than "for" the other.[158] Religious undertones are in fact present insofar as the series of "miracle[s]" unfolding from here to *Le Havre*'s double happy ending is configured in part through secularized Christian references, inspired perhaps by De Sica's *Miracle in Milan* (*Miraolo a Milano*, 1951).[159] However, the Christian tradition is deployed playfully—at small humorous distances—as well. Marcel's witty commentary declares the shoe shiners not only to be closest to the people but also to be "the last to respect the Sermon on the Mount." At another occasion, he indirectly personifies Idrissa as the risen Jesus (and himself as Peter) by asking him, "Quo vadis?" When Idrissa does not get the biblical allusion, his irritation solicits a more mundane translation: "Where are you going?" In drawing on the imaginative resources of religion in the cultural and cinematic archive, *Le Havre* secularizes them. Like De Sica's film, which stages a collective uprising of the homeless against the capitalist would-be developers of their shanty town, *Le Havre* underlines that its miracles are brought about by "collective action."[160] But where De Sica's film deploys magic doves and special effects that allow people to fly on broomsticks, *Le Havre* foregoes such devices of explicit supernatural intervention on both the diegetic level and that of cinematic worldmaking.[161]

As I have argued throughout this study, the "might" of the collective cinematic imagination is never actually godlike or sovereign. Kaurismäki's fiction actively foregrounds many of the networked mediators it deploys, including the actors not fully inhabiting their characters, the props loaded with cultural fantasies, and the affectively charged intertextual citations. None of this, however, should make us underestimate the films' quasi-magical power in defiantly reassembling real-world chunks through the antirealist vectors of genre. More precisely, the particular force of Kaurismäki's fiction is in how it simultaneously deploys the unreal against the real and the real against the unreal, or interventionist design to document the force of human dignity and resilience against dominant political realities. In commenting on the container sequence, the director balances his decision against "realism" by underlining that many of the actors are actual undocumented immigrants, and a reviewer echoes him by attesting an "almost documentary force" to the "linger[ing]" shots of the people in the container.[162] A later sequence replays this intertwining of fictional defiance and documentary force, starting from what is, at first glance, a more conventional assembly of fiction with documentary protocol: a report on the demolition of an actual immigrant camp unofficially called "the Jungle" playing on an old-fashioned TV inserts a dose of socio-discursive actuality into the film's world.[163] When the interviewed immigration secretary claims that the official action was not directed against the immigrants themselves, the owner of the bar turns off the TV with a resolute remote click. Her defiant gesture against the reality of official hypocrisy makes room for different actualities configured through fiction's indirect references: with the secretary silenced, Marcel engages his fellow shoe shiner Chang in a conversation about the boy who escaped from the container. Initially, Chang responds that it is difficult for him to comment because, as another undocumented immigrant, he does "not exist," but then he proceeds to tell his story. Thus, official discourse is replaced with the voice of the "subaltern" who may not be able to speak without mediation (as classically outlined by Gayatri Spivak) but who can be figuratively endowed by fiction's defiance with an opportunity to be heard.[164]

As indicated by the reviews quoted earlier, *The Other Side of Hope* further expands this interweaving of pronounced fictionality with documentary form and force. When Khaled's request for asylum is rejected, a contemporary flat-screen TV in the asylum home features a UN report from Syria that dramatizes the outright denial of reality in the official verdict, with its conceit that the security situation in Aleppo was not bad enough to justify a claim to subsidiary protection. To be sure, that official denial of reality is no less filled with reality: as Kaurismäki underlines in an interview, Khaled's deportation communication is a "word by word" quotation from a nonfictional case; in assembling the character's story, he merely changed the city of origin.[165] A visual equivalent of *Le Havre*'s forceful container sequence is presented by a series of lingering shots that show individual men resting on their beds during Khaled's first night at the reception center. Their expressions are more melancholic and resigned than those of the newly arrived immigrants in *Le Havre*—but no less haunting in their documentary intensity. The shots are without narrative purpose in a narrow sense: the men thus introduced will not be further developed as characters. As shots of real people belonging to the film's and our own world, however, they contribute to Kaurismäki's multidimensional assemblage with affective vectors

FIGURE 3.6 *The Other Side of Hope* (dir. Aki Kaurismäki, 2017).

fleshing out Khaled's fictional story and intensifying *The Other Side of Hope*'s transactions with its audience.[166]

This buildup of documentary intensity peaks when Khaled tells his life story during the first interview for his asylum procedure. A (medium) close-up that lasts almost two minutes shows Khaled's face and shoulders against the bare gray wall of the interview room; additional structure is provided only by an out-of-focus file cabinet in the background to the left (figure 3.6). Looking directly at the film audience, Khaled talks about his professional background as a car mechanic, the destruction of his home that killed most of his family, and the subsequent escape with his sister, the only other survivor, from whom he was eventually separated on the eastern European refugee route. He speaks in a calm voice, with minimal facial movements, and is uninterrupted by any diegetic translation (there are subtitles for the film audience). Only after this narration is eventually punctured by a cut to the blonde interviewer (in a dress a shade lighter than the wall behind her) do we see that a translator is also present in the room, who mediates the conversation, traced now in a more conventional shot-countershot format. Gently defamiliarized by the minimalist acting and mise-en-scène, the long take of the monologue artificially brackets the realistic contours of diegetic context for the sake of a heightened immediacy effect, as it invites the film audience to relate affectively to the horrors of Khaled's life.

MUSICAL AFFECT ALCHEMY

Through what miracles of affective alchemy can such a minimalist evocation of actual horror not merely succeed in inciting intense audience affect but also contribute to the overall positive affect ascribed to *The Other Side of Hope* as well as *Le Havre*? The key to this puzzle, I argue, is the film's use of the "affective code" of music along with "color, texture, movement."[167] A cut directly from the interview scenario brings the close-up of a stylish brown steel guitar played by someone in a red shirt and black jacket with white patterns. The following, more distanced take retroactively integrates the shot into the action as an instance of diegetic live music: the musician plays at the shabby Wall Street Bar where Khaled drinks coffee after his interview. His demeanor and expression are still calm but exude concern and sadness. As his gaze acknowledges the musician, the "vital force" of music provides both a counterpoint to and an affective fleshing out of the minimalist acting.[168] Intensified in mediation (including through the close-up of the beautiful instrument), the music supplements—and, in the audience, facilitates—the strong affectivity that is at best evoked by the understated character performance, and it reassembles negative diegetic feelings with aesthetic pleasure or joy. In the terms of musical scholarship, the genre's "intensity" is in its ability to "present complex or unpleasant feelings . . . in a way that makes them seem . . . direct and vivid," an ability contingent precisely on its reflexive form.[169]

"Remelting" heterogeneous affects in the montage of direct audience address and—characteristically retrospective—diegetic embedding, Kaurismäki's recourse to musical form elements facilitates some of the complex affective transactions required for holding onto hope in *The Other Side*'s world, with its more developed documentary facets. To a lesser degree, the underlying dynamic of complex affective assembly is present in *Le Havre* as well: the latter's stronger bent toward the fairy tale can be characterized as a higher degree of narrative integration with regard to its own musical elements. *Le Havre* features only one live music performance, and it has a developed plot motivation. The mission of helping Idrissa requires a benefit concert, which first requires reuniting an estranged couple: the aging rock icon Little Bob will play only with the happiness of private love restored. Side mission completed, the extended concert sequence unleashes the bliss of this happiness via musical and visual performance, prominently foregrounding Little Bob's gorgeous red leather jacket, which matches the color of a band member's guitar. Just as in *The Other Side of Hope*, the use of music combines affective counterpoint and intensification, here by superimposing the minimalist, awkward romantic performance of the film's lead romantic couple with a more flamboyant (and queer-inclusive) image of love.[170] In this sense, the live concert sequence performs the film's unconditional junction of political solidarity and private love.[171]

In less spectacular ways, music facilitates the affective alchemy of the fairy tale—or the miracle of assembling a 99 percent solidarity collective out of established structures of hegemony—in other moments as well. For example, there is the sequence in which Marcel travels to an immigrant camp to find information on Idrissa's grandfather. Upon his arrival at the dreary seaside camp, the white visitor is greeted with suspicious stares: two sustained, almost frozen shots recalling Fassbinder's mapping of social hostilities in *Ali—Fear Eats the Soul* present a theatrical reminder of the real divisions that might stand in the way of a life-world coalition along the lines of the collective imagined in *Le Havre*. But the mood projected through this opening shifts with a cut to a close-up of the simple but colorful stew prepared by one of the immigrants. The shot is accompanied by the onset of upbeat music, which at first seems extradiegetic (and thus functions as an element of foregrounded affective narration), but in the usual Kaurismäki manner, the music is located within the diegesis in the following take of a small, ancient radio next to the can of tomato soup used for the stew. The music proceeds to accompany and perhaps derealize the subsequent dialogue unfolding during the meal itself, or just affectively lighten it with a fairy touch: when Marcel explains why he needs the requested information on Idrissa's grandfather, his interlocutor asks directly, "Why should I believe you?" Whether by way of simple recourse to the clichés of everyday racism or by way of an attempted joke about them, Marcel responds, "Because of my blue eyes." Marcel's eyes are quite visibly brown in the shot at hand. Faced with the absurdity of his response, the immigrant starts to laugh loudly, incredulously. Perhaps it doesn't even matter at whose expense the joke is. Whether the immigrant is—and whether we are potentially—laughing with or at Marcel here, the assembly of the scene facilitates a reflexive reminder of the real socio-affective divisions recast into its fairy-tale resolution. Marcel's interlocutor has in fact no reason to believe him, as suggested also by the unmoved faces of the other men. But perhaps having been unburdened by laughter and music or encouraged by the barely noticeable nod of one of his companions, the immigrant nonetheless proceeds to offer information, which will enable Marcel to find Idrissa's mother.

To sum up, *Le Havre* assembles its unlikely solidarity collective by boldly cutting through the webs of complexification that it does spin, including in its nodes of lighthearted humor. Gaining joy from the force of fiction's defiance against layered contrary circumstances, this assembly does not annul the audience's knowledge of a much more complicated world outside the cinema. As I have detailed, the "overwhelming feel for a better world" that the film projects can be analyzed as a composite from multiple charges and cinematic techniques, but it is a composite more smoothly fused together than in the second part of the trilogy.[172] Less affectively polar, *The Other Side of Hope* develops incongruity by unfolding the breaks in register and mood afforded by its musical form elements. A concluding look at one more sequence from the film allows me to tie this point back to the form of the collective established here. After his request for asylum has been denied, Khaled flees the detention facility on the morning of his planned deportation. From the moment he starts running outside onward, Finnish singer-songwriter Tuomari Nurmio's "Skulaa tai delaa" accompanies the action: Khaled's climb across the fence and his subsequent tram ride. Subtitles relate the defiant lyrics: "I play, Or I die. . . ." While the music presents a smooth extradiegetic background for the situation at hand, Kaurismäki once more changes its status and interrupts the action by abruptly cutting to footage of the live performance of the piece to which we have evidently been listening. The extended concert coverage includes multiple close-ups of electric guitars, a contrabass, and polished shoes along with full ensemble shots and views of the audience, the largest actual crowd shown in the film. This performance insert is reintegrated with the protagonist's escape only with a delay, and precariously, when after a while Khaled appears in the crowd. (We did not see him approach or get any information motivating his attendance.) The narrative discontinuity thus flaunted translates into affective disruption when three neo-Nazis whose leather jackets identify them as members of the "Liberation Army Finland" show up in the crowd behind Khaled. With the soundtrack continuing in the background, they follow him outside, assault him, and threaten to set him on fire but are interrupted just in time by another group of men who seem to have been drinking around the corner. With unkempt hair and one of them on crutches, they successfully fight back with broken bottles.

The crowd, perhaps still tainted by its association with violence in the wake of fascism, thus does not equal the solidarity collective in Kaurismäki's films either. Its infiltration with hate distinguishes *The Other Side of Hope*'s embrace of affective incongruity from *Le Havre*'s straightforward fairy-tale environment—where we notably never get to see a full-fledged crowd. The overwhelming success of the benefit concert is instead suggested by shots of a moving ticket line whose end we cannot see; inside the concert venue, the camera focuses on the performance itself. (Of course, it is entirely possible that Kaurismäki mostly wanted to save on extras, but the staging choice nonetheless has worldmaking effects.) Qualifying my earlier statement, we might conclude that Deleuze's dictum regarding the people missing in modern political cinema does apply even to Kaurismäki's trilogy insofar as we understand it in terms of making physical collectivity directly visible. In contrast, De Sica's *Miracle in Milan* actually did show collective action via crowd movements. In this sense, Kaurismäki's refugee trilogy indirectly reaccentuates Massumi's optimistic politics of transindividual affect. Short of showing a large group of bodies immediately aligned by a shared affective-political orientation, the refugee trilogy assembles its collectives of political action from the collaborative movements of a network of smaller groups—sometimes more loosely assembled in bars, with or without live music—and a range of "misfit" members.[173] In *Le Havre*, this solidarity collective prominently includes immigrants and local rock stars along with old-fashioned neighborhood volunteers and the enigmatic noir detective. In *The Other Side of Hope*, it is composed of Khaled's boozy rescuers (and the nonhuman actors endowing them with force: crutches and bottles), the seemingly unmoved restaurant crew iconographically imported from Kaurismäki's earlier films, the tech-savvy hipster who charges good money for forging papers, and a trafficker who does not charge for bringing Khaled's sister into the country because, he says, he made money on the outbound trip.[174]

Reemphasizing Massumi's event formula, we might say that odd individuals, even where not immediately "shocked in concert," are linked "differentially" to the "cut" of another individual's appearance.[175] In their sometimes grumpy ways and with their diverging sets of professional, (sub)cultural, and other attachments, regular(ly odd) humans do show up for solidarity even in this second installment of the trilogy, with its partially heightened sense of reality. In other words, the imagined diegetic collective is an impure, radically inclusive, egalitarian one, which forcefully cuts through our real-world knowledge (and prejudices) about class and racial divides in contemporary society—without making concessions to hate or institutional contempt. (Neo-Nazis remain excluded, and the female social worker who helps Khaled escape is the only unambiguously positive state employee.) On the extradiegetic level, this collective of networked individuals is virtually doubled in the dispersed audience community whose partial alignment into an artistic experience of imagined solidarity is facilitated by our shared expectations of genre: of cinematic Kaurismäki-land, comedy, the musical, and the fairy forces of fiction. While awareness of these antirealist nodes of mediation is crucial to our imaginative buy-in, it does not undo all reality of affective reshuffling. The collective joy and hope facilitated by the trilogy films comes about not via immediate real-life applicability or straightforward character identification (although empathy with Khaled certainly plays a role in *The Other Side of Hope*) but through the intricate assembly of heterogeneous feelings: of pain and enjoyment, despair and defiance, ridiculousness and respect, chuckling appreciation and cinephilic awe. Fused together, they give us a glimpse at how differently our world(s) could feel if we (unaligned humans) did show up for solidarity rather than pity.[176] In the following chapter, I investigate how such counterhegemonic worldmaking glimpses are complicated beyond the realm of genre: How can we imagine shared worlds in the mediating folds of realism?

CHAPTER FOUR

Tenderly Cruel Realisms

Objectfull Assembly and the
Horizon of a Shared World

With its unique imbrication of comedy, musical, and documentary realism, *The Other Side of Hope* sits at the intersection of two contemporary
trends: critics have diagnosed not only the turns to genre in arthouse
cinema discussed in the last chapter but also various (re)turns to realism.
Skeptics, to be sure, rate the latter proclamations as old news. The label
of realism has been used and abused, both programmatically and critically, for so many different epistemological and aesthetic positions and
styles at different historical junctures that the diagnosis of its resurgence
seems to indicate little but the phenomenon's undead ontology: realism
haunts just about every period anew.[1] However, the specter of realism
does return with a particular vengeance at certain historical junctures,
and despite my own skepticism about some of its invocations, I argue that
it has actually materialized in productive ways in contemporary cinema.
Realism's twenty-first-century appearances can in part be contextualized with ongoing attempts—across cultural spheres and disciplines—
to overcome postmodernist critiques of representation or (de)construc-
tivist epistemologies and aesthetic practices of theatricality, reflexivity,
or subjectivism. Philosophically, these attempts have found prominent
articulations in new materialisms, object-oriented ontology, and "speculative realism."[2] Bruno Latour's actor-network theory provides an alternative conceptualization, on which this chapter draws substantively.
In cinema and cinema studies, realism's contemporary returns began

as early as the 1990s, with the previously mentioned "new" new waves from Dogme 95 to the Berlin School and the Nuevo Cine Mexicano and with the renewed theoretical interests in phenomenology and ontology cited throughout this study.[3]

The range of realist projects and forms that has evolved since then cannot be exhaustively mapped in a single chapter. In the following, I engage three—very different—films from the 2000s and 2010s to indicate some of this multiplicity of contemporary realist practices. Simultaneously, I locate resonances that allow me to outline a programmatic reconceptualization of these films' realist practices oriented at their productivity in affectively reshuffling collectivity claims. At first glance, the three films—Michael Haneke's *The White Ribbon* (*Das weiße Band*, 2009), Gianfranco Rosi's *Fire at Sea* (*Fuocoammare*, 2016), and Alejandro González Iñárritu's *Biutiful* (2010)—in fact indicate the indiscriminate uses of the label of realism, as it is applied across genres and production contexts to make a broad range of ontological, epistemological, and aesthetic claims. *Biutiful* alone activates several competing notions of realism. A Mexican-Spanish coproduction dramatizing European histories of undocumented migration in its Barcelona setting, it can be described as moving the Mexican new wave onto European shores, but Iñárritu's repeated move in and out of American production contexts also foregrounds questions of cooptation or confluences between independent traditions and postclassical Hollywood form in the era of "intensified" continuity or "postcontinuity."[4] Arguably, the "gritty" or "heightened realism" of Iñárritu's oeuvre, which fragments "classical perspective" to evoke "immediacy and 'heightened emotional proximity,'" is also inflected by "the aesthetic conventions of horror."[5] Within the director's oeuvre, the transition from *Babel*'s multiplot drama (resonant with *The Edge of Heaven*) to *Biutiful*'s primary focus on one protagonist further brings a notion of subjective realism into play: the camera not only follows its protagonist, Uxbal (Javier Bardem), on his walks and public transportation rides through the city of Barcelona but also dramatizes his battle with illness and imminent death by showing dreams, visions, or hallucinations along with his movements and everyday perceptions.[6]

To complicate matters further, concepts of realism cross the border between fiction and documentary in ways that indicate both this border's porousness in contemporary cinema and its continued policing.

Thus, a critic described Iñárritu's heightened realism as "one we associate less with fiction and more with a documentary or *vérité* style," while the generic status of *Fire at Sea* has been questioned on the grounds that it operates through the wrong kind of realism: Rosi's documentary on the diverging worlds of residents and refugees on the Mediterranean island of Lampedusa does not project "immediacy"; it "looks like a neorealist" fiction "classic," with its adolescent protagonist, Samuele, "a descendant of Enzo Staiola as young Bruno in De Sica's *Bicycle Thieves.*"[7] Vis-à-vis these critical suspicions, Rosi insists that the film actually contains only one staged scene, and he dissociates his style from postmodern theatricalizations of documentary.[8] Programmatically, he adds that the "truthfulness in a documentary . . . is as close as you can get to the reality of the people that it represents."[9] Intriguingly, this ethos connects Rosi's documentary method to the historical realism of Michael Haneke's fictional *The White Ribbon.* The latter film may constitute the least evident fit for this chapter. In line with the director's reputation and in stark contrast with the high-affect forms of *Biutiful* and *Fire at Sea*, most initial reviewers read the film, with its stark black-and-white aesthetics and temporally removed voice-over narrator, as a belatedly modernist, Brechtian critique of the emergence of fascism in an authoritarian German village cosmos on the eve of World War I.[10] Several critics, however, diagnosed a break with Haneke's signature "modernist techniques of distanciation" in conjunction with *The White Ribbon*'s historical realism.[11] For the director, the film's gestus of "observation" and its "meticulous attention to detail" supported by extensive research present not only an effort "to get" the look of things "right" but also—as if echoing Rosi—an attempt to get close to the historical "reality of the people."[12] Notwithstanding his own insistence on the "alienation" effects of the voice-over, Haneke situates the film's narration in the genealogy of nineteenth-century literary realism rather than aesthetic modernism or postmodernism.[13]

Despite the widely different reference points and techniques of realism in *Biutiful*, *Fire at Sea*, and *The White Ribbon*, I argue that we can in fact locate some common ground among their respective worldmaking practices: a shifting but not fatally swampy ground for productive realist contributions to the project of affectively reshuffling the claims of collectivity in our twenty-first-century moment. As indicated, I develop this reconceptualization of realism by returning to the philosophy of Latour and adapting his notion of onto-epistemological realism as an intervention into cinema studies.[14] The respective promise of Latour's approach, I argue, is in how it allows me to reconfigure the critical fault lines between modernist and postmodernist critiques, on the one hand, and contemporary returns to realism, on the other. Latour distinguishes his world-building project from the deconstructive approaches to which his initial science studies approach was often assimilated. In contrast to traditional as well as other contemporary philosophies of realism, however, he does so not by renouncing "constructivism" but by situating constructivism as an "*increase* in realism."[15] More specifically, Latour positions his world-building project as a nonpositivist "realism dealing with . . . *matters of concern*, not *matters of fact*."[16] While "highly uncertain and loudly disputed," he explains, matters of concern are nonetheless "real" and "objective"; they should be taken as "*gatherings*" rather than simple "objects" by a "more talkative, active, pluralistic, and more mediated" empiricism.[17]

Latour's "more mediated" realism challenges the critical legacy of defining the notion through motifs of immediacy, as echoed, for example, in the quoted reviews that question *Fire at Sea*'s documentary status on the basis of its aesthetic "failure" to project immediacy. In cinema studies, these motifs of immediacy and contact with the real have been prominently associated with André Bazin's discussion of film ontology. Based on "the essentially objective character of photography," Bazin famously declared, and facilitated merely through the "instrumentality of a non-living agent," film forces us "to accept as real the existence of the object reproduced."[18] Today these motifs of immediacy and contact continue to circulate both in the critique of realism and in some of its returns, also with reference to Bazin's contemporary Siegfried Kracauer.[19] They further resonate in film-theoretical debates on the index, which seems to have attained new promise as a media-specific anchor for the desire for referentiality precisely in today's "post-medium" condition.[20] Latour's intervention helps to complexify these concepts of contact and trace. If you will, his mediated realism simultaneously empowers Bazin's instrumental actor and acknowledges the transformative impact of the human hand holding the camera, along with the many other agencies involved.[21] Furthermore, I draw on Latour to disentangle the controversial promise of indexicality from its associations with the ontology of film and to integrate its (quite mundane) operations into a broader spectrum of material-semiotic processes, which principally—if differentially—operate across disciplines, media, and genres.[22] While detailing field-specific assembly procedures and protocols, Latour emphasizes analogies, "commerce," and "crossings" among them.[23] In his model, scientific graphs, scholarly writing, and more or less realist artistic practices are all constituted through an interplay of continuity/contact and discontinuity/symbolic mediation in translational chains; as I emphasize, they all operate along a spectrum of *productive referentiality*.[24]

In other words, Latour's onto-epistemological realism is anchored in the aesthetics of assembly. Vice versa, aesthetics is anchored in the world: Latour's imbrications of mediacy and the real do not retreat into the discussion of the mere realism effects diagnosed by postmodern critiques of representation but endow aesthetic procedure with epistemological productivity and ontological force.[25] The respective—realist—success of individual world-building acts can be evaluated based on criteria for good *"composition."*[26] This emphasis on criteria makes Latour's proposal more convincing to me than other twenty-first-century reconceptualizations of filmic realism, including reinterpretations of Bazin that have disentangled his legacy from narrow conceptualizations of indexicality, immediacy, and media specificity. Thus, Thomas Elsaesser aligns Bazin with the "post-epistemological" ontologies of Gilles Deleuze, Jean-Luc Nancy, and Stanley Cavell to gesture at the possibility of displacing controversies about "truth and falsehood" with affirmations of "belief and trust"; Hilsabeck Burke analogously describes "'true realism'" as "satisfying a need for what Cavell calls conviction in our shared reality."[27] But where Cavell simply substitutes "acceptance" for "evidence," Latour methodologically strengthens the latter by specifying how different *"truths"* are produced through different kinds of "evidence" in the assembly of controversial matters of concern via language, image, or sound.[28] Enabled rather than undone by visual or verbal intervention, Latour's compositional realism is based on methodological standards of complexity, care, and caution: oriented toward a goal of "objectivity, or rather *objectfullness*," it *"traces a network"* by giving agency to a range of nonsovereign participants and multiplying the associations among actors, attachments, and events or among sights, sounds, and words.[29] The authority of realist worldmaking is thus anchored in the intersubjective—and interobjective—networks of composition and reception.

The ethics of such an *objectfull* assembly of plural truths through aesthetic procedure, I argue in this chapter, forms a common denominator among the different forms of realism in play in Haneke's, Rosi's, and Iñárritu's films. In an interview about *The White Ribbon*, Haneke distinguishes his work from genre filmmaking by suggesting that he tries to build "models 'filled with the world'" or "steeped in a verifiable reality," whereas genre "de-realiz[es] . . . reality" by reducing "the world . . . to a model."[30] Praised for its "richness," *The White Ribbon* develops its objectfull historical realism not through a pretense at immediacy but through interventionist techniques that film scholars have persistently associated with antirealist theatricality: the voice-over and a bold regime of montage in the inclusive sense of both shot composition and editing.[31] Haneke himself explicitly wants the voice-over to signal that the story is not unmediated "'reality' but a memory, an artifact."[32] As I argue, however, this does not mean that it functions primarily as a device of destabilization. Instead, my reading positions the voice-over as a nonsovereign Latourian narrator, which contributes to *The White Ribbon*'s objectfull assembly of controversial matters of concern along with the film's other key techniques: its complex shots—in particular, the interplay of incongruous bodily and verbal performances—and an editing regime that weaves an intricate net of associations between different scenarios in the film's village cosmos. This objectfull assembly, I argue further, enables us to follow the film's diegetic actors in the violent world of their village collective and creates an affective ethos as removed from the modernist coldness and sadism associated with Haneke's authorial signature as it is from the joy projected in Aki Kaurismäki's refugee trilogy.[33] However, *The White Ribbon* does resonate with the alternative modernisms discussed in chapter 2: we might situate it as a contemporary transformation of *Katzelmacher*'s project of critical intensity through realist form. In facilitating a closer tracing of diegetic attachments, *The White Ribbon*'s realist method engages audiences in an intense experience of affective incongruity that assembles shock, discomfort, and outrage with tenderness, respect, sympathy, empathy, and hope. Without glossing over the brutality of the film's diegetic actions or affirming the authoritarian collective it traces, this viewing experience affectively unsettles the viewer's critical judgments. Powerfully disturbing but not exclusively negative, it facilitates a reconfigurative critique of the film's historical world of religious authority for our own postcritical times.

Iñárritu's and Rosi's realisms share aesthetic ground with *The White Ribbon* in how they deploy montage to assemble a larger world from diverging takes and perspectives, while combining montage with more conventional realist methods. As I detail in the following, they generate affective intensity in part through the conceit of documentary presence at the scene of a humanitarian emergency (*Fire at Sea*) and a powerful cinematography of postcontinuity (*Biutiful*). In contrast to *The White Ribbon*, both *Fire at Sea* and *Biutiful* tackle contemporary crises of collectivity and thereby more urgently pose questions of political intervention than Haneke's film. *The White Ribbon*'s Latourian method of patiently assembling a virtual shared horizon from the actors' own takes facilitates a different sensibility for historical scenarios and their contemporary resonances, but (in line with as chapter 3's argument) it does not easily translate into imaginations of political change or resistance. I therefore turn to Jacques Rancière's more forceful imbrications of aesthetics and politics to show how *Fire at Sea* and *Biutiful* take up the challenge of imagining politically and reshuffling the "sensible" toward "shared" horizons—here within the limitations of a realist aesthetics.[34]

These limitations, I demonstrate further, assert themselves differently in relation to each film's navigation of its respective status as documentary or fiction. As indicated in the introduction, my model of affective cinematic worldmaking resituates but does not undo the border between fiction and documentary. Resonant with Latour, Rancière underlines that there is no "'real world' that functions as the outside of art" but rather "a multiplicity of folds in the sensory fabric of the common": the "real always is a matter of construction."[35] Documentary and fiction, I propose in this spirit, operate on an ontologically continuous spectrum of worldmaking practices. In Latour's words, they are made "of the same material, the same figures."[36] Fiction does not operate beyond real-world reference altogether or (as Rancière reminds us) as "the imaginary as opposed to the real."[37] Documentary and fiction do, however, "differ through the treatment to which we subject" their materials and figures, including the disciplinary standards of reference we apply to documentary.[38] As indicated, Rosi's documentary ethos is not about immediacy, but it translates into aesthetic standards for mediating truths—or respectfully tracing matters of concern. In *Fire at Sea*, he aims to document the reality of people's lived experience of the (politically produced) gulf between Lampedusa's residents and the immigrants. Therefore, the film refrains from forcefully visibilizing the "shared world" that is demanded by its normative horizon of affective humanism. More subtly, however, the film's objectfull assembly of historical memories and contemporary vulnerabilities projects such a shared world: it establishes virtual links unredeemed in contemporary reality.[39] In contrast, *Biutiful's* fiction is not disciplined by documentary standards, and its high-affect realism more radically challenges hegemonic distributions of the sensible.[40] Even more objectfull in its rapidly edited assembly of plot details and perspectives than the chapter's other two films, *Biutiful* subjectively aligns us with its dying protagonist—but no less insistently embeds this protagonist in a larger world, or the "myriad lives and stories" surrounding him.[41] In doing so, I suggest, the film challenges us to experientially explore the ethical significance of imagining a shared world—and to do so in ways that provocatively exceed liberal concepts of humanism.

COMPLEX SHOTS, NONSOVEREIGN NARRATION, AND LOCAL EDITING: *THE WHITE RIBBON*

Years ago, when I first taught *The White Ribbon* in an interdisciplinary graduate seminar in the Midwest, several students shocked me by declaring their emotional alignment with the village pastor, whom I, along with most critics, was initially inclined to call "a tyrant."[42] After all, it is the pastor's method of constituting his religiously based family collective that gave the film its title: the white ribbon as a stigma and marker of temporary exclusion for presumed impurity. Puzzled, I engaged the class in a joint attempt to make sense of our diverging alignments through a closer look at the film's form. Starting from conventional associations between spatial and emotional closeness or distance, we quickly established that camera positioning was of limited diagnostic value in *The White Ribbon*. At moments, the immobile camera known to experienced Haneke audiences is unsurprisingly installed at an observer's distance, where it presents a social tableau, sometimes through a door or other framing device, and arguably to a more or less Brechtian effect.[43] Thus, the first scene in the pastor's house, which introduces his character to the film audience, features a long take on the family assembled for dinner. Shot from diagonally behind the pastor, it analyzes the family's operation through hierarchy and violent threats of exclusion: the two oldest children, who are about to be punished for coming home late, are positioned in the background, and the silent mother is almost as removed at the other end of the table. However, a fair number of close-ups and even conventional shot-countershot framings—unusual for Haneke's cinema—balance these distanced framings.[44] In fact, the very first shot on the pastor is a close-up, in a series thereof that foregrounds the faces of the individual family members while he begins his disciplinary speech. Later scenes variously present the pastor along with his family members in unobtrusive, near-classical close and medium shots that make it difficult to trace any implied camera commentary or allegiance.

More important clues for understanding the different readings in my classroom turned out to lie in the complex interplay between different elements of audiovisual shot composition—specifically, bodily and verbal performance, including character speech and voice-over narration.[45] A closer look at the village pastor's rhetoric during his disciplinary monologues foregrounds a contrast between his overall inexpressive body language (and calm, disengaged voice) and the fact that his words almost constantly reference his own emotional engagement. In the initial family scene, for example, he not only talks about the mother having cried but also dramatically declares that they will both have a bad night because "the strokes" to which he just sentenced his two oldest children "will hurt us more than they hurt you." Like me, some of my students decoded these words—unaccompanied by a corresponding affective bodily habitus—as techniques of emotional manipulation from the repertoire of authoritarian education that Haneke extensively researched for the film.[46] The absence of the same decoding impulse in some of my younger students, however, alerted me to the fact that it *is* a critical imposition, mediated by the antiauthoritarian discourses with which I grew up in post-1968 Germany. Cautioning that the pastor appears as a tyrant only from today's perspective, Haneke offers a historical corrective:

"highly representative of the period's attitude towards education," he is "a father who loves his children and is 100 percent convinced that his way of raising them is right."[47] In response to the film's invitations of historically realist form, my students deployed the pastor's "own world-making activities":[48] following his verbal rhetoric of affect, they seem to have historicized his unemotional body language with the normatively restrained habitus of bourgeois masculinity in modern Europe and concluded that he is a well-meaning educator. To be sure, it may be harder for many of us to sustain such generosity when the pastor, also in the initial family scene, cruelly claims that "I don't know what's sadder, your absence or your coming back."[49] The director indicates his own critical take when he characterizes German fascism precisely through the "absolute belief in the 'right thing'" he then attributes to the pastor.[50] At the intersection of these diverging vectors, the film's ethos of historical realism amounts to a modification rather than a full-fledged abdication of critique. Entwining post-Brechtian techniques with invitations to trace the attachments of the pastor and other actors in its complex world, *The White Ribbon* replaces (in Latour's terms) *iconoclastic* critique with "*diplomacy*" by enabling us to tangentially "*share* the experience" of its actors' values, while nonetheless "*modify*[ing] the account."[51]

A later series of scenes in the pastor's house further indicates how the film's often incongruous interplay between bodily affect and language unfolds emotional complexity, reminiscent of Rainer Werner Fassbinder's use of affective incongruity but without the extreme defamiliarization effects of *Katzelmacher*'s theatrical mise-en-scène.[52] When one of the younger boys asks for the father's permission to foster an injured yard bird, the pastor once more references affect in a performative of threat: as if intending to deny this permission, he sternly warns that his son will "be attached" to the bird by the time it is ready to be released again. When the boy counters by reminding the pastor of his own pet bird we see in its cage next to his desk, the pastor argues that the pet bird is used to captivity. Then, for the first time, however, the pastor softens in tone and facial muscle as he asks the child whether he is really prepared for the "heavy responsibility" of standing in as "father and mother" for the yard bird. In response, the little boy's face lights up in joy (figures 4.1 and 4.2). We can read this sheer happiness at the prospect of a situational role shift in the hierarchical family configuration as a forceful

FIGURE 4.1 *The White Ribbon* (dir. Michael Haneke, 2009).

exemplification of Lauren Berlant's "cruel optimism": it demonstrates the boy's attachment to a structure that hurts him but also his "pleasure" and nonsovereign agency in pursuing "promise[s] of intimacy" in a circumscribed world.[53] Toward the end of the film, when the pastor's oldest daughter crucifies his pet bird in revenge for his public shaming of her, the younger son offers the fostered bird as a replacement gift to

FIGURE 4.2 *The White Ribbon* (dir. Michael Haneke, 2009).

"Herr Vater" (as he formally addresses his dad). While the medium close-up shows the sadness on the boy's face accompanying this self-sacrificial act of love, he motivates the gift with the *father's* sadness. The gesture of verbal connection invites the film audience to see the former child in the pastor, whose (perfunctory or anxious) "thank you" sounds rather cold but whose face, my students underlined, seems to betray genuine emotion here. The complexity thus generated does not untwist the film's knot of love and brutality. As the formerly free bird enters captivity for good, the pastor's situational performance of affect fails to connect with the child. Apparently disappointed by the relative lack of response, he turns to leave, painfully underlining that the pastor can show his love for his son as love for a pet only.

The White Ribbon's antithetical deployment of language and physical performance potentially complicates our relationship not only with the pastor but also with the village teacher, whose attempts to solve the mystery of a series of violent incidents and whose off-screen identity as the much older narrator remove him from the cruel village world to a degree. In my own initial reading, he was the only credible candidate for emotional audience alignment. In a scene from one of the film's other plot threads, we see his younger on-screen persona ask for the hand of Eva, whom he shyly courted during her earlier employment as a nanny for the baron's children. In a tableau shot of the dark family living room in the midst of winter, Eva's father openly articulates his skepticism about the financially unpromising applicant. After an inappropriate joke about the significant age distance between them, he asks Eva directly, "Do you want him?" When Eva fails to answer, her mother—who, unlike the pastor's wife, speaks up against her husband—steps in. Underlining the gendered dimension of the film's disconnects between language and bodily performance, she insists, "Of course she wants him. Don't you have any feeling?" The father snaps back, "How can I tell if she clams up?" As Eva flees the room, followed by her mother, he adds a condescending "Women!" (Weiber!).

Now the film does not simply resolve this conflict by asserting the authenticity of nonverbal communication, which would invite us to critically denounce the patriarchal organization of its world while unhesitatingly feeling with the couple. Eva's subdued body language is not easy to read for the twenty-first-century film audience. Painful to watch,

Haneke's careful worldmaking assembly rather suggests that Eva's full consent may in fact be unattainable in the hierarchical configuration at stake, which circumscribes her agency even more brutally than that of other characters. (Her father has a point about the age difference between her and the teacher.) When the prospective couple is finally alone for a moment after Eva's father has declared a mandatory waiting period, the teacher once more asks Eva, "Is that all right with you?" Before providing gestural affirmation by taking his hand, she returns the question to him, notably using the formal mode of address that he has repeatedly asked her to abandon with him: "Ist es Ihnen recht?" (Is it with you, Sir?). The audience unease invited here acknowledges that the teacher's relationship with Eva is not immune from the over-whelming realities of hierarchy and affective disconnect around them, even if their awkward flirtation initially seemed to offer us a break from the dominance of cruelty and sadness in the film's world.[54] At moments paternally condescending, the teacher, like the pastor, talks about his love but often fails to clearly demonstrate it through facial gesture or voice. During a rare outing, Eva's fear at his suggestion of a picnic in the woods underlines that she does not trust him.

In his narrator function, the teacher characteristically includes himself in the village collective by using the first-person plural. When the pastor restores his family community by freeing the children of their ribbon stig-mata for New Year's, for example, the narrator accompanies the images of this family scenario with words that articulate doubt only indirectly: "We thought of ourselves as united in the belief that life in our community was God's will, and worth living." Rather than presenting a full-fledged outside perspective, his account is removed from the world he traces only by the grammatical marker of the past tense. In this sense, the character narrator is a Latourian actor with the—limited—privilege of hindsight, whose historical remove does not equal full-fledged critical distance. Even the voice-over, as the film's arguably strongest Brechtian device, follows Latour's methodological recipe of carefully tracing the actors' attach-ments to their shared world. Another narrator comment reports that the baron's speech in the church after his son was mistreated "frightened the locals": the baron threatened that the "peace of our community" would be lost if the perpetrator was not found. The narrator's words offer an interpretation for the—in part attentive, in part withdrawn—expressions on the villagers' faces that we have just seen in a series of medium close-ups. As he explains, the baron "wasn't popular, but as a social authority and employer of nearly the entire village he was respected."

Importantly, this alignment of the narrator's reports with the perspective of the village does not mean that he loses all narrative authority. While he is marked as nonsovereign by his own introductory references to the limits of his memory as well as his tentative rhetoric, critical habit too quickly equates such nonsovereignty with (the narratologically much more developed concept of) "unreliability."[55] But the narrator's introductory self-positioning also serves to authorize his account as an honest sense-making attempt:

> I don't know if the story I want to tell you is true in all details. Some of it I only know by hearsay. After so many years, a lot of it is still obscure, and many questions remain unanswered. But I think I must tell of the strange events that occurred in our village. They could perhaps clarify some things that happened in this country.[56]

The film subsequently presents intimate detail about village family life to which the narrator could hardly have had access, but he could have certainly imagined these scenes based on the hearsay he references. More generally, such transgressions against the "natural" limits of (human) narrator knowledge have been made acceptable (as realist) to audiences through the history of modern narrative techniques, including the ways in which fictional narrators freely enter multiple minds. In Haneke's film, the narrator's gender and age that we hear in his voice are conventional authority generators, and his measured language in the style of nineteenth-century literary realism generates "dignity."[57] Along with his structural privilege as a voice-over and his significant presence, these features make it likely that we will believe him as long as the other elements of the film do not clearly signal otherwise.[58] And overall they do not. Momentary tonal discrepancies (such as the peaceful landscape shots accompanying the first news of war) might just indicate historical incongruity from a local perspective. While the narrator withholds full evaluation, there is no large-scale "opposition" between him and "the film" (as critics have claimed); rather, voice-image congruity dominates in the unfolding of its world.[59]

In this sense, the narrator's nonsovereign account embodies Latour's realist worldmaking practice of careful and cautious assembly. Eventually, the process does stabilize the matters of concern at hand: the audience is certainly invited to assume that most of the "strange events" in the village find their explanation in the children. And if the subjects of the pastor's regime of torture have thus turned into torturers themselves, the narrator's reconstruction of this process provides us—at our additional historical distance—with indications for critically elaborating this story. Thus, we may conclude that the pastor has interpellated his children into a regime of community violence, as presumably backed by divine law, with his techniques of enforcing consent: "You surely agree with me that I can't leave your offense unpunished."[60] But apart from the narrator's initial hint at the genealogy of fascism, the mode of this assembly does not conceptually explicate such critical conclusions to the effect of foreclosing "local" investigation with historical allegory.[61] Rather than didactically demonstrating "social pathology," the film draws its audience close to its cruel collective.[62]

The film's techniques for doing so include classical empathy generators, especially the close-ups on the younger children's faces. Its most striking tool for bringing us close is, however, the montage editing, which I propose to describe as a thoroughly *local* recording along the lines of Latour's methodological prescriptions for deploying controversies—or, more precisely, as "Localizing the Global" (Latour's first move) combined with "Redistributing the Local."[63] Again and again, a cut takes us from one family scenario to the next in the midst of dramatic situations, mostly without establishing shots or other means of narrative preparation.[64] Haneke's earlier work—specifically, *Code Unknown* (*Code inconnu*, 2000)—is known for emphasizing the autonomy of the shot by separating narratively similarly incomplete sequence shots with black screens. In contrast, the scenario-to-scenario cuts in *The White Ribbon* intertwine rupture with association, establishing linkages between heterogeneous situations and assembling the film's world from there. On the day after the initial dinner in the pastor's house, for example, the wife of a small farmer is killed in a work accident. The film intercuts that plotline with an encounter between the teacher and the pastor's oldest son, Martin, who is dangerously balancing on a bridge. As Martin explains, he wanted to give God a chance to kill him—in response, we may gather, to the pastor's disciplinary speech. Martin's agitated plea not to tell his father is ended by a cut to the location of the accident. Inspecting it, the farmer's oldest son asks questions about the baron's potential responsibility before the editing returns us first to the teacher, who meets Eva on his way home, and then to the house of the doctor, whose children talk about the accident of the farmer's wife, and finally back to the pastor's, where we join the mother's preparations for the spanking ritual in *medias res*.

If this local recording technique, at first glance, operates in stark contrast with the voice-over as a distancing and generalizing tool, the editing collaborates with the narrator in tracing associations—or "redistributing" local impressions. With their implied comparisons or analogies, the (often disorienting) surprise cuts contribute to assembling the village collective.[65] They just do so in a different way than the actual community shots with which the film also presents us at moments, particularly in the church. Usually aligned with the pastor's view, the church shots of the assembled collective function like the narrator's most generalizing comments: they produce seemingly complete visual accounts of the hierarchical community. In contrast, the "local" editing associations between individual scenarios establish (with a fitting distinction by Nancy) "contact," not "congregat[ion]."[66] Exploring multiple links constituting partial assemblages, they can be compared to the narrator's less assertive, suggestive, but not fully evaluative verbal gestures of connection. Generating questions and possibilities rather than ready accounts, they deploy "matters of concern" rather than "matters of fact" in a decidedly nonsovereign but critically engaged manner.

In the terms of cinematic montage theory, the resulting complexity is won through layered effects of similarity, analogy, juxtaposition, and counterpoint. The film's editing regularly activates several of these associative vectors simultaneously in presenting a world of unsettled—and unsettling—connections. For example, a cut takes us from the scene in the pastor's study discussed earlier, in which the boy brings in the injured yard bird, to the house of the small farmer. At the dinner table, the farmer questions his son about the baron's cabbages, which were cut during the harvest festival. In contrast both to the pastor's little boy, who is eager to reproduce existing family structures, and to the film's "mysterious" acts of violence, for which we merely assume the older children are responsible, the farmer's son explicitly defies authority. He asserts that he is "proud" of his deed, thus challenging the baron along with his own father, whom he blames for his passive reaction to the mother's death. In response, his father slaps him in front of the entire assembled family. The simultaneously contrastive and connective associations with the scenario of discipline in the pastor's house facilitated here arguably encourage diverging audience responses. On the one hand, we may be eager to align ourselves with the son's—in the film's world, lone—act of antiauthoritarian resistance. On the other hand, his father's—spontaneous, affective—act of corporeal punishment and his own failure to resist make sense when he demands that his son think about the consequences of his rebellion: the family will not be able to survive without the support of the baron. Furthermore, he insists, it is impossible to establish whether the baron is actually responsible for the accident. The film audience is not given any clear indications as to whether negligence was involved either. Or have the children had their hands in this mystery as well?

While noticeably constructed in its discontinuous, often abrupt mode, the film's narrative world assembly certainly fulfills Latour's criteria for approximating "objectfull" truthfulness through a cautious tracing of diverging perspectives. If anything, the film proceeds *more* cautiously in that it refrains from settling many controversies. This caution does not undo *The White Ribbon*'s critique of authority.[67] While its assembly encourages us to experientially acknowledge the complexity inherent in authority's intricate, layered workings from the perspective of different actors, this local recording does not produce a conciliatory effect; instead, it highlights the cruelty of the attachments it pursues.[68] For example, another abrupt cut between scenarios connects the pastor's cruel rhetoric of affect to the midwife's relationship with the doctor, who abuses her. Telling horrifying stories about the degenerative effects of masturbation, the pastor insists that his respective disciplinary intervention against Martin is motivated solely by love. Immediately after the scared adolescent eventually confesses to touching himself, we join an apparently rather unpleasurable dining room sex act between doctor and midwife in midaction, followed by verbal abuse. In the course of this and a subsequent encounter, the film pushes its explorations of the knot of violence, sex, and emotion to the point where the midwife's cruel optimism unravels: she openly charges the doctor with sexually abusing his daughter and calls herself "ridiculous" for "loving" him, before comparing him to her disabled son.

More so than the "mysterious" acts of violence, it is the close confrontation with these twisted and incapacitated affects that produces the cruelty of Haneke's film. The counterpoint effect of the editing in the described sequence may invite us to get some relief by focusing blame on the doctor. Doing so, those of my students eager to defend the pastor affectively approximated the resolution attempts of the diegetic collective on which the narrator reports at the end of the film: after the disappearance of doctor and midwife, the "village gossips" accused them of all sorts of things, including the unsolved crimes. In this instance, however, the narrator's distanced rhetoric clearly deauthorizes the simple act of scapegoating. Reorienting the film audience toward the complex circulations of violated affect and attachment that the film traced for us, he indirectly challenges us to explore our own affective responses—from potential complicity with the protagonists' violent performances to no less discomforting empathy for the midwife's prolonged holding onto a twisted promise of intimacy.[69] As indicated, there is no comfortable emotional anchor point in the film's world. Even the doctor's children, who seem to be uninvolved in the group violence, have been looped into the circulations of violated affect. Another play of complex association presents the adolescent Anni, the new object of the doctor's sexual affection, as an eerily similar double of the midwife in posture and overall appearance.[70] Anni's largely tender interactions with her little brother offer a contrast with the harsher demeanor of the midwife as well as with that of the pastor's oldest daughter, Anni's age companion. However, such tenderness is inescapably entangled with violence in the village world. In the dialogue between Anni and her brother after the death of the farmer's wife, her gentle habitus increasingly ruptures as she tries to console the little boy, and presumably herself, in answering his insistent, wide-eyed questions about death. Most of the scene is rendered in a close shot-countershot mode, but the visual closeness also foregrounds Anni's verbal distancing gestures. As her initially warm tone shifts, temporal reassurance—yes, he will die, too, but "not for a very long time"—tilts into a stance of defense—yes, their mother "is dead, too. But that was a long time ago." In response to this harsher attempt at rendering death less present, Anni's little brother defiantly pushes his plate off the table, and a cut takes us to the pastor's wife, who wipes off a tear while preparing for her children's punishment.

Thus tracing the seeds of violence in mutilated tenderness, Haneke's film invites thorough disturbance as part of an audience experience of partial and shifting alignments with the film's ensemble of tenderly cruel actors. As I would emphasize, this process amounts less to a "paradoxical affirmation that the meaninglessness of things . . . may actually be our best hope" than to a careful sorting through of meaningful layers of painful experience.[71] Although actual viewers may strive to reduce the offered complexity of engagement—for example, by underlining the contrast between doctor and pastor and excusing the latter as a loving instance of authority—the multiple specific associations evoked by the film's rich narrative worldmaking enable more intricate practices of affective reflexivity. This reflexivity's underlying ethos, I suggested, resonates with that of Fassbinder's modernist affective critique, but it is unfolded beyond *Katzelmacher*'s gestural indications through Haneke's world-filled historical modeling or his objectfull tracing of controversies by way of layered montage.

As I argue in this chapter, this notion of an objectfull tracing of matters of concern provides a promising starting point for reconceptualizing realism beyond postmodern critiques of representation and moving toward the horizon of assembling a shared world from current controversies about affect and collectivity. *The White Ribbon*'s particular project of historical realism contributes to contemporary controversies only indirectly insofar as it invites us to translate our disturbance into (com)passionate questions about the affective ties structuring our own fraught world(s). Haneke himself has suggested that the story resonates beyond its specific historical context in tracing the genealogies of "radicalism" and "fundamentalism."[72] However, we might want to refrain from settling on any definite allegorical translation. As I have demonstrated, the film's "localized" techniques of narration draw us close to the specific scenario unfolded; rather than offering the gratifications of abstract analytical closure, they ask us to explore the links between its historical affects and our twenty-first-century tenderly cruel attachments as matters of concern rather than fact.

Furthermore, *The White Ribbon*'s indirect contribution to larger twenty-first-century conversations invites pause rather than indicating any resolution. In a moment in which the forceful (post)modernist critique of barons and pastors has given way to new hegemonies of nationalist and religious closure, *The White Ribbon*'s affective worldmaking cautions equally against such new affirmations of authority and against arrogant, iconoclastic disregard for the complicated orientations of nonsovereign actors navigating authoritarian worlds. In following—if not outdoing—Latour's methodological insistence on not prematurely resolving any controversies, *The White Ribbon* indirectly alerts us to what is arguably a gap in Latour's argument. Namely, through which means does the cautious tracing of controversies actually lead to the eventual "unification of the collective into a common world acceptable to those who will be unified" that Latour optimistically projects?[73] As indicated, his aesthetic model of compositional realism principally makes room for scholarly or artistic intervention through the translational forces of rhetoric and form. Some of Latour's concrete suggestions, however, are less helpful. At one moment, he affirmatively describes the "master narratives with which we are disciplined" as reservoirs of "metaphors for what 'binds us together,'" which "offer a preview of the collective."[74] In stark contrast to chapter 3's theoretical fairy tales of revolution, Latour's (also politically) realist method does not indicate a clear path from collective violence to collective solidarity. The following two readings therefore develop Rancière's suggestions for redistributing the sensible as a countermethod for imagining differently on realist terrain.

ASSEMBLING VIRTUAL LINKS BETWEEN
TWO WORLDS: *FIRE AT SEA*

As Rancière sets out to programmatically conceptualize the relationship of politics and aesthetics in *Dissensus*, he defines politics as a "*specific break*" not only with the established distribution of political agency but also with the "'distribution of the sensible' . . . that defines the forms of partaking by first defining the modes of perception in which they are inscribed."[75] The "dividing-up of the world (*de monde*) and of people (*du monde*), . . . upon which the *nomoi* [laws] of the community are founded," he reminds us, is "determined in sensory experience" and "presupposes a distribution of what is visible and what not, or what can be heard and what cannot."[76] Rancière associates the political act of challenging the distribution of the sensible with democracy; its subject is the *"people"* in the sense not of any existing community but of a supplementary figure that makes it *"possible to identify 'the count of the uncounted' with the whole of the community."*[77] Rancière's definition is resonant with but more stringently poststructuralist than Alain Badiou's notion of the people referenced in chapter 3: Badiou sees a dynamic, potentially revolutionary people form around the "nonexistent mass" of those excluded from the "official people"—today, in particular, the "newly arrived workers" described as "'immigrants.'"[78] In contrast, Rancière cautions against any positive fleshing out of his "abstract" supplementary figure.[79] My own spin on these questions is less purist: the following readings do continue to engage Badiou's association of the people as political actor with the empirical actors who are "uncountable" insofar as they cross borders irregularly.[80] In Europe's—as well as North America's—current hegemonic regime, I want to underline, this association and the acts of (recon)figuration it affords constitute forceful political provocations in their own right. We urgently need acts of redistributing the sensible that place "one world in another" by making "visible the fact that" immigrants "belong to a shared world that others do not see."[81] As poststructuralism taught us, however, such concrete acts of inclusion remain haunted by the exclusions they themselves perform. In the critical discussions of *Fire at Sea* and *Biutiful* I am about to detail, this problematic unfolds around the politics of humanism—specifically, the purported failure of humanist inclusions to operate politically in Rancière's sense. Against that backdrop, his refusal to solidify the political actor of the people beyond the interventionist gesture it performs challenges me to explore how the act of inclusion can remain dynamic, or productively unstable, in continuously challenging its own limits. Of this chapter's two remaining films, I argue, *Biutiful's* fictional worldmaking presents a more radical answer to this problematic, but Rosi's documentary realism attends to it in its own way.

At the height of public discourse around the so-called refugee crisis (that is, the moment when northern European states could no longer ignore the state of emergency south and east of their borders), Rosi's poetic—"beautiful, mysterious and moving"—documentary on the

Mediterranean island of Lampedusa became a major success: it won the Golden Bear at the 2016 Berlinale, was nominated for the Academy Award for Best Documentary Feature, and holds a 94 percent approval rating from Rotten Tomatoes.[82] Nonetheless, reviewers also articulated concerns. In particular, they commented on the asymmetries in the film's depiction of the "two parallel worlds" on the island, which "clash like two hermetic blocks."[83] While the filmmaker spends significant time with individual island inhabitants, including the twelve-year-old Samuele, who is more interested in his slingshot than school, Rosi does not, they charge, afford us a personal connection with the immigrants. As they come into view only through the "technical operations" of the Navy rescue missions and the subsequent bureaucratic "processing," the immigrants (to one reviewer) appear as an "anonymous mass" rather than as subjects recounting their own story.[84] The refusal "to so much as ask the name of a single refugee," another summarizes, forces "us to sympathize with the crisis . . . from the perspective . . . of Lampedusa and, by extension, the West."[85] The diegetic anchor of such asymmetrical sympathy would be the island doctor, who is the film's only diegetic point of contact between its worlds and, in the words of yet another reviewer, its "moral center of gravity."[86] At one point, Dr. Bartolo articulates a grand-scale humanist proclamation: "It's the duty of every human being to help these people." Abstract and asymmetrical, this juxtaposition recalls Badiou's critique of the neocolonial scene of perception split between active (white) witness and passive victim (see chapter 3). In line with the hegemonic gender codings of this scene, Dr. Bartolo repeatedly foregrounds the suffering of "women and children." With Pooja Rangan's recent *Immediations: The Humanitarian Impulse in Documentary*, we could extend this critique to worry that such humanism invents "the very disenfranchised humanity it claims to redeem," exemplifying an "'emergency thinking'" that suspends politics.[87]

My reading of the film acknowledges these concerns (some of which crossed my own mind upon first viewing it) but develops a more generous interpretation. Politically, my wish to rethink Rangan's critique of documentary humanism stems from my discomfort with wholesale critiques of humanism in an age in which right-wing politics has increasingly exchanged humanist legitimizing promises for unapologetic celebrations of national or religious particularity. In the early

2000s, when human rights discourses provided key ideological support for the "War on Terror," corresponding critiques of humanism had a different political urgency. Today, as the controversial closure of Lampedusa's harbor by prime minister Matteo Salvini has made even the much more recent rescue operations shown in *Fire at Sea* feel historical, a complementary move seems worth exploring.[88] Rather than letting go entirely of a (however compromised and unsatisfactory) legacy of imagining more inclusive notions of political collectivity, might we instead try to transform this legacy? In this spirit, I propose that *Fire at Sea*'s humanism is exemplified not by Dr. Bartolo's grand-scale asymmetrical proclamation but by the affective vulnerability that the film traces underneath his awkward attempts to verbalize his painful experience of treating rescued immigrants—or certifying the deaths of those who did not survive. In other words, I argue that the film develops a creaturely humanism of (however differentially) shared exposure to conditions of violence, precarity, and death. The stark contrast between *Fire at Sea*'s "two worlds" is punctuated by how its objectfull assembly—of historical memories, spatial practices, and nonhuman agency—spins a web of virtual connections that is mostly ignored in the critical reviews.[89] That Rosi does not fully actualize these virtual links between the island's two worlds, I argue further, is a matter of documentary ethics and aesthetics—although not of the immediations that Rangan holds responsible for performing apolitical humanism.

In interviews, Rosi spells out the practical constraints that explain some of the film's asymmetrical design. At the time of the Ebola epidemic, his permission to film the rescue operations was contingent on his wearing a full hazmat suit; this severely limited interactions with the immigrants, who could not even see his face. Furthermore, the immigrants stayed on Lampedusa for only two days; they were sent on to the mainland after initial health checks and immigration processing.[90] But rather than treating these constraints as limitations to be cinematically outsmarted, Rosi's documentary ethos is built on reflecting them. Asked why he didn't bring his protagonist, Samuele, down to the migrant center, he responds that "this never happens in reality": with the institutionalization of migration over the preceeding few years, the "parallel lives" of immigrants and residents have become "the reality in Lampedusa."[91] The ethical stakes of this claim to the real are heightened in the director's response to a further critical concern: to one reviewer, the inclusion of footage of dead bodies in the underbelly of a boat toward the end of the film borders on the "voyeuristic."[92] In response to a resonant interviewer question, Rosi exclaims affectively, "The hard part is that these things should not fucking happen. People cannot die like that. This is the hard part—not me filming."[93]

Importantly, this recourse to the real does not attempt to silence critical questions by erasing the decisions underlying documentary representation. In the same interview, Rosi spells out that he initially resisted the insistence of his navy interlocutors that the horror of these deaths needed to be shown but let himself be convinced.[94] In line with the concept of a more mediated realism proposed at the outset of this chapter, Rosi's documentary ethos grounds a deliberate practice of collective artistic worldmaking. In addition to interhuman negotiations on what needs to be shown, this includes a programmatic sharing of agency between the filmmaker and the world to be documented. Rosi outlines his aesthetics as one that avoids interviews and voice-over, instead grabbing "moments of reality that become very strong narration" in their assembly: the filmmaker's "strong point of view" forms in watching, as he allows "reality to unfold itself and follow[s] that in its own expression."[95] In film-theoretical discussions from Bazin to today, this cuts (at least) two ways. On the one hand, it vetoes unilaterally interventionist aesthetics, from traditional documentary didacticism to the postmodernist techniques of theatricality, that have flamboyantly challenged dominant "documentary's claim to an unmediated encounter."[96] On the other hand, Rosi makes no such claim himself. In actively deploying mediation as a means of approaching the realities of the Mediterranean emergency, his affective realism modifies the "sensations of temporal urgency" and "spatial presence" produced by Rangan's documentary immediations.[97] Nor does Rosi aim to surrender *all* worldmaking authority. Such—mediated—surrender is the second counterstrategy explored by Rangan—for example, in radical experiments in which recording devices are attached to animals. Instead, Rosi's poetics generates representational authority via a Latourian "following" of other actors.

The emphasis on mediation as the facilitating condition for presence and encounter characterizes *Fire at Sea*'s cinematic practice on more than one level. Poetologically most explicit, the filmmaker's assembly turns the medical reality of an eye exam into a metaphor: Samuele's "lazy" eye dramatizes his—and, by extension, our—inability or unwillingness to see.[98] In analogy to the prescribed glasses, *Fire at Sea*'s cinematography simultaneously acknowledges and aims to correct these challenges—for example, with a range of shots reminiscent of *A Separation*'s techniques for foregrounding mediation and blockage as part of nonsovereign perception (see chapter 1). In a sequence at the refugee center, we see immigrants using the few available phone booths in a shot that leaves their faces and upper bodies blurry behind the partially opaque glass panels surrounding the phones. More intense is a sequence in which individual refugees in the small space of a moving rescue boat are seen in haunting close-ups that visually emphasize the play of foil covers in front of the faces. With all sound muted for a moment, these shots entwine an eerie conceit of heightened experientiality with a simultaneous emphasis on mediation. In yet different ways, this emphasis is inscribed in the sequences with Dr. Bartolo, whom we first meet during the examination of a pregnant immigrant. Indicating that the "cultural mediator" has not yet arrived, he gestures at his ultrasound images to communicate with the patient in the absence of a shared language, while ambiguously verbally addressing us or the filmmaker, who is not openly interfering but is implicitly acknowledged as coconstituting the everyday moment recorded.

The doctor's running commentary on his difficulties in determining the sex of the woman's entangled twins momentarily lightens the film's drama with a touch of comicality before he details the visual effects of his patient's suffering. Dr. Bartolo's testimony continues to unfold through narration rather than immediate dialogue (with either the filmmaker or the diegetic interlocutors) in the subsequent—crucial—scene in which he looks at the photograph of a recently arrived boat on his computer. His explanation of the three-class system that crams the poorest immigrants into the hold of the boat has the informative function of an interview, but it is presented more as a personal recollection to which we are listening (figure 4.3). This format allows for an unfolding of affective urgency short of any conceit to immediacy. Indirectly preparing us for the horrifying images we will see toward the end of the film, Dr. Bartolo tells of the people he had to bring to the emergency room: "dehydrated," "malnourished," "exhausted," and (he brings up a

FIGURE 4.3 *Fire at Sea* (dir. Gianfranco Rosi, 2016).

picture of an adolescent boy) badly burned from fuel-water mixtures on the unsound rubber boats. As indicated, I propose that the ethical force of the doctor's presence in the film is felt less in his discursive attempts to come to terms with this experience than in how his words (punctured by silences), his glances down, and his affective hand gestures indicate the affective impact of the "awful things" he sees. Dr. Bartolo, my students have suggested, is himself traumatized by this rescue work. Whatever his colleagues may say, he reports that he cannot not get used to examining dead bodies, to putting them into bags or taking samples: "after death, another affront." "All this leaves you so angry," he continues, "with emptiness in your gut, a hole," and with nightmares, which he experiences frequently.

The film's concluding rescue sequence, which culminates in the footage of the dead bodies in the hold of the boat, is the film team's attempt to share a few glimpses of that experience with the audience, intentionally "without becoming voyeuristic or pornographic."[99] The sequence starts from an image we have seen many times: the extreme long shot of a crowded blue boat in the sea iconographically recalls mainstream media coverage of the European refugee crisis. The camera then tracks the gradual evacuation of the boat onto a larger navy ship, where a medical professional in a full hazmat suit (presumably Dr. Bartolo) attends to severely dehydrated men on the ground while others, barely standing, are subjected to bureaucratic procedure. About ten minutes into the sequence, we hear that "forty dead bodies" have been found, then another "fifteen." The arrival of the first body bags on the navy ship is followed by a cut to survivors sitting under a roof on the navy ship; the camera closely traces their mourning for more than two minutes—in part *so* closely spatially that it made me more uncomfortable than the footage of the bodies to follow. Does the camera have a right to record these tears? Another distance shot of the boat, now almost empty, is abruptly followed by a shot of entangled limbs, fabrics, and empty water bottles in its hold. A total of three still shots of this kind, each held for a number of seconds, records the reported deaths: just slow enough to give us time to look, or to urge us to see, without excessive lingering. The following sustained take of the empty sea, with mostly muted sound, indicates the camera(person)'s mourning, in turn followed by views of a partial eclipse of the sun. Surely another moment "of reality," the eclipse footage is assembled to become "very strong narration," an affective metaphor for the filmmaker's plea to attend to the realities of (in Christina Sharpe's terms) death and life "in the wake" or the contemporary condition of systemic violence against racialized immigrants that secures the fortress Europe.[100]

Intense metaphor on the one hand, the eclipse is, on the other hand, one of the many details through which *Fire at Sea*'s poetics of creaturely humanism embeds the humanitarian catastrophe at stake in a larger world or emphatically *our* larger *real* world—from a local angle. (The local vantage point presents a stark contrast to Ai Weiwei's very differently universalizing *Human Flow*.)[101] The film's sustained interest also in the island population attains its significance as part of its assembly of nonsovereign life practices, exposed to the elements not only in the attempt to enter Europe. Rosi's assembly foregrounds the locals' vulnerability to the sea as they struggle to make a living through fishing, from the dangerous nightly diving outings of an irregular urchin fisherman to Samuele's seasickness, which he is instructed to overcome to become a fisherman himself. This does not mean that *Fire at Sea* relativizes the sharply asymmetrical distribution of life chances: the introductory titles alert us immediately that an estimated 15,000 immigrants have died in the attempt to cross the Straight of Sicily in the last two decades. It does mean that the film complicates the identification of Lampedusa with "the West": the opening titles also specify that the island is closer to the African coast than to Sicily, and Lampedusa's tourism industry, which has been impacted by Europe's fear of immigrants, is absent from the film.[102]

Starting from the political actuality of two parallel worlds that the filmmaker identifies as a crucial matter of concern, *Fire at Sea* reassembles this actuality by tracing links between the lives of the locals and those of the immigrants: partial and virtual links unredeemed in contemporary reality. The introductory sequence artfully layers motifs of both contrast and connection. First, it introduces Samuele on a search for slingshot wood. Mostly very long shots and takes embed the adolescent in the stark winter landscape of the island, a bare and rough environment in muted colors that is very different from a tourist's cliché image of sunny southern Italy. Then a cut brings the island's radar device into view as we overhear a radio communication between the attendant on duty and a desperate migrant voice. The nature-technology contrast between Samuele and the contemporary world of European Union border control operations is thus superimposed with the contrast between the two voices: the attendant's monotonous, repetitive demand for position details and numbers (250 people) and the migrant's panicked plea for help. After the connection is ominously interrupted, we get glimpses of the rescue operation, with several shots foregrounding the ship's high-tech equipment without any crew member captured in the image. Human and technology are visually assembled in a third scenario, introducing a local radio host with computers, mixing board, and microphone but also a soft face and voice, as underlined in a sustained close-up of his singing along to the music. Yet another cut takes us to one of his listeners, an older woman preparing food in her kitchen as the local news interrupts the music: 206 people were pulled from the sea and (so far) 34 bodies recovered. "Poor souls," the woman mutters.

As the film unfolds, we may notice that this older resident's electronic (non)connection with the "distant" world of the immigrants who are dying just a few miles away simultaneously seems to be her primary (tenuous) connection with her "own" social world, or local collective. The film shows her almost exclusively alone in her daily activities around the house, accompanied by the radio host, whom she calls to request music. In stark contrast to Jakob Brossmann's 2015 documentary *Lampedusa in Winter*, which foregrounds collective assemblies (town hall meetings as well as outdoor crowds) in detailing protests against the exploitative ferry company, *Fire at Sea* restricts its indications of local collectivity almost exclusively to the radio host's repeated brief appearances.[103] This focus on the virtuality, or mediatized ontology, of the island collective simultaneously dramatizes and relativizes the opposition between resident and immigrant worlds: on the one hand, it contrasts Lampedusa's individualized residents with the migrants' almost constant visual embedding in their collective; on the other, it suggests that the residents are cut off from direct contact not only with the immigrants—while virtually connected to them as well as their own families.

Introducing herself as "Auntie Maria," the elderly resident later asks the radio host to play the song that gives the film its title, "Fire at Sea," and dedicate it to her son, who cannot go out fishing in the current bad weather. Extending the dedication to all fishermen listening, the radio host complies, thus anchoring the film's musical title motif in its diegetic world. In the narration established by editing, this moment follows another use of the title phrase, which indirectly established the song's historical backdrop. Sitting by the window in the storm, Samuele's grandmother tells him of how she would bring food to his grandfather, who was out on the boat all day but also of how they would be scared to go out at night because it was wartime: the navy ships would fire rockets, and "it was like there was fire at sea."[104] In some respects, the locals' history with war, which is echoed by today's immigrant deaths at sea, is not fully in the past: right afterward, we see Samuele and his friend enacting shooting fantasies out on the coast, with their bare hands standing in for weapons. At some point, the friend interrupts Samuele's obsessively repetitive gestures: "Enough. You killed 'em all." If Samuele seems unaware of the current war at Europe's borders, the trauma of past wars lives on in his games, and *Fire at Sea*'s cinematic worldmaking contrasts the reality of present separation with the inter-world connections that come into view on a historical axis.

Unlike the virtual island collective, the immigrants live (and die) under enforced conditions of physical crowding; Rosi, however, includes glimpses of the everyday humanity of individual perseverance, survival, and nonsovereign agency. At moments, his characteristically immobile camera conveys the impression of just being present while a few immigrants, for example, arrange their reflective foil blankets for comfort on the floor. A sequence documenting the procedures at the processing facility more dramatically highlights individuality as a counterpoint to the collectivization imposed by the bureaucratic machinery. Following extensive coverage of how the arriving group is counted and serially body scanned, a close-up introduces a woman wearing a hijab as she is instructed to adjust her scarf for an official picture. Initially resistant, she consents after a moment, apparently relieved as she understands that the request is not to take off her hair covering entirely but merely to make visible her hairline. Panning to the left, the camera shows the number positioned next to her head as the picture is taken; in stepping out of the light, she nods a "thank you." With variations, the following shots of other immigrants in the moment of having their picture taken repeat this contrastive arrangement of bureaucratic deindividuation, the individuality of demeanor and facial expression, and the nonsovereign agency of communication under conditions of asymmetrical power distribution. As these shots assemble, for example, an adolescent girl's withdrawn look with an adult man's apparent pleasure in posing, the tangential alignment of immigration authority and film camera reflects on the underlying process of representation in an open-ended manner: we may wonder whether the presence of the second, extradiegetic camera provided arrival operations with a lighter touch for this man; whether the navy photographer, whom we do not see any more than the filmmaker, aimed at creating a relaxed atmosphere; or whether we are just witnessing the immigrant's joyful relief at having made it. Short of actually tilting into humor, however, the film's serial assembly of expressive faces culminates in the haunting seriousness of an adolescent boy looking directly at us for an extended moment (figure 4.4). Inviting neither asymmetrical sympathy nor facile empathy, his expression demands recognition of another human's traumatic experience we do not share.

Finally, the interplay of individuality and collectivity is also dramatized in the "single shot" highlighted positively by the most critical reviewer cited earlier: listening in on the call-and-response performance of a group of Nigerian men, *Fire at Sea* most emphatically "gives voice" to the immigrants and "makes the suffering as forceful as it could be for those who didn't live through it."[105] Rangan, to be sure, warns that the "language of documentary immediacy is most insidious" where it supports the conceit of authentic self-representation in participatory

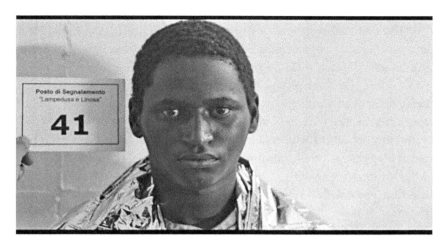

FIGURE 4.4 *Fire at Sea* (dir. Gianfranco Rosi, 2016).

documentary.[106] But Rosi's compositional choices demonstrate once more that the affective force of expressive performance and mise-en-scène does not have to be premised on pretend immediacy. In close-up, we see the face of the main speaker on the right side of the screen, with a few other participants visible behind him to the left. As the camera doubles the mediation entailed in the speaker's own narrative performance, his act of working through lived experience operates analogously to the narrative testimony of Dr. Bartolo. Against the backdrop of dangerously overloaded boats and administrative deindividuation, however, the extended coverage of this call-and-response performance presents an affirmation of the collective as a space of spirituality, support, and creativity—without playing the collective against the individual. After announcing "This is my testimony," the speaker alternates third- and first-person plural forms throughout most of his narration ("many," "we"). Punctuated by the collective responses of his audience, his performance shows the individual as embedded in and enabled rather than obliterated by the collective. For the film audience, his English-language testimony also provides glimpses of the specific histories of some of the people we have seen arrive: the speaker tells of bombs in Nigeria; of the flight through the desert, where many died; and of the terrible conditions in Libya, where ISIS ruled and the locals "would not save us because we are Africans." They had to risk the sea route, where many more would die.[107]

The call-and-response performance culminates in a celebration of survival before a cut to Samuele's experience of getting sick on the fishing boat facilitates a far less dramatic echo in the film's other world. Later, after the final rescue sequence discussed earlier, the film once again returns to Samuele. On one of his outdoor excursions, we see him turn on a flashlight at dusk, this time to find a bird that he caresses with a little branch. But the film's layered configurations of contrast and partial analogy do not thus culminate in a metaphorical pretense to change. After another scene with Auntie Maria and a final shot of the radio host, the film ends with Samuele out on the dock. As he acts out another shooting fantasy, the credits start rolling, accompanied by the title song. The filmmaker, who has demanded political interventions in interviews, makes the distinction that the "issue," not the "film," is "political": *Fire at Sea* is "about sensations, . . . about emotions, . . . about encounters."[108] Of course, I insist with Rancière that these sensations, emotions, and encounters *are* political; with Rangan, the film becomes "a political act" in *"reading* emergency."[109] But Rosi's distinction makes sense insofar as it indexes the restraint inscribed in his poetics of documentary realism. Its mode of cautious assembly tasks us with deciphering partial and virtual links, as it insists on the actual divergences between life worlds along with the shared vulnerability of collectively embedded humans across this divide.

ASSEMBLING THE "COUNT OF THE UNCOUNTED": *BIUTIFUL*

The different assembly protocols of fiction enable Iñárritu to challenge this divide between life worlds more forcefully. In its "reframing of the 'real,'" Rancière argues, fiction can change "existing modes of sensory presentations" and build "new relationships between . . . the individual and the collective."[110] In *Biutiful*'s respective endeavor, montage plays a crucial role once more, along with intensified (and intensifying) techniques of world detailing: Iñárritu's film exemplifies Latour's methodology of objectfull realism even more fully than the other two films discussed in this chapter. In thus accumulating links between its Barcelona-based family drama and the worlds of irregular Chinese and African immigrants, the film sensibilizes "a shared world that others do not see" in highly provocative ways.[111] *Biutiful* couldn't be further removed from any cheerful cosmopolitanism. With its visceral high-affect aesthetics—the close camera regime, the focus on abject as well as beautiful detail, and the at times disorientingly elliptic narration—the film draws its audiences into an experience so "bleak" and "intense" that it is thoroughly disturbing upon first viewing.[112] Reminiscent of *The White Ribbon* in its insistence on cruelty as part of its realist ethos and in its firm refusal to prematurely resolve any controversies, *Biutiful* is in some respects perhaps *less* activist than *Fire at Sea*.[113] At the same time, I argue that *Biutiful's* uncompromising fictional assembly of contemporary real-world horrors is more radical than any of the films discussed so far in how it challenges the hegemonic "dividing-up of the world (*de monde*) and of people (*du monde*)" or the "sensory experience" on which the norms of "the community"—and corresponding acts of exclusion—are founded.[114]

Once again, this reading is not uncontroversial. Notwithstanding its two Oscar nominations and overall worldwide success, *Biutiful* has received somewhat mixed reviews in the English-language world, and some of my students and colleagues (on the occasion of talks) have chimed in with—in part diverging—concerns.[115] These include, on the one hand, worries about the relatively mainstream status of Iñárritu's filmmaking, with its Hollywood connections and melodrama inflections, and charges that the film perpetuates stereotypes of the immigrant groups it features.[116] On the other hand, some (re)viewers have felt alienated by how the film violates mainstream standards for empathy management and moral closure. They complain, for example, that "no one in the movie is apprehended by the law," that "the only cops visible are corrupt ones," and that the protagonist, Uxbal, "is a nasty piece of work by any yardstick, surely, a guy who makes his money exploiting poor people, and yet repeatedly we are invited to sympathise with him."[117] I grant that *Biutiful* confronts us with an imposition. In my reading, however, it is in how the film radicalizes humanist concerns beyond "simple" demands for transcontinental sympathy. More precisely, *Biutiful* forcefully sensibilizes a horizon of *shared implication*—and *responsibility*—in cinematically confronting us with Uxbal's ethical failures, conflicts, and concerns in a network of nonsovereign actors, against the backdrop of neoliberal precarity, racism, and heteronormativity—or a world in which social solidarity structures have fallen apart even as modern regimes of violent normativity continue to hold power.[118]

Creating complexity in its dense network of associations, *Biutiful* dramatizes the ethical instability of Uxbal's position in the world of irregular labor he inhabits as a middleman between Chinese immigrants manufacturing counterfeit-label accessories and Senegalese immigrants selling them on the street. On the diegetic level, the charge that Uxbal is "exploiting" the immigrants is explicated by the police officer whom Uxbal bribes to facilitate that business. Once their deal breaks down, and a number of Senegalese sellers are arrested in a raid (and face deportation), Uxbal confronts the officer. The latter's utter lack of moral authority is underscored by his blatantly racist rhetoric: "The blacks had to be taken down." In the shot-countershot staging of their exchange, Uxbal's facial mimicry indicates his disgust, and his insistence on the human impact of deportation verbalizes dissent. He defends himself against the exploitation charge by claiming that he is, rather, "helping" the immigrants "get work," and his often attentive, personal interactions with individual immigrants lend credibility to this defense. Nonetheless, the sharp reply of the corrupt law's unsympathetic representative contains a truth: "for a cut, like everyone else." In its breathless rhythm of quick, elliptic montage, *Biutiful* contours this truth through the interplay with another sequence in which Uxbal talks warmly to Lili, one of the Chinese immigrants, who has been babysitting his children, before he gets into a fight with their agents, Hai and Liwei. Pointing to the conditions he just observed in the unfinished basement where the workers are housed, Uxbal charges Hai and Liwei with exploitation before he suddenly declares, "I don't give a shit," and physically attacks Liwei for withholding Ubxal's share of the profit: "It's fucking mine. It's mine. . . . It's my money." Hai steps in, disentangles the fighters, and pays Uxbal.

Uxbal's ethics of care is thoroughly entangled in the logic of profit. The film dramatizes his outburst of aggression as an overwhelmed, utterly nonsovereign actor's stress response to a neoliberal world in which collective support structures are absent. The film's fictional reconfiguration of respective life-world actualities weaves local conditions into a transnational horizon. Based on a year of research, including interviews with a large number of recent immigrants to Spain, *Biutiful*'s diegetic world closely reflects specific immigration patterns, employment trends, and the increased crackdowns on irregular migration triggered by the 2008 economic crisis.[119] At the same time, the film bypasses Spain's comparatively generous immigration policies up to that point: the granting of social rights (education and health care) to irregular residents and the successive waves of legalization in the 1990s and 2000s.[120] There is also no mention of any state support on which Uxbal's own family might be able to rely. In the wake of his diagnosis with terminal cancer, he desperately tries to assemble resources for his two children. By underlining the instability of Uxbal's ethics as he juggles that commitment with his concern for the immigrants, the film's complex worldmaking forcefully drives home the point that compassion cannot be relied on as a market corrective or a mode of community formation in the world of neoliberalism.[121] And if the promises of family and faith are ideologically hailed (and perhaps experienced) as leftover havens for solidarity in that world, the film underlines that they do not remain untouched by the realities of exploitation either.[122] Just minutes before the fight with Hai and Liwei, a camera close-up of another cash exchange underlines that Uxbal accepts money even for the spiritual services he performs on occasion: he is apparently able to communicate with the dead and sells that capacity as the promise of facilitating their peaceful rest to surviving family members.

As in *The White Ribbon*'s historical world, the performance of religion is thus entangled in the portrayed regime of collective violence. At the same time, the two films differ significantly in how they treat (what Latour calls) the "beings" of faith.[123] During the question-and-answer period following one of the talks I gave on *The White Ribbon*, an audience member (with, I understood, a religious background) asked me whether the logic of my Latourian reading did not require me to go further and take seriously the possibility of divine agency in the film's world. While having to grant the theoretical legitimacy of the question, I find it difficult to imagine a coherent reading along these lines. *The White Ribbon* encourages us to displace a distant ideology critique with a tracing of its historical actors' worldmaking processes, but the director's stated interest in a carefully historicizing critique seems to be reflected in the narrator's humanist perspective and to be at odds with the divine cruelty we would have to postulate as ruling the film's world. In contrast, *Biutiful*'s aesthetics of subjective realism, or the way in which it assembles its larger world partly from Uxbal's perceptions, in fact invites us to accept the challenge of "ontological pluralism."[124] Often letting us see with the protagonist—floating images of (un)dead souls, strange insects on the ceiling, and his father in a snowy forest as he passes away—the film does not definitively categorize these views as either supernatural visions or dreams and hallucinations. Rather than limiting "our inquiry to" the "'social dimensions'" of religion, *Biutiful* thus asks us to consider "the strange nature of what" is "'given into experience'" as a virtual reality among others.[125]

Importantly, this ontological pluralism does not resolve but rather sharpens *Biutiful*'s materialist and ethical concerns as well as the problematic of nonsovereign agency that connects them in the film's complex cosmos of controversies.[126] When Uxbal turns to his spiritual mentor, Bea, for guidance, she tries to calm his worries by displacing his agency with an assertion of spiritual community: "You think you take care of the children? [. . .] The universe takes care of them." In a slightly impatient tone, Uxbal counters, "But the universe doesn't pay the rent." That Bea's wholesale spiritual surrender offer remains unconvincing does not yet legitimize Uxbal's fraught attempts at individually shouldering earthly responsibility for material care. He insists that Hai and Liwei get heaters installed for the workers in the basement. Then, in a moment when his body is noticeably fighting the stress of his latest chemotherapy treatment, he buys the least expensive heaters in the store. The significance of this decision is highlighted through the lyrical staging of the transaction: the accompanying melancholic music drowns out the dialogue. One morning soon thereafter, the Chinese workers are found dead in the basement, suffocated by gas leaking from the cheap heaters. As Uxbal is now consumed by guilt, Bea once more tries to calm him down by reminding him that their death was an "accident."

What exactly is the role of human agency in a universe apparently prone to accidents? (Another accident is featured in the earlier sequence in which the Senegalese street sellers are chased by the police in a forceful mise-en-scène of the chaos, disorientation, and panic that characterizes *Biutiful*'s overall positioning of both protagonists and audiences.)[127] A reviewer circumscribes *Biutiful*'s treatment of Uxbal's responsibility by calling the film "a tragedy in the classical sense of the term."[128] I agree that the classical concept captures part of *Biutiful*'s dramatization of "overtaken" human agency against a horizon of ambiguously transcendental contingency—in particular, in the narrative emphasis on Uxbal's flawed decision and the resulting death of the workers. Like the world assembly in *Fire at Sea*, *Biutiful*'s fictional world assembly foregrounds the shocking actuality of death, not least as the absolute limit of agency and indicator of its radically asymmetrical distributions. Here we have a strikingly beautiful shot of the sea at dawn, from which the bodies of the Chinese workers are washed ashore a moment later. (Liwei had tried to dispose of them too close to the beach.) All narrative emphasis notwithstanding, however, *Biutiful*'s world is ultimately too complex to be able to isolate one individual misstep, character flaw, or event as a central narrative turning point along the lines of genre theory. Thus, I propose that the film disassembles the concept of tragedy into its intricate dramatization of how the "responsibility for action" is "shared" in a network of (caring and exploiting) humans, things (such as heaters), and other forces (perhaps constituting the universe).[129] In detailing this distribution of agency, I suggest further, *Biutiful* encourages us to complicate wholesale moral judgments without abandoning moral *concerns*—including Uxbal's own.

After the terrible death of the Chinese immigrants, Uxbal falls apart further, increasingly compromising even his family, for whose benefit he became so ruthless. The film's tracing of the violent conflicts with his bipolar (ex-)wife Marambra makes for some of *Biutiful*'s most gruesome moments. After a night of drinking and drugs, into which his irresponsible brother tempted him in his despair, Uxbal finds seven-year-old Mateo all by himself with a black eye. As the boy explains, Marambra "punished" him for bad behavior and left with his older sister for a planned trip, on which Uxbal had believed all of them to be. Upon their return, Marambra wants to "explain" herself, while Uxbal, who has custody, tries to leave with the children. When Marambra doesn't let go of Mateo, Uxbal chokes her, thus perpetuating the circle of abuse from which he wants to protect the boy. The camera pans back and forth between the dramatic scene and the frightened older daughter, who overhears the struggle in the next room. For the film audience, this is extremely painful as well. Granting us even less distance from the agents of violence than Haneke's artfully composed, retrospective historical narration, *Biutiful*'s unabashedly affective aesthetics of presence simultaneously heightens the sensations of tenderness and brutality. Closely following its actors' perspectives while foregrounding the effects of their violence, the film enmeshes subjective with intersubjective, or collective, realism. The degree of our overall narrative and spatial alignment with Uxbal makes it difficult to fully withdraw our allegiance from him even while he acts out, but the camera also foregrounds the pain of his wife, with whom we stay for a moment after the abuse. Marambra did get to explain herself in an earlier scene: her being overwhelmed with the responsibilities of child care is coinduced by hurt from the boy's acting out against her—he called her a whore—and by her rational fears—Mateo's failure to listen to her has endangered him before. Fully spelling out the layers of the portrayed situation might take another page: the assembly of the film's "entire created world" from countless significant mise-en-scène, dialogue, and sound details interwoven in its elliptic narration is too objectfull not to frustrate audiences longing for clear-cut allegiance.[130]

Most importantly for my argument, the film's assembly does not play the family unit against the larger world. Their interweaving has multiple layers. On the plot level, the dysfunctional family is embedded in historical contexts of migration insofar as Uxbal lost his father when he had to flee the Franco regime before Uxbal's birth. Furthermore, the protagonist's own name resonates as Native American rather than Castilian or Catalan.[131] On the level of casting, both Uxbal's daughter and his father are played by actors with North African backgrounds.[132] On that of cinematography, the camera often embeds Uxbal in the crowds of a visibly globalized urban space, and at key moments, it adds other subjective perspectives. To be sure, the overall focus on Uxbal does allow for gradations of allegiance, which can tempt us to get relief by constructing contrast: Unlike Uxbal, does Liwei not cry over the dead workers primarily out of fear for his own future when the first words we hear him say—in tears—are "We are ruined"? But if we engage more closely with the film's layered worldmaking invitations, it is difficult to stabilize such impressions toward categorical differentiations between a more or less "saintly protagonist" and (harmfully stereotyped) "unfeeling sweatshop owners."[133] Like Uxbal's, Hai's and Liwei's nonsovereign worldmaking is compromised by the logic of profit. Additionally, their lives are impacted by the collective pressures of heteronormativity. Throughout the film, we have received glimpses at Hai and Liwei's love relationship, which Hai juggles with his family commitments. After the first round of tense negotiations with Uxbal, a bathroom scene shot almost entirely in close-ups—mostly of their faces, if momentarily also of the action of a zipper opening—foregrounded Liwei's insistence on his love vis-à-vis Hai's reminders of his family. For a few moments, we are experientially exposed to Liwei's tender caresses and Hai's own desire, visible in his facial mimicry and audible in his moans even before he begins to passionately return the kiss. In another scene, the camera stays with Liwei for a moment, who smokes at the window of his apartment in his underwear, after Hai has abruptly left him to go "home." A third scene balances perspective by introducing us to Hai's family. Initially, they seem united in joyful laughter around the dinner table, but when Liwei disrupts their meal with a sudden appearance in the door and Hai leaves the room with him, the camera focuses on his quietly unsettled wife. This indication of yet another personal world of drama underlines the workings of narrative ellipsis in *Biutiful* more generally: rather than effecting aesthetic reduction (of world to model), the hints at motivations and back stories suggest that what is left out could be detailed toward an even fuller world assembly.

After all of this, a striking sequence toward the end of the film takes us from a long, intensely emotional hug between Uxbal and his daughter, who just confronted him about the increasingly undeniable signs of his illness and imminent death, to a city shot out of an apartment window, with curtains flattering in the wind underlining the mood of mourning, and then to a close-up of Hai looking out of a window (figures 4.5–4.7). Judging by the curtains and light, it is not the same window, but the elliptic editing strongly suggests that the previous shot could have been Hai's subjective vision, establishing an equivalence of melancholic views. As he turns to leave, we realize that Hai contemplates another horrific scene that comes as a shock to the audience: Liwei is stretched out naked on the bed in his own blood. A preceding, quickly shot montage sequence may allow us to puzzle together an explanation: Liwei's uncontrolled emotional response to the accident seems not only to have fully blown Hai's cover with his family but also to have exposed Liwei's aging parents to armed police. The affective imposition of this deathbed scenario for the audience is, however, created not only by the

FIGURE 4.5 *Biutiful* (dir. Alejandro González Iñárritu, 2010).

FIGURE 4.6 *Biutiful* (dir. Alejandro González Iñárritu, 2010).

FIGURE 4.7 *Biutiful* (dir. Alejandro González Iñárritu, 2010).

elliptic narration of the diegetic story but also by how it is tied together with the preceding moment of emotional intensity between Uxbal and his daughter by Gustavo Santaolalla's melancholic sound track. The slow guitar tune first set in as the father-daughter hug got closer, supplanting the amplified sound of heartbeats, which had aligned us multisensorially with their intensity.[134]

For one reviewer, the affective connection thus established between the two scenarios was simply too much: he complains that the montage makes the resolution of the Hai-Liwei plot "ring 10 times more falsely than" it would have without the preceding "naked," "unadorned depiction of human frailty."[135] But, of course, Iñárritu's radical insistence on human frailty is constituted precisely by cuts—or, with Rancière, breaks—such as this one. Rather than relying on Latour's hope that a patient tracing of controversies may ultimately succeed in assembling a more inclusive collective, *Biutiful* stages forceful dissent as "an intervention in the visible," audible, and sensible that "places one world in another" by identifying those "without part . . . with the whole of the community."[136] *Biutiful*'s "count of the uncounted," like that in *Fire at Sea*, emphatically includes irregular migrants in its reconfiguration of contemporary Europe, but *Biutiful* radicalizes the gesture of inclusion beyond the call for sympathy without regard to race or faith.[137] By placing the limit figure of the murderer mourning his queer love into the "universal" drama of family love and loss, the film not only endows him with "a world of experience" but also demands that we see, and hear, the world we share with him.[138] In the mood of mourning, this provocation does not sugarcoat violence, but it poses questions about all of our involvement in (structural, if not physical) acts of murder while honoring the vulnerability shared by deeply compromised actors across diverging socio-symbolic positionalities. *Biutiful*'s bleak worldmaking thus reconfigures a virtual collective in the mode of counterpoint.

No less importantly, the sequence does not end here. With the soundtrack continuing, another cut adds a third perspective to the film's assembly of the collective by making the connection to Ige, a Senegalese immigrant whose husband, Ekweme, has been deported. Ige's world of experience has also been contoured throughout the film. For example, an earlier cut from a happy moment in Uxbal's family to her living quarters showcases their family pictures on the wall, shortly after Uxbal had an emotional response to the analogous pictures on Marambra's wall. Interweaving similarity and counterpoint, the camera tracks the basic conditions in the immigrants' living quarters and a fight with Uxbal, who has come to offer Ige money after her husband's arrest. Blaming Uxbal for the arrest, Ige initially refuses to take the money, angrily declaring that "if you didn't have children, I'd kill you." But his sharp reminder that the arrested men "knew what they were doing"—dealing drugs in addition to purses—makes her anger dissipate into despair. Uxbal, now also gentle in tone, does not have a quick answer to her question: "What am I going to do with my baby?" During a prison visit, Ekweme then talks Ige out of her resistance against staying in Barcelona with the Spanish-born infant, countering her fear that "we don't belong here" with the reminder that there is no work at all in Senegal and assuring her that Uxbal will help. Uxbal in fact offers to have Ige stay in his own apartment, and Ige begins to take care of his children. Shortly before the concluding montage sequence, Uxbal shows Ige the money he has scraped together, asking her to take it and stay with his children after his death. Ige, however, resists yet again: she explains that she still plans to return to Senegal once *she* has some money together.

Now, in the third scenario assembled by the ongoing melancholic soundtrack, we see Ige with Uxbal's money; she packs her bag, safely delivers Mateo to his school and tenderly bids him good-bye, and then goes to the train station, where we see her contemplating the timetable. In conjunction with Ige's earlier threat against Uxbal, her apparent plan to take off with Uxbal's savings may uncomfortably remind us of the story that the racist police officer told Uxbal when asked to prevent the deportation of Ige's husband: a story about tigers attacking their caretaker, with the point that it was "dangerous to trust a man who is hungry." Of course, this plot echo thoroughly reconfigures the story: Ige herself has become the caretaker, and her nonviolent, melancholic departure at worst acts out a materialist translation stripped of the aggressively racist implications of the officer's animal allegory. Furthermore, Ige's apparent departure entails an ethical challenge to Uxbal's plan: Did he, a comparatively privileged European, not try to appropriate her life for his needs while she told him that her own community takes precedence?

But this is not the end of the sequence either, even if the following events remain less than certain: audience perception becomes ever more fragile as the "grainy film stock and dark background lighting" increasingly subordinate "vision to other sensory stimuli" toward the end of the film.[139] A brief shot captures a figure, unrecognizable but ambiguously identified by what might be Ige's blue bag, walking on a dark street in (it seems) Uxbal's neighborhood, before the editing returns us to a close-up of the protagonist, who is self-medicating with a needle. We hear a door close, and Uxbal asks "Ige?" At first, there is no response, but when he asks again, her voice confirms her return, and we see a shade walking by the bathroom door. If Uxbal, whose perspective guides the remainder of the film, is not hallucinating, Ige has returned after all. Arguably, some ontological uncertainty remains, given that he now also sees his own specter up on the ceiling, indicating his imminent death in analogy to his earlier visions of other (un)dead people. Even if we trust the indications of Ige's return, this concluding counterpoint is hardly developed as a certain victory of human solidarity. Perhaps it just announces a grace period of reflection. In not making a more clear-cut decision on her behalf, the film affirms Ige's (however circumscribed) nonsovereign agency. Any redemption remains bracketed, as we do not get a fuller final view of Ige to heroic or sentimental effect. In this film's brutal world, the promise of solidarity can perhaps take the form of spectral counterpoint only.[140] In *Biutiful*'s affective poetics, collectivity thus operates in analogy to its aesthetic counterpart, the beauty announced in the film title. Diegetically introduced through the daughter's English spelling exercise following Uxbal's diagnosis, the film's visual as well as verbal insistence on the phonographically accented "biutiful" not only resists standard conceptions of beauty but also haunts us as a counterpoint to violence and decay—from the discussed shot of the bodies being washed ashore at sunrise to Uxbal's insect visions.[141] With its contrastive insistence on nonstandard shared worlds, Iñárritu's redistribution of the sensible underlines simultaneously, and with equal force, the compromised conditions under which solidarity fails to materialize in our contemporary world *and* a horizon of alternative imagining. More fully than *The White Ribbon*, *Biutiful* gestures beyond the omnipresence of violence in its world, without tempering the brutality that its tender scenarios share with Haneke's.

As I have demonstrated in this chapter, it is the objectfull realism of all three films' narrative worldmaking that enables their powerful explorations of affect and collectivity. An alternative to lingering conceptions of realism through notions of immediacy, the notion of objectfull assembly as the common denominator of Haneke's historical realism, Rosi's neorealist documentary, and Iñárritu's aesthetics of sensation allowed me to show how deliberate but nonsovereign construction—prominently including techniques of montage—unfolds a realist ethos through the careful tracing of controversies in Latour's sense. The three films discussed in this chapter differ in the degree to which they develop interventionist dissent into the real they reconfigure. Through the affordances of fiction, *Biutiful* most radically poses the question of solidarity. Short of imagining a full-fledged answer, however, even *Biutiful*'s active reshuffling of the sensible operates at a far cry from Kaurismäki's imaginatively activist refugee trilogy. For all of realism's productivity in working through contemporary enmeshments of affect and collectivity, it may in fact not easily lend itself to full-blown imaginations of resistance. The epilogue therefore takes up that question of resistance once more.

Epilogue

Reconfiguring Resistance

Outside the fairy tale and the musical, "the people" in the emphatic sense of a collective of political action do seem to remain largely missing in contemporary European cinema.[1] Most of the films highlighted in this study attain their promise in reshuffling the sensible as scenarios of intricate realignment rather than straightforward revolution or collective resistance. Furthermore, even the miraculous solidarity collectives that Aki Kaurismäki assembles through the forces of genre are cinematically embodied as networks of mostly dispersed and heterogeneous individuals rather than as larger groups visibly or audibly "acting in concert."[2] I could just accept this observation as evidence for my overarching theoretical framework: with Bruno Latour, I have underlined that collectivity per se is best understood not in terms of any original unity, identity, or tradition but (metaphorically) as a "wasp's nest," a moving configuration of nonsovereign actors, each of whom is simultaneously attached to multiple shifting objects and groupings.[3] However, my sociopolitical starting point was in the alarming contemporary resurgence of seemingly smoothly aligned collectives of hate, as visualized in the vernacular video of an anti-immigration protest crowd. The crowd had its theoretical as well as cinematic heyday in the earlier twentieth century as a figure of infectious, dangerously uncontrolled—or programmatically revolutionary—collectivity.[4] But today's return of political populisms has reactivated some of the fears attached to the crowd in earlier social theory, while resonant positive theoretical counterfigurations have been developed under alternative names: those of the "multitude" or transsubjective "becoming."[5] Even theorists who remain skeptical of the unconditional celebration of such collective bodily potential, such as Judith Butler, have emphasized the significance of the body—or, better, plural bodies—in acts of political assembly.[6] How then do, or could, these phenomena of collective world(mak)ing as physical assembly look and sound in the cinema? In focusing my investigations on film's imaginative work of complicating and tentatively reshuffling hateful claims of collectivity, what did I miss? What other imaginations of "We" are out there?

I could have turned—or might in a future study turn—to the archive of largely vernacular and news media films documenting political uprisings throughout the last decade in different (trans)national contexts: Occupy Wall Street, the Arab Spring, the Istanbul Gezi Park protests, and the Hong Kong Umbrella Movement, among others. After one of my recent talks on the present book, an audience member asked me whether I had studied how the affective assemblies of right-wing political videos differ from the cinematic counterimaginations I champion. Comparing vernacular and news videos from different political contexts, I could, perhaps, answer this question by detailing how activists and journalists assemble the movements, gestures, shouts, and chants of different twenty-first-century protest crowds to engage audiences in diverging or parallel ways. In the U.S. context, Spike Lee's powerful *BlacKkKlansman* (2018) offers a potential entry point into such a comparative endeavor, in a format closer to my other examples here: another artful imbrication of documentary with genre, the film links two historical counterparts, the Ku Klux Klan and civil rights movement to the 2017 white supremacist rally in Charlottesville, Virginia, and the Black Lives Matter movement.

In this epilogue to a book on transnational European arthouse cinema that is largely focused on the imaginative affordances of fiction, however, I cannot do justice to such broader archives. Instead, I turn to one more European fiction film, which echoes the outlined questions in two ways. Deniz Gamze Ergüven's *Mustang* (2015) unfolds subtle resonances with the 2013 Istanbul Gezi Park protests, as it stages a fictional small resistant collective as a physical assembly: the playful, tussling, sensual, rebellious "becoming together" of five adolescent sisters subjected to increasingly rigid codes of behavior in rural Turkey. *Mustang* offers itself as a reference point for my concluding remarks also by how its unique aesthetics brings together a number of poetological questions discussed in this book. As I will detail, it entwines elements of realism, genre, and more or less post-Brechtian technique in ways that allow me to summarize my efforts at reassembling conventional aesthetic categories to better conceptualize the intricate affective transactions and ethico-political interventions of contemporary cinema.

Mustang has been linked to Sofia Coppola's *The Virgin Suicides* (1999), based on Jeffrey Eugenides's novel of the same title, which dramatizes the impact of Christian religious conservatism in the sexually more liberal U.S. culture of the 1970s.[7] While these transnational parallels are intriguing, the intertextual comparison highlights the formal and affective differences between Coppola's turn-of-the-century film with its postmodern, pop-cultural inflections and Ergüven's contemporary aesthetics of sensation. *Mustang* has common ground with the high-affect realisms (especially of Alejandro González Iñárritu's *Biutiful*) discussed in chapter 4: its close, fast-paced, elliptic, and sometimes disorienting cinematography and editing deploy cinema's potential for affectively reshuffling collectivity by forcefully engaging (all of) our senses. *The Virgin Suicides* emphasized perspectival distance by restaging Eugenides's literary "We" narration as the retrospective voice-over of the outside observer collective of neighborhood boys. *Mustang* has a voice-over, too, but it is that of the youngest sister, Lale. Her first-person (singular and plural) account is charged with the force of a vivid memory experientially visualized—we are to understand—in the film's affective images. In particularly striking ways, these images radicalize Coppola's play with the collective appearance of five physically similar sisters. In fact, Ergüven indicates that her starting point was in "a visual idea, of having a body with five heads and 10 arms and 10 legs."[8]

This emphasis on collective physicality is crucial to the film's imagination of resistance against a regime of oppression. More precisely (and in stark contrast to *The Virgin Suicides*, with its focus on death), *Mustang* imagines a spectrum from the nonconscious articulation of bodily unruliness to explicit resistance.[9] In the opening sequence, we see the girls' celebratory running along the beach at the end of the school year and a game of playful wrestling in the sea, which will become the diegetic occasion for their imminent confinement to the house. Sitting on the shoulders of boys their age, they fight each other, fall, laugh, argue, wrestle, and laugh again. Mostly in close-ups and medium close-ups (interspersed with long shots of the entire play collective), the camera traces the girls' movements, the splashing water, and the soaked school uniforms and wet long hair sticking to their bodies. This cinematography of physical joy and energy invites a concluding return to Brian Massumi's conceptualization of affect as "a dimension of life . . . which indirectly carries a political valence."[10] Among the twenty-first-century contributions to rethinking affect's intersections with collectivity discussed in these pages, Massumi's proposal is the one that most fully develops the promise of collective physicality, as associated with "vitality," "joy," and the ethical call to "really experience our belonging to this world."[11] In *Mustang*'s diegetic world, to be sure, the adults interpret the wrestling game in the sea as sexual and drastically curtail the girls' freedom of movement. The success of these disciplinary measures, however, remains limited: the camera tracks the sisters' continued running around inside the house and their entangled limbs as they keep playing and wrestling, be it for fun or in anger over one of them taking the other's things. At other moments, they rest entangled on the same bed or comfort each other. Massumi specifies that affect's affirmation of "relational intensities of experience" should not be "misunderstood as a celebration of good feeling": affect's "micropolitical" force is attached not solely to "positive emotions."[12] It does, however, facilitate "an aesthetic politics" in which "resistance is of the nature of a *gesture*, . . . an invitation to mutual inclusion in a collective movement."[13]

Mustang's cinematic worldmaking explores a broad spectrum of such gestures of nonsovereign resistance, including the "creative conversion" of disciplinary "constraints."[14] Angrily, the second-youngest sister, Nur, responds to the charge of the girls "pleasuring themselves" on the boys' shoulders by setting out to burn chairs in the yard (after all, they touched their behinds—"That's disgusting!"). Later the older sisters decide to "improve" the shapeless, "shit-colored" dresses they are now supposed to wear by tearing them on one side, playfully testing the poses they can strike. A momentary return to boundless collective joy is facilitated by a secret escape to a soccer game open to female audiences only, where we see the girls dance ecstatically in a larger

FIGURE 5.1 *Mustang* (dir. Deniz Gamze Ergüven, 2015).

crowd. In close-ups and medium close-ups from varying angles—eye level, up above and near the ground—the camera records their moving feet, upper bodies, flowing hair, hands up in the air, and open mouths (figure. 5.1). This sequence has been read as an homage to Jafar Panahi's *Offside* (2006), which revolves around the temporary imprisonment of a group of cross-dressed female teenagers who tried to sneak into a World Cup qualification game from which they are banned due to their sex. Of course, the association highlights differences between Iran and Turkey along with resonances. In *Mustang*, the camera's celebration of the girls dancing at the game presents their movement as unrestricted once they escape the house.[15] The action ostensibly revolves around familial rather than official state repression—although we will see that the film also traces the ways in which this repression is encouraged by Turkey's contemporary Islamist government.

In any case, the comparison underlines the significance of questions that Massumi eschews as a feature of more traditional approaches: those of "ideology."[16] While my investigations have followed his, and other affect scholars', lead in foregrounding the fundamental importance of affect to collective worldmaking processes in the cinema and beyond, I have equally insisted that we need to theorize affect's entanglements with the forces of history, culture, and politics. In the case of *Mustang*, some of these entanglements are indicated by the film's polarized reception. The diverging voices evidence (what I call) the culturalist closures of our historical moment: the ever more hegemonic framing of social and political conflict in the neo-Orientalist terms of essential, asymmetrical differences between East and West, "Muslim" and "secular Christian" societies.[17] Generally enthusiastic, Western critics have summarized *Mustang*'s intervention, for example, as "a tantalizing meditation of what it means to be a woman in Turkey."[18] Turkish (and Turkish German) reactions were more mixed, with significant support for the film but also charges of showing a false image of the country, catering to Western tastes, and engaging in exploitative sexualization—in the tradition of classical Orientalist imagery.[19]

Ergüven counters the sexualization charge by insisting that *Mustang* presents the world through the eyes of a thirteen-year-old girl in a cinematic language that aims to disrupt the male "lens" through which most films objectify women.[20] Her plea not to short-circuit her cinematography of sensual delight with the critical categories established by Laura Mulvey's classical analysis of mainstream cinema speaks to the questions of reading methodology that this study has explored in the wake of the postcritical turn. In line, for example, with my discussion of *My Life to Live* in chapter 2, can we bracket suspicion and imagine the possibility that the camera held by two male cinematographers (David Chizallet and Ersin Gök) in fact traces Lale's experience? I do emphatically believe that we should allow for that possibility in taking seriously cinematographic attempts at facilitating perspective change. I also believe that *Mustang*'s cinematography offers support for the director's perspectival claim with its elliptic, mobile takes and, at moments, point-of-view shots from Lale's angle. Nonetheless, the instabilities faced by *Mustang*'s project are indicated by Ergüven's own snippy remark about how men have trouble with the thirteen-year-old lens.[21] Complicating matters, I have also heard the sexualization charge articulated from a "Western" feminist perspective.[22] Meanwhile, the director's own cultural and political suspicions make her comment further on the "constant sexual projection on everything in Turkey."[23] Asserting that the conflict about the film "is *exactly* the conflict . . . in the film," she attributes the negative responses to sympathies for Recep Tayyip Erdoğan.[24]

While some of the latter suspicion is probably appropriate, it under-lines the vicissitudes of collective worldmaking in the loops of cinematic composition and reception. Mediating between form- and spectatorship-based approaches, the reading methodology proposed in these pages draws on the diverging, equally nonsovereign perspectives of directors, team members, and critical and lay audiences to (re)assemble a film's layered worldmaking as a heterogeneous, multivectoral assemblage that enmeshes artistic intentions with (non- or half-conscious) affects, real-world memories, fantasies, intertextual and other associations, discursive topoi, and genre tropes. The unruly bodies of *Mustang*'s girls operate in a context—or, more precisely, in multiple overlapping, diegetic and extradiegetic contexts. In tracing how worlds are made within such contexts, I have argued, we do not have to choose between a "politics of affirmation" and the "well-oiled machine" of suspicious critique that has come under fire in affect studies and the contemporary humanities more generally.[25] Rather, we can develop careful modes of *reconfigurative* critique balancing generosity and contextual awareness, imagination and knowledge, radical hope and realism. In that spirit, I will caution that *Mustang* does lend itself to a culturalist reception in some respects: its forceful feminist celebration of collective affect as unruly, sensual girlhood does not as forcefully challenge hegemonic divisions of the world via categories of culture and religion (categories deeply entangled with those of gender and sexuality). While the charge of Orientalism ignores the director's stated project and insistence on not reducing affect to sex, it pinpoints how the film unfolds its thematic focus on sensual rebellion and sexual oppression in a particular world. *Mustang* resonates with Michel Foucault's analysis of European moder-nity: the familial regime of discipline saturates every corner of the house with desire, as the younger siblings play with provocative gestures.[26] However, the film develops this story in a cultural context marked as "other" for Western audiences. With its title metaphor simultaneously orienting us to a fantasy of "untamed" Western freedom, *Mustang* invites associations reinforcing the ways in which mainstream twenty-first-century European discourses have projected sexual and gender oppression as a defining feature of Muslim culture.[27]

These interferences of ideology are supported by some elements of *Mustang*'s aesthetics. Like Kaurismäki's trilogy discussed in chapter 3,

Mustang has been classified as a "modern fairytale."[28] The label fits only halfway in that *Mustang* is less flamboyantly antirealist and optimistic throughout, but it captures the components of reduction in its narrative form. With its premise of foregrounding collective structures of discipline and rebellion through the fivefold adolescent protagonist(s), the film deliberately models a clear-cut conflict rather than an unfolding of an "objectfull" world in the spirit of Latour's concept of realism (see chapter 4). After the girls' escape to the soccer game, the adults move to marry them off one by one. We might call this narrative concentration to critical effect "post-Brechtian," keeping in mind the ways in which I reworked Brecht's key concept of *Verfremdung* in chapter 2: certainly not distanciating, *Mustang* incorporates elements of aesthetic defamiliarization into its sensual form to sharpen its tale into a critically affective parable. At the same time, realist horizons are not entirely abandoned. Ergüven cites her own childhood memories along with stories she heard to assert that "the situations" at "the basis of each scene are real."[29] Integrating her comments with Latour's vocabulary, we might say that the film develops actual "matters of concern" in "fragmentary" and "condensed" form, while "fiction" (or more free-floating inventiveness) comes into play with "the way the girls react."[30]

In principle, this interplay of real-world reference and defiant imagination parallels Kaurismäki's revolutionary fairy-tale worldmaking. However, *Mustang*'s condensed fictional assembly of historical situations invites audience associations with available cultural schemata in less idiosyncratic, less theatricalized, and less consistently humorously bracketed ways than Kaurismäki's refugee trilogy. Thus, narrative ellipsis works toward a one-dimensional character in the case of *Mustang*'s evil uncle, who not only has a major role in enforcing the regime of discipline on the sisters but also turns out to be a rapist: guided by Lale's half-understood observations, we can gather that his nightly excursions into the room of the third sister, Ece, contribute to her eventual suicide. At this point, the two oldest sisters have been married, and Ece's wedding was imminent. As the adults proceed to arrange that of Nur, the fourth sister, Lale's resistance takes on more decisive form—and *Mustang* finds its closure in a culturalized narrative trope of (more or less individual) escape. Our empathy for the ingenious and courageous young narrator is rewarded when Lale and Nur make it to Istanbul's

"Western" Beyoğlu neighborhood, where they incidentally walk by a sex shop before reuniting with Lale's beloved schoolteacher, who had left for Istanbul at the outset of the film.

Rather than escaping ideology, *Mustang*'s aesthetics of bodily sensation is thus framed by clear-cut narrative integration. As indicated, this paradigmatically underwrites the premise of this book: the operation of affective gestures needs to be studied as part of multidimensional worldmaking processes, including the fictional cosmos constituted by a film along with the life worlds grounding its production and reception. However, this emphasis does not have to undo the audience joy facilitated by *Mustang*'s vivid gestures of resistance. Narrative, I have also insisted, is not exhausted by the presumably linear vectors of plot and closure. Instead, the multivectoral nature of worldmaking processes—as an assembly of affects and associations, bodies, gestures, memories, objects, perceptions, and discourse chunks via images, sounds, and words in the loops of composition and reception—affords imaginative openings perhaps even more than closures. If Ergüven's film is glorious at first sight and not free from hegemonic ideology upon second thought, third and fourth takes offer themselves as well. Namely, *Mustang*'s techniques of aesthetic reduction are matched by an array of diverging elements that complexify its fairy-tale-style modeling.

As I have emphasized in a number of readings, narrative can operate as a force of unfolding complexity even on the comparatively straightforward level of plot and character design. On this level, *Mustang*'s fairy-tale modeling is complicated by how the five-headed creature is unfolded into individual trajectories in the course of the film.[31] Before the concluding escape, the sisters' different responses to the collective situation at hand indicate a spectrum of nonsovereign worldmaking practices of resistant adaptation. When asked to serve tea to a suitor's family in the living room, Sonay, the oldest, threatens to scream. With the force of a quick impromptu demonstration, she negotiates to marry her actual lover. During the wedding, Sonay's exuberant happiness contrasts with the despondency of Selma, who was next in line to be advertised to the suitor and now turns to everyone's half-empty raki glasses. When Selma does not bleed on the wedding night and is taken to a doctor for a virginity test, a frontal shot from above shows the image of an immobilized bride with a disaffected face. Selma's voice, however, defies the muted body as she tells the doctor that she "slept with the entire world." The doctor's calm professionalism indicates that he will honor his confidentiality promise—or that not all men in the Turkish provinces are evil. When he finds the hymen intact and asks Selma why she would say such a thing, her response indicates more resignation than Sonay might show but indirectly asserts her demand to be heard: "When I say I am a virgin, no one believes me."

The character of the grandmother, who has been raising the siblings after the early death of their parents, also has layers. Her hair is more often uncovered than that of the women around, and as she is pressured into more rigorous education methods by her restrictive environment, she alternates between punishing and protecting the girls.[32] While the grandmother is thus awarded the dignity of an indicated worldmaking perspective of her own, the nonsovereignty of her action is dramatized, for example, in the close-ups of an early sequence. The grandmother's hands, apparently in concert with those of an aunt not even fully introduced as a character yet (and not clearly identified by a face shot), sort through all the things—the nonhuman actors—that might have the power to "pervert" the girls, as Lale's narrative grammar has it. However, the family's female hands also lend themselves to defiant acts in Ergüven's fictional world. When the grandmother faints upon seeing the girls on TV during the soccer game (while the family men are preparing to watch it next door), the more modestly dressed Aunt Emine resolutely steps in with a stone to effect an electricity outage in the entire village. Of course, this is one of the moments in which the mode of comedy does contribute to opening up *Mustang*'s narrative worldmaking. Now in analogy to Kaurismäki's refugee trilogy again, genre mediations infuse the fairy-tale parable with the kind of productive affective incongruity that I have repeatedly foregrounded as a means of reshuffling the sensible. In boldly asserting possibilities of resistant agency in unexpected places, the invited laughter layers the film's grand-scale opposition between "Western" sensuality and provincial repression with recognition for the aunt's bold practicality as it further shakes up the film's heterogeneous configuration of (melodramatic and celebratory) moods. In showcasing fictionality, these moments also remind us not to (mis)read the film's real-world resonances literally: *Mustang*'s diegetic world is deliberatively, if nonsovereignly shaped into an imaginative intervention.

Even more important qualifications to the outlined concerns about *Mustang*'s culturalist resonances, however, emerge from an opposite vector of complexification. Namely, *Mustang*'s stylized model is (in Michael Haneke's words quoted in chapter 4) "filled with the world" in that its fictional assembly operates through piecemeal reference to contemporary public life worlds.[33] To begin, the film's soccer game scenario indexes the Turkish Football Federation's banning of male fans from certain games in 2011 in an effort to curb fan violence.[34] For local audiences, this detail contributes to anchoring *Mustang*'s story in the contemporary Turkey of Erdoğan's unprecedented Islamist regime rather than any seemingly timeless world of cultural tradition. If Ergüven's statements that the film's inspirations come partly from her own childhood memories seem to situate its world in the backward Turkish provinces, she also discusses her worries about how Erdoğan's autocratic regime is changing the "heterogeneous country."[35] Audiences familiar with contemporary Turkish politics can in fact decipher a number of more specific political references. Once more resonant with Kaurismäki's trilogy, it is, not least, the TV that fastens the diegetic world to the twenty-first century, if in a less obtrusive way. Whereas Kaurismäki stages a theatrical clash between highlighted retro objects and equally showcased current events, electronics casually but consistently indicate that *Mustang*'s world is a twenty-first-century world. Less foregrounded—at key moments even off-screen—the film's deployment of media requires us to listen closely to make specific connections.

For example, a brief scene shows Ece binge eating after her engagement, while we hear the voice of Erdoğan, probably on the flat-screen TV we have seen in the house. Here the film uses a quote from his speech at the International Women and Justice Summit in November 2014, according to which feminists "refuse motherhood."[36] Such piecemeal documentary actuality takes on a crucial role in the plot with a dinner scene in which the uncle ardently listens to then deputy prime minister Bülent Arınç's controversial 2014 speech on female chastity.[37] While we see the uncle's keen face, we hear Arınç: "Women must be chaste and pure, know their limits, and mustn't laugh openly in public. . . ." Apparently, this speech triggered a lot of public laughing at the deputy prime minister in the world of social media.[38] In *Mustang*'s diegetic world, Ece develops a counterdiscourse. Her gestural mockery is enjoyed by her younger sisters and seems to be tolerated by the grand-mother. However, when Ece asks, "Can you read between the lines?" and Nur bursts out laughing, the uncle belatedly picks up on their rebellion and orders Ece to leave the table. Momentarily, the sound of a shot indicates her suicide outside. The girls' preceding laughter in the publics facilitated by the film's exhibition awards historical specificity to Ece's shocking death: the fictive event points less to an unbroken tradition of patriarchal domination in the Turkish countryside than to the provincial resonances of a transnational moment of politicized Islam. As indicated, to be sure, this conclusion requires interpretative audience labor: reminiscent of *The White Ribbon*, *Mustang* does not develop its political allusions into a full-fledged critical narrative. We have to draw our own analytical conclusions regarding the interplay of patriarchy and religion, tradition and contemporary politics.

In puzzling together *Mustang*'s layers of meaning, audiences might attribute significance also to details such as the #DirenGezi (#Resist-Gezi) hashtag, which we glimpse when the grandmother opens the closet with the banned items, in conjunction with the fact that in the end Nur and Lale arrive by bus at Istanbul's Taksim Square. An establishing shot affords a view north to Gezi Park, the site of the 2013 resistance against the neoliberal city planning of Erdoğan's government. In the film, the square is scarcely populated, and the course of the narrative has mostly dissolved the five-headed creature through which *Mustang* celebrated resistant physical assembly—although the prior shot showed its remainders: Nur's and Lale's faces and hair together against the bus window. What kind of associations are we invited, or likely, to make? One of the features of the Gezi Park protests that gathered international media attention was their broad coalitional basis, including—along with "regular" neighborhood people, Kurdish and LGBT organizations—Istanbul's generally inimical major soccer teams and their fans. In *Mustang*'s soccer game, the girls cheered for one of these Istanbul teams, Galatasaray SK. An alternative news media documentary on the Gezi protests assembles footage of the soccer fans' rhythmic chanting, clapping, jumping, and marching with shots of group dancing, lines of people passing water bottles, and drone footage of a huge crowd to support the voice-over argument that people of "many different political backgrounds organized together in unprecedented manners."[39] How does such historical footage echo in *Mustang*'s fictional soccer game celebration and, more generally, in its cinematography of collective physical joy?

To avoid misunderstandings, my argument is not that that we should read the film allegorically—straightforwardly from the Gezi angle. Instead, my insistence on the different layers of (diegetic and extradiegetic) context is an effort to heed warnings such as Butler's not to glorify "the ostensible vitality of surging multitudes" as such: "Feeling alive is not quite the same as struggling for a world in which life becomes livable for those who have not yet been valued as living beings."[40] My readings of *Mustang* and the other films featured in these pages have aimed to flesh out such distinctions in mapping associations carefully. At the same time, I have emphasized the forceful productivity of mediatized affect in cinematic processes of reshuffling the sensible toward counterhegemonic reevaluations—and the more egalitarian worlds they allow us to imagine.[41] *Mustang* does not directly tell the story of the Gezi Park uprising. Many nonlocal audience members may not even have picked up on the subtle resonances, and the film's culturalized representations of gendered violence and rebellion have made some critics worry about claiming the film as a work allied with Gezi's political bid to reconfigure "We, the people" against Erdoğan's Islamist, neoliberal nationalism.[42] All of this granted, I do think that *Mustang*'s elliptic aesthetics encourages us to unfold the outlined political allusions. (Their onto-epistemological status is no different from that of the uncle's hideous nighttime activity, of which we also get only minimal glimpses.) While *Mustang* does not tell the story of Gezi as such, its celebration of resistant physicality reads politically in multiple ways.

In showing us a world that unfolds layers once we start looking and listening more closely, *Mustang* certainly presents a fitting concluding example for my methodological plea in this study: the plea to attend to and sharpen our critically imaginative sensorium for the different modes and techniques through which contemporary cinema productively reconfigures affective assemblies of collectivity. *Mustang* also serves as a reminder not to play different worldmaking tactics against one another but to appreciate how they can support each other. The ever more urgent task of opening up hateful and authoritarian assemblies in our world of collective closures cannot forego any of them: the imagination of radically defiant gestures, which I located in Kaurismä-ki's refugee trilogy and (differently) in Ergüven's cinematography of collective affect, needs to be supplemented with a more cautious tracing of the ways in which these gestures operate in layered worldmaking contexts. Simultaneously, the patient following of links and intricate affect assemblages, on which most of my readings of have centered, requires backup with the resistant, provocative energy provided by bold gestures of alternative collective possibility. Perhaps viewerly imagination allows us to see Lale and Nur wildly dance in the next Gezi uprising—or the next Berlin protest march against right-wing hegemony.

Acknowledgments

This book has been in the making for a very long time, and I cannot hope to account anywhere near fully for all the humans (or nonhumans, for that matter) that helped to shape it in so many ways. Most importantly perhaps, the project moved with me from the Midwest to New York and has been equally shaped by two different (if overlapping) worlds—or institutional environments, support networks, and conversations and collaborations with colleagues and friends.

In the Bloomington, Indiana, world, to begin somewhere, Ilana Gershon, Lara Kriegel, Micol Siegel, Stephanie DeBoer, and (within driving radius) Tanja Nusser not only have been wonderful friends but also have read early versions of the introduction and the book prospectus. In my Indiana University home department, I particularly wish to thank Benjamin Robinson and Fritz Breithaupt for our intellectual conspiracies and fights over the years (empathy! complexity!); Bill Rasch for amicable challenges; Johannes Türk for encouraging interest and feedback; Mark Weiner and Susanne Even for friendship; Brigitta Wagner for bringing more cinema into our world; and Jill Giffin for her patience with my occasional lack thereof and her tireless administrative support. Chapter 2 benefited from feedback at the departmental colloquium. Beyond German Studies, I appreciated the opportunity to discuss the project at a Media School brown bag. For exchanges at this occasion and beyond in the vibrant intellectual environment of what was, for most of my time at Indiana, the Department of Communication and Culture, I am grateful to Barb Klinger, Greg Waller, Joan Hawkins, John Lucaites, Jon Simons, Joshua Malitsky, Marissa Moorman, Michael Martin, Ryan Powell, and Tim Bell (along with Ilana and Steph again). Less directly involved with the book, the Gender Studies folks were another crucial part of this world (with particular shout-outs to Brenda Weber, Colin Johnson, Justin R. Garcia, LaMonda Horton-Stallings, Steph Sanders, and Barb Black-Kurdziolek). Around campus and town, I owe so much to many others (not least for the basics: food, housing/home remodeling support, free therapy), including Agnieszka Drobniak, Alex Lichtenstein, David Fischer, Purnima Bose, and Sam DeSollar—and, of course, Ilana, Lara, Micol, Steph DeBoer, and Tanja again. I miss you all.

At Columbia, I am grateful to Andreas Huyssen, Dorothea von Mücke, Jeremy Dauber, Mark Anderson, Oliver Simons, and Stefan Andriopolous and also to Bill Dellinger and Peg Quisenberry for bringing me on board, supporting the move, and welcoming me in so many ways. Beyond the Department of Germanic Languages, I much appreciate having been initiated so quickly into a sometimes overwhelmingly rich transdisciplinary environment, including but not limited to IRWGS/IGS, ICLS, Comparative Media Studies, and the Heyman Center—with particular thanks among others to Eileen Gillooly, Jack Halberstam, Marianne Hirsch, and Noam Elcott. Most directly pertinent to this manuscript, I am very grateful for having had the opportunity to present on this project at both the Sites of Cinema and the Affect Studies university seminars. Particular thanks (for feedback and hosting) to Brian Larkin, Jane Gaines, Lauren Mancia, Nico Baumbach, Patricia Dailey, Rob King, Thomas Dodman, Thomas Elsaesser, Ekin Erkan, and Valeria A. Tsygankova along with Oliver and Stefan once more. New York–based friendship networks are still in the making, but food and hiking should never go unacknowledged: a particular nod to Andrea Krauss, Elisabeth Strowick, Gil Hochberg, and Susan Bernofsky.

No less importantly, I owe a lot to my students at both Indiana and Columbia, whose observations, interpretations, knowledge, and, at moments, unexpected responses reverberate through these pages. In particular, I thank the participants in my Indiana graduate seminars on Intertwining Distanciation and Intensity: Complex Affectscapes in European Independent Cinema (fall 2012), Making Worlds: Form,

Affect, and Narrative in Contemporary European Film (spring 2015), and Collectivity (fall 2016) and the undergraduates in two courses on contemporary cinemas of migration (fall 2014, 2016). In New York, I am thinking of the participants in two semesters of the Berlin-Istanbul seminar (fall 2017, spring 2019) and the joint graduate-undergraduate courses on Postwar German Cinema—one focusing on Feelings (spring 2018) and the other on 21st-Century Transnational Cinema (spring 2019). Some of my former graduate students have become friends and have remained crucial interlocutors. For this book, Olivia Landry has been a particularly important one: a source of intellectual inspiration and specific material references alike. Of my current doctoral students, Hazel Rhodes has had the most in-depth engagement with it all. As my research assistant (and fellow interworld traveler), she has seen the project come together and has provided invaluable, critically appreciative writing feedback at different stages along with style sheet, indexing and tech support toward the end.

In the larger world of North American and European academia, the project has much benefited from the opportunity to present early versions of individual readings as well as theoretical conceptualizations in a number of invited talks: early on, at the Postcolonizing Europe conference in Munich, in Ann Arbor (twice), in Tübingen, at a Contemporary Narrative Theory plenary panel at the Chicago Narrative Society conference, at the Friedrich Schlegel Graduiertenschule as well as the Public Spheres of Resonance conference at the FU Berlin, in Pittsburgh, and at the ZfL Berlin. For inviting, hosting, and critically engaging me, I thank, among others (and very elliptically on all but the most recent events), Andreas Gailus, Ann Cvetkovich, Anne Fleig, Christian von Schewe, Eva Geulen, Frauke Berndt, the German Studies graduate students at the University of Michigan (in 2010 and 2018), Irene Kacandes, Irmela Krüger-Fürhoff, John B. Lyon, Kira Thurman, Kristin Dickinson, Marie-Luise Angerer, Olivia Landry, Peter McIsaac, Randall Halle, Sabine von Dirke, Sue Lanser, Teresa Kovacs, and Tobias Döring. I also thank the (co)organizers of and discussants on a number of conference panels—at GSA 2011 and 2012, ACLA 2012, Narrative 2012, the Affect Theory Conference 2015, SCMS 2016, and MLA 2017—including but not limited to Corina Stan, Gregory J. Seigworth, Heather Love, Hunter Bivens, Lisa Maria Blackman, Katrin Pahl, Marc Silberman, Peter Rehberg,

Shane Denson, and Yi-Ping Ong along with Randall once more. Finally, via electronic exchange, thank you to Dan Yacavone for a generous response to a not-so-generous early citation.

With regard to money and time, my 2015–2016 sabbatical made a crucial contribution to the writing process. I am tempted to underline that it was "fully earned" with regular teaching and service obligations, but I am much aware of the privilege of having held positions in which I qualify for sabbaticals. At Columbia, I also specifically wish to thank Sarah Cole for a book subsidy contribution. At Columbia University Press, I thank Philip Leventhal for his interest, engagement, and feedback throughout the process as well as Monique Briones for logistical support. Sherri Goldecker's careful copyediting was very helpful, as was Ben Kolstad's management of the project. I am also very grateful to James Cahill and the second anonymous reader for their time and (supportive and challenging) comments, which helped me to make the manuscript stronger.

Indicative of the limitations of two world frameworks (with a nod to Leslie Adelson), some of the most important people have not yet been mentioned. I have spent far too little time in the Berlin-centric universe in recent years, but some of you have been part of my life for a long time: Annett Ballschmiede, Christiane Leidinger, Gabriele Mietke, Sonja Klocke, Stefanie Diekmann, and Tanja again. Before everyone else, I remain indebted to my parents, who made it all possible with their love, dreams, and practical sense, and to my sister and her family, including Elisa and Mattis, the coolest niece and nephew in the world. Last but not least, I don't know how I would have gotten it all together without Gregg: your love, faith, and food throughout the daily grind of writing and revising, your patience with the proverbial absent-mindedness and the recurring insistence that Sunday is a workday. Thank you for coming into my world.

Finally, I am grateful for the permission to reprint parts of previously published articles in revised (and reframed) form: "Configuring Affect: Complex Worldmaking in Fatih Akın's *Auf der anderen Seite* (*The Edge of Heaven*)," *Cinema Journal* 54, no. 1 (Fall 2014): 65–87, copyright 2014 by the University of Texas Press, all rights reserved; "Simple Truths, Complex Framings, and Crucial Specifications: Aki Kaurismä-ki's 'Le Havre,' " *Modern Language Notes* 130, no. 3 (April 2015): 506–27,

Notes

INTRODUCTION

1. Döbeln wehrt sich: Meine Stimme gegen Überfremdung (@DLwehrtsich), *Update aus #Clausnitz*, February 18, 2016, video, 0:33, https://www.facebook.com/DLwehrtsich/videos/837057433070266/; see "Clausnitz: Video zeigt rabiates Vorgehen der Polizei," *Zeit Online*, February 19, 2016, sec. Gesellschaft, https://www.zeit.de/politik/deutschland/2016-02/sachsen-clausnitz-fluechtlinge-markus-ulbig.

2. The slogan has been reappropriated by the right-wing Pegida/ movement more generally. See Judith Butler, *Notes Toward a Performative Theory of Assembly* (Cambridge, MA: Harvard University Press, 2015), 3. On this appropriation and the slogan's history see also Richard Herzinger, "Intervention: Ergo totgeschlagen," *Perlentaucher*, September 14, 2019, https://www.perlentaucher.de/intervention/der-ruf-wir-sind-das-volk-ist-in-einer-demokratie-eine-drohung.html.

3. In this sense, my project presents a respectful counteremphasis to recent interventions such as Christina Sharpe's *In the Wake: On Blackness and Being* (Durham, NC: Duke University Press, 2016). Despite essential long-term continuities, including mass-scale incarceration and the everyday possibility of being "killed for simply being black," I do think it is important to underline that "Black death" is a "constitutive aspect of this democracy" (or whatever is left of it) under Trump in a different way than it was under Obama (7, 16).

4. See chapter 1 on how the emergence of now dominant culturalist paradigms can nonetheless be traced back to the 1990s.

5. See, e.g., Kwame Anthony Appiah, *Cosmopolitanism: Ethics in a World of Strangers* (New York: Norton, 2007); Judith Butler, *Precarious Life: The Power of Mourning and Violence* (London: Verso, 2004); Paul Gilroy, *Postcolonial Melancholia* (New York: Columbia University Press, 2005); Nina Glick Schiller and Andrew Irving, eds., *Whose Cosmopolitanism? Critical Perspectives, Relationalities and Discontents* (Oxford: Berghahn, 2014). See chapter 1 for detail on these discussions.

6. See, e.g., Jane Bennett, *Vibrant Matter: A Political Ecology of Things* (Durham, NC: Duke University Press, 2010); Bruno Latour, *Reassembling the Social: An Introduction to Actor-Network-Theory* (Oxford: Oxford University Press, 2005); Brian Massumi, *Parables for the Virtual: Movement, Affect, Sensation* (Durham, NC: Duke University Press, 2002); and critically, Arjun Appadurai, "Mediants, Materiality, Normativity," *Public Culture* 27, no. 2 (2015): 221–37. For detail, see the following sections of this introduction.

7. The diagnosis of the "affective turn" as such is often attributed to Patricia Ticineto Clough, with Jean Halley, eds., *The Affective Turn: Theorizing the Social* (Durham, NC: Duke University Press, 2007). Attesting to its pervasiveness, Eugenie Brinkema even speaks of our twenty-first-century "Episteme of the Affect," with reference to Michel Foucault's notion of an episteme in the sense of a historical a priori grounding the production of knowledge. *The Forms of the Affects* (Durham, NC: Duke University Press, 2014), xi.

8. There has been a vibrant discussion among historians about whether and how the fascism label is or is not appropriate for analyzing contemporary right-wing populisms; see, e.g., Jennifer Evans and Elizabeth Heineman, eds., "Syllabus," New Fascism Syllabus: Exploring the New Right Through Scholarship and Civic Engagement, accessed March 16, 2019, http://www.thehistoryinquestion.com /syllabus/interrogating-the-past/the-syllabus/. I would generally err on the side of caution in using the label, but I do think that there is significant overlap with earlier twentieth-century fascisms regarding authoritarianism, demagogic styles of masculinist leadership, and antipluralist assertions of aggressively exclusionary ideas of the nation.

9. Alain Badiou, "Alain Badiou: Reflections on the Recent Election," *Verso* (blog), November 15, 2016, https://www.versobooks.com/blogs/2940-alain-badiou -reflections-on-the-recent-election; Carolin Emcke, *Gegen den Hass* (Frankfurt am Main: Fischer, 2016), 38–39; see similarly Markus Metz and Georg Seeßlen, *Der Rechtsruck: Skizzen zu einer Theorie des politischen Kulturwandels* (Berlin: Bertz + Fischer, 2018).

10. Firas Alshater, *Wer Sind Diese Deutschen? ZUKAR 01*, January 27, 2016, video, 3:06, https://www.youtube.com/watch?v=ZozLHZFEblY.

11. Alshater's *Wer Sind Diese Deutschen?* cites a resonant 2015 Toronto-based video performance as inspiration; see *I'm a Muslim, I Trust You, Do You Trust*

Me?, M. Remaili, February 7, 2015, video, 2:58, https://www.youtube.com/watch?v=2lvTNjQhO8o.

12. "Berührungsängste." Firas Alshater, *Clausnitzer & Flüchtlingsbaby! Ich Glaubs Nicht! ZUKAR 03 (Der Workshop)*, February 25, 2016, video, 2:39, https://www.youtube.com/watch?v=aCEohihEuiI.

13. Alshater had first explored the cat theme in yet another video made for an anti-hate campaign, shot between the films explored here. Firas Alshater, *Ich Habe Nix Gegen Katzen . . .#YouGeHa2016, ZUKAR Mini 01*, February 5, 2016, video, 2:17, https://www.youtube.com/watch?v=Cp3JGmhLUXc.

14. As detailed below, my investigations overall have some affinity with the larger, 90+-minute formats of cinema. With that caveat, my use of the notion of cinema is intended to include postcinematic aesthetic practices as well as the recognition that contemporary viewing happens across different screen formats and physical locations. See Steven Shaviro, *Postcinematic Affect* (Washington, DC: Zero Books, 2010); Shane Denson and Julia Leyda, "Perspectives on Post-cinema: An Introduction," in *Post-cinema: Theorizing 21st-Century Film*, ed. Shane Denson and Julia Leyda (Falmer: Reframe Books, 2016), 1–18. However, I hold onto the notion of cinema also to foreground the communicative loops of production, distribution, and reception across technologies and platforms, including festivals and awards, professional review, and fan practices (for their significance to my endeavor, see the section on nonsovereign agency). Alternatingly, I use the notion of *film* in an inclusive sense. Many of the works discussed in subsequent chapters have been shot in nondigital formats, and I attend to these formats for how they contribute to the making of specific cinematic worlds, but my focus is on aesthetic composition and reception more than media specificity.

15. Jacques Rancière, *Dissensus: On Politics and Aesthetics*, ed. and trans. Steven Corcoran (London: Continuum, 2010), 36.

16. See L. A. Alexander, *Fictional Worlds: Traditions in Narrative and the Age of Visual Culture* (Charleston, SC: Createspace Independent Publishing Platform, 2013); Alice Bell and Marie-Laure Ryan, eds., *Possible Worlds Theory and Contemporary Narratology* (Lincoln: University of Nebraska Press, 2019); Marta Boni, ed., *World Building: Transmedia, Fans, Industries* (Amsterdam: Amsterdam University Press, 2017); Pheng Cheah, *What Is a World?* (Durham, NC: Duke University Press), 2016; Mari Hatavara et al., eds., *Narrative Theory, Literature, and New Media: Narrative Minds and Virtual Worlds* (New York: Routledge, 2016); Eric Hayot, *On Literary Worlds* (New York: Oxford University Press, 2012); Bo Pettersson, *How Literary Worlds Are Shaped: A Comparative Poetics of Literary Imagination* (Berlin: de Gruyter, 2018); Marie-Laure Ryan and Jan-Noël Thon, eds., *Storyworlds Across Media: Towards a Media-Conscious Narratology* (Lincoln: University of Nebraska Press, 2014);

Mark J. P. Wolf, ed., *Revisiting Imaginary Worlds: A Subcreation Studies Anthology* (New York: Routledge, 2016).

17. Daniel Yacavone, *Film Worlds: A Philosophical Aesthetics of Cinema* (New York: Columbia University Press, 2015). See also Alberto Baracco, *Hermeneutics of the Film World: A Ricoeurian Method for Film Interpretation* (New York: Palgrave Macmillan, 2017).

18. Yacavone, *Film Worlds*, 40.

19. On the Spinoza connection in Deleuzian approaches, see, e.g., Gregory J. Seigworth and Melissa Gregg, "An Inventory of Shimmers," in *The Affect Theory Reader*, ed. Melissa Gregg and Gregory J. Seigworth (Durham, NC: Duke University Press, 2010), 3. Cognitive worldmaking concepts variously draw on Nelson Goodman's *Ways of Worldmaking* (Indianapolis: Hackett, 1978), possible worlds theory, and classical and postclassical narratology. In the last field, see Monika Fludernik, Towards a "Natural" Narratology (London: Routledge, 1996); Marie-Laure Ryan, *Narrative as Virtual Reality: Immersion and Interactivity in Literature and Electronic Media* (Baltimore: Johns Hopkins University Press, 2001); David Herman, *Basic Elements of Narrative* (Oxford: Wiley-Blackwell, 2009), and David Herman, *Storytelling and the Sciences of Mind* (Cambridge, MA: MIT University Press, 2013). While Yacavone's model is also syncretic, Deleuzian notions of worlding do not play a significant role for him.

20. Phenomenology is itself multiple. Important reference points for recent work include Martin Heidegger, Hannah Arendt, and Maurice Merleau-Ponty. On Heidegger, see, e.g., Cheah, *What Is a World?*; on Arendt, see, e.g., Annamarie Jagose, "Queer World Making: Annamarie Jagose Interviews Michael Warner," *Genders* 31 (2000), https://www.colorado.edu/gendersarchive1998-2013/2000/05/01/queer-world-making-annamarie-jagose-interviews-michael-warne; on Merleau-Ponty, see, e.g., Sara Ahmed, *Queer Phenomenology* (Durham, NC: Duke University Press, 2006); Vivian Sobchack, *The Address of the Eye: A Phenomenology of Film Experience* (Princeton, NJ: Princeton University Press, 1992); and Laura U. Marks, *The Skin of the Film: Intercultural Cinema, Embodiment, and the Senses* (Durham, NC: Duke University Press, 2000), who also draws on Gilles Deleuze. Cognitive scholars have explored intersections with phenomenology, while Deleuzians and new materialists often distance themselves from phenomenology for its focus on humans and consciousness. For the former, see, e.g., Carl Plantinga, *Moving Viewers: American Film and the Spectator's Experience* (Berkeley: University of California Press, 2009); Robert Sinnerbrink, *Cinematic Ethics: Exploring Ethical Experience Through Film* (New York: Routledge, 2016); for the latter, see, e.g., Bennett, *Vibrant Matter*, 30. For alternatives, c.f. Marks, *The Skin*, and Mark B. N. Hansen, *Feed-Forward: On the Future of Twenty-First Century Media* (Chicago: University of Chicago Press, 2015). Less central to my

project are Stanley Cavell's cinematic worlds with their inspirations in Ludwig Wittgenstein in addition to Heidegger; see *The World Viewed*, enl. ed. (Cambridge, MA: Harvard University Press, 1979).

21. For the increasing reception of Latour in literary studies, see, e.g., David Alworth, *Site Reading: Fiction, Art, Social Form* (Princeton, NJ: Princeton University Press, 2016); Yves Citton, "Fictional Attachments and Literary Weavings in the Anthropocene," *New Literary History* 47, no. 2–3 (Spring/Summer 2016): 309–29, https://doi.org/10.1353/nlh.2016.0016; Rita Felski, *The Limits of Critique* (Chicago: University of Chicago Press, 2015); Stephen Muecke and Rita Felski, eds., "Recomposing the Humanities—with Bruno Latour," special issue, *New Literary History* 47, no. 2–3 (Spring/Summer 2016); Elizabeth S. Anker and Rita Felski, eds., *Critique and Postcritique* (Durham, NC: Duke University Press, 2017); Heather Love, "Close But Not Deep," *New Literary History* 41, no. 2 (2010): 371–91, http://doi.org/10.1353/nlh.2010.0007; Matthew Mullins, *Postmodernism in Pieces: Materializing the Social in U.S. Fiction* (Oxford: Oxford University Press, 2016). In media studies, see, e.g., Georg Kneer, Markus Schroer, and Erhard Schüttpelz, eds., *Bruno Latours Kollektive* (Frankfurt am Main: Suhrkamp, 2008); Lorenz Engell, Joseph Vogl, and Bernhard Siegert, eds., *Agenten und Agenturen* (Weimar: Verlag der Bauhaus-Universität Weimar, 2008); Ilka Becker, Michael Cuntz, and Astrid Kusser, *Unmenge: Wie verteilt sich Handlungsmacht?* Mediologie 16 (Munich: Fink, 2008). In cinema studies, see Joshua Malitsky, "A Certain Explicitness: Objectivity, History, and the Documentary Self," *Cinema Journal* 50, no. 3 (2011): 26–44; Ilana Gershon and Joshua Malitsky, "Actor-Network-Theory and Documentary Studies," *Studies in Documentary Film* 4, no. 1 (2010): 65–78; and, more recently, Jerome P. Schaefer, *An Edgy Realism: Film Theoretical Encounters with Dogma 95, New French Extremity, and the Shaky-Cam Horror Film* (Cambridge: Cambridge Scholars Publishing, 2015); Eric Herhuth, "The Politics of Animation and the Animation of Politics," *Animation: An Interdisciplinary Journal* 11, no. 1 (March 1, 2016): 4–22; and my own contributions: Claudia Breger, "Cruel Attachments, Tender Counterpoints: Configuring the Collective in Michael Haneke's *The White Ribbon*," *Discourse: Journal for Theoretical Studies in Media and Culture* 38, no. 2 (2016): 142–72; Claudia Breger, "Cinematic Assemblies: Latour and Film Studies," in *Latour and the Humanities*, ed. Rita Felski and Stephen Muecke (Baltimore: Johns Hopkins University Press, forthcoming).

22. David Bordwell, *Poetics of Cinema* (New York: Routledge, 2008), 90, 110–11 (Bordwell's emphasis).

23. Bordwell, *Poetics*, 111.

24. Bordwell foregrounds audience activity, but see *Poetics*, 123 (and the following pages) on the filmmaker side. More forcefully on filmmaker intention, see, e.g., Noël Carroll, *The Philosophy of Motion Pictures* (Malden, MA: Blackwell,

2008): 157. In intermedial narratology, see Herman's focus on the intentional dimensions of worldmaking in *Storytelling and the Sciences of Mind*. Plantinga attempts a more balanced approach; see *Moving Viewers*, 54–57.

25. Plantinga, *Moving Viewers*, 9.

26. See, e.g., Carroll, *Philosophy*, 134; Gregory Currie, *Image and Mind: Film, Philosophy and Cognitive Science* (Cambridge: Cambridge University Press, 1995). In Steven Shaviro's polemical summary, cognitivists privilege the "normal" over "any form of deviation, mutation or invention." "The Cinematic Body Redux," *Parallax* 14, no. 1 (2008): 51. This is a bit harsh. Plantinga's cognitive-perceptual approach and Bordwell's interests in historical poetics make for significantly more complexity, short of abandoning the outlined foci. See, e.g., Bordwell, *Poetics*, 32, 50–51, 110–20; Plantinga, *Moving Viewers*, 44, 78. Of particular interest to my modeling is Bordwell's use of the notion of worldmaking for a contemporary aesthetic trend—see chapter 1.

27. Plantinga, *Moving Viewers*, 31.

28. Massumi, *Parables*, 28; Brian Massumi, *The Power at the End of the Economy* (Durham, NC: Duke University Press, 2015), 105.

29. Massumi, *Parables*, 28. The underlying definitions of affect vs. emotion are quite similar in Deleuzian and cognitive approaches but with opposite inflections: cognitive approaches privilege the "higher" functions of "emotions proper" instead of (biologically bound) affect. Carroll, *Philosophy*, 151; less categorically, see Plantinga, *Moving Viewers*, 29; Yacavone, *Film Worlds*, 165. Importantly, the affect-emotion polarization is not without alternatives in the Deleuzian tradition. Although Brian Massumi's early contrastive definition has remained influential (as indicated by its reappearance in *The Power*, 105), he provides less polarizing wordings in interviews. See *Politics of Affect* (Malden, MA: Polity, 2015). Deleuze did not oppose affect to the social as clearly. See Marie-Luise Angerer, *Vom Begehren nach dem Affekt* (Zurich: Diaphanes, 2007), 66.

30. Seigworth and Gregg, "An Inventory of Shimmers," 3; Massumi, *The Power*, 14.

31. Steven Shaviro, *The Cinematic Body* (Minneapolis: University of Minnesota Press, 1993), 3, 4, 5, 9.

32. Massumi, *Parables*, 28, 27.

33. Massumi, *The Power*, 66. According to Massumi, only "a trial-and-error approach" can solve the problem of how to mobilize affect politically "without fostering a fascism" (94). I believe we need better answers.

34. Brinkema, *The Forms*, xiii, xiv. For an early critique of the move beyond ideology and signification in affect studies, see Ruth Leys, "The Turn to Affect: A Critique," *Critical Inquiry* 37, no. 3 (2011): 434–72; in cinema studies more recently, Nico Baumbach, *Cinema/Politics/Philosophy* (New York: Columbia University Press, 2019), 6. The insistence on "immediacy" is exemplified by Shaviro's theory

of cinematic perception. *The Cinematic Body*, 25. With Deleuze and Félix Guattari, Shaviro does acknowledge mediation as a necessary condition of *natural* perception but claims that images "on the screen are violently torn away from any external horizon or context." *The Cinematic Body*, 28. Instead, my model traces precisely the multitude of (affective, associative, etc.) links in operation also in the cinema.

35. Kathleen Stewart, "Afterword: Worlding Refrains," in Gregg and Seigworth, *The Affect Theory Reader*, 342; Massumi, *The Power*, 107–8. While the pervasive antinarrative rhetoric reflects lingering (post)modernist inflections across the humanities, Massumi's plea for "a semiotics willing to engage with continuity" and his definition of "change" as that "which includes rupture but is nevertheless continuous" resonate with my notion of narrative. *Parables*, 4, 51.

36. Seigworth and Gregg, "An Inventory of Shimmers," 3 (emphasis removed), 11.

37. Latour probes the notion of world-building as an alternative to Goodman's (primarily symbolic and arguably voluntarist) world*making*, although he uses the latter notion as well. *Reassembling*, 24–25; see, e.g., 57, 103. The notion of "worlding" as such is rare in Latour's texts (see, however, Bruno Latour, *Down to Earth: Politics in the New Climatic Regime*, trans. Catherine Porter [Cambridge: Polity, 2018], 12, 54, with reference to Donna Haraway), but Latour has long emphasized ontology as a corrective to primarily symbolic accounts. See, e.g., Bruno Latour, *An Inquiry Into Modes of Existence* (Cambridge, MA: Harvard University Press, 2013), 19–20. Importantly, both world and knowledge are "articulated." *An Inquiry*, 87; see 93–95, 144–46 on mediation; see also Bruno Latour, *Pandora's Hope: Essays on the Reality of Science Studies* (Cambridge, MA: Harvard University Press, 1999), 69.

38. Sara Ahmed, *The Cultural Politics of Emotion* (Edinburgh: Edinburgh University Press, 2004), 7, 12.

39. Ahmed, *The Cultural Politics*, 13.

40. Sobchack, *The Address*, xvii.

41. Gilles Deleuze speaks of "recollection-images, dream-images and world images." *Cinema 2: The Time-Image*, trans. Hugh Tomlinson and Robert Galeta (Minneapolis: University of Minnesota Press, 1989), 68.

42. For similarly less categorical distinctions between affect and emotion, see Sianne Ngai, *Ugly Feelings* (Cambridge, MA: Harvard University Press, 2005), 27; Ann Cvetkovich, *Depression: A Public Feeling* (Durham, NC: Duke University Press, 2012), 4. Of course, it is sometimes useful to specify phenomena on different points of this spectrum through the conventional terminologies of affect and emotion. The inclusion of the *un*conscious in my definition reflects the belief that we do not need to move beyond psychoanalysis as radically as suggested by both Deleuzian and cognitive theorists (see chapter 2). Syncretic perspectives

are also developed by Ahmed and Lauren Berlant, even as they disagree on terminology: Ahmed's interest in subjectivity and historicity makes her opt for the notion of "emotion," while Lauren Berlant distances herself from it. See Lauren Berlant, *Cruel Optimism* (Durham, NC: Duke University Press, 2011), 12–13. However, Ahmed's use of the notion differs from neuroscientific concepts by emphasizing many of the features I find productive in concepts of affect, including the insistence on instability along with capture and attachment. *The Cultural Politics*, 6, 11–12.

43. On cuteness, see Sianne Ngai, *Our Aesthetic Categories: Zany, Cute, Interesting* (Cambridge, MA: Harvard University Press, 2012).

44. In Deleuze's writings, the notion of assemblage describes the work of cinematic montage as the "composition, the assemblage [*agencement*] of movement images" but also more generally the process of making complex, multiple connections between "interwoven forces" or always already entangled heterogeneous elements. See Gilles Deleuze, *Cinema 1: The Movement-Image*, trans. Hugh Tomlinson (London: Athlone Press, 1986), 30, 70; Jasbir Puar, "Queer Times, Queer Assemblages," *Social Text* 23, no. 3–4 (2005): 121–39. Deleuze's specification that "assemblages" include "states of things, bodies, various combinations of bodies, hodgepodges" along with "utterances, modes of expression, and whole regimes of signs" further counteracts the oppositional mappings of "bodies/affect vs. signification" that have marked some of his work and its reception in affect studies. Gilles Deleuze, "Eight Years Later: 1980 Interview," in *Two Regimes of Madness: Texts and Interviews 1975–1995*, ed. David Lapoujade and trans. Ames Hodges and Mike Taormina (New York: Semiotext(e), 2006): 177.

45. My insistence on communication and rhetoric may still raise eyebrows. Bordwell protests against a notion of communication as "the transmission of an idea or concept from mind to mind," although he accepts that cinema presents an "experience of *representations*." *Poetics*, 124. My use of the notion of communication is closer to the latter idea than to that of conceptual transmission, and "rhetoric" for me designates processes of affective-semiotic mediation exceeding intentional design.

46. See Brinkema, *The Forms*, xiii–xiv, 37 (Brinkema's emphasis); see, e.g., 25, 36, 46. In stripping away all those dimensions, Brinkema's own readings at moments return us to the (negative, interruptive) motifs her initial discussion problematizes so convincingly.

47. Specifically, he brings together Goodman's symbolic-constructivist concept and more recent cognitive work with Mikel Dufrenne and, to a lesser degree, with Hans-Georg Gadamer and Paul Ricoeur. The intersection between phenomenology and hermeneutics has been further fleshed out by Baracco, *Hermeneutics*, 2017.

48. Yacavone, *Film Worlds*, 16, 230.

49. Yacavone, *Film Worlds*, 195–96, 230–31. In literary theory, the interest in totality has also had a comeback. See, e.g., Hayot, *On Literary Worlds*, 44.

50. For example, Marie-Laure Ryan stipulates that "fictional texts do not share their reference worlds with other texts." "Postmodernism and the Doctrine of Panfictionality," *Narrative* 5, no. 2 (1997): 167. More recent rhetorical conceptualizations emphasize that fictional discourse "is not making referential claims." Henrik Skov Nielsen, James Phelan, and Richard Walsh, "Ten Theses About Fictionality," *Narrative* 23, no. 1 (2015): 61–73, 68.

51. See Ryan, "Postmodernism," for a critique of postmodern scholarship's tendency to dissolve this distinction.

52. The quote is from Rancière, *Dissensus*, 141. I develop the notion of piecemeal reference with Ricoeur and Latour. On literary fiction, see Claudia Breger, "Affects in Configuration: A New Approach to Narrative Worldmaking," *Narrative* 25, no. 2 (May 2017): 227–51; on film, see chapter 4.

53. Yacavone, *Film Worlds*, 214, 219. Yacavone qualifies that the "single" author "personality" projected by a film world is not to be equated with the empirical director.

54. See Firas Alshater, "It's Not My Dream Job, However, to Be a Refugee: An Interview with Firas Alshater," interview by Ulla Brunner, trans. Goethe-Institut Brüssel, Goethe-Institut, August 2016, https://www.goethe.de/en/kul/med/20819516 .html; also Firas Alshater, *Ich komm auf Deutschland zu: Ein Syrer über seine neue Heimat* (Berlin: Ullstein extra, 2016), 197.

55. Latour, *Reassembling*, 77; see 63–74; Gershon and Malitsky, "Actor-Network-Theory," on the sun rays and microphones. See also in the section "Following the Actors" on Sobchack's phenomenological notion of film's nonhuman/human-like agency as developed against apparatus theories. Philosophically, the agency and even the perspective and experience of nonhumans have been further explored in new materialism and speculative realism. See Bennett, *Vibrant Matter*; Steven Shaviro, *The Universe of Things: On Speculative Realism* (Minneapolis: University of Minnesota Press, 2015).

56. Drawing on Latour among others, Bennett speaks of "*distributive*" agency. *Vibrant Matter*, 21 (Bennett's emphasis). She includes "the human narrator" in her list of things that make up actant assemblages (22). Gershon and Malitsky describe Latour's theory as "fundamentally a theory of relationality." "Actor-Network-Theory," 66.

57. Latour, *Reassembling*, 43.

58. Latour, *Reassembling*, 45 (Latour's emphases).

59. Latour, *Reassembling*, 44–45.

60. On collective reception, see Marks, *The Skin*, 62–65.

61. See, e.g., Lorenz Engell, "Eyes Wide Shut. Die Agentur des Lichts—Szenen kinematographischer verteilter Handlungsmacht," in *Unmenge—Wie verteilt sich*

Handlungsmacht?, ed. Ilka Becker, Michael Kuntz, and Astrid Kusser (Munich: Fink, 2008), 75–92. Critically, on the overemphasis on nonhumans, see Appadurai, "Mediants."

62. Butler describes the human as an "agentic creature." *Notes*, 44. Hansen develops part-resonant ideas from a media-theoretical angle. *Feed-Forward*. But as I would emphasize, humans' networked nature predates Facebook and Siri.

63. For resonant readings of Latour, see, in particular, Felski, *The Limits*; Anker and Felski, *Critique and Postcritique*. In line with Deleuzians, Latour has distanced himself from phenomenology due to its traditional foci on consciousness and "human intentionality." *Pandora's Hope*, 9. However, contemporary phenomenologies provide alternatives. See, e.g., Marks, *The Skin*, 150, 152. Beyond film studies, see Ahmed's and Eve K. Sedgwick's postclassical phenomenologies and Hansen's call for "reinventing phenomenology." *Feed-Forward*, 26. See Ahmed, *Queer Phenomenology* and *The Cultural Politics of Emotion*; Eve K. Sedgwick, *Touching Feeling: Affect, Pedagogy, Performativity* (Durham, NC: Duke University Press, 2003).

64. Latour, *Reassembling*, 161, 236 (Latour's emphasis).

65. See Nathalie Karagiannis and Peter Wagner, "Introduction: Globalization or Worldmaking?," in *Varieties of Worldmaking: Beyond Globalization*, ed. Nathalie Karagiannis and Peter Wagner (Liverpool: Liverpool University Press, 2007), 3; Hannah Arendt, *The Human Condition* (Chicago: University of Chicago Press, 1998)

66. Arendt, *Human Condition*, 184. I thus disagree with Cheah's charge that Arendt effectively reintroduces "the sovereignty of human self-determination." Cheah, *What Is a World?*, 139. On her break with Heidegger over questions of agency and politics, see Arendt, *Human Condition*, 96.

67. Arendt, *Human Condition*, 184.

68. In what she describes as a "vulgarization" of Heidegger's notion, Gayatri Chakravorty Spivak reminds us that "worlding" can be a force of imperialism. "Three Women's Texts and a Critique of Imperialism," *Critical Inquiry* 12, no. 1 (Autumn 1985): 243, 260. See Alshater, *Ich komm*, e.g., 182–86, 197–98, and in the next section on the mixed reception of the *Workshop* video.

69. Arendt, *Human Condition*, 5. Heidegger and contemporary approaches drawing on him (sometimes via Jacques Derrida) leave little room for human agency. Underlining that worlding "exceeds all human calculations," Cheah instead emphasizes the world-opening power of the "inhuman gift of time." *What Is a World?*, 8, 14; see 11. I find this eschatological perspective very unsatisfying and instead foreground concrete affective transformations—yesterday, today, tomorrow.

70. Berlant, *Cruel Optimism*, 97–98.

71. See Arendt, *Human Condition*, 2; critically, see, e.g., Kelly Oliver, *Earth and World: Philosophy After the Apollo Missions* (New York: Columbia University Press, 2015), 74, 85. Latour would take issue, for example, with Arendt's claim

that action "goes on directly between men without the intermediary of things or matter." Arendt, *Human Condition*, 7. But see also, e.g., Arendt, *Human Condition*, 183, for an acknowledgment of continuity between action and the world of things, speech, and the body.

72. Oliver, *Earth and World*, 112; see also Cheah, *What Is a World?* From my angle, Heidegger is a poor guide toward more contemporary perspectives also insofar as he is the source of Arendt's anthropocentric distinctions: he speaks of the "worldless" stone and the animal "poor in world." Martin Heidegger, *Der Ursprung des Kunstwerkes* (Stuttgart: Reclam, 1960), 41.

73. Cheah separates Heidegger's philosophy from his politics, charging diverging evaluations with a "sociological-historical deterministic view of philosophy." *What Is a World?*, 134. I disagree: we can specify conceptual resonances without drawing deterministic conclusions. Bruno Latour, for his part, distances himself from Heidegger's investments in immediacy, intuition, and a nature conceptually opposed to culture. "Why Has Critique Run Out of Steam," *Critical Inquiry* 30, no. 2 (2004): 233.

74. Latour, *Reassembling*, 254. In his new work, *Down to Earth*, he reiterates his commitment to a "*common world*"—a world, he insists, abandoned by "the ruling classes" (2; Latour's emphases). In the face of Trump's election, Latour rearticulates his worldmaking project here as that of uncoupling attachments to the earth from the "return to identity and the defense of borders" (2, 92).

75. On Heidegger, see Oliver, *Earth and World*, 22. Oliver's own notion of world remains perhaps too close to the idea of distinct cultural traditions, as indicated by her "guiding question": "How can we share the earth with those with whom we do not even share a world?" (4).

76. Latour, *Reassembling*, 45.

77. Latour, *Reassembling*, 254.

78. Thus, he acknowledges inspirations in narrative theory and compares his "world-building enterprise" to the "construction sites" of film production as well as aesthetic practice more generally. Latour, *Reassembling*, 103; see 55, 88–89. See also Latour, *An Inquiry*, for a fuller engagement of different disciplinary modes and contexts, including fiction; on writing and textuality, see Bruno Latour, "Life Among Conceptual Characters," *New Literary History* 47, no. 2–3 (Spring/Summer 2016): 463–76; on Latour as an artist, see Francis Halsall, "Actor-Network Aesthetics: The Conceptual Rhymes of Bruno Latour and Contemporary Art," *New Literary History* 47, no. 2–3 (Spring/Summer 2016): 439–61; on Latour's work specifically with film and filmmakers, see David D., "Bruno Latour's Artistic Practices: Writing, Products and Influence," *Toronto Film Review* (blog), February 5, 2016, http://torontofilmreview.blogspot.com/2016/02/bruno -latours-artistic-practices.html.

79. Latour, *Reassembling*, 14 (Latour's emphasis), 227.

80. Latour, *Reassembling*, 12; see Latour, "Why Has Critique"; and on "care and caution," see *Pandora's Hope*, 288.

81. Latour, *Reassembling* 103; see 5.

82. On collective emergence, see Marks, *The Skin*, 55.

83. With reference to Latour's call for abandoning the modernist ethos of distanced critique, see, in particular, Felski, *The Limits*; Anker and Felski, *Critique and Postcritique*; and Muecke and Felski, "Recomposing the Humanities." Other crucial reference points for these discussions on postcritical reading include Sedgwick's call for "reparative" instead of "paranoid" epistemologies in *Touching Feeling*, 145; the discussions on "surface" vs. "symptomatic" reading and new practices of description in Stephen Best and Sharon Marcus, "Surface Reading: An Introduction," *Representations* 108, no. 1 (2009): 1–21, with reference to Jameson, https://doi.org/10.1525/rep.2009.108.1.1; Heather Love, "Close but Not Deep: Literary Ethics and the Descriptive Turn," *New Literary History* 41, no. 2 (2010): 371–91, http://doi.org/10.1353/nlh.2010.0007; and Sharon Marcus, Heather Love, and Stephen Best, "Building a Better Description," *Representations* 135, no. 1 (2016): 1–21.

84. Shaviro, *The Cinematic Body*, 10. Shaviro's postcritical stance resonates with Massumi's dictum that affect is "resistant to critique" and his call for more "*affirmative* methods." Massumi, *Parables*, 28, 12 (Massumi's emphasis).

85. Sobchack, *The Address*, 263, xviii.

86. Sobchack, *The Address*, 22.

87. Marks, *The Skin*, xi. On synesthesia, see also Sobchack, *The Address*, 76–77, and, more recently, Jennifer M. Barker, *The Tactile Eye: Touch and the Cinematic Experience* (Berkeley: University of California Press, 2009).

88. See Felski, *The Limits*, 176, with reference to Marielle Macé.

89. On empathy and sympathy, see, e.g., Murray Smith, "Altered States: Character and Emotional Response in the Cinema," *Cinema Journal* 33, no. 4 (1994): 34–56; Plantinga, *Moving Viewers*. Sympathy features (differently) in Massumi's work also (see chapter 3).

90. Alshater generally takes pride in reaching out to different audiences, and the initial hugging video did prompt articulations of respect from self-identified antirefugee viewers. See Kate Connolly, "Firas Alshater: The YouTube Star Who Became Germany's Most Hugged Refugee," *The Guardian*, March 20, 2016, sec. World News, https://www.theguardian.com/world/2016/mar/20/firas-alshater-interview-youtube-zukar-refugee; Alshater, *Ich Komm*, 182. The online comments on the *Workshop* video, however, show a split between largely enthusiastic fans (occasionally using strong anti-Nazi rhetoric) and opponents ranting against refugees; one viewer specifically critiques the video for a double standard in fighting prejudices against "foreigners" with other prejudices. Alshater, *Clausnitzer & Flüchtlingsbaby!*

91. My respective disagreement with Felski is part terminological: I do not equate all "critique" with the negative "hermeneutics of suspicion," while I embrace much of Felski's counterproposal, including the Latourian emphasis on (re)*con*figuration over "*deconstruction.*" Felski, *The Limits*, 2, 17; on the hermeneutics of suspicion, see Paul Ricoeur, *The Rule of Metaphor* (Toronto: University of Toronto Press, 1978), 285. Latour modifies his own critique of critique, suggesting, for example, that we aim for "critical proximity" instead of "critical distance." *Reassembling*, 253.

92. See Lauren Berlant on "dedramatizing the performance of critical and political judgement" by way of such slowing down. "Starved," in *After Sex? On Writing Since Queer Theory*, ed. Janet Halley and Andrew Parker (Durham, NC: Duke University Press, 2011), 80.

93. Latour introduces these vectors as the two methodological moves of "Localizing the Global" and "Redistributing the Local." See *Reassembling*, 173, 191. He polemicizes against context(ualization) as a mode of large-scale reductive social explanation (173). However, see Heather Love for a defense of the category using the work of Donna Haraway, on whom Latour draws. "The Temptations: Donna Haraway, Feminist Objectivity, and the Problem of Critique," in Anker and Felski, *Critique and Postcritique*, 56–57.

94. Latour, *An Inquiry*, 8.

95. See, e.g., Mark Lilla, "The Liberal Crackup," *Wall Street Journal*, August 11, 2017, sec. Life, https://www.wsj.com/articles/the-liberal-crackup-1502456857.

96. This paragraph is in dialogue with in part more critically weighted assessments in Muecke and Felski's coedited special issue on "Recomposing the Humanities."

97. I am thinking of cognitive preferences for measurement evidence but also, e.g., Franco Moretti's quantitative methods. See *Distant Reading* (London: Verso, 2013).

98. See Latour, *An Inquiry*, on the contours of such inquiry within and across academic domains and chapter 4 on real and imagined worlds.

99. On the effects of globalization on European film production, distribution, and exhibition since the 1990s, see Randall Halle, *German Film After Germany* (Champaign: University of Illinois Press, 2008); on the shifting and contested borders of Europe, see Halle, 6; on Europe as an overlapping of geographical categories at the intersection of postcolonial flows, see Etienne Balibar, "The Borders of Europe," in *Cosmopolitics: Thinking and Feeling Beyond the Nation*, ed. Pheng Cheah and Bruce Robbins (Minneapolis: University of Minnesota Press, 1998), 225.

100. On these debates, see, e.g., Lúcia Nagib, Chris Perriam, and Rajinder Dudrah, eds., *Theorizing World Cinema* (London: Tauris, 2012); also, Steven Rawle, *Transnational Cinema: An Introduction* (London: Red Globe Press, 2018), 1.

101. Aihwa Ong, *Flexible Citizenship: The Cultural Logics of Transnationality* (Durham, NC: Duke University Press, 1999), 4; Tim Bergfelder, "Love Beyond the Nation: Cosmopolitanism and Transnational Desire in Cinema," in *Europe and Love in Cinema*, ed. Jo Labanyi, Luisa Passerini, and Karen Diehl (New York: Intellect, 2012), 61; on scale, see Rawle, *Transnational Cinema*, 15, and on the debates, see Nagib, Perriab, and Dudrah, *Theorizing World Cinema*. Bergfelder acknowledges the outlined use while critiquing some of the effectively reessentializing uses of the notion of transnationalism.

102. See Halle, *German Film After Germany*, 7.

103. On interculturality, see Marks, *The Skin*, 6, 9; on transnationalism as emphasizing these contingencies, see, e.g., Young-sun Hong, "The Challenge of Transnational History," forum post, *H-German Discussion Network*, H-Net, January 19, 2006, https://lists.h-net.org/cgi-bin/logbrowse.pl?trx=lm&list=H-German.

104. On this danger, see Halle, *German Film After Germany*, 8.

105. On the transcontinental inspirations of European modernisms, see, e.g., Kobena Mercer, "Diaspora Aesthetics and Visual Culture," in *Black Cultural Traffic: Crossroads in Global Performance and Popular Culture*, ed. Harry J. Elam Jr. and Kennell Jackson (Ann Arbor: University of Michigan Press, 2005), 146. Specifically on New German Cinema in relation to not only the French New Wave but also the Brazilian Cinema Novo, see, e.g., Lúcia Nagib, *World Cinema and the Ethics of Realism* (New York: Continuum, 2011), chap. 2.

106. On contemporary European cinema as transnational and world cinema, see also, e.g., Isolina Ballesteros, *Immigration Cinema in the New Europe* (Bristol: Intellect, 2015); Daniela Berghahn and Claudia Sternberg, eds., *European Cinema in Motion: Migrant and Diasporic Film in Contemporary Europe* (New York: Palgrave Macmillan, 2010); Yosefa Loshitzky, *Screening Strangers: Migration and Diaspora in Contemporary European Cinema* (Bloomington: Indiana University Press, 2010).

107. Karagiannis and Wagner, "Introduction: Globalization or Worldmaking?," 3, 8.

108. On the planetary as an alternative to expansionist globalization, see Gilroy, *Postcolonial Melancholia*, 75, 79.

109. In Rancière's words, "strategies of critical clash" have been displaced by those of "testimony, archive and documentation," oriented at restoring "a certain sense of community." *Dissensus*, 145–46.

110. Massumi, *The Power*, 37.

111. Deleuze, *Cinema 2*, 216.

112. Deleuze, *Cinema 2*, 216.

113. Marks, *The Skin*, 55, with reference to Deleuze.

114. Deleuze, *Cinema 2*, 215 (Deleuze's emphasis).

115. Latour, *Reassembling*, 133.

116. Gerda Roelvink, *Building Dignified Worlds: Geographies of Collective Action* (Minneapolis: University of Minnesota Press, 2016), 6.

117. Latour, *Reassembling*, 45.

1. AFFECTS IN CONFIGURATION: CONTROVERSY AND CONVIVIALITY IN FATIH AKIN'S *THE EDGE OF HEAVEN* AND ASGHAR FARHADI'S *A SEPARATION*

1. Samuel P. Huntington, "The Clash of Civilizations," *Foreign Affairs* 72, no. 3 (Summer 1993): 22–49, https://doi.org/10.2307/20045621.

2. See, e.g., Graham Huggan, "Perspectives on Postcolonial Europe," *Journal of Postcolonial Writing* 44, no. 3 (2008): 241–49; Arjun Appadurai, *Modernity at Large: Cultural Dimensions of Globalization* (Minneapolis: University of Minnesota Press, 1996); Paul Gilroy, *Postcolonial Melancholia* (New York: Columbia University Press, 2005). In the German context referenced in the first half of this chapter, this hope was supported by the important reform of the citizenship law effective in 2000: now, finally, children born in the country to long-term residents would grow up as citizens. See, e.g., Deniz Göktürk, David Gramling, and Anton Kaes, "Introduction: A German Dream?," in *Germany in Transit: Nation and Immigration 1955–2005*, ed. Deniz Göktürk, David Gramling, and Anton Kaes (Berkeley: University of California Press, 2007), 4.

3. The "postsecular" is a constitutive component of European modernity. See Hent de Vries, "Introduction: Before, Around, and Beyond the Theologico-Political," in *Political Theologies: Public Religions in a Post-secular World*, ed. Hent de Vries and Lawrence E. Sullivan (New York: Fordham University Press, 2006), 2–3, 7. Without implying that European modernity was ever purely secular, my historicizing use of the term foregrounds recent shifts in discursive, institutional, perceptive, and material practices. This includes the ways in which German Turks and British Pakistanis have been relabeled as Muslims, the frequency of official recourse to religious tradition, and the defringing of right-wing populism in alliance with major Christian churches (see, e.g., Norbert Blech, "Der Anti-Gender Aufstand: Der neue gemeinsame Kampf von christlichen Aktivisten und Neurechten gegen Aufklärung und Emanzipation" [working paper, Deutsche Aidshilfe, *Magazin.hiv*, August 2016, https://magazin.hiv/wp-content/uploads/2016/08/2016-Homophobie-Grundlagenpapier-Norbert-Blech.pdf]). It also includes growing observance numbers in immigrant communities, often correlated with length of stay in the host country—indicative of marginalization pressures. See Faruk Şen, "The Historical Situation of Turkish Migrants in Germany," *Immigrants & Minorities* 22, no. 2–3 (2003): 208–27.

4. The quote is from Sara Ahmed, *The Cultural Politics of Emotion* (Edinburgh: Edinburgh University Press, 2004), 44. In the German context, the prevalence of these feelings became apparent in the 2010 controversy about Thilo Sarrazin's racist anti-immigration bestseller *Deutschland schafft sich ab* (Germany abolishes itself); a survey suggested that his supporters included a relative majority of respondents affiliated with *all* major parties except the Green Party. See Consumerfieldwork GmbH, "Meinungsumfrage zur Buchveröffentlichung von Thilo Sarrazin: Hohe Zustimmung für Sarrazin in der Bevölkerung," *openPR*, September 6, 2010, https://www.openpr.de/news/463082/Meinungsumfrage-zur -Buchveroeffentlichung-von-Thilo-Sarrazin-Hohe-Zustimmung-fuer-Sarrazin-in -der-Bevoelkerung.html.

5. See, e.g., Martha C. Nussbaum, "Patriotism and Cosmopolitanism," *Boston Review* 19, no. 5 (October 1, 1994): 3, http://bostonreview.net/martha-nuss-baum-patriotism-and-cosmopolitanism; Pheng Cheah, "Introduction Part II: The Cosmopolitical Today," in *Cosmopolitics: Thinking and Feeling Beyond the Nation*, ed. Pheng Cheah and Bruce Robbins (Minneapolis: University of Minnesota Press, 1998), 21; Sheldon Pollock et al., "Cosmopolitanisms," in *Cosmopolitanism*, ed. Carol A. Breckenridge et al. (Durham, NC: Duke University Press, 2002), 2–3.

6. Judith Butler, *Precarious Life: The Power of Mourning and Violence* (London: Verso, 2004), 12, 30.

7. Gilroy, *Postcolonial Melancholia*, 2, 4. Gilroy is careful to distinguish his own programmatic notion of multiculturalism from affirmative culturalisms advocating tolerance for seemingly given differences (see 2): multiculturalism does not have to be about the coexistence of separate worlds.

8. Gilroy, *Postcolonial Melancholia*, 4.

9. Gilroy, *Postcolonial Melancholia*, 4.

10. Aihwa Ong, *Neoliberalism as Exception: Mutations in Citizenship and Sovereignty* (Durham, NC: Duke University Press, 2006), 18; Aihwa Ong, *Flexible Citizenship: The Cultural Logics of Transnationality* (Durham, NC.: Duke University Press, 1999), 14. On "neoliberal cosmopolitanism," see Pollock et al., "Cosmopolitanisms," 5. See also Gilroy, *Postcolonial Melancholia*, 4; more generally, Nina Glick Schiller and Andrew Irving, eds., *Whose Cosmopolitanism? Critical Perspectives, Relationalities, and Discontents* (Oxford: Berghahn, 2014).

11. Gilroy, *Postcolonial Melancholia*, 4.

12. See Homi Bhabha, "Unsatisfied Notes on Vernacular Cosmopolitanism," in *Text and Narration*, ed. Peter C. Pfeiffer and Laura García-Moreno (Columbia, SC: Camden House, 1996), 191–207. On the emergence of James Clifford's concept of "discrepant" cosmopolitanism, see Bruce Robbins, "Comparative Cosmopolitanisms," in Cheah and Robbins, *Cosmopolitics*, 253–60. Paul Rabinow's "critical

cosmopolitanism" aims to account for the "inescapabilities and particularities of places, characters, historical trajectories," quoted in Ong, *Flexible Citizenship*, 14.

13. Bruce Robbins, "Introduction Part I: Actually Existing Cosmopolitanism," in Cheah and Robbins, *Cosmopolitics*, 2–3. On today's cosmopolitanisms of the displaced, see Pollock et al., "Cosmopolitanisms," 5, 10.

14. Robbins, "Comparative Cosmopolitanisms," 253, with reference to Spivak's notion of worlding; Bruno Latour, *Down to Earth*, trans. Catherine Porter (Cambridge: Polity, 2018), 39, 53; on "cosmopolitics," see also Bruno Latour, *An Inquiry Into Modes of Existence* (Cambridge, MA: Harvard University Press, 2013), 481.

15. Critically, on today's negative rebranding of cosmopolitanism, see Ilja Trojanow, "Verbale Umerziehung," *die tageszeitung*, August 23, 2017; Robbins, "Introduction Part I," 1.

16. The quotes are from Mark Lilla, whose critique of the politics of identity downplays histories of group-based discrimination. "The Liberal Crackup," *Wall Street Journal*, August 11, 2017, https://www.wsj.com/articles/the-liberal -crackup-1502456857.

17. Gilroy, *Postcolonial Melancholia*, 9.

18. Gilroy, *Postcolonial Melancholia*, 8.

19. Barbara Mennel, "Criss-crossing in Global Space and Time: Fatih Akın's *The Edge of Heaven* (2007)," *Transit* 5, no. 1 (2009): 22, http://escholarship.org/uc /item/28x3x9r0; with reference also to Levent Tezcan; Fatih Akın, "Ich wollte die Frauen entdecken," interview by Birgit Glombitza, *die tageszeitung*, September 25, 2007, http://www.taz.de/!5167.

20. Tim Bergfelder, "Love Beyond the Nation: Cosmopolitanism and Transnational Desire in Cinema," in *Europe and Love in Cinema*, ed. Jo Labanyi, Luisa Passerini, and Karen Diehl (New York: Intellect, 2012), 63 (with Mica Nava), 75, 78. On the cosmopolitanism of postmillennium Turkish German cinema, see also Sabine Hake and Barbara Mennel, eds., *Turkish German Cinema in the New Millennium: Sites, Sounds, and Screens* (Oxford: Berghahn, 2012), 5.

21. Bruno Latour, *Reassembling the Social: An Introduction to Actor-Network-Theory* (Oxford: Oxford University Press, 2005), 227 (see the introduction to this volume).

22. Akın was born in 1973 in Germany to Turkish immigrants. *Head On* was awarded the Golden Bear at the Berlin International Film Festival, or Berlinale, and several European film prizes.

23. Ingo Arend, "Wir trinken auf den Tod," *Der Freitag*, September 28, 2007, http:// www.freitag.de/kultur/0739-rueckwaertsgang. (Unless otherwise noted, all translations from non-English sources are my own.) On intensified continuity, see David Bordwell, *The Way Hollywood Tells It: Story and Style in Modern Movies* (Berkeley: University of California Press, 2006); on the cinema of sensations,

see Ágnes Pethő, ed., *The Cinema of Sensations* (Newcastle: Cambridge Scholars, 2015); on *The Cut*, see chapter 3.

24. On the connection to European auteur cinema, see Bergfelder, "Love Beyond the Nation," 74; Thomas Elsaesser, "Ethical Calculus: The Cross-cultural Dilemmas and Moral Burdens of Fatih Akın," *Film Comment*, May–June 2008, 36, http://www.filmcomment.com/article/the-edge-of-heaven-review/; Deniz Göktürk, "Mobilität und Stillstand im Weltkino digital," in *Kultur als Ereignis: Fatih Akıns Film "Auf der anderen Seite" als transkulturelle Narration*, ed. Özkan Ezli (Bielefeld: Transcript Verlag, 2010), 22, 35. On the Berlin School, see Marco Abel, *The Counter-cinema of the Berlin School* (Rochester, NY: Camden House, 2013); Roger F. Cook et al., eds., *Berlin School Glossary: An ABC of the New Wave in German Cinema* (Bristol: Intellect, 2013); and my own discussions in Claudia Breger, *An Aesthetics of Narrative Performance* (Columbus: Ohio State University Press, 2012). On space and movement in *The Edge of Heaven*, see Mennel, "Criss-crossing."

25. Arend, "Wir trinken auf den Tod."

26. On the prison portrayal, see the interview by Lars-Olav Beier and Matthias Matussek, "Regisseur Fatih Akin: 'Erst mit zwei Frauen wurde die Geschichte sexy,'" *Der Spiegel*, September 26, 2007, http://www.spiegel.de/kultur/kino/regisseur-fatih-akin-erst-mit-zwei-frauen-wurde-die-geschichte-sexy-a-507996.html.

27. David Gramling, "On the Other Side of Monolingualism: Fatih Akın's Linguistic Turn(s)," *German Quarterly* 83, no. 3 (2010): 357; more generally, see Mennel, "Criss-crossing"; Bergfelder, "Love Beyond the Nation."

28. See Akın in discussion with Beier and Matussek, "Regisseur Fatih Akin"; on the Egoyan connection, Christian Buß, "Jedem seine eigene Heimat," *Der Spiegel*, September 25, 2007, http://www.spiegel.de/kultur/kino/0,1518,507815,00.html.

29. Warren Buckland, "Puzzle Plots," in *Puzzle Films: Complex Storytelling in Contemporary Cinema*, ed. Warren Buckland (Malden, MA: Blackwell, 2009), 1–12.

30. See Bordwell, *The Way Hollywood Tells It*, 80–82; cf. Matthew Campora, *Subjective Realist Cinema: From Expressionism to* Inception (Oxford: Berghahn, 2014); also, Buckland, "Puzzle Plots," 5.

31. Bordwell, *The Way Hollywood Tells It*, 58–59, with reference to Ridley Scott for the notion of layering.

32. See Alexandra Stäheli on *The Edge of Heaven*, "Liebe ist stärker als der Tod," *Neue Zürcher Zeitung*, October 4, 2007, 49; also, on the intertitles specifically, see Bergfelder, "Love Beyond the Nation," 74.

33. Mennel, "Criss-crossing," 10–11; see also Göktürk, "Mobilität."

34. Göktürk highlights the irony of us hearing this statement on the DVD audio commentary. "Mobilität," 23. However, I am interested in the return of complex narrative forms in the age of new media.

35. Fatih Akın, "Ich wollte die Frauen entdecken." Elsewhere, he specifies that he does not want to "manipulate" audiences and is critical of violence and exploitation also in left-wing contexts. Fatih Akın, "Keine Angst vor Islamismus in der Türkei," interview by Andreas Kilb and Peter Körte, *Frankfurter Allgemeine Zeitung*, September 3, 2007, https://www.faz.net/aktuell/feuilleton/kino /interview-mit-fatih-akin-keine-angst-vor-islamismus-in-der-tuerkei-1103163 .html.

36. David Bordwell modifies the cliché that "classical" narration is invisible; instead, he claims, it is "covert." *Narration in the Fiction Film* (Madison: University of Wisconsin Press, 1985), 160.

37. Fatih Akın does mention the more self-reflexive forms of New Hollywood as a model in "Ich wollte die Frauen entdecken."

38. On literary omniscience, see Paul Dawson, *The Return of the Omniscient Narrator: Authorship and Authority in Twenty-First Century Fiction* (Columbus: Ohio State University Press, 2013). For Brechtian narration, Roland Barthes identifies "the Law of the Party" as the worldly authority that "cuts out the epic scene" in line with Marxist concepts of history. "Diderot, Brecht, Eisenstein," trans. Stephen Heath, *Screen* 15, no. 2 (1974): 38. On cinema, with a focus on voice-over as the medium's most notorious technique of foregrounded narration, see Sarah Kozloff, *Invisible Storytellers: Voice-Over Narration in American Fiction Film* (Berkeley: University of California Press, 1988). Of course, Hollywood's presumably covert narration has equally been associated with claims to sovereignty, indicating the need to further specify the effects of specific configurations of formal elements. See, e.g., Bordwell, *Narration*, 160.

39. See Dawson, *The Return of the Omniscient Narrator*, 32, with reference to Sternberg.

40. On collective authorship in the cinema in this first sense, see also Markus Kuhn, *Film-Narratologie: Ein erzähltheoretisches Analysemodell* (Berlin: de Gruyter, 2013). On nonhuman and networked agency (also in the second sense spelled out in the next paragraph), see Ilana Gershon and Joshua Malitsky, "Actor-Network-Theory and Documentary Studies," *Studies in Documentary Film* 4, no. 1 (2010): 65–78. The proposal, I hope, resolves the old debate between Bordwell and Seymour Chatman: we can emphasize narrative agency in the cinema without anthropomorphizing narration into a coherent human(-like) agent. See Bordwell, *Narration*, 62, in dialogue with Chatman.

41. Fatih Akın, "Keine Angst"; Monique Akın, dir., *Fatih Akın—Tagebuch Eines Filmreisenden* (Hamburg: Norddeutscher Rundfunk, 2007).

42. Latour, *Reassembling*, 44–45. As Nelson Goodman emphasizes, worldmaking is always "a remaking." *Ways of Worldmaking* (Indianapolis: Hackett, 1978), 6. See Daniel Yacavone, *Film Worlds: A Philosophical Aesthetics of Cinema* (New York:

Columbia University Press, 2015), chaps. 4 and 8, even as Yacavone ultimately foregrounds filmmaker intention and the alterity of the aesthetic world.

43. Latour, *Reassembling*, 44, 52.

44. See Latour, *Reassembling*, 12 and passim.

45. Consistently distributing agency grammatically gets tiresome, and I pragmatically alternate in endowing the film (as a composite textual actor) and the director with representative agency. Conventional director privileges are reflected in access asymmetries, including the availability of interview statements. However, I supplement their voice with those of other team members as available. On the reception side, I concretize the involved plurality of worldmaking actors by drawing on reviews along with student and my own responses.

46. Fatih Akın, "Keine Angst."

47. In the realm of literary theory, the dialogicity of storytelling has been forcefully explored by Mikhail Bakhtin along with scholars of African diaspora aesthetics. *The Dialogic Imagination: Four Essays*, trans. Caryl Emerson and Michael Holquist (Austin: University of Texas Press, 1981); see, e.g., Lisa Baker, "Storytelling and Democracy (in the Radical Sense): A Conversation with John Edgar Wideman," *African American Review* 34, no. 2 (2000): 263–72.

48. See Latour, *Reassembling*, 173, 191, on the moves of "Localizing the Global" and "Redistributing the Local" (two of Latour's chapter titles).

49. Fatih Akın, "Die Welt besteht aus Zyklen," interview by Syd Thompson, *Filmreporter.de*, May 28, 2007, https://filmreporter.de/stars/interview/794-Die-Welt-besteht-aus-Zyklen.

50. E.g., Peter Schneider, "The New Berlin Wall," *New York Times Magazine*, December 4, 2005, 66–71; critically, see Beverly Weber, *Violence and Gender in the "New" Europe: Islam in German Culture* (New York: Palgrave, 2013).

51. See Deniz Göktürk, "Turkish Women on German Streets: Closure and Exposure in Transnational Cinema," in *Spaces in European Cinema*, ed. Myrto Konstantarakos (Exeter: Intellect, 2000), 64–76, with a focus on cinema.

52. The notion is used, e.g., by Katja Nicodemus, "Zwei Särge und die Liebe," *Die Zeit*, September 27, 2007, https://www.zeit.de/2007/40/Fatih-Akin-Film/.

53. The quote is from Ahmed, *The Cultural Politics*, 58.

54. See, e.g., Noël Carroll, *The Philosophy of Motion Pictures* (Malden, MA: Blackwell, 2008), 175–76.

55. Where I don't specify empirical responses, my use of "we" designates the implied film audience as constituted by the invitations of form. Actual viewer responses depend on many other factors as well.

56. Eberhard Seidel, "Gesundes Volksempfinden 2006," *die tageszeitung*, October 7, 2006, 12, http://www.taz.de/!368434/.

57. Furthermore, Günter Wallraff used the name for his undercover documentary persona as the immigrant "other" in the 1985 best-seller *Ganz unten* (Cologne: Kiepenheuer & Witsch, 1985).

58. See Gramling, "On the Other Side," 358, with different interpretative emphasis.

59. Steven Shaviro uses the notion of "atomized" actors to critique the neoliberal inflections of cognitive theory. "The Cinematic Body Redux," *Parallax* 14, no. 1 (2008): 51. Cognitive accounts emphasize the stability of characters, as based on either evolutionarily grounded motivations or cultural scripts, in line with the assumption that films "economically" sculpt characters for effortless audience access. Carroll, *Philosophy of Motion Pictures*, 176; more complexly, see Carl Plantinga, *Moving Viewers: American Film and the Spectator's Experience* (Berkeley: University of California Press, 2009), e.g., 83.

60. Lauren Berlant, *Cruel Optimism* (Durham, NC: Duke University Press, 2011), 14–16.

61. See Latour, *Reassembling*, 45, as detailed in the introduction.

62. Murray Smith, "Altered States: Character and Emotional Response in the Cinema," *Cinema Journal* 33, no. 4 (1994): 34, 36, with reference to Richard Wollheim for the distinction between central and acentral forms of imagining. While Smith argues for abandoning the psychoanalytic (and vague folk) concept of identification altogether, I still find it useful for describing some aspects of some cinematic transactions—namely, to emphasize how affective experience can impact the identity of viewers. I agree with Smith on displacing the notions of "*belief*" and "'subjection'" that characteristically accompanied psychoanalytical accounts of identification with terms of "*attention, imagination, perception and sensation.*" Murray Smith, "Film Spectatorship and the Institution of Fiction," *Journal of Aesthetics and Art Criticism* 5, no. 2 (1995): 113 (Smith's emphases); Murray Smith, "Altered States," 49.

63. Murray Smith, "Altered States," 39–41.

64. Plantinga has qualified Smith's distinction: audience responses are "usually mixtures of both shared feelings and 'feelings for.'" Plantinga, *Moving Viewers*, 99. See also Robert Sinnerbrink on "cinempathy" or "the dynamic movement between poles of empathy and sympathy." *Cinematic Ethics: Exploring Ethical Experience Through Film* (New York: Routledge, 2016), 94.

65. See, e.g., Carroll, *Philosophy of Motion Pictures*, 183; Plantinga, *Moving Viewers*, 44, 78.

66. See Homi Bhabha, *The Location of Culture* (New York: Routledge, 1994), 85–92. Akın references the caricaturized teacher Daniel in his earlier comedy *In July* (*Im Juli*, 2000). See Fatih Akın, "Mein Heimatgefühl hat sich ausgebreitet," interview by Katharina Dockhorn, *epd Film*, no. 10 (2007), http://www.epd-film.de/33178_51923.php.

67. On dominant conceptualizations of the migration experience, see Leslie Adelson, "Against Between: A Manifesto," in *Unpacking Europe*, ed. Salah Hassan and Iftikhar Dadi (Rotterdam: NAI, 2001), 244–55.

68. Stäheli, "Liebe ist"; Arend, "Wir trinken auf den Tod"; on the film's transnational configuration, Göktürk, "Mobilität"; Gramling, "On the Other Side"; Mennel, "Criss-crossing."

69. For the (quite different) context of precarious Filipino service labor, Martin F. Manalansan, "Servicing the World: Flexible Filipinos and the Unsecured Life," in *Political Emotions: New Agendas in Communication*, ed. Janet Staiger, Ann Cvetkovich, and Ann Reynolds (New York: Routledge, 2010), 217.

70. In Monique Akın's *Fatih Akın—Tagebuch eines Filmreisenden* (2007), Fatih Akın comments on the making of these images with reference to footage of a 1996 incident in which left-wing radicals beat up a police officer.

71. The film never explicitly mentions the Kurdistan's Workers Party (PKK), but Akın has supported this contextualization in interviews; see, e.g., Fatih Akın, "Ich wollte die Frauen entdecken."

72. See Göktürk, "Mobilität," 25. I don't think we can identify this playful fictional quotation with the film's position.

73. Anna Parkinson, *An Emotional State: The Politics of Emotion in Postwar West German Culture* (Ann Arbor: University of Michigan Press, 2015).

74. The quote is from Noah Isenberg, "Fatih Akın's Cinema of Intersections," *Film Quarterly* 64, no. 4 (2011): 58.

75. See Dipesh Chakrabarty, *Provincializing Europe: Postcolonial Thought and Historical Difference* (Princeton, NJ: Princeton University Press, 2000), 4.

76. Gilroy, *Postcolonial Melancholia*, 4, 75; see xv.

77. Quoted from Huggan, "Perspectives on Postcolonial Europe," 244.

78. The 1993 reform introduced the notion of "safe third countries" as specified by German law and allowed the "presumption" (*Vermutung*) that the claim of an applicant from that country is unfounded. The judge cites this clause in her rejection of Ayten's petition. See Article 16a, *Grundgesetz für die Bundesrepublik Deutschland*, rev. pub. ed., in *Bundesgesetzblatt*, Teil III, Gliederungsnummer 100–101, July 19, 2017, http://www.gesetze-im-internet. de/gg/GG.pdf.

79. Beier and Matussek, "Regisseur Fatih Akin."

80. Ahmed, *The Cultural Politics*, 126, 139, 164.

81. Ahmed's opposition highlights theoretical genealogies I tackle in chapter 2: the category of affect has taken on many of the promises attached to liberated or revolutionary sex in the twentieth century. See Marie-Luise Angerer, *Vom Begehren nach dem Affekt* (Zürich: Diaphanes, 2007).

82. Ahmed, *The Cultural Politics*, 30.

83. A less generous interpretation is that the film's death "sentence" for two of its female protagonists remains trapped in traditional misogynist topoi. See, e.g., the interviewers' respective question in Fatih Akın, "Keine Angst." Akın responds that he didn't intend to punish them. I do not argue that the film escapes problematic topoi, only that the complexity of its foregrounded configuration layers these links with different possibilities.

84. See, e.g., Bridget McNulty, "Chekhov's Gun: What It Is and How to Use It," *Now Novel* (blog), January 28, 2014, https://www.nownovel.com/blog/use-chekhovs-gun/.

85. Bruno Latour details nonhuman agency through the example of the gun in *Pandora's Hope: Essays on the Reality of Science Studies* (Cambridge, MA: Harvard University Press, 1999), 179–80.

86. Gilroy, *Postcolonial Melancholia*, 80.

87. Isolina Ballesteros, *Immigration Cinema in the New Europe* (Bristol: Intellect, 2015), 251.

88. "Einfühlung"; see Nicodemus, "Zwei Särge und die Liebe."

89. This insistence on the weight of individual form elements resonates with Eugenie Brinkema's intervention. I do not, however, as radically isolate these elements as forces of "a nonintentional formal affect" beyond "narrative thematics," character, and spectator response. Eugenie Brinkema, *The Forms of the Affects* (Durham, NC: Duke University Press, 2014), 98–99. We do have a character grieving here, and I think that the film (as the composite actor invested by director and crew) cares about audience response to this "powerful and unsettling" scene. Isenberg, "Fatih Akin's Cinema of Intersections," 58.

90. E.g., David Bordwell, *Poetics of Cinema* (New York: Routledge, 2007), 100.

91. Fritz Breithaupt, *Kulturen der Empathie* (Frankfurt am Main: Suhrkamp, 2009), 142, 148.

92. Ahmed, *The Cultural Politics*, 26, with reference to Leder. Suzanne Keen discusses literary foregrounding as a means of furthering empathy by slowing the reader's pace; see *Empathy and the Novel* (New York: Oxford University Press, 2007), 87, with reference to Miall and Kuiken.

93. The English subtitles of the Strand DVD edition use *repent*, linking the scene to Yeter's encounter with the Islamists and adding to the religious interpretation also put forward by the English film title (see later in this section). The Turkish notion, however, is not the same in both scenes. Whereas the Islamists' "tövbe etmek" (repent) has religious connotations, the 1999 law, Pişmanlık yasası, to which Ayten is referred, does not (thank you to Olivia Landry and Ihsan Topaloglu for help with this detail).

94. Thomas Elsaesser reads the film's "ethical turn" through Levinas, Rancière, and Badiou. *European Cinema and Continental Philosophy: Film as Thought Experiment* (New York: Bloomsbury, 2019), 215–24.

95. Thus Göktürk, "Mobilität," 25, on whose analysis of these sequences I otherwise draw.

96. Gilroy, *Postcolonial Melancholia*, 6.

97. The performance of the song in the concluding sequence differs from that in the introductory sequence. On the soundtrack, see now also Berta Gueneli, *Fatih Akın's Cinema and the New Sound of Europe* (Bloomington: Indiana University Press, 2019).

98. Gilroy, *Postcolonial Melancholia*, 75.

99. Gramling, "On the Other Side," 355.

100. The film further won the Golden Globe for Best Foreign Language Film and was nominated for the Academy Award for Best Original Screenplay.

101. Rahul Hamid, "Freedom and Its Discontents: An Interview with Asghar Farhadi," *Cineaste* 37, no. 1 (Winter 2011): 40; see also Stephen Holden, "A Family Coming Apart at the Seams," *New York Times*, January 1, 2012.

102. Thus Hamid, "Freedom and Its Discontents," 40.

103. Hamid Naficy, *A Social History of Iranian Cinema*, vol. 4, *The Globalizing Era, 1984–2010* (Durham, NC: Duke University Press, 2012), 259.

104. James Bell, "Scenes from a Marriage," *Sight and Sound* 21, no. 7 (July 2011): 38–39.

105. James Bell, "Scenes from a Marriage."

106. Bert Rebhandl, "Ein schwebendes Verfahren," *die tageszeitung*, July 14, 2011; Godfrey Cheshire, "Scenes from a Marriage," *Film Comment* 48, no. 1 (2012): 60; Naficy, *A Social History of Iranian Cinema*, 4:259.

107. Rebhandl, "Ein schwebendes Verfahren"; Naficy, *A Social History of Iranian Cinema*, 4:259. Farhadi confirms the intention of having the audience judge the characters specifically with respect to the introductory sequence. James Bell, "Scenes from a Marriage," 38.

108. Philip Kemp, "A Separation," *Sight and Sound* 21, no. 7 (July 2011): 77.

109. Rebhandl, "Ein schwebendes Verfahren"; Kemp, "A Separation," 77.

110. Kemp, "A Separation," 77.

111. Vivian Sobchack, *The Address of the Eye: A Phenomenology of Film Experience* (Princeton, NJ: Princeton University Press, 1992), 263, 265, 308.

112. Sobchack, *The Address of the Eye*, 308.

113. Sobchack, *The Address of the Eye*, 264–65 (with reference to Jean-Louis Baudry specifically), 363, 68.

114. Sobchack, *The Address of the Eye*, 119, 99; see 56.

115. Rob White, "Editor's Notebook: Institutionalized," *Film Quarterly* 65, no. 3 (Spring 2012): 4.

116. Sobchack herself acknowledges that the "body is always also a [historically] qualified body." *The Address of the Eye*, 144. She more fully attends to "historical

and cultural" experience in Vivian Sobchack, *Carnal Thoughts: Embodiment and Moving Image Culture* (Berkeley: University of California Press, 2004), 2.

117. Laura U. Marks, *The Skin of the Film: Intercultural Cinema, Embodiment, and the Senses* (Durham, NC: Duke University Press, 2000), xi, 2, 1; Laura U. Marks, *Hanan al-Cinema: Affections for the Moving Image* (Cambridge, MA: MIT Press, 2015), 1; see 9.

118. Marks, *The Skin*, 62.

119. Naficy, *A Social History of Iranian Cinema*, 259; Shahab Esfandiary, *Iranian Cinema and Globalization: National, Transnational and Islamic Dimensions* (Bristol: Intellect, 2012), 77. According to Esfandiary, Farhadi was warned by friends that *A Separation* would "not be successful outside Iran" (103). See Christopher Gow, *From Iran to Hollywood and Some Places In-Between: Reframing Post-revolutionary Iranian Cinema* (London: Tauris, 2011), 11.

120. Marks, *The Skin*, 63.

121. Marks, *Hanan al-Cinema*, 9.

122. Marks, *Hanan al-Cinema*, 8, 87.

123. Naficy, *A Social History of Iranian Cinema*, 105, 126.

124. Sobchack, *Carnal Thoughts*, 6. Farhadi has claimed not to differentiate between local and transnational audiences because their concerns "are largely the same," but he added that it may be "easier for an Iranian audience to have a more complex and complete reaction to this film" because of their understanding of the "nuances of the language" and "the social context." James Bell, "Scenes from a Marriage," 39. I am aware of my own limitations to a higher degree here than with the other films discussed in this study: I have little prior research experience in Iranian cinema and zero linguistic competence. However, Marks pointedly charges that "the lazy assumption"—supported by a "bastardized form" of postmodern ethics—that "one should not even try" to "understand the experience of the other" is not a valid conclusion. Marks, *Hanan al-Cinema*, 13.

125. Godfrey Cheshire, "Iran's Cinematic Spring," *Dissent* 59, no. 2 (2012): 78; Naficy, *A Social History of Iranian Cinema*, 333.

126. See, e.g., Gerd Gemünden, "Adding a New Dimension: The 61st International Film Festival Berlin," *Film Criticism* 36, no. 1 (2011): 87; Christina Nord, "Mit besten Grüßen nach Teheran," *die tageszeitung*, February 21, 2011.

127. See Daniel Kothenschulte, "Berlinale: Auszeichnung für den Turbo-Dostojewski," *Frankfurter Rundschau*, February 21, 2011; Dave Itzkoff, "Ceremony in Iran for 'Separation' Director Is Canceled," *New York Times*, March 13, 2012. Naficy first introduces the film in the category of "underground" cinema, while detailing the range of official reactions from criticism to praise and post-Oscar appropriations. *A Social History of Iranian Cinema*, 72, 259–61.

128. See Farhadi in Rahul Hamid, "Freedom and Its Discontents," 42. A few days before the international premiere, *A Separation* reaped the Audience Award for Best Film and the awards for best director, best cinematography, and best screenplay at the Fajr International Film Festival in Tehran; it went on to become "a major box office hit in Iran." Cheshire, "Iran's Cinematic Spring," 78. The year before, Farhadi had excused himself from serving on the Fajr jury along with others in a covert act of protest. See Naficy, *A Social History of Iranian Cinema*, 332.

129. Cheshire, "Iran's Cinematic Spring," 79; Cheshire, "Scenes from a Marriage," 60.

130. Naficy, *A Social History of Iranian Cinema*, 103. The required treatment of all cinematic space as public space, with hijabs in place (see 115), may help to explain a difficulty that White cites in support of his argument: he had increasing trouble "distinguishing between government" and home space in the film ("Editor's Notebook," 4). But my viewer's experience does not confirm that experience: *A Separation* carefully underlines demarcations by emphasizing character gestures of adjusting or changing scarves and adding or taking off chadors in the transition between private and public spaces.

131. Naficy, *A Social History of Iranian Cinema*, 164; see chap. 2 there.

132. Cheshire, "Iran's Cinematic Spring," 79; Nord, "Mit besten Grüßen nach Teheran."

133. John Petrakis, "On Film: A Separation," *Christian Century*, April 18, 2012, 43.

134. Naficy, *A Social History of Iranian Cinema*, 259.

135. Gow, *From Iran to Hollywood*, 42, citing Bill Nichols; Kothenschulte, "Berlinale: Auszeichnung für den Turbo-Dostojewski"; Hamid, "Freedom and Its Discontents," 40.

136. Sobchack, *The Address of the Eye*, 121–22.

137. James Bell, "Scenes from a Marriage," in dialogue with Farhadi.

138. Sinnerbrink's reading of the film is mostly focused on one scene but is congruent with my reading in the interest in perception across obstacles and "cinempathy" as a "kinetic-cinematic practice of alternating perspective-taking." *Cinematic Ethics*, 101.

139. On the impossibility of a complete phenomenological "reduction" or "bracketing" of context, see Sobchack, *Carnal Thoughts*, 2; critically, on Husserl (with Merleau-Ponty) also Sobchack, *The Address of the Eye*, 35–49.

140. See Sobchack, *The Address of the Eye*, 36–38 (Sobchack's emphasis).

141. Sobchack, *The Address of the Eye*, 131; see also 243.

142. Marks, *The Skin*, 131; see 137.

143. I quote Sobchack's reconceptualization of the film-theoretical notion of "point of view" here. See *The Address of the Eye*, 62.

144. Sobchack, *The Address of the Eye*, 286 (Sobchack's emphases); see also Marks, *The Skin*, 164, on haptic cinema. These phenomenological takes resonate with

the cognitive notions of empathy and sympathy detailed above in their shared goal of reworking the psychoanalytic legacy.

145. Sobchack, *The Address of the Eye*, 287, 194 (Sobchack's emphases).

146. Holden, "A Family Coming Apart." Naficy uses the notion of unreliability in discussing "Iranian hermeneutics" as marked by the regime of the veil. *A Social History of Iranian Cinema*, 105.

147. Naficy, *A Social History of Iranian Cinema*, 105, explicitly comparing both.

148. See Latour, *Reassembling*, first 16.

149. Anthony Lane, "Tehran Tales," *New Yorker* 87, no. 43 (2012): 78. On mood as the way in which "a (fictional) world is expressed or disclosed via a shared affective attunement orienting the spectator within that world," see Robert Sinnerbrink, "*Stimmung*: Exploring the Aesthetics of Mood," *Screen* 53, no. 2 (2012): 148.

150. Cheshire, "Scenes from a Marriage," 60; Roger Ebert, cited in Alexa Dalby, "A Separation Wins Iran's First Oscar," *The Middle East*, no. 431 (April 2012): 60–61.

151. Rebhandl, "Ein schwebendes Verfahren."

152. Latour, *Reassembling*, 45.

2. CRITICAL INTENSITY: JEAN-LUC GODARD'S AND RAINER WERNER FASSBINDER'S DEFAMILIARIZED WORLDMAKING PRACTICES

1. André Bazin, *What Is Cinema?*, trans. Hugh Gray, vol. 1 (Berkeley: University of California Press, 2005), 29.

2. The characterization of neorealism as a "phenomenological realism" was proposed by Amédée Ayfree in a 1952 *Cahiers* article, quoted by George Lellis, *Bertolt Brecht, "Cahiers du Cinéma" and Contemporary Film Theory* (Ann Arbor: University of Michigan Research Press, 1982), 19. Lellis begins to question the film-theoretical opposition between Bertolt Brecht and Bazin—in particular, regarding their shared interest in realism's "moral" dimension and a "participating spectator" (see 19–20, 37–38). See also Angelos Koutsourakis who, however, holds onto a traditional conceptualization of Brechtian *Verfremdung* as "polemical." *Rethinking Brechtian Film Theory and Cinema* (Edinburgh: Edinburgh University Press, 2018), 19.

3. Rita Felski, *The Limits of Critique* (Chicago: University of Chicago Press, 2015), 76; see 2–3. See also—not only on negative affects—Jean-Michel Rabaté, *The Pathos of Distance: Affects of the Moderns* (New York: Bloomsbury, 2016).

4. I thus conceptualize defamiliarization as a set of aesthetic techniques, not just a general property of art, as Murray Smith suggests. "The Logic and Legacy of Brechtianism," in *Post-theory: Reconstructing Film Studies*, ed. David Bordwell and Noël Carroll (Madison: University of Wisconsin Press, 1996), 134.

5. Brian Massumi, *Parables for the Virtual: Movement, Affect, Sensation* (Durham, NC: Duke University Press, 2002), 28.

6. Andrew Dudley with Hervé Joubert-Laurencin, eds., *Opening Bazin: Postwar Film Theory and Its Afterlife* (New York: Oxford University Press, 2011); see also Hilsabeck Burke, "The 'Is' in What Is Cinema? On André Bazin and Stanley Cavell," *Cinema Journal* 55, no. 2 (2016): 25–42; Steven Shaviro, *The Cinematic Body* (Minneapolis: University of Minnesota Press, 1993), 11; Murray Smith, "The Logic"; and Vivian Sobchack's resonant critique of 1970s film theory in *The Address of the Eye: A Phenomenology of Film Experience* (Princeton, NJ: Princeton University Press, 1992), as discussed in chapter 1.

7. Murray Smith, "The Logic," 130–31.

8. See also Koutsourakis, *Rethinking Brechtian Film Theory*, 96. Smith takes the "feeling and reason" binary from the table contrasting "dramatic" and "epic" forms of theatre in Brecht's 1930 "Notes on the Opera *Rise and Fall of the City of Mahagonny*." See Murray Smith, "The Logic," 131; Bertolt Brecht, "Notes on the Opera *Rise and Fall of the City of Mahagonny*," in Bertolt Brecht, *Brecht on Theatre*, ed. Marc Silberman, Steve Giles, and Tom Kuhn, 3rd ed. (London: Bloomsbury, 2015), 65. This text became one of the central reference points of 1970s filmic "Brechtianism" after having been published in 1972 in *Cahiers du Cinema*. Even here, Brecht qualifies his oppositions as indicating "shifts of accent" rather than "absolute antitheses." Brecht, "Notes on the Opera *Rise and Fall of the City of Mahagonny*," 65. But the opposition of "feeling" vs. "rationality" (see 65) is altogether absent from the 1935 revision of the table. Bertolt Brecht, "Theatre for Pleasure or Theatre for Instruction," in Brecht, *Brecht on Theatre*, 111. Defending "the role of emotions," Brecht now underlines affective incongruity: whereas the dramatic theater's spectator says, "I weep when they weep, I laugh when they laugh," the epic theater's spectator says, "I laugh when they weep, I weep when they laugh." See Marc Silberman, "Exile Years: Introduction to Part Two," in Brecht, *Brecht on Theatre*, 102; Brecht, "Theatre for Pleasure or Theatre for Instruction," 112. Even the charge of simplified reception is arguably too sweeping: Peter Wollen emphasizes the importance of pleasure for radical cinema in "Godard and Counter-cinema: Vent d'Est," in *Readings and Writings: Semiotic Counter-strategies* (London: Verso, 1982), see, in particular, 80; Stephen Heath acknowledges Brecht's interest in "a new basis" for "artistic pleasure" in "Lessons from Brecht," *Screen* 15, no. 2 (1974): 109; and Dana Polan forcefully dissents from the "formalist" Brecht already in the 1970s in "A Brechtian Cinema? Towards a Politics of Self-Reflexive Film," in *Movies and Methods*, ed. Bill Nichols (Berkeley: University of California Press, 1985), 2:661–72.

9. The cognitive evaluation–focused model of emotions resonates with Brecht's focus on judgment; see, e.g., Brecht, *Brecht on Theatre*, 183, and Murray

Smith, "The Logic" 132–33. Their emphasis on filmmaker intention and audience guidance has common ground with Brecht's programmatic notion of artistically controlling emotions. See, e.g., Noël Carroll, *The Philosophy of Motion Pictures* (Malden, MA: Blackwell, 2008), 211, 158–59; Brecht, *Brecht on Theatre*, 163.

10. Steve Cannon, " 'Not a Mere Question of Form': The Hybrid Realism of Godard's *Vivre sa vie*," *French Cultural Studies* 7, no. 21 (1996): 283.

11. Jean-Luc Godard, quoted in Douglas Morrey, *Jean-Luc Godard* (Manchester: Manchester University Press, 2005), 39; see, e.g., David Sterritt, *The Films of Jean-Luc Godard: Seeing the Invisible* (Cambridge: Cambridge University Press, 1999). A few recent academic readings have begun to question this legacy. Maureen Turim's focus on the face, in particular, resonates with my reading of the film. See "Three-Way Mirroring in *Vivre sa vie*," in *A Companion to Jean-Luc Godard*, ed. Tom Conley and T. Jefferson Kline (Chichester: Wiley-Blackwell, 2014). 89–107. Turim also introduces a notion of "intensity," if without further conceptual development (92).

12. Cannon, "Not a Mere Question of Form," 285.

13. There is little close reading evidence for these interpretative moves. Harun Farocki cites the spatial distance in one of the film's *very* few extreme long shots—namely, as Nana loses her apartment—as indicative of "a certain emotional distance" to Nana; see Kaja Silverman and Harun Farocki, *Speaking About Godard* (New York: NYU Press, 1998), 9. Morrey's attempt to revise the standard Brechtian reading makes him opt for more careful wordings, but he still suggests that the film "seemingly" reserves "little warmth . . . for the character." Morrey, *Jean-Luc Godard*, 42; see 39. In reversing these takes, my concern is not just with the function of distanciation—the political overestimation of which Cannon targets—but also with the question of distance generation as such. See Cannon, "Not a Mere Question of Form," 283–84.

14. See Laura Mulvey, "Visual Pleasure and Narrative Cinema," *Screen* 16, no. 3 (1975): 6–18.

15. Silverman and Farocki, *Speaking About Godard*, 7; see 11, 14, 30.

16. Heath, "Lessons from Brecht," 104, 110 (Heath's emphasis).

17. Silverman and Farocki, *Speaking About Godard*, 14; see 29.

18. Laura Mulvey and Colin MacCabe, "Images of Woman, Images of Sexuality," in *Godard: Images, Sounds, Politics*, ed. Colin MacCabe with Mick Eaton and Laura Mulvey (Bloomington: Indiana University Press, 1980), 94, 101.

19. Andreas Busche, "Die Illusion vom Tod als Befreiung," *die tageszeitung*, September 19, 2001; Rainer Gansera, "Pflanzlich bewegt," *Süddeutsche Zeitung*, December 20, 2001; Clauss Loeser, "Der Weg nach unten," *Berliner Zeitung*, September 20, 2001; "A Love Song," *Time* 82, no. 15 (October 11, 1963): 131. Here I draw on

the press archive of the library of the Deutsche Kinemathek in Berlin, which includes a number of international reviews from 1963 and others written upon a 2001 rerelease of the film in Germany. Academic critics have at moments acknowledged this "love" without changing their take on "the brutality of the film." See Jeremy Mark Robinson, *Jean-Luc Godard: The Passion of Cinema* (Kent: Crescent Moon, 2009), 143, 158.

20. See Michel Foucault, *History of Sexuality*, trans. Robert Hurley, vol. 1, *An Introduction* (New York: Vintage, 1978).

21. See Marie-Luise Angerer, *Vom Begehren nach dem Affekt* (Zurich: Diaphanes, 2007); Janet Halley and Andrew Parker, eds., *After Sex? On Writing Since Queer Theory* (Durham, NC: Duke University Press, 2011); and my own attempt at mediation in *Nach dem Sex? Sexualwissenschaft und Affect Studies*, Hirschfeld-Lectures no. 5 (Göttingen: Wallstein, 2014). The critique of desexualization was articulated already in response to Foucault's historicization of sex and the emergence of queer studies, prominently by Leo Bersani in *Homos* (Cambridge, MA: Harvard University Press, 1996). Foucault, of course, stipulated that the Christian *dispositif* of sexuality, which would culminate in psychoanalysis, sacrificed *pleasure* to the obsession with *desire* in the first place. See Michel Foucault, "On the Genealogy of Ethics," in *The Foucault Reader*, ed. Paul Rabinow (New York: Pantheon, 1984), 347, 359. On mending the perceived gulf between psychoanalysis and affect studies, see also José Esteban Muñoz, "Introduction: From Surface to Depth, Between Psychoanalysis and Affect," *Women & Performance: A Journal of Feminist Theory* 19, no. 2 (2009): 123–29.

22. Lauren Berlant, "Starved," in Halley and Parker, *After Sex?*, 80.

23. See Lutz Koepnick on the long take as a means of reconstructing "spaces for the possibility of wonder," as associated with "curiosity," "rapt attention," and "affirmation and amazement," vs. "the dominant rhetoric of sovereign viewership." *The Long Take: Art Cinema and the Wondrous* (Minneapolis: University of Minnesota Press, 2017), 1, 9, 14, 25.

24. Mulvey, "Visual Pleasure and Narrative Cinema," 14.

25. On the soundtrack, see Cannon, "Not a Mere Question of Form," 285.

26. Turim, "Three-Way Mirroring," 89.

27. Silverman and Farocki, *Speaking About Godard*, 2.

28. Mulvey, "Visual Pleasure and Narrative Cinema," 14.

29. Turim mentions (in passing) the notion of defamiliarization for situating Godard's Brechtianism, based on Martin Esslin's early English-language study of Brecht. This adds to the genealogy I suggest, although for Turim, *My Life to Live*'s Brechtianism amounts to an unpolitical emphasis on theatricality. "Three-Way Mirroring," 96–97.

30. Brecht, *Brecht on Theatre*, 143.

31. See Lellis, *Bertolt Brecht*, 31. The Bazin influence in *My Life to Live* has been noted: see Cannon, "Not a Mere Question of Form," 286; more generally, on Godard, see also Morrey, *Jean-Luc Godard*, 3.

32. Quoted from Lellis, *Bertolt Brecht*, 41; see 19.

33. Bernhard Dort, "Towards a Brechtian Criticism of Cinema," in *Cahiers du Cinéma: 1960–1968: New Wave, New Cinema, Reevaluating Hollywood*, ed. Jim Hillier (Cambridge, MA: Harvard University Press, 1986), 238–39 (Dort's emphasis). See Bazin, *What Is Cinema?*, 102.

34. Dort, "Towards a Brechtian Criticism of Cinema," 239.

35. On Brecht's (epistemological, critical) realism, see Polan, "A Brechtian Cinema?," 664; Silberman, "Exile Years: Introduction to Part Two," 107; Lellis, *Bertolt Brecht*, 47; Sylvia Harvey, "Whose Brecht? Memories for the Eighties: A Critical Recovery," *Screen* 23, no. 1 (1982): 45–59; Roswitha Mueller, "Brecht the Realist and New German Cinema," *Framework* 25 (1984): 42–51; see Koutsourakis, *Rethinking Brechtian Film Theory*, 88, briefly on Dort and, in particular, chap. 3.

36. I develop Latour's notion of realism more fully for the context of cinematic aesthetics in chapter 4.

37. The quote is from Lellis, *Bertolt Brecht*, 44 (Lellis's emphasis), with reference to Dort, "Towards a Brechtian Criticism of Cinema," 244. Of course, Bazin himself modifies his rhetoric of realism as an erasure of style. In his chapter on "Theater and Cinema," some common ground with Brecht emerges from Bazin's unease with the apparent implications of his own distinctions—namely, that the cinema seems aligned with the dramatic theater of illusion and passive spectatorship. Haunted by high-cultural suspicions of cinema spectatorship, which turns "the audience into a 'mass'" and renders "emotion uniform," Bazin shifts his focus from media ontology to aesthetics—specifically, techniques of counteracting the passivity effect (*What Is Cinema?*, 98–100). In fact, these very techniques of provoking "self-awareness at the height of illusion"—especially deep focus—become emblematic of Bazin's notion of cinematic realism (113; see also 1, 35–36). Twenty-first-century recovery efforts have emphasized these aspects of Bazin's work. See, e.g., Thomas Elsaesser, "A Bazinian Half-Century," in Andrew with Joubert-Laurencin, *Opening Bazin*, 3–12.

38. Colin McCabe, *Godard: A Portrait of the Artist at Seventy* (New York: Farrar, Straus, and Giroux, 2004), 79; Godard as attributed via Jacques Pétat, with reference to Brecht, quoted in Lellis, *Bertolt Brecht*, 54. MacCabe notes that Godard's intellectual genealogy is "unthinkable without Bazin," although Godard refused to oppose realism to active mediation as early as 1952, emphasizing that "all positioning of a camera is already editing." *Godard*, 58, 78.

39. Jean-Luc Godard, "Interview, December 1962," in booklet included with *Vivre sa vie* Criterion Collection DVD (New York: Criterion Collection, 2010), 28–31.

40. Dort, "Towards a Brechtian Criticism of Cinema," 239 (Dort's emphasis), quoting Brecht's *The Exception and the Rule*.

41. Marc Silberman, Steve Giles, and Tom Kuhn, "General Introduction," in Brecht, *Brecht on Theatre*, 5. Brecht started using the term after his visit to Moscow in 1935, first in the essay on "Verfremdung Effects in Chinese Acting." See Silberman, "Introduction to Part Two," 104. His Moscow host, Sergei Tretiakow, may have introduced him to Shklovsky's concept. See Brecht, *Brecht on Theatre* 158–59. Polan uses the term in passing in "A Brechtian Cinema?," 671.

42. Silberman, Giles, and Kuhn, "General Introduction," 5. Jacques Rancière's reading of "distanciation" (including in Godard) integrates these poles by arguing that it "aims to produce a sensory clash . . . in order to engender an awareness of the underlying reasons" for the presented strangeness. *Dissensus: On Politics and Aesthetics*, ed. and trans. Steven Corcoran (London: Continuum, 2010), 143.

43. On Bazinian resonances in Gilles Deleuze, see Dudley Andrew, "A Binocular Preface," in Andrew with Joubert-Laurencin, *Opening Bazin*, xi; Elsaesser, "A Bazinian Half-Century," 10–11. Morrey also deploys the Joan of Arc connection in developing his reading of *My Life to Live* in relation to Robert Bresson's practice of making "ordinary objects appear alien." Morrey, *Jean-Luc Godard*, 40–41. Bresson's *The Process of Joan of Arc* was in French cinemas in 1962.

44. Bazin, *What Is Cinema?*, 109, 133. Bazin compares Dreyer to Bresson here.

45. Gilles Deleuze, *Cinema 1: The Movement-Image*, trans. Hugh Tomlinson (London: Athlone Press, 1986), 106, 108.

46. McCabe, *Godard*, 63, summarizing Bazin. On the "imbrication of fiction and documentary" throughout Godard's career, see Morrey, *Jean-Luc Godard*, 4. Nora M. Alter and Timothy Corrigan cite *My Life to Live* as one of Godard's "essay films," characterized by "the mixing of art- and documentary-film styles." See Nora M. Alter and Timothy Corrigan, eds., *Essays on the Essay Film* (New York: Columbia University Press, 2017), 3, 5.

47. I discuss Brecht's concept of fabula in my reading of Fassbinder below.

48. Silverman uses the notion "mimetic" and Turim, that of "identification." See Silverman and Farocki, *Speaking About Godard*, 11; Turim, "Three-Way Mirroring," 90.

49. Bertolt Brecht, "A Short, Private Lecture for My Friend Max Gorelik," in Brecht, *Brecht on Theatre*, 148; Bertolt Brecht, "The Threepenny Lawsuit," in *Brecht on Film and Radio*, trans. and ed. Marc Silberman (London: Methuen, 2000), 171. Portions of this latter essay were reprinted in the 1960 special issue of *Cahiers*. See Lellis, *Bertolt Brecht*, 12; Koutsourakis, *Rethinking Brechtian Film Theory*, 20.

50. Brian Massumi, *What Animals Teach Us About Politics* (Durham, NC: Duke University Press, 2014), 35–36 (Massumi's emphasis); see 78–79. For Brecht, the "gestus" as a "purely animal category" is "not yet a social gestus." Bertolt Brecht, "On Gestic Music," in Brecht, *Brecht on Theatre*, 168.

51. See Bertolt Brecht, "Notes on the Threepenny Opera," in *Brecht on Theatre*, 75; Bertolt Brecht, "On Experimental Theatre," in *Brecht on Theatre*, 142. Brecht repeatedly underlines that he does not aim to renounce empathy entirely: e.g., Bertolt Brecht, "Short Description of a New Technique of Acting That Produces a Verfremdung Effect," in Brecht, *Brecht on Theatre*, 184; see also Bertolt Brecht, "The Progressiveness of the Stanislavsky System," in Brecht, *Brecht on Theatre*, 133, on Stanislavsky. Polan introduces a distinction between "empathetic" and "critical" identification. "A Brechtian Cinema?," 670.

52. See Bertolt Brecht, "On Experiments in Epic Theatre," in Brecht, *Brecht on Theatre*, 118; Bertolt Brecht, "The German Drama: Pre-Hitler," in Brecht, *Brecht on Theatre*, 122. On crowds, see, e.g., Sigmund Freud, "Group Psychology and the Analysis of the Ego," in *The Standard Edition of the Complete Psychological Works of Sigmund Freud*, ed. James Strachey et al., vol. 18 (1920–1922) (London: Hogarth Press and the Institute of Psychoanalysis, 1955), 65–144. Canetti's later, ambiguously more positive take constitutes a virtual bridge with today's revolutionary multitudes (see chapter 3).

53. Bertolt Brecht, "*Verfremdung* Effects in Chinese Acting," in Brecht, *Brecht on Theatre*, 154; see 152.

54. Brecht, "*Verfremdung* Effects in Chinese Acting," 153; see also, e.g., 186; Bertolt Brecht, "Three Notes on *Verfremdung* and the Elder Breughel," in Brecht, *Brecht on Theatre*, 159; Bertolt Brecht, "Notes on *Pointed Heads and Round Heads*," in Brecht, *Brecht on Theatre*, 163.

55. Brecht overall emphasizes techniques of restrained acting toward the goal of not melting emotions but does indicate other possibilities on occasion. For example, he underlines that "each gesture . . . must have the full embodiment of a human gesture" and "render all the quotation's overtones." "Short Description of a Technique of Acting," in Brecht, *Brecht on Theatre*, 186.

56. Silverman and Farocki, *Speaking About Godard*, 11.

57. In an interview on *My Life to Live*, Jean-Luc Godard claims: "I have always traced a character's history from an emotional point of view, trying to make the audience understand and become involved with him." See "Jean-Luc Godard and *Vivre sa vie*: Interview with Tom Milne," in *Jean-Luc Godard: Interviews*, ed. David Sterritt (Jackson: University Press of Mississippi, 1998), 7.

58. As noticed by Silverman, in Silverman and Farocki, *Speaking About Godard*, 4.

59. Yet another intertextual connection repeatedly mentioned (e.g., in Turim, "Three-Way Mirroring," 103) is that to Kenji Mizoguchi's *Street of Shame* (1956). Notably, none of the five sex workers shown in *Street of Shame* dies. In balancing emphases on violence and social stigma with an exploration of character agency, the film rather resonates with my reading of *My Life to Live*.

60. Cannon, "Not a Mere Question of Form," 288; see also Robinson, *Jean-Luc Godard*, 159.

61. Cannon claims that Nana is "treated throughout as an object . . . rather than as a conscious subject" and that "Anna Karina" is "objectified" also; see "Not a Mere Question of Form," 286, 291. For Robinson, Nana's turn to sex work is signaled by her objectification through the camera. *Jean-Luc Godard*, 150.

62. Jean-Luc Godard, "*Vivre sa vie* Scenario," in booklet included with *Vivre sa vie* Criterion Collection DVD (New York: Criterion Collection, 2010), 10–14; Silverman and Farocki, *Speaking About Godard*, 7. See also Julien Zanetta, "Portrait of a Lady: Painting Emotion in Jean-Luc Godard's *Vivre sa vie*," in *Exploring Text and Emotions*, ed. Lars Saetre (Aarhus: Aarhus University Press, 2014), 228–39 vs. 236.

63. Loeser, "Der Weg nach unten." The first two quotes are from Cannon, "Not a Mere Question of Form," 291, and from David Bordwell, *Narration in the Fiction Film* (Madison: University of Wisconsin Press, 1985), 281.

64. In 1985, Bordwell develops the category of "parametric," or "style centered," narration through a reading of *My Life to Live*—as well as cross-references to *Katzelmacher*, in *Narration in the Fiction Film*, 281; see 286, 289. Bordwell warns against assigning "thematic" or self-reflexive "meanings" to these variations of style, instead postulating "a richness and texture that resists interpretation" (282, 289).

65. On the state of the marriage, including Karina's miscarriage and suicide attempts and Godard's violence and jealousy, see MacCabe, *Godard*, 141–42, 162. Turim concludes that the film is marked by a "passion" filled with "biographical, imagistic, sociological and philosophical ambiguities." "Three-Way Mirroring," 106. My own insistence on the interference of real-world affective charges does not aim to ground filmmaking in a coherent biographical scenario but—again—to underline the porous, open nature of artistic worlds as the assembly of radically heterogeneous materials.

66. Enno Patalas, "Nana S. philosophiert," *Die Zeit*, October 12, 1962, 41, https://www.zeit.de/1962/41/nana-s-philosophiert.

67. Cannon, "Not a Mere Question of Form," 287; Patalas, "Nana S. philosophiert." According to Silverman, the original French version ended with a two-minute "close-up" on the corpse, which was "brutally" cut down to a few seconds in the English and German versions. See Silverman and Farocki, *Speaking About Godard*, 1. I have not seen a copy with this two-minute shot; in the Criterion Collection edition, the final glance at the corpse is in a long shot.

68. Patalas, "Nana S. philosophiert."

69. For the ironic reading of the title see, e.g., Cannon, "Not a Mere Question of Form," 286. On literal reading as an alternative to symptomatic reading, see

Stephen Best and Sharon Marcus, "Surface Reading: An Introduction," *Representations* 108, no. 1 (2009): 12–13. For me, the point is not to privilege the presumably direct in bracketing all rhetorical moves of interpretation but to explore close reading alternatives to more or less automatized moves of meaning construction.

70. Bruno Latour, *Reassembling the Social: An Introduction to Actor-Network-Theory* (Oxford: Oxford University Press, 2005), 45 (Latour's emphasis).

71. The quote is from Arthur Rimbaud's "Lettres du voyant" (1871); see Anna Levett, "Shouldn't Love Be the One True Thing? Godard and the Legacy of Surrealist Ethics," *Quarterly Review of Film and Video* 34, no. 8 (2017): 687. Situating Godard's film between Deleuze and Emmanuel Levinas, Levett develops a more positive interpretation of this "becoming other" that modifies the diagnosis of objectification. Levett, "Shouldn't Love Be the One True Thing?," 688, 693.

72. See, e.g., Cannon, "Not a Mere Question of Form," 286.

73. Her tone is playful but hardly "ritualistic." Sterritt, *The Films of Jean-Luc Godard*, 78.

74. Compare Morrey, *Jean-Luc Godard*, 39, and Susan Sontag, who did endorse the claim to freedom in her 1964 essay preceding the formation of the standard critical reading. "Godard's *Vivre sa vie*," in *Against Interpretation: And Other Essays* (New York: Picador, 2001): 196–208.

75. Silverman and Farocki, *Speaking About Godard*, 16.

76. See Turim, "Three-Way Mirroring," 102.

77. The sound of shots first punctures the sustained close-up on Raoul's notebook, which lists the clients of his women and which Nana opens while waiting for him; after she closes it quickly, the screen goes to black for a moment. The next take shows Nana from a greater distance, without the book. As the gunshots begin again and a hurt man enters the café, she flees. If this assembly once more associates sex work with death, it simultaneously highlights the arbitrary nature of the narrative connection established.

78. If read classically as revealing Nana's inner life, Silverman notes, the letter would show this life to be "astonishingly banal." See Silverman and Farocki, *Speaking About Godard*, 18. Instead of the negative conclusion that the film deconstructs romantic notions of subjectivity, however, we can take seriously the ways in which affective subjectivity is coconstituted through strategic worldmaking orientations.

79. Silverman and Farocki, *Speaking About Godard*, 22; Morrey, *Jean-Luc Godard*, 43; see also Cannon, "Not a Mere Question of Form," 289.

80. Cannon, "Not a Mere Question of Form," 289; Lauren Berlant, *Cruel Optimism* (Durham, NC: Duke University Press, 2011), 98. The question whether Nana's optimism is cruel in Berlant's sense—as an attachment to something that will

hurt her—is answered less conclusively than in Fassbinder's *Katzelmacher* (see section "Collective Assemblies" below). It *is* cruel insofar as we follow the association of the young man with Poe's painter developed in tableau twelve and with the filmmaker, whose voice reads Poe's story in another foreshadowing of Nana's death as murder by means of art. The film's layering of incongruous elements, however, also allows me to insist on contrary vectors: diegetically, the relationship with the young man does seem to open a different future for Nana, but it is cut short by Raoul's revenge. The reason he states for selling her is that Nana refused to accept all clients: she defended her agency throughout her sex work.

81. The Jack the Ripper connection is noticed by Farocki. Silverman and Farocki, *Speaking About Godard*, 28.

82. See, e.g., Turim, "Three-Way Mirroring," 103. Excerpts of the documentary are made available in the Criterion Collection edition.

83. Tableau ten recounts another distinctly negative experience with a client who does not actually want her. Silverman dramatizes this encounter as a confirmation that prostitution represents "the most extreme form of subjective negation: as the eradication both of desire and the self" but recognizes that the affective close-up on Nana/Karina's melancholy response at the end of the tableau extradiegetically affirms her. Silverman and Farocki, *Speaking About Godard*, 24.

84. Cannon, "Not a Mere Question of Form," 290.

85. Mizoguchi's *Street of Shame* is a crucial reference point here, with its more extensive exploration of the conflicted but often supportive sociality among the brothel workers.

86. Thus even Bordwell, *Narration in the Fiction Film*, 314, despite his expressed resistance to interpretation.

87. Levett, "Shouldn't Love Be the One True Thing?," 694.

88. The allusion has been decoded as a reference to the OAS (Organisation armée secrète) campaign of bombings and shootings after the March 1962 independence of Algeria. See Turim, "Three-Way Mirroring," 95.

89. The film was awarded the TV prize of the Akademie der Darstellenden Künste in 1969 and German Film Awards in five categories, including best film, best screenplay, and best cinematography (in part shared with other productions), in 1970.

90. The newspaper reviews upon the film's initial cinematic release explain the title to non-Bavarian audiences: with its sexual connotations, it is used for southern Europeans, including "guest workers." See, e.g., Peter W. Jansen, "Der Griech aus Griechenland: Fassbinders zweiter Film 'Katzelmacher' läuft in Mannheim," *Frankfurter Rundschau*, October 4, 1969; Michael Lentz, "Eine Ordnung muß wieder sein: Faßbinders Film 'Katzelmacher' uraufgeführt," *Handelsblatt*, November 24, 1969.

91. See the section, "Collective Assemblies"; on Godard's overall influence on Fassbinder, see Laura McMahon, "Imitation, Seriality, Cinema: Early Fassbinder and Godard," in *Companion to Rainer Werner Fassbinder*, ed. Brigitte Peucker (Hoboken, NJ: Wiley-Blackwell, 2011), 79–96.

92. This may indicate that dominant Brechtian frameworks were quite established by 1969 in Germany.

93. Martin Brady, "Brecht in Brechtian Cinema," in *"Verwisch die Spuren!": Bertolt Brecht's Work and Legacy: A Reassessment*, ed. Robert Gillett and Godela Weiss-Sussex (Amsterdam: Rodopi, 2008), 297.

94. See, e.g., Michael Töteberg, "Introduction," in Rainer Werner Fassbinder, *The Anarchy of the Imagination: Interviews, Essays, Notes. Rainer Werner Fassbinder*, ed. Michael Töteberg and Leo A. Lensing and trans. Krishna Winston (Baltimore: Johns Hopkins University Press. 1992), xvii.

95. On this reception, see also Thomas Elsaesser, *Fassbinder's Germany: History, Identity, Subject* (Amsterdam: Amsterdam University Press, 1996), 45. Elsaesser makes the case for a more complex reading but still underlines the film's "didacticism" (270; see 33). Resonant with my own intervention is that of David Barnett, who, from the angle of theater rather than cinema studies, underlines the role of Artaud in Fassbinder's previous reception. *Rainer Werner Fassbinder and the German Theatre* (Cambridge: Cambridge University Press, 2005), 5–6; see 71 for the acknowledgment that cinema scholars have instead focused on Brecht. Barnett then argues for the importance of Brecht in a more "sensual" interpretation (see 6–7, 71–73). He does not detail his reading for the film but discusses defamiliarization and slowness in the theater production (see 48–53).

96. McMahon, "Imitation, Seriality, Cinema," 92.

97. See Rainer Werner Fassbinder, "Die Gruppe, die trotzdem keine war," interview by Corinna Brocher, 1973, in *Fassbinder über Fassbinder: Die ungekürzten Interviews*, ed. Robert Fischer (Berlin: Verlag der Autoren, 2004), 130–31.

98. Ursula Frohne, "Expanded Fassbinder—On the Aesthetic Legacy of Cinema in Contemporary Art," in *Fassbinder Now: Film and Video Art*, ed. Deutsches Filminstitut and the Rainer Werner Fassbinder Foundation (Frankfurt am Main: Deutsches Filminstitut, Filmmuseum, 2013), 31; Claire Kaiser, "Exposed Bodies, Evacuated Identities," in Peucker, *Companion to Rainer Werner Fassbinder*, 112. For the later works, Elena Del Río proposes a different reading of Fassbinder's tableaux as a "vital," "intense locus of force." *Deleuze and the Cinemas of Performance: Powers of Affection* (Edinburgh: Edinburgh University Press, 2012), 68. In her syncretic reading at the intersection of Brecht with Artaud, distanciation becomes the precondition for the emergence of a different kind of affect, as opposed to sentimentality (72–73).

99. Del Rio, *Deleuze and the Cinemas of Performance*, 73. See also Frohne on the film's "anti-narrative structures" in "Expanded Fassbinder," 31. Hermann Kappelhoff revises the Brechtian reading by underlining how Fassbinder (even in the early *Katzelmacher*) relates Brecht's techniques to the gestural repertoire of Hollywood melodrama. "Gestische Emblematik: Fassbinder's *Katzelmacher* und Brecht's 'sozialer Gestus,'" in *Schauspielen und Montage: Schauspielkunst im Film*, ed. Knut Hickethier (St. Augustin: Gardez!, 1999), see 196, 198. However, he ties this conceptualization back into the film's dominant reading by postulating the complete separation of rhetoric from body in the film (see 204). Later, he ends up rewording the diagnosis of a frozen gaze: the "film's staging conducts a kind of autopsy" that presents the ensemble's acting "to the dissector's scientific gaze"; *Katzelmacher*'s montage presents "but a series of fragmentary scenes." Hermann Kappelhoff, *The Politics and Poetics of Cinematic Realism* (New York: Columbia University Press, 2015), 120, 124. See similarly Anne Marie Freybourg, *Bilder lesen: Visionen von Liebe und Politik bei Godard und Fassbinder* (Vienna: Passagen, 1996), 76.

100. Roland Barthes, "Diderot, Brecht, Eisenstein," trans. Stephen Heath, *Screen* 15, no. 2 (1974): 35; Stephen Heath, "Lessons from Brecht," *Screen* 15, no. 2 (1974): 122; Mulvey, "Visual Pleasure and Narrative Cinema," 14. Brecht's own writings resonate with this emphasis at moments (see, e.g., his comments on Alfred Döblin's "epic" writing in "Theatre for Pleasure or Theatre for Instruction," 110). Overall, however, he is far less antinarrative. Critically, on the antinarrativity of 1970s Brechtianism, see Polan, "A Brechtian Cinema?," 663, as well as Nenad Jovanovic, who outlines that Brecht's concept of montage draws on Pudovkin among the Soviet theorists, who emphasized plot. See *Brechtian Cinemas: Montage and Theatricality in Jean-Marie Straub and Danièle Huillet, Peter Watkins, and Lars v. Trier* (Albany: State University of New York Press, 2017), 12, 24–26.

101. Lauren Berlant and Lee Edelman, *Sex, or the Unbearable* (Durham, NC: Duke University Press, 2014), viii, 3, 57. Explicitly in response to Eve Kosofsky Sedgwick's notion of reparativity, Edelman continues to advocate for modernist shock techniques and for a politics of "irony" as "the negativity of dissent." Berlant and Edelman, *Sex, or the Unbearable*, 48, 8, 70.

102. See Muñoz, "Introduction," 123.

103. Massumi, *Parables*, 25–26; see 28; Brian Massumi, *The Power at the End of the Economy* (Durham, NC: Duke University Press, 2015), 105. As indicated in the introduction, Massumi does introduce alternative concepts of temporality in calling for a non-Saussurian "semiotics willing to engage with continuity" and foregrounding the themes of "variation" and "transformation" (*Parables*, 3, 4, 9) as well as "worlding" as such (*The Power*, 107).

104. Berlant, *Cruel Optimism*, 5 and passim; Elizabeth Freeman, *Time Binds: Queer Temporalities, Queer Histories* (Durham, NC: Duke University Press, 2010), xxii, 21, 15.

105. Freeman, *Time Binds*, xxi, xvii, xiii.

106. Freeman, *Time Binds*, 14.

107. Berlant, *Cruel Optimism*, 14, 5, 10; Berlant and Edelman, *Sex, or the Unbearable*, 20. Their exchange underlines how Berlant's emphases on historical context, situation, and scene complicate Edelman's temporalities. *Sex, or the Unbearable*, 4–14.

108. Berlant, *Cruel Optimism*, 21, 27, 198, 228, 263; see, e.g., 199.

109. On how to rethink narrative as including modernist forms, see my earlier *An Aesthetics of Narrative Performance Transnational Theater, Literature and Film in Contemporary Germany* (Columbus: Ohio State University Press, 2012); on narrative and montage during the Weimar Republic, see Patrizia McBride, *The Chatter of the Visible: Montage and Narrative in Weimar Germany* (Ann Arbor: University of Michigan Press, 2016).

110. Roswitha Mueller, "Brecht the Realist and New German Cinema," *Framework* 25 (1984): 47. Mueller situates Fassbinder's early work as in line with Brecht's own early radical experiments and emphasis on the relative autonomy of the gestus, as opposed to both his and New German Cinema's later shift "towards audience expectations" and an increased emphasis on the "fable" (45–46). Intriguingly, however, a reviewer in 1969 characterized *Katzelmacher* as "almost a commercial film in aesthetic terms." Jansen, "Der Griech aus Griechenland." Certainly not just "pure succession" without "any progressive chain of events" (Kappelhoff, *The Politics*, 123–24), *Katzelmacher* clearly tells "a story." Jansen, "Der Griech aus Griechenland."

111. Mueller, "Brecht the Realist," 47.

112. On slow modernism as intertwining space and time in assembling heterogeneous elements, see Lutz Koepnick, *On Slowness Toward an Aesthetic of the Contemporary* (New York: Columbia University Press, 2014), 21 and passim; on *Katzelmacher*, see Koutsourakis, *Rethinking* (in passing).

113. Berlant, in Berlant and Edelman, *Sex, or the Unbearable*, 25.

114. Berlant, "Starved," 81; Berlant, in Berlant and Edelman, *Sex, or the Unbearable*, 56; see 19. "Queer" resonates literally as well as metaphorically here. Berlant plays on how the notion has been conceptualized against identity-centered approaches, and my reading analogously situates Fassbinder's cinema as one in which affects, attachments, desires, and identifications do not line up neatly. See Eve Kosofsky Sedgwick, *Tendencies* (London: Routledge, 1994), 6–8.

115. Freybourg explicates the negative affect underlying concepts of distanciation in arguing that *Katzelmacher* uses film's possibilities for evoking feelings as

"aggressive violence." *Bilder lesen*, 84. Fassbinder himself repeatedly qualified his interest in Brecht, suggesting, for example, that he (Fassbinder) was interested in "people" (die Menschen) and that his use of *Verfremdung* was stylistic rather than "intellectual," as was the case with Brecht or Alexander Kluge. See Rainer Werner Fassbinder, "Meine Filme handeln von Abhängigkeit," interview by Christian Braad Thomsen, 1971, in Fischer, *Fassbinder über Fassbinder*, 224.

116. The latter effect was diagnosed by the *New York Times* reviewer quoted on my DVD edition. My affective response can be bolstered by appealing to the (equally nonsovereign) authority of the director: Fassbinder talks about making his films "beautiful" in 1969, of wanting to do something else than "simply using alienation technique" and of hoping for audiences to "experience the kind of rage I feel." Rainer Werner Fassbinder, "The Kind of Rage I Feel," in Fassbinder, *The Anarchy of the Imagination*, 3, 5.

117. Elsaesser acknowledges the "visually sumptuous" quality of Fassbinder's films (from *Katzelmacher* onward) and the ways in which they provide audiences with a "tactile sensation of bodies agonizingly and violently in contact with each other." *Fassbinder's Germany*, 240.

118. For a more sustained theoretical exploration of affect and mess, see Katrin Pahl, "What a Mess," *Modern Language Notes* 130, no. 3 (2015): 528–53. I use the notion in a methodologically more limited way than Pahl insofar as I argue that a focus on the details of a film's configuration does allow for *some* sorting out, if—again—slowly.

119. The terminology of "guest work" conveyed the official expectation that West Germany's postwar labor recruitment from a number of Mediterranean countries (1955–1973) would not result in permanent immigration, while it was to provide a "positive" alternative to the country's tradition of *Fremdarbeit* (alien labor), including massive-scale forced labor practices during both world wars. Some of *Katzelmacher*'s 1969 reviewers keep reverting to the notion of *Fremdarbeit*, along with most of the film characters, who are at one point corrected by Elisabeth, who hosts the Greek.

120. Freybourg, *Bilder lesen*, 77; see also, e.g., Alexandra Ludewig, *Screening Nostalgia: 100 Years of German Heimat Film* (Berlin: Transcript, 2011), 247.

121. Elsaesser, *Fassbinder's Germany*, 29. Elsaesser highlights Fassbinder's "apparently non-judgmental relation to destructive or evil characters" (29), in line with the director's expression of love for his characters, including those who do "bad things" (böse Sachen). Rainer Werner Fassbinder, "Hollywoods Geschichten," interview by Christian Braad Thomsen, in Fischer, *Fassbinder über Fassbinder*, 236. See also Frohne, "Expanded Fassbinder," 37.

122. Thus, "plot" is "an elaborate conjugation of interdependent couples." Elsaesser, *Fassbinder's Germany*, 270.

123. Berlant, *Cruel Optimism*, 5.

124. Decoding increasingly explicit allusions, we may eventually understand that the plan is that of pimping out Marie and Helga; see Rainer Werner Fassbinder, "Alles Vernünftige interessiert mich nicht," interview by Wolfgang Limmer and Fritz Rumler, 1980, in Fischer, *Fassbinder über Fassbinder*, 513. However, the delay is crucial for the film's assembly of affects and its poetics of parallels and contrasts between scenarios. In the exposition sequence, the focus is on the women's expressed concern for their men.

125. Even Elsaesser claims that the "deadpan, deliberately wooden dialogue is intended to point to the characters' stark emotional isolation from each other." *Fassbinder's Germany*, 270.

126. "Eine Liebe und so, das hat immer mit Geld was zu tun." *Katzelmacher*'s language can be traced back to Marieluise Fleisser, to whom the film is dedicated. See, e.g., Wallace Steadman Watson, *Understanding Rainer Werner Fassbinder: Film as Private and Public Art* (Columbia: University of South Carolina Press, 1996), 81; Michael Töteberg, *Rainer Werner Fassbinder* (Reinbek: Rowohlt, 2002), 36.

127. Frohne, "Expanded Fassbinder," 35; see Özkan Ezli, "Peripherien zwischen Repräsentation und Individuation: Die Körper der Minderheiten in Fassbinders *Katzelmacher* und *Angst Essen Seele auf*," in *Prekäre Obsession: Minoritäten im Werk von Rainer Werner Fassbinder*, ed. Nicole Colin, Franziska Schößler, and Nike Thurn (Bielefeld: Transcript, 2012), 104; Koutsourakis, *Rethinking*, 218.

128. When Fassbinder describes the shared "theme" of his films as "the exploitability of feelings within the system that we live in," his analysis starts from the presence of feelings. Rainer Werner Fassbinder, "'I've Changed Along with the Characters in My Films'; A Discussion with Hella Schlumberger," in Fassbinder, *The Anarchy of the Imagination*, 28.

129. The film's approximation of sexual and romantic feeling is explicated in the recurring use of the expression *etwas fühlen* (to feel something) in relation to both. In the first of the film's shots of walking couples (for more generally on these scenes, see toward the end of my reading), for example, Maria and Helga use the phrase linked, in quick succession, to claims about their men being *lieb* (good/endearing/nice) as well as *gut* (good, related to sexual attraction or performance).

130. During one of their encounters, Franz asks Rosy, "Couldn't we do a little more, as though it was love or something?" (Kann man nicht ein bisschen mehr machen, als wärs Liebe oder so?), as well as whether she has "a desire/pleasure with me" (eine Lust mit mir). Her defensive response, "I don't know anything about that, I have to make a living," is in tension with her repeated tender gestures. Later Rosy implicitly acknowledges Franz's romantic framework: sitting closely next to him, she asks him not to have hopes for the relationship

because she is "different." He replies, "Everyone needs a love," and her response, "Nicht gewöhnlich darf es sein" (It may not be ordinary), ambiguously opens the fantasy of a nonordinary relationship between them. Erich, Rosy's former boyfriend, dramatizes her resistance against feelings by complaining that there was no *Zärtlichkeit* (tenderness) with her, while underlining that she did not ask him for money. Simultaneously, he defends Rosy against the others' moral indignation about her work relationship with Franz. Diegetically, this fits with Erich's own interest of profiting from Marie's beauty, but extradiegetically, it also fits with the director's expressed nonjudgmental take on sex work; see Fassbinder, "Alles Vernünftige," 513–14. In short, money, sex, and feeling mix freely in *Katzelmacher*'s world of everyday behaviors.

131. Brecht, "Notes on Pointed Heads and Round Heads," 163.

132. Kappelhoff, *The Politics*, 126; Karl Korn, "Die Unbehausten: Eine filmische Bestandsaufnahme von R. W. Fassbinder," *Frankfurter Allgemeine Zeitung*, no. 282, December 5, 1969.

133. André Green, *The Fabric of Affect in the Psychoanalytic Discourse*, trans. Alan Sheridan (London: Routledge, 1999), xv.

134. Green, *The Fabric of Affect*, 182.

135. See Green, *The Fabric of Affect*, 166, 178.

136. Eve Kosofsky Sedgwick, *Touching Feeling: Affect, Pedagogy, Performativity* (Durham, NC: Duke University Press, 2003), 128–38; Eve Kosofsky Sedgwick, "Melanie Klein and the Difference Affect Makes," in Halley and Parker, *After Sex?*, 283–301.

137. The reviewer uses the Brechtian notion *Lehrstück*; see J. S., "Die deutschen Kleinstädter: Fassbinder's 'Katzelmacher' ab Freitag im 'Cinema Paris,'" *Abend*, June 30, 1970. See also Jansen, "Der Griech aus Griechenland."

138. On bracketing as a phenomenological technique of defamiliarization, see Bert O. States, "The Phenomenological Attitude," in *Critical Theory and Performance*, ed. Janelle G. Reinelt and Joseph R. Roach, rev. ed. (Ann Arbor: University of Michigan Press, 2007), 26–36.

139. The quote is from Green, *The Fabric of Affect*, 184.

140. In recent humanities debates around reading practices, my insistence on multivectorality thus departs from Heather Love's plea for "thin" description. See Heather Love, "Close Reading and Thin Description," *Public Culture* 25, no. 3 (2013): 401–34. Love argues not against using thick description per se but for probing the reading of behavior without "intention, emotion, cognition and depth, as well as cultural context" (403). Given my interest precisely in these along with other "affective and aesthetic qualities," I nonetheless reverse the emphasis, even as I join Love's efforts to deprivilege the linear vectors of "depth hermeneutics." Love, "Close Reading," 403, 411.

141. Berlant, *Cruel Optimism*, 14.

142. See Berlant, *Cruel Optimism*.

143. The quote is from Kappelhoff, who acknowledges this quality of the film even while denying *Katzelmacher* "living" expression. *The Politics*, 130; see 119–20. He explains the intensity effect exclusively through the poetics of delay (129–30). His argument is in part media-ontological: unlike Brecht's stage, film "always already" fictionalizes the "physical appearance of the actors," as the camera "occup[ies]" the narrating position with which the actors are endowed in Brecht's theater (120). I disagree: narrative authority can be shared, and "living" or real and affecting expression is not restricted to the theater or even to more naturalized forms of film acting.

144. Erich tells Helga, "Zu einer Liebe, da gehört schon ein Schmerz," when she protests his roughness during a sexual encounter between them, after Marie has left Erich. Marie later describes her love for Jorgos as a sensation also of pain.

145. The exact wording in *My Life to Live* is less forward looking: *recommencer à vivre* (to live again). See Berlant, *Cruel Optimism*, 4 and passim.

146. McMahon, to be sure, sees "the pleasure of rhythm and movement" counteracted by "the static, frontal framing" and "lack" of "music." See "Imitation, Seriality, Cinema," 93. See also Svetlana Svyatskaya, "The Overwhelming Moments of Misfortune: Jesper Just and Rainer Werner Fassbinder," in Deutsches Filminstitut and the Rainer Werner Fassbinder Foundation, *Fassbinder Now*, 237. In visual terms, the intertextual "quotation" is very loose and reads as such perhaps only if we have deciphered the earlier explicit verbal citation.

147. Gunda talks about a boyfriend who is away "on construction" but we never see him, and the others doubt his existence or commitment. The shot preceding Rosy's dance emphasizes Gunda's spatial isolation at the railing in-between couples.

148. A subsequent scene shows Gunda returning to Rosy's apartment to ask for money Rosy owes her, alluding to Rosy's new sex work earnings. The shot further curtails the possibility of escape in establishing a visual counterpoint to the dance scene, as both women tensely walk around each other against the bare wall.

149. Brecht, "On Experiments in Epic Theatre," 118 (Brecht's emphasis).

150. Brecht, "The German Drama," 122.

151. Sara Ahmed, "Affective Economies," *Social Text* 79 (2004): 117.

152. Ahmed, "Affective Economies," 120; see 121. Ahmed spells out how she both draws on and departs from Freud in opening up the psychic toward social processes and foregrounding "sideways" over the linear "backward" movement of symptomatic reading (120, 126).

153. Ahmed, "Affective Economies," 117; see also Ezli, "Peripherien zwischen Repräsentation und Individuation," 104.

154. Ahmed, "Affective Economies," 119.

155. On this threat of proximity, see Ahmed, "Affective Economies," 117.

156. Ahmed, "Affective Economies," 119, 121.

157. "Eine Ordnung muss wieder her." "Eine Rache muss sein." "Da gehören wir her und sonst nix."

158. Ahmed, "Affective Economies," 127.

159. Ahmed, "Affective Economies," 26.

160. Peter's affective mutedness first ruptures when he tries to buy violent sex with Rosy, who asserts her transactional agency when he tears her bra: this is not worth the money. Later Peter hits Elisabeth at the dinner table in front of Jorgos and participates in beating him up.

161. These three techniques have been associated too closely in debates on critique and postcritique; see Elizabeth S. Anker and Rita Felski, eds., *Critique and Post-critique* (Durham, NC: Duke University Press, 2017), 1.

162. The quote is from Anker and Felski, *Critique and Postcritique*, 4.

163. ". . . als die alten bis zur allgemeinen Bewusstlosigkeit zu konstituieren."

164. The motif is first introduced with Gunda's failed attempt at seducing Jorgos (which will result in her fantasy of violence), if in even more minimalist fashion: the trees in the background of their encounter are bare. But if Gunda's dreams do not bloom the way Marie's do, might the montage effect of layered association and contrast still acknowledge them as the barest of dreams?

165. Joe McElhaney, "A Nagging Physical Discomfort: Fassbinder and Martha," in Peucker, *Companion to Rainer Werner Fassbinder*, 206.

166. See similarly McMahon, "Imitation, Seriality, Cinema," 95; Elsaesser, *Fassbinder's Germany*, 270.

167. Fassbinder, "I've changed," 19. Elsaesser makes this point similarly for Fassbinder's films more generally in *Fassbinder's Germany*, 32.

3. GENRE ASSEMBLAGES: AFFECTIVE INCISIONS IN FATIH AKIN'S *THE CUT* AND AKI KAURISMÄKI'S REFUGEE TRILOGY

1. See Rüdiger Suchsland, "Langsames Leben, schöne Tage: Annäherungen an die 'Berliner Schule,'" *Film-Dienst* 58, no. 13 (2005): 6–9.

2. "Genre movies are not acceptable." See Lars von Trier and Thomas Vinterberg, on behalf of Dogme 95, "The Vow of Chastity," *Dogme95.dk*, accessed May 18, 2019, http://www.dogme95.dk/the-vow-of-chastity/. Since then, dogme cofounder Lars von Trier has experimented with just about everything from musical (*Dancer in the Dark*, 2000) to "German romance" (*Melancholia*, 2011); see Lars von Trier, "Director's Statement: *Melancholia*,"

Melancholia press kit, TrustNordisk, April 13, 2011, http://www.trustnordisk.com/film/2010-melancholia.

3. On this brand, see, e.g., Andrew Nestingen, *The Cinema of Aki Kaurismäki: Contrarian Stories* (London: Wallflower Press, 2013). To be sure, a more complex story can be told for Fatih Akın's films also. While *The Cut* does read as an actual turn to genre in relation to *The Edge of Heaven*, Akın's earliest features also had crime, comedy, and road movie affiliations (*Short Sharp Shock*, 1998; *In July*, 2000). Rather than being an art director who "lapsed" into genre in the 2010s, Akın is a multimode filmmaker who has developed strikingly different forms for different projects. The "refugee trilogy" label was introduced by Aki Kaurismäki in a press conference on *The Other Side of Hope*. See Barbara Möller, "Flüchtling, kommst du nach Finnland," *Die Welt*, February 15, 2017, https://www.welt.de/print/welt_kompakt/kultur/article162089830/Fluechtling-kommst-du-nach-Finnland.html.

4. E.g., A. O. Scott, "Finding Solace, Oceans from Home," *New York Times*, October 20, 2011, sec. Movies, https://nyti.ms/2BuvdDn.

5. *The Cut* had its premiere at the 2014 Venice Film Festival. It was quickly released in Germany, where it was nominated for 2015 German film prizes in three categories, and in Turkey, but it had only a very limited run in the United States.

6. Daniel Kothenschulte, "Der Tod fährt manchmal mit der deutschen Bahn," *Die Welt*, August 31, 2014; "Ein süffiges Epos mit allen Vor- und Nachteilen," according to Rüdiger Suchsland, "Die 40 Tage des Fatih Akin. Venedig-Blog, 3. Folge," *Negativ* (blog), September 1, 2014, http://www.negativ-film.de/2014/09/die-40-tage-des-fatih-akin-venedig-blog-3-folge; see similarly Peter Bradshaw, "*The Cut* Review: Fatih Akin's Armenian Genocide Epic Draws Blood," *The Guardian*, August 31, 2014.

7. Andreas Busche, "Tränen und majestätische Landschaften," *die tageszeitung*, October 15, 2014.

8. Fatih Akın, "Q&A: Fatih Akın Discusses His New Film *The Cut*," interview by Stephen Heyman, *New York Times*, August 26, 2014.

9. "Verbeugung vor der Anmutung der großen Kinos der Vergangenheit," according to Kothenschulte, "Der Tod."

10. In 2014 (in the press notes for *The Cut*), Akın hopefully speaks of a gradual lifting of the social taboo, but the controversy has since been reheated. Fatih Akın, "An Interview with Fatih Akin, Director & Screenwriter," press notes for *The Cut*, Strand Releasing, 2014, https://strandreleasing.com/films/cut/; see, e.g., Deutsche Presse-Agentur et al., "Erdogan: Turkey Will 'Never Accept' Genocide Charges," *Deutsche Welle*, June 4, 2016, https://p.dw.com/p/1Jof5; Raffi Khatchadourian, "Remembering the Armenian Genocide," *New Yorker*, April 21, 2015, https://www.newyorker.com/news/daily-comment/remembering-the-armenian-genocide.

11. Akın, quoted in Jochen Kürten and Oliver Glasenapp, "Processing a Collective Trauma," *Quantara.de*, September 11, 2014, https://en.qantara.de/node/18318.

12. Fatih Akın, "Mit Leibwächtern würde ich mich besser fühlen," interview by Hanns-Georg Rodek and Peter Praschl, *Die Welt*, October 13, 2014; see Akın as quoted in Kürten and Glasenapp, "Processing a Collective Trauma." The German Amazon video and DVD reviews are also clearly positive (4.2/5), and the audience reviews on Rotten Tomatoes are better than, if not as radically different from, the critical ones (with a score of 65 percent vs. 60 percent as of May 26, 2019).

13. According to Susanne Ostwald, Akın's attempt to produce "a contemporary historical cinema of great emotions" (großes zeitgeschichtliches Gefühlskino) fails to actually incite emotional involvement; see "Fatih Akın scheitert mit *The Cut*," *Neue Zürcher Zeitung*, September 1, 2014, http://www.nzz.ch/feuilleton/kino/fatih-akin-scheitert-mit-the-cut-1.18374179. In contrast, some of the audience reviews on Rotten Tomatoes do assert the film's "very emotional" or "heart pounding" character. Aleksandra M. and Griffin J., "The Cut Reviews," Rotten Tomatoes, April 22, 2017/April 3, 2016, https://www.rottentomatoes.com/m/the_cut/reviews?type=user.

14. Jacques Rancière, *Dissensus: On Politics and Aesthetics*, ed. and trans. Steven Corcoran (London: Continuum, 2010), 33, 36.

15. Rancière, *Dissensus*, 32.

16. See Bruno Latour, *Reassembling the Social: An Introduction to Actor-Network-Theory* (Oxford: Oxford University Press, 2005), 217–18.

17. The quote is from Brian Massumi, *The Power at the End of the Economy* (Durham, NC: Duke University Press, 2015), 37.

18. Bertolt Brecht, "On Experimental Theatre," in Bertolt Brecht, *Brecht on Theatre*, ed. Mark Silberman, Steve Giles, and Tom Kuhn, 3rd ed. (London: Bloomsbury, 2015), 143.

19. Gilles Deleuze, *Cinema 2: The Time-Image*, trans. Hugh Tomlinson and Robert Galeta (Minneapolis: University of Minnesota Press, 1989), 216 (Deleuze's emphasis).

20. Fatih Akın, "An Interview."

21. All English translations here are mine; my DVD edition has only German titles.

22. Bertolt Brecht, "Theatre for Pleasure or Theatre for Instruction," in Brecht, *Brecht on Theatre*, 109.

23. See *100 Armenian Tales*, collected and edited by Susie Hoogasian Villa (Detroit: Wayne State University Press, 1996, 58); Barbara Pflegerl, *Es war einmal, es war keinmal. Türkische Volksmärchen* (Vienna: Böhlau, 1992).

24. Fatih Akın, "Q&A: Fatih Akın Discusses His New Film *The Cut*"; Fatih Akın, "An Interview." Yilmaz Güney wrote *Yol* while imprisoned; the film was banned in Turkey for its negative portrayal of the country and pro-Kurdish theme.

25. Fatih Akın, "An Interview."

26. In the interview in the press notes, Akın references Wolfgang Gust's research on the role of the German Empire (see http://www.armenocide.de/). Fatih Akın, "An Interview." The Germans were aware of the genocide plans and minimally became complicit in not stopping and in variously justifying the actions of their Ottoman allies. More recent research also supports the charge that German army officers had a significant role in the initial recommendations to deport Armenenians for supposed security concerns. There is less evidence for larger-scale direct involvement in the atrocities. See Carl-Alexander Krethlow, "Deutsche Militärs und die Armenier 1835–1916: Demographische Konzepte, Sicherheitsmaßnahmen und Verstrickungen," in *Das Deutsche Reich und der Völkermord an den Armeniern*, ed. Rolf Hosfeld and Christin Pschichholz (Göttingen: Wallstein, 2017), 149–71; Isabel V. Hull, "Deutsche Militärs und der Völkermord an den Armeniern," in Hosfeld and Pschichholz, *Das Deutsche Reich und der Völkermord an den Armeniern*, 182–214. The film's allusions to the German presence on the scene have been highlighted by reviewers: see Kothenschulte, "Der Tod"; Suchsland, "Die vierzig Tage des Fatih Akin." More generally on the film's historical detailing of setting, costume, etc., see Anke Westphal, "Der Genozid und das Schweigen: Fatih Akins *The Cut*," *Berliner Zeitung*, September 1, 2014.

27. Charles J. Maland, *Chaplin and American Culture: The Evolution of a Star Image* (Princeton, NJ: Princeton University Press, 1989), 59.

28. Walter Serner, "Cinema and Visual Pleasure," trans. Don Reneau, in *The Promise of Cinema: German Film Theory 1907–1933*, ed. Anton Kaes, Nicholas Baer, and Michael Cowan (Berkeley: University of California Press, 2016), 41.

29. Serner, "Cinema and Visual Pleasure," 44, 42.

30. Hermann Duenschmann, "Cinematograph and Crowd Psychology: A Sociopolitical Study," trans. Eric Ames, in Kaes, Baer, and Cowan, *The Promise of Cinema*, 257 (Duenschmann's emphasis).

31. André Bazin, *What Is Cinema?*, trans. Hugh Gray, vol. 1 (Berkeley: University of California Press, 2005), 99.

32. I am alluding to Althusser's concept of interpellation here. See Louis Althusser, "Ideology and Ideological State Apparatuses," in *On Ideology*, trans. Ben Brewster (London: Verso, 2008), 1–60.

33. On these standards, see David Bordwell, *The Way Hollywood Tells It: Story and Style in Modern Movies* (Berkeley: University of California Press, 2006), 129.

34. *The Cut's* Armenians speak an accented English underlining their minority status, but oral communication with other groups in the Ottoman Empire is not shown to be an issue. In this sense, the film emphasizes the multicultural normalcy interrupted by the genocide. Akın explains that he decided to use English in part to facilitate his own work with the actors, as he does not speak Armenian.

But he also references Roman Polanski's *The Pianist*, where English is made "a language of identification" by having the Polish but not the German characters speak it. See Fatih Akın, "Q&A: Fatih Akın Discusses His New Film *The Cut*."

35. The plot also drives home the point: when in Cuba, Nazaret's host pressures him to go to church, and Nazaret explicitly consents only for the sake of their human connection, not that with God. Worse, the church community assembly turns into a prelude for violence: Nazaret identifies, follows, and beats up the prospective husband of one of his daughters because Nazaret had heard he did not follow through on his marriage proposal and thus prompted the daughters' further migration before Nazaret's arrival.

36. Akın, as quoted in Kothenschulte, "Der Tod." On the use of both the Anatolian and the Baghdad railways in the Armenian genocide, see Peter Balakian, *The Burning Tigris: The Armenian Genocide and America's Response* (New York: Perennial, 2003), 190–96.

37. David Bordwell, *Poetics of Cinema* (New York: Routledge, 2007), 294.

38. To be precise, when Nazaret escapes, he is initially accompanied by the Turkish deserter who saves his life in the group execution, and they briefly join a group of Turkish robbers. But when the gang targets a rich Armenian acquaintance from Nazaret's hometown in the first holdup we see, Nazaret walks off into the desert by himself, revoking allegiance with both sides.

39. On how the return to so-called classical staging historically "normalized" widescreen cinematography after the first few years, see Bordwell, *Poetics*, 306; see also David Bordwell, "Widescreen Aesthetics and Mise en Scene Criticism," *Velvet Light Trap* 21 (Summer 1985): 25.

40. The quote is from Bordwell, *Poetics*, 308 (Bordwell's emphasis).

41. See Adrian Danks, "'People Are Waiting': Elia Kazan's *America America*," *Senses of Cinema* 62 (2012), http://sensesofcinema.com/2012/cteq/people-are-waiting-elia-kazan-and-america-america; see also Fatih Akın, "An Interview." Filmed from less extreme angles (and minus the widescreen format), *Yol* also features resonant scenes of exposure in nature.

42. *America America* opens in the late 1800s, but the anti-Armenian pogroms shown foreshadow the genocide. Stavros stabs the Turk with the knife that his singularly fierce grandmother had pressed on him, against his own earlier convictions, but he does so only after the Turk threatened Stavros with murder, taunting him with racist slurs about the Greeks' supposed meekness. Akın's reassembly unsettles Kazan's ethnic codings. Whereas Stavros offers his shoes to Hohannes in the first of the scenes discussed, this gesture is echoed by Mehmet, the Turk who saves Nazaret by (only) cutting his throat, in a gesture of asking for forgiveness, which Nazaret accepts. *The Cut*'s emotional simplicity thus does not translate into a reethnicizing of conflict.

43. Kelly Oliver, *Earth and World: Philosophy After the Apollo Missions* (New York: Columbia University Press, 2015), 31, with reference to Hannah Arendt's use of the desert metaphor.

44. Colin Root, "Stretching the Screen: Horizontality, the CinemaScope Film, and the Cold War," *Quarterly Review of Film and Video* 32, no. 5 (2015): 464, 459.

45. Bazin, as quoted in Bordwell, "Widescreen Aesthetics," 19. Bordwell cites Bazin's claim that the midcentury innovations toward spatial unity went "beyond convention" to explore "phenomenal reality." Of course, other scholars have objected: the "monumentally baroque medium" of CinemaScope increased "artifice" along with realism. See James Spellerberg, "CinemaScope and Ideology," *Velvet Light Trap* 21 (1985): 30–32. Akın's self-aware deployment of widescreen as a technology of experiential storytelling annuls the controversy.

46. Douglas Pye, "The Western (Genre and Movies)," in *Film Genre Reader IV*, ed. Barry Keith Grant (Austin: University of Texas Press, 2012), 251; Gilles Deleuze, *Cinema 1: The Movement-Image*, trans. Hugh Tomlinson (London: Athlone Press, 1986), 146.

47. See John White, *Westerns* (New York: Routledge, 2011), 7.

48. The first quote is from Brian Massumi, *Politics of Affect* (Malden, MA: Polity, 2015), 6. Oliver foregrounds Martin Heidegger's critique of technological globalization as the source of unworlding/desertification but also references a text set in a Russian prison-of-war camp; see *Earth and World*, 33.

49. See, e.g., Massumi, *The Power*.

50. Balakian, *The Burning Tigris*, 192, 257. Ras-ul-Ain (Balakian's spelling) was a station on the Baghdad Railway (257). The camp inhabitants had been deported there both by train and on foot; many were dying even upon arrival from starvation, illness, exhaustion, and abuse, including mass-scale rape. See also the documents collected by the Institute of History, Armenian National Academy of Sciences, *Die armenische Frage und der Genozid an den Armeniern in der Türkei (1913–19): Dokumente des politischen Archivs des Auswärtigen Amts Deutschlands*, ed. Wardges Mikaeljan (Yerevan: Armenian National Academy of Sciences, 2004), http://www.aga-online.org/german-records/attachments/deutscheAktenStuecke.pdf.

51. A German reviewer singles out this sequence as the visually "strongest" of the film. See Jan Schulz-Ojala, "Armenien-Drama von Fatih Akın *The Cut*: Der stumme Schrei," *Der Tagesspiegel*, October 15, 2015. Historical records cited by Balakian mention black tents and blue caftans, which underlines that the film's color palette in this sequence is an artistic choice; see *The Burning Tigris*, 257–58.

52. Giorgio Agamben, *Homo Sacer: Sovereign Power and Bare Life*, trans. Daniel Heller-Roazen (Stanford, CA: Stanford University Press, 1998), 166. The notion of "letting die" is, of course, Michel Foucault's. Agamben seeks to bring together

Foucault's biopolitical paradigm and Hannah Arendt's conceptualizations of totalitarianism. See Michel Foucault, *History of Sexuality*, vol. 1, *An Introduction*, trans. Robert Hurley (New York: Vintage, 1978). For Agamben, the camp is the vanishing point of a longer biopolitical process in which biological life displaced "the free man" as the "subject of politics." *Homo Sacer*, 124.

53. Agamben, *Homo Sacer*, 171.

54. Agamben, *Homo Sacer*, 171, 153.

55. Agamben, *Homo Sacer*, 185.

56. Ben Singer, *Melodrama and Modernity: Early Sensational Cinema and Its Contexts* (New York: Columbia University Press, 2001), 53. Importantly, the heightened emotionality associated with melodrama cannot be described as "excessive relative" to the diegetic "situation" in *The Cut* or as an expression of ideological conflicts repressed by the narrative (see 57, 39). Linda Williams critiques these scholarly tropes of excess by underlining that melodrama "is the fundamental mode of popular American moving pictures," not an embarrassing deviation from the norm: "supposedly realist cinematic *effects* . . . most often operate in the service of melodramatic *affects*." "Melodrama Revised," in *Refiguring American Film Genres: History and Theory*, ed. Nick Browne (Berkeley: University of California Press, 1998), 42 (Williams's emphasis).

57. The film's overall emphasis on fictional mediation reads as a cautionary move in relation to the debate on historical and artistic representation in the wake of the Holocaust here: the visual presentation of Akın's camp offers anchoring points for imagining the horrors portrayed rather than direct access.

58. Fatih Akın, "An Interview." See also Fatih Akın, "Mit Leibwächtern würde ich mich besser fühlen," where Akın mentions Klausmann's objections to other Western remakes. For a rethinking of the traditional concept of dignity for an anthropocenal humanism premised on "vulnerability and coexistence or belonging with others," see Gerda Roelvink, *Building Dignified Worlds: Geographies of Collective Action* (Minneapolis: University of Minnesota Press, 2016), 147.

59. Singer, *Melodrama and Modernity*, 40.

60. Dietmar Dath, "Fatih Akin in Venedig: Dem Kranich folgen," *Frankfurter Allgemeine Zeitung*, August 31, 2014.

61. This point about affective "orientation toward" builds on Olivia Landry's resonant argument in *Movement and Performance in Berlin School Cinema* (Bloomington: Indiana University Press, 2019), 80. The early, non-genre-affiliated Berlin School films that Landry discusses also feature walking characters and (less extremely) distant camera work. Simultaneously, these films are quite different from *The Cut*: as Landry suggests, they show their minority characters as "organically connected to the spaces" through which they move and empower them as points of perspectival authority, which phenomenologically undoes the distance between

viewer and character (90; see 93). In *The Cut*, the exposed character on screen does not have such worldmaking power. Rather than undoing the pronounced camera distance, the emphasis on movement merely facilitates an affective turning "toward" on our part.

62. Kothenschulte, "Der Tod."

63. Kothenschulte, "Der Tod."; Suchsland, "Die vierzig Tage des Fatih Akin."

64. On mood, see Robert Sinnerbrink, *"Stimmung*: Exploring the Aesthetics of Mood," *Screen* 53, no. 2 (2012): 148; also, Jonathan Flatley, *Affective Mapping: Melancholia and the Politics of Modernism* (Cambridge, MA: Harvard University Press, 2008), 19–24.

65. Wendy Brown, *Undoing the Demos: Neoliberalism's Stealth Revolution* (New York: Zone Books, 2015), 37.

66. On conviviality in this sense, see Paul Gilroy, *Postcolonial Melancholia* (New York: Columbia University Press, 2005).

67. Aki Kaurismäki, interview by Christine Masson, pressbook for *Le Havre*, Sputnik Oy, Pyramide International, and Pandora Film Produktion, 2011, 6.

68. Malcom Lewis, "Le Havre," *New Internationalist*, no. 451 (April 2012): 41; Peter von Bagh, "Common People: Aki Kaurismäki," *Film Comment* 47, no. 5 (September–October 2011): 38; see also Laura Rascaroli, "Becoming-Minor in a Sustainable Europe: The Contemporary European Art Film and Aki Kaurismäki's *Le Havre*," *Screen* 54, no. 3 (2013): 333. In Cannes, *Le Havre* won the FIPRESCI prize of the International Federation of Film Critics. The film was also nominated for the European Parliament's Lux Prize and served as the Finnish entry for the Best Foreign Language Film at the Eighty-Fourth Academy Awards.

69. Kaurismäki, quoted in von Bagh, "Common People," 40.

70. Ryan Gilbey, "Ocean's Heaven," *New Statesman* 141, no. 5100/5101 (April 9–22, 2012): 84; Roger Ebert, "Review of *Le Havre*," *RogerEbert.com*, November 2, 2011, https://www.rogerebert.com/reviews/le-havre-2011; Nick James, "Shelter from the Storm," *Sight and Sound* 21, no. 7 (July 2011): 24–29.

71. Kaurismäki, quoted in von Bagh, "Common People," 41.

72. Von Bagh, "Common People," 41.

73. Kaurismäki, quoted in Bert Cardullo, "Finnish Character: An Interview with Aki Kaurismäki," *Film Quarterly* 59, no. 4 (Summer 2006): 8.

74. Vladimir Propp, *Morphology of the Folktale*, 2nd rev. ed. (Austin: University of Texas Press, 1968); for an overview, see Dmitry Olshansky, "The Birth of Structuralism from the Analysis of Fairy-Tales," *Toronto Slavic Quarterly* 25 (Summer 2008), http://sites.utoronto.ca/tsq/25/Olshansky25.shtml.

75. See Propp, *Morphology of the Folktale*, 25–65.

76. Patrick Colm Hogan, *Affective Narratology: The Emotional Structure of Stories* (Lincoln: University of Nebraska Press, 2011), 1, 80, 33 (Hogan's emphasis).

77. Hogan defines home as the "center toward which we tend" and underlines that his notion of " 'normalcy' " is "defined by emotional response, not by objective conditions." *Affective Narratology*, 30, 77. Nonetheless, the assumption that all human beings share emotional proclivities for a state of normalcy should be marked as such: an assumption. Further complications abound if we engage Hogan's typology of genres, which aims to map the variety of narrative forms across cultures and periods onto three major plot types grounded in individual, separate emotions. *Le Havre* would have to be characterized as a combination of the romantic plot, based on love and attachment, and the heroic one, based on pride in relation to collective belonging (see 19, 129–30). But the latter does not make much sense here, especially because for Hogan, heroic pride is "obviously in conflict with" empathy (133). Notably, elements of Hogan's third, "sacrificial" genre, which restores normalcy through "punishment," are entirely absent (134). In foregoing the cruelty associated with the fairy-tale genre, Kaurismäki's contemporary fairy tale similarly undercuts William Flesh's even more reductive evolutionary attempt at generalizing the "human capacity for and delight in narrative" through the function of "comeuppance." See *Comeuppeance: Costly Signaling, Altruistic Punishment, and Other Biological Components of Fiction* (Cambridge, MA: Harvard University Press, 2009), 5.
78. Lauren Berlant, *Cruel Optimism* (Durham, NC: Duke University Press, 2011), 6.
79. Berlant, *Cruel Optimism*, 6. Hogan's "event" encompasses a "cause and response to an incident." *Affective Narratology*, 33. More generally, the event has been a key element of narrative theory since its structuralist beginnings.
80. Berlant, *Cruel Optimism*, 5.
81. Massumi, *The Power*, 37 (Massumi's emphasis).
82. Massumi, *The Power*, 42.
83. Massumi, *The Power*, 19, 72, 109.
84. Massumi, *The Power*, 35, 42.
85. Massumi, *The Power*, 35, 71, 64, 70–72. Massumi opposes affective joy to "pleasure" in the field of emotion.
86. "The multitude is the real productive force of our social world, whereas Empire is a mere apparatus of capture that lives off the vitality of the multitude." Michael Hardt and Antonio Negri, *Empire* (Cambridge, MA: Harvard University Press, 2001), 62.
87. Massumi, *The Power*, 76, 66; see Brian Massumi, *What Animals Teach Us About Politics* (Durham, NC: Duke University Press, 2014), 36. As indicated in the introduction, Massumi does acknowledge the complementary danger of "fascist contagion." *The Power*, 66.
88. Alain Badiou, *Ethics: An Essay on the Understanding of Evil*, trans. Peter Hallward (New York: Verso, 2000), see, in particular, 12, 43.

89. Badiou, *Ethics*, 41; see 13.

90. Badiou, *Ethics*, 28, 40, 46.

91. Badiou, *Ethics*, 53. What "arises from a truth-process," Badiou claims, "cannot be communicated" (50–51). Massumi characterizes sympathy as "immediate communication," insisting that this "communication" is "not a mediation" but "an archiving of affective immediacy." *The Power*, 64, 84.

92. Badiou, *Ethics*, 42–43.

93. I introduce Latour's notion (*Reassembling*, 45) in the introduction.

94. Stuart Klawans, "Times Squared," *The Nation*, November 28, 2011, https://www .thenation.com/article/times-squared/.

95. Badiou, *Ethics*, 51 (Badiou's emphasis).

96. Massumi, *The Power*, 60, 61.

97. See Rancière on the people vs. the multitudes divide in contemporary theory. *Dissensus*, 84–90. While the "Deleuzians" avoid the notion of the people, Deleuze himself does use it, as cited earlier, if with the emphasis that the people are "missing" in modern cinema. *Cinema 2*, 216.

98. Alain Badiou, "Twenty-Four Notes on the Uses of the Word 'People,'" in Alain Badiou, et al., *What Is a People?*, trans. Jody Gladding (New York: Columbia University Press, 2016), 21–22, 24, 26.

99. Badiou, "Twenty-Four Notes on the Uses of the Word 'People,'" 28.

100. Rascaroli, "Becoming-Minor in a Sustainable Europe," 334. Rascaroli's reading of *Le Havre* draws on Deleuze and Guattari's concept of minor literature.

101. Massumi, *The Power*, 43, 109 (Massumi's emphasis); Badiou, *Ethics*, 16.

102. The film was awarded a Silver Bear for Best Director.

103. See, e.g., Daniel Kothenschulte, "Von Hoffnung und anderen Gefühlen," *Frankfurter Rundschau*, February 8, 2017, sec. TV & Kino, https://www.fr.de/kultur /tv-kino/hoffnung-anderen-gefuehlen-11645127.html; Georg Seeßlen, "*Die andere Seite der Hoffnung*: Erst einmal eins auf die Nase," *Die Zeit*, March 26, 2017; Möller, "Flüchtling, kommst du nach Finnland"; Thomas Groh, "Es zählt der einzelne Mensch: Aki Kaurismäki's *Die andere Seite der Hoffnung* (Wettbewerb)," *Perlentaucher*, February 14, 2017; Elmar Krekeler, "Film: Der neue Kaurismäki. Was heißt Einwanderungsbehörde auf Finnisch?," *Die Welt*, March 30, 2017, https://www .welt.de/kultur/kino/article163258578/Was-heisst-Einwanderungsbehoerde -auf-Finnisch.html.

104. Groh, "Es zählt der einzelne Mensch"; Seeßlen, "*Die andere Seite der Hoffnung*" ("von Polizeimacht über Amtsgewalt bis hin zu den mörderischen Nazis"); see Milan Zibula, "Chronik der Gefühle. Reduktion: In Aki Kaurismäki's trübseliger Retrowelt kommt mit der *Anderen Seite der Hoffnung* Realität an," *Freitag*, no. 12 (March 23, 2017), https://www.freitag.de/autoren/der-freitag/chronik -der-gefuehle; Möller, "Flüchtling, kommst du nach Finnland."

105. In comic mode, this sequence is staged as a masculinity competition. Wikström's emerging respect for Khaled seems to result partly from the power of his fist.

106. Aki Kaurismäki, "Aki Kaurismäki: 'Meine Filme sind nur Illusionen,'" interview by Dominik Kamalzadeh, *Der Standard*, February 25, 2017.

107. As far as I can see, this label has not been applied to the film, and, of course, the film does not activate all genre conventions fully. The role of diegetic live music in Kaurismäki's oeuvre has received some attention. See, e.g., Jörn Barkemeyer, *Filmmusik bei Aki Kaurismäki: Eine Analyse der Musik und ihrer Verwendung als dramaturgisches Gestaltungsmittel* (Berlin: VDM, 2011); Nestingen, *The Cinema of Aki Kaurismäki*, 26.

108. Seeßlen, *"Die andere Seite der Hoffnung."*

109. Möller, "Flüchtling, kommst du nach Finnland"; Richard Dyer, *Only Entertainment* (London: Routledge, 1992), 26.

110. Dyer, *Only Entertainment*, 18, 24.

111. Jane Feuer, *The Hollywood Musical*, 2nd ed. (Basingstoke: Macmillan, 1993), 33, 25, 36.

112. See Rascaroli, "Becoming-Minor in a Sustainable Europe," 331; Nestingen, *The Cinema of Aki Kaurismäki*, 4. A number of scholars have cautioned that comedy may be better designated as a "mode," *"quality,"* or "vision" than as a proper "genre" with distinguishing elements of setting, iconography, and a shared plot structure. See Kristine Brunovska Karnick and Henry Jenkins, eds., "Introduction: Funny Stories," in *Classical Hollywood Comedy* (New York: Routledge, 1995), 65, 71; McFadden and Corrigan, as quoted in Andrew Horton, ed., "Introduction," in *Comedy/Cinema/Theory* (Berkeley: University of California Press, 1991), 3 (McFadden and Corrigan's emphasis); Geoff King, *Film Comedy* (London: Wallflower Press, 2002), 5. My reading does emphasize the generic element of a happy end but also deploys the notion of comedy more generally to gesture at affective transactions that cross generic structures.

113. Rascaroli, "Becoming-Minor in a Sustainable Europe," 327; Jaakko Seppälä, "Doing a Lot with Little: The Camera's Minimalist Point of View in the Films of Aki Kaurismäki," *Journal of Scandinavian Cinema* 6, no. 1 (2016): 7–8; Lawrence Smith, "Readymades, Rejects and the *Ready-to-Hand*: Found Objects in the Films of Aki Kaurismäki," *Scandinavian-Canadian Studies* 19 (2010): 230–60.

114. Nestingen, *The Cinema of Aki Kaurismäki*, 5. On the Bresson connection, e.g., James, "Shelter from the Storm," 25; Seppälä, "Doing a Lot with Little," 9. The French actress Arletty played Garance in Carné's *Children of Paradise* (*Les enfants du paradis*, 1945); see, in particular, his *Port of Shadows* (*Le quai des brumes*, 1938). For the other references, see James, "Shelter from the Storm," 25;

Kaurismäki, quoted in von Bagh, "Common People," 40; Rascaroli, "Becoming-Minor in a Sustainable Europe," 339.

115. The band's career was initiated by Kaurismäki's *Leningrad Cowboys Go America* (1989).

116. See Möller, "Flüchtling, kommst du nach Finnland." Kaurismäki's *Leningrad Cowboys* referenced *Go West*, also known as *The Marx Brothers Go West* (1940).

117. See Nestingen, *The Cinema of Aki Kaurismäki*, 4.

118. See Rascaroli, "Becoming-Minor in a Sustainable Europe," 331.

119. See Rascaroli, "Becoming-Minor in a Sustainable Europe," 335; Lawrence Smith, "Readymades, Rejects and the *Ready-to-Hand*," 4; Nestingen, *The Cinema of Aki Kaurismäki*, 89, 92. Inspector Monet's connection to the past is explicated when, during their first encounter, Marcel disrespectfully comments that Monet's ID looks as if it was a "pensioner's metro card." "No metro in Le Havre," the inspector responds dryly, adding a spatial layer to Marcel's provocative gesture of temporal removal. In this sense, the film's real-world fairy tale of antiracist community action finds its imaginative resources in the sedimentations of history at the periphery of today's Europe.

120. Gilbey, "Ocean's Heaven." Kaurismäki's own playfully pragmatic answer to the question of period dates *Le Havre*'s action to "2007 or earlier, but not much earlier," with reference to the 2008 French ban on smoking in bars it disrespects. Quoted in von Bagh, "Common People," 40.

121. Möller, "Flüchtling, kommst du nach Finnland."

122. Klawans, "Times Squared."

123. See Kaurismäki, quoted in von Bagh, "Common People," 38.

124. Kaurismäki, quoted in von Bagh, "Common People," 43.

125. Nestingen, *The Cinema of Aki Kaurismäki*, 92, 95; see Elizabeth Freeman, *Time Binds: Queer Temporalities, Queer Histories* (Durham, NC: Duke University Press, 2010).

126. Gilbey, "Ocean's Heaven"; Lukas Stern, "Die andere Seite der Hoffnung-Kritik," critic.de, February 14, 2017, https://www.critic.de/film/the-other-side-of-hope -10640/; Rascaroli, "Becoming-Minor in a Sustainable Europe," 328; Groh, "Es zählt der einzelne Mensch"; Lawrence Smith, "Readymades, Rejects and the *Ready-to-Hand*," 3; see Möller, "Flüchtling, kommst du nach Finnland."

127. Bruno Latour, "Why Has Critique Run Out of Steam?," *Critical Inquiry* 30, no. 2 (2004): 236, 233. The horizon of authenticity is projected by Lawrence Smith's Heideggerian reading of Kaurismäki. See "Readymades, Rejects and the *Ready-to-Hand*," 8. Latour references Heidegger's notion of the "Thing" but distances himself from Heidegger's interest in immediacy and the playing of the Thing against the object. See "Why Has Critique," 232–34.

128. Von Bagh, "Common People," 38.

129. Latour uses these notions in *Pandora's Hope* for the processes of mediation misrepresented as straightforward representation in Western culture's hegemonic epistemology of transparence. See Bruno Latour, *Pandora's Hope: Essays on the Reality of Science Studies* (Cambridge, MA: Harvard University Press, 1999), 251.

130. Nestingen, *The Cinema of Aki Kaurismäki*, 45; Seppälä, "Doing a Lot with Little," 9, 11; see also, e.g., Zibula, "Chronik der Gefühle."

131. Kati Outinen, interview by Peter von Bagh, in booklet included with *Le Havre* Criterion Collection DVD (New York: Criterion Collection, 2011).

132. Klawans, "Times Squared," 36.

133. See, e.g., Nestingen, *The Cinema of Aki Kaurismäki*, 13, 15, 64.

134. Seppälä, "Doing a Lot with Little," 5, 8, with reference also to Roger Connah.

135. Seppälä, "Doing a Lot with Little," 19, 9.

136. Seppälä, "Doing a Lot with Little," 11.

137. Rascaroli, "Becoming-Minor in a Sustainable Europe," 328–29. Unlike the portrayal of Jeanne d'Arc (discussed in chapter 2), however, *Le Havre*'s close-ups are not characteristically shot from below. In the container sequence discussed in the next section, the exception is when Idrissa stands up to flee.

138. See Rascaroli, "Becoming-Minor in a Sustainable Europe," 329, 331 (where she emphasizes that the container sequence is not parody).

139. With reference to Kaurismäki's own comparisons, we might say that he fuses Bresson's and Douglas Sirk's methods by "blowing up" minimalism; see Kaurismäki in Nestingen, *The Cinema of Aki Kaurismäki*, 146. The first encounter between Marcel and his wife, for example, is performatively understated to the degree of indicating their mutual love only minimally. Right afterward, a camera zoom closes in on her gesture of holding a hand to her hurting stomach to dramatize the intensity of pain underneath her collected façade.

140. The quote is from Horton, *Comedy/Cinema/Theory*, 9, who in turn quotes Kenneth McLeish (McLeish's emphasis). Parody arguably always intertwines homage and critique (see Linda Hutcheon, *The Politics of Postmodernism* [New York: Routledge, 1989], 101), but it has been characterized primarily through its vectors of "assault" (e.g., King, *Film Comedy*, 107). Humor, laughter, and comedy more generally have been variously theorized in terms of both distance and "affective immediacy" (e.g., Henry Jenkins, summarized in Karnick and Jenkins, "Introduction: Funny Stories," 84). However, the two accounts that have most influenced twentieth-century theories, Freud's and Bergson's, both emphasize the forces of negativity, arguably in line with Mikhail Bakhtin's diagnosis of the modern reduction of laughter to "cold humor, irony, sarcasm." Quoted in William Paul, "Charles Chaplin and the Annals of Anality," in Horton, *Comedy/Cinema/Theory*, 113. In detailing the mediations of pleasure in the joke's battle

against repression and critique, Sigmund Freud certainly underlines aggression, satire, and divestiture. E.g., "Der Witz und seine Beziehung zum Unbewussten," *Studienausgabe IV: Psychologische Schriften* (Frankfurt am Main: Fischer, 1970), 92. Meanwhile, Henri Bergson postulates "the *absence of [positive] feeling*" in foregrounding laughter's "collective" workings to enforce norms. See *Laughter: An Essay on the Meaning of the Comic*, trans. Cloudesley Brereton and Fred Rothwell (New York: Macmillan, 1914), 4 (Bergson's emphasis), 2; see 6. My alternative emphasis on playful reparation resonates with John Bruns's revisionary account; see *Loopholes: Reading Comically* (New Brunswick, NJ: Transaction, 2009), 23–24, 28, with reference to Eve Kosofsky Sedgwick's concept of reparative reading.

141. Bruns, *Loopholes*, 11 (with reference to Bakhtin), xiii, 14. I remain unconvinced by Bruns's attempt to depoliticize Bakhtin's account of carnival (see xiv, 2, 10, 37).

142. Friedrich Schlegel's irony opens up "the possibility of the infinity of other perspectives," demonstrating "the feeling for the universe" (Sinn fürs Weltall). See Allen Speight, "Friedrich Schlegel," in *The Stanford Encyclopedia of Philosophy*, ed. Edward N. Zalta (Stanford, CA: Stanford University, 1997–), published online March 19, 2007, and revised November 30, 2015, https://plato.stanford.edu/archives/win2016/entries/schlegel/; Friedrich Schlegel, "Philosophische Lehrjahre 1796–1806, Erster Teil," in *Kritische Friedrich-Schlegel-Ausgabe*, vol. 18, ed. Ernst Behler (Munich: Schöningh, 1963), 128.

143. The quotes are from Bruns, *Loopholes*, 52, with reference to Martha Nussbaum; my wording attempts to open up Bruns's primarily cognitive focus on comedy as a "mode of thought." See Bruns, *Loopholes*, xi.

144. *Drifting Clouds* (1996), *The Man Without a Past* (2002), and *Lights in the Dusk* (2006) have been grouped together as the Loser Trilogy.

145. On the importance of incongruity to comedy theory, see, e.g., King, *Film Comedy*, 5; on the balance of "the plausible and the implausible" or "absurd," see *Film Comedy*, 14. In an analogous but tonally darker scene in *The Other Side of Hope*, Khaled is assaulted as a "Jew."

146. Debjani Ganguly, *This Thing Called the World: The Contemporary Novel as Global Form* (Durham, NC: Duke University Press, 2016), 2.

147. Badiou, *Ethics*, 13.

148. At moments, the child trope does seem to institute relations of authority. Taken literally, these relations are as offensive as the film's retro staging of 1950s gender roles in Marcel's marriage. When Marcel returns from locating Idrissa's grandfather in a detention facility, for example, Marcel admonishes the boy, who incautiously ventured out of the house during his absence, by declaring that the grandfather had instructed Idrissa to obey Marcel. At other moments, the film reverses these relations, for example, with a dialogue in which Marcel

touches on racist tropes in mocking Idrissa's formality: he comments on Idrissa's apparently "civilized/cultured" (*cultivée*) family. With indignation and gravitas, Idrissa replies that his father was a professor, thus dressing down his host by insisting on the class difference between them, which is not undone by Idrissa's situational need. In a reviewer's words, the boy's empowerment makes us wonder whether he ultimately "save[s] them from their little world of nostalgia and miserabilist avant-garde absurdism." See Klawans, "Times Squared," 36.

149. Rascaroli, "Becoming-Minor in a Sustainable Europe," 330.

150. Kaurismäki, quoted in von Bagh, "Common People," 40.

151. Badiou, *Ethics*, 11–12.

152. See, e.g., "Idrissa," Name Meaning, https://www.thenamemeaning.com/idrissa/.

153. Badiou, *Ethics*, 12; see 40. This resonates with Badiou's insistence "to think beyond the affect" in countering new fascisms. See Alain Badiou, "Alain Badiou: Reflections on the Recent Election," *Verso* (blog), November 15, 2016, https://www.versobooks.com/blogs/2940-alain-badiou-reflections-on-the-recent-election. He does, however, qualify the idea of transcending human animality: every subject's techniques of revolutionary "consistency" depend on her "animal traits." Badiou, *Ethics*, 48.

154. E.g., Judith Butler, *Precarious Life: The Power of Mourning and Violence* (London: Verso, 2004).

155. Declaring that "every definition of Man based on happiness is nihilist," Badiou ambiguously positions his ethics of immortality as "ascetic," worrying that it "always demand[s] of us a renunciation." *Ethics*, 37, 53.

156. Rascaroli, "Becoming-Minor in a Sustainable Europe," 330.

157. Butler, *Precarious Life*, 131, with reference to Lévinas.

158. On this distinction, see Murray Smith, "Altered States: Character and Emotional Response in the Cinema," *Cinema Journal* 33, no. 4 (1994): 34–56.

159. Badiou analogously configures revolutionary departure from the world as is through a Christian model in *St. Paul: The Foundation of Universalism*, trans. Ray Brassier (Stanford, CA: Stanford University Press, 2003).

160. Klawans, "Times Squared."

161. Rascaroli, to be sure, locates "magic realism" in the film's happy ending. "Becoming-Minor in a Sustainable Europe," 332. She cites the inspector's compassion, which, I would caution, is unlikely, but not supernatural, and the flowering of a cherry tree (a possible reference to Yasujiro Ozu), which I don't think is definitively marked as out of season: another tree down the road seems to have a couple of buds, too. Finally, Arletty's recovery reverses the doctor's earlier verdict but also, and even more strikingly, the cinematic management of contrary expectations throughout the sequence.

162. Kaurismäki, quoted in von Bagh, "Common People," 40; Klawans, "Times Squared," 36.

163. Rascaroli traces the clip to an actual 2009 news report of one of the (repeated) crackdowns on that camp. "Becoming-Minor in a Sustainable Europe," 332.

164. Gayatri Chakravorty Spivak, "Can the Subaltern Speak?," in *Marxism and the Interpretation of Culture*, ed. Cary Nelson and Larry Grossberg (Chicago: University of Illinois Press, 1988), 271–313.

165. Kaurismäki, "Meine Filme sind nur Illusionen."

166. Roland Barthes might diagnose a "reality effect," but the "detail" included through deviation from linear progression is not "insignificant." See "The Reality Effect," in *The Rustle of Language*, trans. Richard Howard (New York: Hill and Wang, 1986), 142–43.

167. Dyer, *Only Entertainment*, 18.

168. The quote is from Nestingen, *The Cinema of Aki Kaurismäki*, 48. On the affective fleshing out of understated performance in Kaurismäki's films more generally, see Barkemeyer, *Filmmusik bei Aki Kaurismäki*, 22; on *The Other Side of Hope*, see Krekeler, "Der neue Kaurismäki."

169. Dyer, *Only Entertainment*, 23; Feuer, *The Hollywood Musical*, 30; see 35.

170. In an interview included in the Criterion Collection DVD, André Wilms comments on how Little Bob has been increasingly mistaken for a woman as he has aged; I did in fact read him as a butch lesbian upon first viewing the film. Intentionally or not, the iconography of this love story signals affirmation of a romance queerer, or differently queer, than Marcel and Arletty's stylized 1950s hetero marriage.

171. The spectacle of Little Bob's happiness forcefully undoes Badiou's question of whether fidelity to the event requires asceticism and renunciation; see *Ethics*, 53.

172. Kaurismäki, quoted in von Bagh, "Common People," 38.

173. A reviewer of *The Other Side of Hope* speaks of the film's "eigenbrötlerischer" community of solidarity, which translates as "misfit" as well as "solitary." See Groh, "Es zählt der einzelne Mensch."

174. In the wake of "Me, Too" debates, the students in my spring 2019 transnational cinema class charged him with having raped her on the way, largely based on her intense, haunted gaze that the camera captures while she hugs her brother. I agree that there is an indication of trauma, but I don't think we have the evidence to blame the trafficker specifically.

175. Massumi, *The Power*, 109, 37.

176. On this distinction, see again Brecht, "On Experimental Theatre," in Brecht, *Brecht on Theatre*, 143.

4. TENDERLY CRUEL REALISMS: OBJECTFULL ASSEMBLY AND THE HORIZON OF A SHARED WORLD

1. Critical fatigue resonated early on in Roman Jakobson's complaint that the realism label functions as an "unendlich dehnbare[r] Sack" (endlessly stretchable bag). Quoted in Rolf Parr, "Realismus—Marianne Wünschs Bestimmung einer Epoche," *kultuRRevolution* 54 (2008): 27–29.

2. On object-oriented ontology and speculative realism, see Steven Shaviro, *The Universe of Things: On Speculative Realism* (Minneapolis: University of Minnesota Press, 2015).

3. E.g., Vivian Sobchack, *The Address of the Eye: A Phenomenology of Film Experience* (Princeton, NJ: Princeton University Press, 1992); Laura U. Marks, *The Skin of the Film: Intercultural Cinema, Embodiment, and the Senses* (Durham, NC: Duke University Press, 2000); along with the revival of André Bazin since the 2000s, e.g., Andrew Dudley with Hervé Joubert-Laurencin, eds., *Opening Bazin: Postwar Film Theory and Its Afterlife* (New York: Oxford University Press, 2011). See the following on the new Mexican wave. Marco Abel influentially described Berlin School realism as an "a-representational" one that heightens intensity precisely through minimalist restraint; see *The Counter-cinema of the Berlin School* (Rochester, NY: Camden House, 2013). For qualifications regarding this minimalism's resistance to representation, see Randall Halle, *The Europeanization of Cinema: Interzones and Imaginative Communities* (Champaign: University of Illinois Press, 2014), chap. 4. I have characterized Berlin School film in terms of an aesthetics of phenomenological observation; see Claudia Breger, *An Aesthetics of Narrative Performance: Transnational Theater, Literature and Film in Contemporary Germany* (Columbus: Ohio State University Press, 2012).

4. On intensified vs. postcontinuity, see David Bordwell, *The Way Hollywood Tells It: Story and Style in Modern Movies* (Berkeley: University of California Press, 2006); Steven Shaviro, "Post-continuity: An Introduction," in *Post-cinema: Theorizing 21st-Century Film*, ed. Shane Denson and Julia Leyda (Falmer: Reframe Books, 2016), http://reframe.sussex.ac.uk/post-cinema/. On Alejandro González Iñárritu, see Dolores Tierney, "Alejandro Gonzáles Iñárritu: Director Without Borders," *New Cinemas: Journal of Contemporary Film* 7, no. 2 (2009): 101–17; Jeff Menne, "A Mexican Nouvelle Vague: The Logic of New Waves Under Globalization," *Cinema Journal* 47, no. 1 (2007): 70–92; Luisela Alvaray, "National, Regional, and Global: New Waves of Latin American Cinema," *Cinema Journal* 47, no. 3 (2008): 48–65. Iñárritu has mentioned Lars von Trier as an influence; see Menne, "A Mexican Nouvelle Vague," 74.

5. Kathleen Honora Connolly, "Spirits and Those Living in the Shadows: Migrants and a New National Family in *Biutiful*," *Revista Canadiense de Estudios*

Hispánicos 39, no. 3 (2015): 545, 551; Tierney, "Alejandro Gonzáles Iñárritu," 105, 106 (quoting Geoff King), 113.

6. On subjective realism, see Matthew Campora, *Subjective Realist Cinema: From Expressionism to* Inception (Oxford: Berghahn, 2014).

7. Tierney, "Alejandro Gonzáles Iñárritu," 108; Susanne Ostwald, "Der Schmerz der Freiheit," *Neue Zürcher Zeitung*, February 14, 2016, https://www.nzz.ch /feuilleton/kino/der-schmerz-der-freiheit-1.18695242; Peter Bradshaw, "*Fire at Sea* Review: Masterly and Moving Look at the Migrant Crisis," *The Guardian*, June 9, 2016, https://www.theguardian.com/film/2016/jun/09/fire-at-sea-review -masterly-and-moving-look-at-the-migrant-crisis. E. Nina Rothe compares *Fire at Sea* to "photorealism"; see "'We Are Facing a Disaster': Berlinale Winner Gianfranco Rosi Talks *Fuocoammare*," *HuffPost* (blog), February 25, 2016, https:// www.huffpost.com/entry/we-are-facing-a-disaster_b_9314334.

8. Granting that he always "wanted to break this barrier between documentary and fiction," Rosi states that he is "glad to call" *Fire at Sea* "a documentary" and distances himself from Michael Moore, whose "films became propaganda and entertainment." Rosi, quoted in Amir Ganjavie, "Berlinale Dispatch #1: Gianfranco Rosi Talks About *Fire at Sea* (*Fuocoammare*) (2016)," *Bright Lights Film Journal*, March 28, 2016, https://brightlightsfilm.com/berlinale-berlin-golden -bear-award-refugees-gianfranco-rosis-fire-sea-fuocoammare-2016/.

9. Rosi, quoted in Ganjavie, "Berlinale Dispatch #1."

10. See, e.g., Daniel Kothenschulte, "Die Logik des Traums," *Frankfurter Rundschau*, May 23, 2009; Daniel Kothenschulte, "Die schrecklichen Kinder," *Frankfurter Rundschau*, October 14, 2009, http://www.fr-online.de/kultur/goldene-palme -cannes-die-schrecklichen-kinder,1472786,3188608.html; Fritz Göttler, "Im Dorf der Verdammten," *Süddeutsche Zeitung*, October 14, 2009, http://www .sueddeutsche.de/kultur/im-kino-das-weisse-band-im-dorf-der-verdammten -1.28208; and on Haneke's "impressively icy" gaze and the film's "exacting scientific study," Karin Luisa Badt, "Cannes 2009: Andrea Arnold's *Fish Tank* Makes the Most Waves," *Film Criticism* 33, no. 3 (2009): 68. Roy Grundmann speaks of anachronism in his "Introduction: Haneke's Anachronism," in *A Companion to Michael Haneke*, ed. Roy Grundmann (Malden, MA: Wiley-Blackwell, 2010), 1; more generally, on Haneke's modernist and/or Brechtian reputation, see Grundmann, "Introduction," 6; Thomas Elsaesser, "Performative Self-Contradictions: Michael Haneke's Mind Games," in Grundmann, *A Companion to Michael Haneke*, 63; Brigitte Peucker, "Games Haneke Plays: Reality and Performance," in Grundmann, *A Companion to Michael Haneke*, 130; Jörg Metelmann, "Fighting the Melodramatic Condition: Haneke's Polemics," in Grundmann, *A Companion to Michael Haneke*, 168. See also the director's own comments on the film's distanciation techniques in Roy Grundmann, "Unsentimental Education:

An Interview with Michael Haneke," in Grundmann, *A Companion to Michael Haneke*, 599–600.

11. Robert Sinnerbrink, "A Post-humanist Moralist: Michael Haneke's Cinematic Critique," *Angelaki: Journal of the Theoretical Humanities* 16, no. 4 (2011): 116. Grundmann also suggests the film is "more realist" than most of Haneke's others, with its "period setting and overt concern with the historical parameters of the time"; the "alienation effect" seems "to be less strong" here. "Unsentimental Education," 592–93, 599. In reviewing *The White Ribbon*, Catherine Wheatley even revises the more general diagnosis that Haneke's "films are 'cold,'" instead comparing their "understated" or "a little austere" way to Dreyer's and Bresson's films. See "The Revenge of Children," *Sight and Sound* 19, no. 12 (2009): 14.

12. Grundmann, "Unsentimental Education," 593; on the lighting, the use of period photographs for the mise-en-scène, and the research, Michael Haneke, "The Revenge of Children," interview by Geoff Andrew, *Sight and Sound* 19, no. 12 (2009): 16–17. On Haneke's research, see also Fatima Naqvi, *Trügerische Vertrautheit: Filme von Michael Haneke* (Vienna: Synema, 2010), in particular, 136–40. Naqvi, however, describes the film's design in terms of "camouflage" as historiography (130).

13. Haneke specifically mentions Theodor W. Fontane, quoted in Alexander Horwath, "The Haneke Code: Talking Shop, Theory and Practice with the Director of *The White Ribbon*," *Film Comment* 45, no. 6 (November–December 2009): 29.

14. On Latour's approximation of epistemology and ontology, see Bruno Latour, *An Inquiry Into Modes of Existence* (Cambridge, MA: Harvard University Press, 2013), 138.

15. Bruno Latour, *Reassembling the Social: An Introduction to Actor-Network-Theory* (Oxford: Oxford University Press, 2005), 92 (Latour's emphasis).

16. Bruno Latour, "Why Has Critique Run Out of Steam?," *Critical Inquiry* 30, no. 2 (2004): 231 (Latour's emphasis); see Latour, *Reassembling*, 114.

17. Latour, *Reassembling*, 114–15. Latour quotes Heidegger's notion of "gathering" here.

18. André Bazin, *What Is Cinema?*, trans. Hugh Gray, vol. 1 (Berkeley: University of California Press, 2005), 13.

19. Jennifer Fay positions Siegfried Kracauer's insistence on cinema's "capacity to reveal an earth outside human feeling" against the artificial worlds of dominant cinematic aesthetics. See *Inhospitable World: Cinema in the Time of the Anthropocene* (New York: Oxford University Press, 2018), 19; see 6–7. For a recent critique of documentary cinema's "immediations," see Pooja Rangan, *Immediations: The Humanitarian Impulse in Documentary* (Durham, NC: Duke University Press, 2017).

20. Mary Anne Doane, "Indexicality: Trace and Sign: Introduction," *differences: A Journal of Feminist Cultural Studies* 18, no. 1 (2007): 2; see Mary Anne Doane, "The Indexical and the Concept of Medium Specificity," *differences: A Journal of Feminist Cultural Studies* 18, no. 1 (2007): 128–52. In addition to Bazin, this discussion of indexicality references Roland Barthes's theory of photography and Charles Sander Peirce's semiotics. In Peirce, the index is the type of sign that works through a direct physical connection with its object—e.g., the bullet hole as the sign of a shot; see Charles Sanders Peirce, *Peirce on Signs: Writings on Semiotic by Charles Sanders Peirce*, ed. James Hoopes (Chapel Hill, NC: University of North Carolina Press, 1991), 239–40. Doane's own critique of the contemporary resurgence of these referentiality desires indicates how even film scholars critical of realism have held onto notions of indexicality and the real. Doane argues that the index functions ambiguously in both a register of "the trace" and one of "*deixis.*" "Indexicality," 2. While the index as trace entertains "an alliance with realism as both style and ideology," the index as deixis evokes "presence" in a referentially empty manner. "Indexicality," 4; "The Indexical and the Concept of Medium Specificity," 136. Although the "dialectic" of these two workings of the index can produce "an almost theological faith . . . in the image," Doane sees a "utopian dimension" in how "the deictic index . . . verifies an existence" beyond the belief in "realistic representations." "The Indexical and the Concept of Medium Specificity," 140, 146.

21. Joshua Malitsky's work on postrevolutionary Russian and Cuban documentary cinema explores this complexification for the realm of film aesthetics. Drawing, in particular, on Latour's *Pandora's Hope*, Malitsky amends the dominant historical narrative of how Soviet montage theorists retracted their avant-garde affiliations under Stalinist pressure by underlining the differently modernist connections of the more "realistic" or "more 'restrained'" forms of documentary in Russian cinema of the late 1920s. See Joshua Malitsky, "A Certain Explicitness: Objectivity, History, and the Documentary Self," *Cinema Journal* 50, no. 3 (2011): 26, 28. The turn beyond "rapid juxtapositions and complex narrative," Malitsky argues, achieved higher "indexical stability" in Latour's sense by way of a "descriptive" aesthetics of "accumulation." Malitsky, "A Certain Explicitness," 41; Joshua Malitsky, "Ideologies in Fact: Still and Moving-Image Documentary in the Soviet Union, 1927–1932," *Journal of Linguistic Anthropology* 20, no. 2 (2010): 358.

22. I would argue that this embedding of indexicality in a broader spectrum of translational processes characterizes the trajectory of Latour's work from *Pandora's Hope* (with its focus on indexicality) to *An Inquiry*. In *Pandora's Hope: Essays on the Reality of Science Studies* (Cambridge, MA: Harvard University Press, 1999), Latour circumscribes indexicality as the paradigm that establishes scientific

reference, whereas his own scholarly writing establishes its links through "allusions and illustrations" (78)—or, in Peirce's semiotic terminology, symbols and icons. In *Reassembling the Social*, Latour mostly abandons indexicality as an explicit concept but implicitly holds onto it with his repeated insistence on continuity (i.e., the physical trace? [see, e.g., 190, 229]). As he refocuses on the differences between institutionalized domains in *An Inquiry*, Latour also reemphasizes the role of *dis*continuity, including material discontinuity in the chains of scientific reference along with the crucial role of figuration or "fiction" across domains (92, 249–50).

23. Latour, *An Inquiry*, 146.

24. On productive referentiality, see Latour, *An Inquiry*, 92.

25. See Jerome P. Schaefer, *An Edgy Realism: Film Theoretical Encounters with Dogma 95, New French Extremity, and the Shaky-Cam Horror Film* (Cambridge: Cambridge Scholars Publishing, 2015), who also draws on Latour to displace ideology-critical approaches with "a film theory of transformations" (15).

26. Latour, *Reassembling*, 254 (Latour's emphasis); see 128.

27. Thomas Elsaesser, "A Bazinian Half-Century," in Andrew with Joubert-Laurencin, *Opening Bazin*, 11; Hilsabeck Burke, "The 'Is' in What Is Cinema? On André Bazin and Stanley Cavell," *Cinema Journal* 55, no. 2 (2016): 26.

28. Stanley Cavell, *The World Viewed*, enl. ed. (Cambridge, MA: Harvard University Press, 1979), 157; Latour, *An Inquiry*, 18–19, 139. See Latour's critique of analytical philosophy for its reliance on language alone, on the one hand, and on fictions of immediacy, on the other (137).

29. Latour, *Reassembling*, 133 (Latour's emphasis). On "care and caution," see Latour, *Pandora's Hope*, 288–92.

30. Haneke, quoted in an interview by Horwath in "The Haneke Code," 31.

31. Rob White, "Three Types of Nothing," *Film Quarterly* 63, no. 4 (2010): 6. On montage in *The White Ribbon*, see James S. Williams, "Aberrations of Beauty: Violence and Cinematic Resistance in Haneke's *The White Ribbon*," *Film Quarterly* 63, no. 4 (2010): 48–55. As Elsaesser highlights, the "pseudo-contradiction between creativity (montage) and integrity (the real)" has, of course, been challenged, including by Gilles Deleuze, *Cinema 1: The Movement-Image*, trans. Hugh Tomlinson (London: Athlone Press, 1986), 81; see Elsaesser, "A Bazinian Half-Century," 11. See also chapter 2 on Jean-Luc Godard.

32. Haneke, "The Revenge of Children," 16.

33. More recent work on Haneke has begun to complicate the assessment of his oeuvre—for example, by exploring how his films rupture audience distance, as "affect perforates the formalist surface of Haneke's films." Peucker, "Games Haneke Plays," 139; see Grundmann, "Introduction," 34–35; Elsaesser, "Performative Self-Contradictions," 62; Eugenie Brinkema, *The Forms of the Affects*

(Durham, NC: Duke University Press, 2014), 99. In exploring these complications, however, Haneke scholarship largely remains focused on the intersection of violence and unpleasure; see also Eugenie Brinkema, "How to Do Things with Violences," in Grundmann, *A Companion to Michael Haneke*, 354–70; Tarja Laine, "Haneke's 'Funny Games' with the Audience (Revisited)," in *On Michael Haneke*, ed. Brian Price and John David Rhodes (Detroit: Wayne State University Press, 2010), 51–60; Martin Blumenthal-Barby, "The Surveillant Gaze: Michael Haneke's *The White Ribbon*," *October* 147 (Winter 2014): 95–116. More resonant with my reading, Laine describes the film's "ethical pursuit" as one of "thinking through affect." "Haneke's 'Funny Games,'" 58. Elsaesser attends to the "glimpses and moments" where Haneke's films attempt to "engage with the world" nonsadistically. "Performative Self-Contradictions," 70–71.

34. Jacques Rancière, *Dissensus: On Politics and Aesthetics*, ed. and trans. Steven Corcoran (London: Continuum, 2010), 36, 38.
35. Rancière, *Dissensus*, 148.
36. Latour, *An Inquiry*, 251.
37. Rancière, *Dissensus*, 141.
38. Latour, *An Inquiry*, 251.
39. On visibilizing a shared world, see Rancière, *Dissensus*, 38.
40. Latour uses the metaphor of discipline for factual narrative. *An Inquiry*, 251.
41. María Del Mar Azcona, "'We Are All Uxbal': Narrative Complexity in the Urban Borderlands in *Biutiful*," *Journal of Film and Video* 67, no. 1 (2015): 3.
42. Grundmann, "Unsentimental Education," 604.
43. On Haneke's oeuvre, see Georg Seeßlen, "Structures of Glaciation: Gaze, Perspective, and Gestus in the Films of Michael Haneke," in Grundmann, *A Companion to Michael Haneke*, 323–36. Seeßlen notably concludes with a hint at the surprising "tenderness . . . behind such seemingly cool observation" (336; see 327, 329).
44. See James S. Williams, "Aberrations of Beauty," 49.
45. For the earlier films, Seeßlen comments on the disconnect between character language and bodily performance. "Structures of Glaciation," 330–31. But the complex and shifting relations between different elements of shot composition cannot easily be summarized in the diagnosis that "the terror of *The White Ribbon* is [primarily] sonically expressed." James S. Williams, "Aberrations of Beauty," 52.
46. Haneke specifically worked with a 1977 antiauthoritarian anthology on bourgeois pedagogy. See Naqvi, *Trügerische Vertrautheit*, 136–40.
47. Haneke, quoted in Grundmann, "Unsentimental Education," 604.
48. Latour, *Reassembling*, 24.
49. My translation (here and in several following quotes); the English subtitles of my DVD edition do not always render the connotations of the original German.

50. Haneke, quoted in Grundmann, "Unsentimental Education," 596.

51. Latour, *An Inquiry*, 189, 8 (Latour's emphasis). See also Bruno Latour, "Life Among Conceptual Characters," *New Literary History* 47, no. 2–3 (2016): 474.

52. For Haneke's earlier films, Seeßlen highlights incongruity in the context of a more traditional Brechtian reading. See "Structures of Glaciation."

53. Lauren Berlant, *Cruel Optimism* (Durham, NC: Duke University Press, 2011), 14, 189; see 98.

54. Their first encounter on the street not only established that both of them are not originally from the village but also was set apart from the surrounding dark interior scenes through the use of full sunlight, the dominance of close shot-counter-shot framings, and the fact that we saw this encounter in its full length up to Eva's departure (see later in this section on the otherwise dominant cutting in the midst of individual scenarios).

55. For a sophisticated treatment of unreliability in narrative theory, see James Phelan, *Living to Tell About It: A Rhetoric and Ethics of Character Narration* (Ithaca, NY: Cornell University Press, 2005).

56. See Grundmann, "Unsentimental Education," 594, 599, against Haneke's own interpretation.

57. Haneke, quoted in an interview by Horwath in "The Haneke Code," 29.

58. In cases of voice-image incongruity, Seymour Chatman insists, the cinematic "convention [is] that seeing is believing." *Coming to Terms: The Rhetoric of Narrative in Fiction and Film* (Ithaca, NY: Cornell University Press, 1990), 136. On voice-over authority generators (potentially overriding this convention), see Sarah Kozloff, *Invisible Storytellers: Voice-Over Narration in American Fiction Film* (Berkeley: University of California Press, 1988); also, e.g., Stella Bruzzi, *New Documentary: A Critical Introduction* (London: Routledge, 2000), 51.

59. James S. Williams, "Aberrations of Beauty," 52, vs. Grundmann, "Unsentimental Education," 594. Against a standard of narration as a practice of autonomous critique, more traditional narratological analysis would characterize the narrator as part "unreliable" in that he *underevaluates* from his participant position, but we have little reason to charge him with *misreporting*. On these distinctions, see Phelan, *Living to Tell*, 49–53. From my angle, the notion of nonsovereign narration better describes the situation.

60. A letter found with the tortured son of the midwife quotes a bible passage about God "visiting the iniquity of the fathers upon the children."

61. Garrett Stewart claims that the film silences "mystery" through "history." "Prewar Trauma: Haneke's *The White Ribbon*," *Film Quarterly* 63, no. 4 (2010): 47. For another reading in terms of allegory, see Margarete Johanna Landwehr, "Voyeurism, Violence, and the Power of the Media: The Reader's/Spectator's Complicity in Jelinek's *The Piano Teacher* and Haneke's *Le Pianiste, Caché, The White Ribbon*,"

International Journal of Applied Psychoanalytical Studies 8, no. 2 (2011): 117–32. For a (perhaps too clear-cut) counterposition, see Oliver C. Speck, *Funny Frames: The Filmic Concepts of Michael Haneke* (New York: Continuum, 2010), 101–2.

62. Garrett Stewart, "Pre-war Trauma," 40.

63. Latour, *Reassembling*, 173, 191.

64. Discussing the film's themes of libidinal frustration, Garrett Stewart states: "There is no foreplay in Haneke's editing either." "Pre-war Trauma," 43.

65. See also Garrett Stewart, "Pre-war Trauma," 41.

66. Jean-Luc Nancy, *The Inoperative Community*, ed. Peter Connor and trans. Peter Connor et al. (Minneapolis: University of Minnesota Press, 1991), 61.

67. "In *The White Ribbon*, the problem is fatherhood, not its absence," Garrett Stewart summarizes. "Pre-war Trauma," 42.

68. In this sense, the film presents less a radical departure from Haneke's earlier work than a shift in degree in how cruelty is embedded in multifaceted audience engagement.

69. On such complicity, see Blumenthal-Barby, "The Surveillant Gaze," 104–5.

70. See Naqvi, *Trügerische Vertrautheit*, 145.

71. The quote is from Elsaesser, "Performative Self-Contradictions," 54.

72. Haneke, "The Revenge of Children," 16.

73. Latour, *Reassembling*, 255.

74. Latour, *Reassembling*, 189.

75. Rancière, *Dissensus*, 30, 36 (Rancière's emphases).

76. Rancière, *Dissensus*, 36. To be precise, Rancière distinguishes between the "aesthetics of politics" and the "politics of aesthetics" in (what he conceptualizes as) the modern "aesthetic regime of art," emphasizing that the framing of any symbolic act as art separates "consequences from intentions" (116, 140, 151). However, Rancière himself outlines the various challenges to the regime of aesthetic autonomy undertaken in modern political art (see 134–51). If the "'aesthetics of politics' consists above all in the framing of a *we*," whereas the "'politics of aesthetics'" revolves around individualities, my films mix both emphases (see 141–42 [Rancière's emphasis]).

77. Rancière, *Dissensus*, 116, 140, 33 (Rancière's emphases).

78. Alain Badiou, "Twenty-Four Notes on the Uses of the Word 'People,'" in *What Is a People?*, ed. Alain Badiou et al. and trans. Jody Gladding (New York: Columbia University Press, 2016), 28.

79. Rancière, *Dissensus*, 33.

80. Carmen González-Enríquez, "Irregularity as a Rule," in *Irregular Migration in Europe: Myths and Realities*, ed. Anna Triandafyllidou (London: Routledge, 2012), 250.

81. Rancière, *Dissensus*, 38.

82. The quote is from Bradshaw, "*Fire at Sea* Review."

83. Peter Goldberg, "Rough Seeing: Gianfranco Rosi's *Fire at Sea*," *Brooklyn Rail: Critical Perspectives on Arts, Politics, and Culture*, November 1, 2016, https://brooklynrail.org/2016/11/film/rough-seeing-gianfranco-rosis-fire-at-sea.

84. Claudia Lenssen, "Die Unmöglichkeit einer Insel," *die tageszeitung*, February 14, 2016; Goldberg, "Rough Seeing."

85. Goldberg, "Rough Seeing."

86. A. O. Scott, "*Fire at Sea* Is Not the Documentary You'd Expect About the Migrant Crisis. It's Better," *New York Times*, October 20, 2016.

87. Rangan argues the latter point with reference to Elaine Scarry and Craig Calhoon. *Immediations*, 1, 3; see 66.

88. On Italy's retreat from sea-rescue operations see, e.g., Matthias Rüb, "Streit über Flüchtlinge: Wie Italien sich aus der Seenotrettung zurückzog," *Frankfurter Allgemeine Zeitung*, July 1, 2019.

89. An exception here is Alessandra Potenza, "How Italy's Gianfranco Rosi Made the Stunning Oscar-Nominated Migrant Doc Fire at Sea," *The Verge*, January 24, 2017, https://www.theverge.com/2017/1/24/14371650/fire-at-sea-gianfranco-rosi-interview-academy-awards-documentary.

90. See Rosi, quoted in Ganjavie, "Berlinale Dispatch #1"; Rosi, quoted in Potenza, "How Italy's Gianfranco Rosi."

91. Rosi, quoted in Ganjavie, "Berlinale Dispatch #1."

92. Ostwald, "Der Schmerz der Freiheit."

93. Rosi, quoted in Ganjavie, "Berlinale Dispatch #1."

94. Rosi would later tell his editor, Jacopo Quadri, that these "30 seconds" of footage had to be in the film and that its structure should in fact be based on arriving there.

95. Rosi, quoted in Potenza, "How Italy's Gianfranco Rosi"; Rosi, quoted in Ganjavie, "Berlinale Dispatch #1."

96. Rangan, *Immediations*, 4. Rangan endorses these postmodern techniques (for example, "ironic performance") as the first part of her own conceptual answer (100).

97. Rangan, *Immediations*, 4.

98. Rosi explicitly makes this connection. Quoted in Potenza, "How Italy's Gianfranco Rosi."

99. Rosi, quoted in Potenza, "How Italy's Gianfranco Rosi."

100. Rosi, quoted in Potenza, "How Italy's Gianfranco Rosi"; see Christina Elizabeth Sharpe, *In the Wake: On Blackness and Being* (Durham, NC: Duke University Press, 2016).

101. *Human Flow*, directed by Ai Weiwei (Germany: Participant Media, Amazon Studios, and AC Films, 2017).

102. Rosi positions the locals as a (third) group "dismissed" by the media drama juxtaposing immigrants with the world of Europe and comprising a point of resistance against the European border regime. Quoted in Potenza, "How Italy's Gianfranco Rosi." Prior to the institutionalization of the refugee flow, he insists, they had been "embracing people and migration," quoting an interlocutor to the effect that "fishermen always welcome anything that comes from the sea." Potenza, "How Italy's Gianfranco Rosi." This borderline romanticizing statement falls short of tracing real-world controversies but is partly echoed in other accounts: Emma Jane Kirby, for example, details the impact of migration on tourism, but her interviewees blame the institutionalization of migration more than the migrants themselves. "Why Tourists Are Shunning a Beautiful Italian Island," *BBC News Magazine*, February 13, 2016. See also Jakob Brossmann's documentary *Lampedusa in Winter* (Austria, Italy, and Switzerland: Taskovski Films, 2015), which indicates some of the local controversy around immigration while foregrounding solidarity efforts in a moment just preceding the complete institutional separation of migrants from inhabitants.

103. A (different) radio host is featured in *Lampedusa in Winter* as well, but in that film, his news broadcasts are merely one among many techniques of assembling local collectivity.

104. The title song is a Sicilian wartime song referring to the 1943 bombing of an Italian ship in port at Lampedusa. See Bradshaw, "*Fire at Sea* Review."

105. Goldberg, "Rough Seeing."

106. Rangan, *Immediations*, 4.

107. On the conditions in Libyan camps and prisons, see, e.g., Arjan Hehenkamp, "Arzt über Flüchtlingslager in Libyen: 'Es sind Orte voller Gewalt,'" interview by Christian Jakob, *die tageszeitung*, February 6, 2017, http://www.taz.de/Arzt-ueber-Fluechtlingslager-in-Libyen/!5381309/.

108. Rosi, quoted in Rothe, "We Are Facing a Disaster."

109. Rangan, *Immediations*, 10 (Rangan's emphasis).

110. Rancière, *Dissensus*, 141.

111. Rancière, *Dissensus*, 38.

112. Iñárritu underlines that audiences were more likely to emphasize the film's positive affective dimensions upon repeated viewings. Mike Fleming Jr., "OSCAR: Alejandro Gonzalez Iñárritu Q&A on 'Biutiful,'" interview, *Deadline Hollywood*, December 19, 2010, https://www.deadline.com/2010/12/oscar-alejandro-gonzalez-inarritu-qa-on-biutiful/. On *Biutiful*'s "spectacular" and "arresting" cinematic language, see Peter Bradshaw, "*Biutiful*—Review," *The Guardian*, January 27, 2011, https://www.theguardian.com/film/2011/jan/27/biutiful-review; on the film's visceral aesthetics, see Elizabeth Anker, "Embodiment and Immigrant Rights in Alejandro González Iñárritu's *Biutiful*," in *Imagining Human*

Rights, ed. Susanne Kaul and David Kim (Berlin: de Gruyter, 2015), 187–99; Del Mar Azcona, "We Are All Uxbal." Laura Podalsky's resonant discussion of Iñárritu's earlier films locates their aesthetic genealogy at the intersection of Mexican traditions of melodrama with global flows in the contemporary (trans) media culture of immediacy and sensation; see *The Politics of Affect and Sensation in Contemporary Latin American Cinema: Argentina, Brazil, Cuba, and Mexico* (New York: Palgrave Macmillan, 2011).

113. The director mentions *The White Ribbon* as kin in spirit—e.g., in the interview with Fleming, "OSCAR: Alejandro Gonzalez Iñárritu Q&A."

114. Rancière, *Dissensus*, 36.

115. *Biutiful*, Iñárritu's first feature in Spanish since his 2000 debut film, *Amores perros*, was nominated for Academy Awards for Best Foreign Language Film and Best Actor; Bardem received the Best Actor Award upon the film's premiere at Cannes in 2010. On Rotten Tomatoes, the film is listed with a 64 percent critical and 75 percent audience score. On the mixed responses—and, in particular, the time it took for the film to find U.S. distribution—see, e.g., Iñárritu, quoted in Fleming, "OSCAR: Alejandro Gonzalez Iñárritu Q&A."

116. Paul Begin, for example, pointedly argues that *Biutiful* casts "the immigrant Chinese entrepreneur as a global villain." "Empathy and Sinophobia: Depicting Chinese Migration in *Biutiful* (Iñárritu, 2010)," *Transnational Cinemas* 6, no. 1 (2015): 1. The melodrama concern was prominent in the discussion following my Sites of Cinema seminar presentation at Columbia University in January 2019. I acknowledge the overlap of genre and realism and aim to deautomatize attached critical judgments (see chapter 3). While I am quite critical of some of Iñárritu's other work, including *Babel* and *The Revenant*, I make a case for *Biutiful*'s complex intervention.

117. Bradshaw, "*Biutiful*—Review."

118. Anker's reading of the film resonates with mine regarding the dissolution of sovereignty presumptions in the film's aesthetics of bodily decomposition; see "Embodiment and Immigrant Rights." Unlike her, I don't position Uxbal as a figure of sovereignty even in the beginning. Del Mar Azcona more generally reads him as a border figure; see "We Are All Uxbal."

119. On the research, see Nicole Sperling, "The Dark Is Just 'Biutiful' to Alejandro González Iñárritu and Javier Bardem," *Los Angeles Times*, December 30, 2010, https://www.latimes.com/archives/la-xpm-2010-dec-30-la-et-bardem-inarritu-20101230-story.html; on irregular migration to Spain, see González-Enríquez, "Irregularity as a Rule." The film does not reflect the statistically most significant irregular migration from Spanish-speaking Latin American countries but focuses on the groups most visible in social controversies on migration (Chinese and Senegalese/more generally sub-Saharan African).

120. See González-Enríquez, "Irregularity as a Rule." The limits to Iñárritu's localization efforts are further indicated by the fact that the characters speak Castilian Spanish, not Catalan.

121. See Lauren Berlant, "Introduction: Compassion (and Withholding)," in *Compassion: The Culture and Politics of an Emotion*, ed. Lauren Berlant (New York: Routledge, 2004), 1–14.

122. See Berlant, "Introduction," 3.

123. Latour, *An Inquiry*, 297.

124. Latour, *An Inquiry*, 181. On subjective realism, see Campora, *Subjective Realist Cinema*.

125. Latour, *Reassembling*, 236, 233.

126. Another ambivalent reviewer situates the film as an "urban version of the Passion" but qualifies that the director lacks "the stringent moral and spiritual vision of authentically (or even experimentally) religious filmmakers like Carl Dreyer, Robert Bresson or the Dardenne brothers." See A. O. Scott, "The Mob Work Is Tough; Then He Has to Go Home," *New York Times*, December 28, 2010. Rather than matters of moral or religious fact, I would say that *Biutiful* traces matters of moral and spiritual concern.

127. On the significance of the accident in Iñárritu's earlier films, see, e.g., Menne, "A Mexican Nouvelle Vague," 75, on *Amores perros*.

128. Maria Delgado, "*Biutiful*," *Sight & Sound* 21, no. 2 (2011): 48–49. The director more cautiously speaks of an experimental "play with tragedy." Iñárritu, quoted in Fleming, "OSCAR: Alejandro Gonzalez Iñárritu Q&A."

129. Latour, *Pandora's Hope*, 180.

130. The quote is from Bradshaw, "*Biutiful*—Review."

131. See Maria DiFrancesco, "Facing the Specter of Immigration in *Biutiful*," *Symposium* 69, no. 1 (2015): 32 (and the corresponding endnote). Iñárritu associates the name Uxbal with an Aztec word.

132. Connolly, "Spirits and Those Living in the Shadows," 548; see DiFrancesco, "Facing the Specter," 32.

133. Dana Stevens, "Life Sucks: The Oscar-Nominated *Biutiful* Is Ready to Depress You," *Slate*, February 3, 2011; see, again, Begin, "Empathy and Sinophobia."

134. See Anker, "Embodiment and Immigrant Rights," 198.

135. Glenn Kenny, "This Can't End Well: How We Live Now, or the New Humanism According to Alejandro Gonzalez Iñárritu," *Film Comment* 46, no. 6 (2010): 49.

136. Rancière, *Dissensus*, 36–38.

137. The quote is from Rancière, *Dissensus*, 35.

138. Jacques Rancière, *The Intervals of Cinema*, trans. John Howe (London: Verso, 2014), 121, on Pedro Costa.

139. Anker, "Embodiment and Immigrant Rights," 196.

140. On the spectral presence of the immigrants in the film, see DiFrancesco, "Facing the Specter"; Connolly, "Spirits and Those Living in the Shadows."
141. On the first point, see Anker, "Embodiment and Immigrant Rights," 196.

EPILOGUE

1. See Gilles Deleuze, *Cinema 2: The Time-Image*, trans. Hugh Tomlinson and Robert Galeta (Minneapolis: University of Minnesota Press, 1989), 216.
2. Judith Butler develops Arendt's idea of "acting in concert" with a focus on the relationship between speech and body in *Notes Towards a Performative Theory of Assembly* (Cambridge, MA: Harvard University Press, 2015), 9, 80, 151. See Hannah Arendt, *The Human Condition* (Chicago: University of Chicago Press, 1958), 200. On Ari Kaurismäki, see chapter 3.
3. Bruno Latour, *Reassembling the Social: An Introduction to Actor-Network-Theory* (Oxford: Oxford University Press, 2005), 45.
4. See the introduction and chapter 3. On the crowd's cinematic history, see also Lorenz Engell, "Eyes Wide Shut. Die Agentur des Lichts—Szenen kinematographischer verteilter Handlungsmacht," in *Unmenge—Wie verteilt sich Handlungsmacht?*, ed. Ilka Becker, Michael Kuntz, and Astrid Kusser (Munich: Fink, 2008), 75–92.
5. The reactivation of old fears of the crowd was highlighted by Deborah Gould in her talk "Passion and Danger in the Age of Trump" (lecture, Columbia University, New York, September 24, 2018). See also Butler, *Notes*, 1; on the multitude, again, Michael Hardt and Antonio Negri, *Empire* (Cambridge, MA: Harvard University Press, 2001); on "local global becoming," Brian Massumi, *The Power at the End of the Economy* (Durham, NC: Duke University Press, 2015), 15.
6. Butler, *Notes*, 7–8; see 182–83 on the multitude; 223–24 on Deleuze.
7. The director underlines other inspirations as well, including Jafar Panahi's *Off-side* (2006). See Rachel Donadio, "Breaking Free of Cultural Confines," *New York Times*, November 22, 2015, AR 15; Despina Ladi, "Wild at Heart," *Sight and Sound* 26, no. 6 (June 2016): 28.
8. Deniz Gamze Ergüven, quoted in Donadio, "Breaking Free."
9. One of the sisters in *Mustang* does take her own life also, but the suicide is rendered through the sound of a gunshot, not elaborately visualized.
10. Brian Massumi, *Politics of Affect* (Malden, MA: Polity, 2015), vii.
11. Massumi, *Politics of Affect*, 6, 10, 45.
12. Massumi, *Politics of Affect*, 140–41, 79.
13. Massumi, *Politics of Affect*, 36, 105 (Massumi's emphasis).
14. Massumi, *Politics of Affect*, 39.

15. Cinematographically, *Offside* gets closest to *Mustang*'s celebration of collective physicality in the concluding sequence, which imagines a loosening of restrictions in the celebratory postgame atmosphere.

16. Massumi cites Deleuze and Guattari's provocative formula that "there is no ideology." *Politics of Affect*, 58. While I agree to Massumi's specification that "no situation is ever fully predetermined by ideological structures," I don't share his optimism that power structures are "secondary effects of affective encounters, and ideologies are secondary expressions of power structures" (58, 93; see also 85).

17. See the introduction and chapter 1; on Orientalism classically, Edward Said, *Orientalism* (New York: Pantheon, 1978).

18. Yonca Talu, "Mustang," *Film Comment* 51, no. 6 (November–December 2015), 73; see also Donadio, "Breaking Free"; Ladi, "Wild at Heart," 28. The film has a 94 percent critical score on Rotten Tomatoes (as of May 31, 2019); it won four Césars in France and an Oscar nomination, significantly for France, not for Turkey.

19. Turkish supporters included *Canım Istanbul*; see Deniz Gamze Ergüven, "Interview with *Mustang* Director Deniz Gamze Ergüven," *Canım Istanbul* (blog), October 21, 2015, http://canimistanbul.com/blog/en/interview-deniz-gamze-erguven/. On the cited charges, e.g., Ladi, "Wild at Heart"; Donadio, "Breaking Free." In Germany, the *Spiegel* reviewer worries that the film could be politically instrumentalized by those who do not believe in Turkey's ability to commit to European values but praises its sensual cinematography along with the ways in which it complicates its narrative. Hannah Pilarczyk, "Oscar-Kandidat *Mustang*: Fünf Mädchen für die Freiheit," *Der Spiegel*, February 23, 2016. The reviewer for the conservative, majority-German paper *Die Welt*, however, who explicitly identifies herself as "half" Turkish, trashes *Mustang* as a "disgrace" (*Zumutung*) for "every Turkish woman, every woman," quipping that Humbert Humbert would leave Lolita for these girls. Iris Alanyalı, "Hier sehen Sie fünf türkische Jungfrauen," *Die Welt*, February 25, 2016.

20. Ergüven, quoted in Paula Mejia, "Two Questions with Deniz Gamze Ergüven," *Newsweek*, March 4, 2016, 59; Ergüven, "Interview."

21. Ergüven, quoted in Mejia, "Two Questions."

22. Thus during the question-and-answer period following the film showing at Columbia University's Maison Française in fall 2017.

23. Ergüven, "Interview."

24. Ergüven, quoted in Mejia, "Two Questions" (Ergüven's emphasis); see also Ergüven, quoted in Ladi, "Wild at Heart."

25. Gerda Roelvink, *Building Dignified Worlds: Geographies of Collective Action* (Minneapolis: University of Minnesota Press, 2016), 6; Rita Felski, *Uses of Literature* (Malden, MA: Wiley-Blackwell, 2008), 1.

26. Michel Foucault, *History of Sexuality*, vol. 1, *An Introduction*, trans. Robert Hurley (New York: Vintage, 1978).

27. See Beverly Weber, *Violence and Gender in the "New" Europe: Islam in German Culture* (New York: Palgrave, 2013); Jin Haritaworn, *Queer Lovers and Hateful Others: Regenerating Violent Times and Places* (London: Pluto, 2015).

28. Ladi, "Wild at Heart," 28; see also Ergüven herself, quoted in Ladi, "Wild at Heart," 29; in negative terms, Alanyalı, "Hier sehen Sie fünf türkische Jungfrauen."

29. Ergüven, quoted in Ladi, "Wild at Heart," 29.

30. Latour, *Reassembling*, 114; Ergüven, quoted in Ladi, "Wild at Heart," 29.

31. As noted, e.g., by Pilarczyk, "Oscar-Kandidat *Mustang*."

32. Despite all the plot emphasis on modest dress, she never makes an attempt at covering the manes of the girls. Of course, we can suspect that this serves the extradiegetic purpose of showcasing their sexual presence. Simultaneously, the film steers clear of the cliché trope of the hijab as a symbol of oppression.

33. Michael Haneke, quoted by Alexander Horwath, "The Haneke Code: Talking Shop, Theory and Practice with the Director of *The White Ribbon*," *Film Comment* 45, no. 6 (November–December 2009), 31.

34. See Travis Waldron, "The Awesome All-Women Crowd at Turkish Soccer Games," *Think Progress*, September 22, 2011, https://thinkprogress.org/the-awesome-all-women-crowd-at-turkish-soccer-games-59599735133/.

35. Ergüven, quoted in Rachel Cooke, "Interview, Deniz Gamze Ergüven: 'For Women in Turkey It's Like the Middle Ages,'" *The Guardian*, May 15, 2016, https://www.theguardian.com/film/2016/may/15/deniz-gamze-erguven-mustang-turkey-interview-rachel-cooke.

36. See Gul Tuysuz, "7 Times Turkish President 'Mansplained' Womanhood," CNN, June 9, 2016, https://www.cnn.com/2016/06/09/europe/erdogan-turkey-mansplained-womanhood/index.html.

37. See Talu, "Mustang," 73.

38. See Wikipedia, s.v. "Bülent Arınç," last modified May 25, 2018, 04:46, https://en.wikipedia.org/wiki/B%C3%BClent_Ar%C4%B1n%C3%A7.

39. Brandon Jourdan and Marianne Maeckelbergh, dirs., *Taksim Commune: Gezi Park and The Uprising in Turkey* (Turkey, Netherlands: Global Uprisings, 2013), http://www.globaluprisings.org/taksim-commune-gezi-park-and-the-uprising-in-turkey/.

40. Butler, *Notes*, 183.

41. Butler's own interest in the role of the body in political assembly remains perhaps too circumscribed by her account of the ("chiasmic") relation between "linguistic" and "bodily performativity." *Notes*, 9; see 76. The notion of assemblage I work with further dissolves this duality and has allowed me to flesh out the agential force of (socially signifying) bodies and affects more fully.

42. Butler reminds us that this "We, the people" is "often a wager, a bid for hegemony." *Notes*, 4.

Bibliography

FILMS AND AUDIOVISUAL MATERIALS

Ali—Fear Eats the Soul (*Angst essen Seele auf*). Directed by Rainer Werner Fassbinder. West Germany: Filmverlag der Autoren/Tango-Film, 1974.

America America. Directed by Elia Kazan. USA: Athena Enterprises, Warner Bros, 1963.

Amores Perros. Directed by Alejandro González Iñárritu. Mexico: Altavista Films, Zeta Film, 2000.

Birdman or (*The Unexpected Virtue of Ignorance*). Directed by Alejandro G. Iñárritu. USA: New Regency Pictures, M Productions, Grisbi Productions, 2014.

Biutiful. Directed by Alejandro González Iñárritu. Mexico, Spain: Televisió de Catalunya et al., 2010.

Bravo! (*Aferim!*) Directed by Janu Rude. Romania, Bulgaria, Czech Republic, France: HU Film Productions, Klas Film, Endorfilm, 2015.

Children of Paradise (*Les enfants du paradis*). Directed by Marcel Carné. France: Société Nouvelle Pathé Cinéma, 1945.

Clausnitzer & Flüchtlingsbaby! Ich Glaubs Nicht! ZUKAR 03 (Der Workshop). Directed by Firas Alshater. February 25, 2016. Video, 2:39. https://www.youtube .com/watch?v=aCEohihEuiI.

Code Unknown (*Code inconnu*). Directed by Michael Haneke. France, Austria, Romania: Arte France Cinéma et al., 2000.

The Cut. Directed by Fatih Akın. Germany, France, Italy, Russia, Poland, Canada, Turkey, Jordan: Bombero International et al., 2014.

Dancer in the Dark. Directed by Lars von Trier. Denmark et al.: Zentropa Entertainments, Trust Film Svenska, Film I Väst, 2000.

Days of Heaven. Directed by Terrence Malick. USA: Paramount Pictures, 1978.

Döbeln wehrt sich: Meine Stimme gegen Überfremdung (@DLwehrtsich). *Update aus #Clausnitz,* February 18, 2016. Video, 0:33. https://ww.facebook.com/DLwehrtsich/videos/837057433070266/.

Drifting Clouds. Directed by Aki Kaurismäki. Finland: Sputnik, 1996.

The Edge of Heaven (Auf der anderen Seite). Directed by Fatih Akın. Germany, Turkey, Italy: Anka Film et al., 2007.

Fatih Akın—Tagebuch Eines Filmreisenden. Directed by Monique Akın. Hamburg: Norddeutscher Rundfunk, 2007.

Fire at Sea (Fuocoammare). Directed by Gianfranco Rosi. Italy, France: Stemal Entertainment, 21 Unofilm, Cinecittà Luce, 2016.

Fireworks Wednesday (Chaharshanbe Suri). Directed by Ashgar Farhadi. Iran: Boshra Film, 2006.

Go West (also known as *The Marx Brothers Go West*). Directed by Edward Buzzell. USA: Metro-Goldwyn-Meyer, 1940.

Gold. Directed by Thomas Arslan. Germany, Canada: Schramm Film Koerner & Weber, Red Cedar Films, Bayerischer Rundfunk, 2013.

The Hateful Eight. Directed by Quentin Tarantino. USA: Visiona Romantica, Double Feature Films, FilmColony, 2015.

Human Flow. Directed by Ai Weiwei. Germany: Participant Media, Amazon Studios, and AC Films, 2017.

Ich Habe Nix Gegen Katzen . . .#YouGeHa2016, ZUKAR Mini 01. Directed by Firas Alshater. February 5, 2016. Video, 2:17. https://www.youtube.com/watch?v=Cp3JGmhLUXc.

I'm a Muslim, I Trust You, Do You Trust Me? Directed by M. Remaili. February 7, 2015. Video, 2:58. https://www.youtube.com/watch?v=2lvTNjQhO80.

In July (Im Juli). Directed by Fatih Akın. Germany: Argos Filmcilik Turizm, Quality Pictures, Wüste Film, 2000.

Katzelmacher. Directed by Rainer Werner Fassbinder. West Germany: Antiteater X-Film, 1969.

Lampedusa in Winter. Directed by Jakob Brossmann. Austria, Italy, Switzerland: Taskovski Films, 2015.

La vie de bohème. Directed by Aki Kaurismäki. Finland, France, Sweden, Germany: Sputnik, Pyramide Productions, Films A2, 1992.

Le Havre. Directed by Aki Kaurismäki. Finland, France, Germany: Sputnik, Pyramide Productions, Pandora Film, 2011.

Leningrad Cowboys Go America. Directed by Aki Kaurismäki. Finland, Sweden: Svenska Filminstitutet (SFI), Villealfa Filmproduction Oy, 1989.

The Little Soldier (*Le petit soldat*). Directed by Jean-Luc Godard. France: Les Productions Georges de Beauregard, Société Nouvelle de Cinématographie (SNC), 1963 (produced 1960).

Lights in the Dusk (*Laitakaupungin valot*). Directed by Aki Kaurismäki. Finland, Germany, France: Sputnik, 2006.

Lola and Billy the Kid (*Lola und Bilidikid*). Directed by Kutluğ Ataman. Germany: Boje Buck Produktion, Westdeutscher Rundfunk (WDR), Zero Film GmbH, 1999.

The Man Without a Past (*Mies vailla menneisyyttä*). Directed by Aki Kaurismäki. Finland, Germany, France: Bavaria Film, Pandora Filmproduktion, Pyramide Productions, 2002.

The Marriage of Maria Braun (*Die Ehe der Maria Braun*). Directed by Rainer Werner Fassbinder. West Germany: Albatros Filmproduktion, Fengler Film, Filmverlag der Autoren, 1979.

Match Factory Girl (*Tulitikkutehtaan tyttö*). Directed by Aki Kaurismäki. Finland: Esselte Video, Finnkino, Svenska Filminstitutet (SFI), 1990.

Melancholia. Directed by Lars von Trier. Denmark, Sweden, France, Germany: Zentropa Entertainments, Memfis Film, Zentropa International Sweden, 2011.

Miracle in Milan (*Miraolo a Milano*). Directed by Vittoria De Sica. Italy: Produzioni De Sica, Ente Nazionale Industrie Cinematografiche, 1951.

Mustang. Directed by Deniz Gamze Ergüven. France, Germany, Turkey, Qatar: CG Cinéma, Vistamar Filmproduktion, Uhlandfilm, 2015.

My Life to Live (*Vivre sa vie*). Directed by Jean-Luc Godard. France: Les Films de la Pléiade, Pathé Consortium Cinéma, 1962.

Nana. Directed by Jean Renoir. France: Les Films Jean Renoir, 1926.

Offside. Directed by Jafar Panahi. Iran: Jafar Panahi Film Productions, 2006.

Once Upon a Time in Anatolia (*Bir Zamanlar Anadolu'da*). Directed by Nuri Bilge Ceylan. Turkey, Bosnia and Herzegovina: Zeynofilm, Production 2006, 1000 Volt, 2011.

The Other Side of Hope (*Toivon tuolla puolen*). Directed by Aki Kaurismäki. Finland: Sputnik, 2017.

Pandora's Box (*Die Büchse der Pandora*). Directed by Georg Wilhelm Pabst. Germany: Nero Film AG, 1929.

The Passion of Joan of Arc (*La passion de Jeanne D'Arc*). Directed by Carl Theodor Dreyer. France: Société génerale du films, 1928.

Pickpocket. Directed by Robert Bresson. France: Compagnie Cinématographique de France, 1959.

Port of Shadows (*Le quai des brumes*). Directed by Marcel Carné. France: Ciné-Alliance, 1938.

The Revenant. Directed by Alejandro G. Iñárritu. USA, Hong Kong, Taiwan: Regency Enterprises, RatPac Entertainment, New Regency Pictures, 2015.

The Searchers. Directed by John Ford. USA: C. V. Whitney Pictures, 1956.

A Separation (*Jodaí-e Nadér az Simín*). Directed by Ashgar Farhadi. Iran: Ashgar Farhadi Film Productions, 2011.

Short Sharp Shock (*Kurz und Schmerzlos*). Directed by Fatih Akın. Germany: Wüste Film, Zweites Deutsches Fernsehen (ZDF), 1998.

Street of Shame (*Akasen chitai*). Directed by Kenji Mizoguchi. Japan: Daiei Studios, 1956.

Taksim Commune: Gezi Park and the Uprising in Turkey. Directed by Brandon Jourdan and Marianne Maeckelbergh. Turkey, Netherlands: Global Uprisings, 2013. http://www.globaluprisings.org/taksim-commune-gezi-park-and-the-uprising -in-turkey/.

Taxi Tehran (*Taxi*). Directed by Jafar Panahi. Iran: Jafar Panahi Film Productions, 2015.

This Is Not a Film (*In film nist*). Directed by Jafar Panahi and Mojtaba Mirtahmasb. Iran: Jafar Panahi Film Productions, 2011.

Timbuktu. Directed by Abderrahmane Sissako. France, Mauretania: Arte France et al., 2014.

Transit. Directed by Christian Petzold. Germany, France: Schramm Film, Neon Productions, Arte France Cinéma, 2018.

The Trial of Joan of Arc (*Procès de Jeanne d'Arc*). Directed by Robert Bresson. France: Agnes Delahaie Productions, 1962.

The Virgin Suicides. Directed by Sofia Coppola. USA: American Zoetrope, Eternity Pictures, Muse Productions, 1999.

Wer Sind Diese Deutschen? ZUKAR 01. Directed by Firas Alshater. January 27, 2016. Video, 3:06. https://www.youtube.com/watch?v=ZozLHZFEblY.

Western. Directed by Valeska Grisebach. Germany, Bulgaria, Austria: Komplizen Film, Chouchkov Brothers, Coop99 Filmproduktion, 2017.

The White Ribbon (*Das weiße Band*). Directed by Michael Haneke. Germany, Austria, France, Italy: X-Filme Creative Pool, Wega Film, Les Films du Losange, Lucky Red, 2009.

Yol. Directed by Yilmaz Güney. Turkey, Switzerland, France: Güney Film, Cactus Film, France 2, 1982.

PRINT AND ONLINE MATERIALS

100 Armenian Tales. Collected and edited by Susie Hoogasian Villa. Detroit: Wayne State University Press, 1996.

"A Love Song." *Time* 82, no. 15 (October 11, 1963): 131.

Abel, Marco. *The Counter-cinema of the Berlin School*. Rochester, NY: Camden House, 2013.

Adelson, Leslie. "Against Between: A Manifesto." In *Unpacking Europe*, ed. Salah Hassan and Iftikhar Dadi, 244–55. Rotterdam: NAI, 2001.

Ahmed, Sara. "Affective Economies." *Social Text* 79 (2004): 117–39.

Ahmed, Sara. *The Cultural Politics of Emotion*. Edinburgh: Edinburgh University Press, 2004.

Ahmed, Sara. *Queer Phenomenology*. Durham, NC: Duke University Press, 2006.

Akın, Fatih. "Die Welt besteht aus Zyklen." Interview by Syd Thompson. *Filmreporter.de*, May 28, 2007. https://filmreporter.de/stars/interview/794-Die-Welt -besteht-aus-Zyklen.

Akın, Fatih. "Ich wollte die Frauen entdecken." Interview by Birgit Glombitza. *die tageszeitung*, September 25, 2007. http://www.taz.de/!5167.

Akın, Fatih. "An Interview with Fatih Akın, Director & Screenwriter." Press notes for *The Cut*. Strand Releasing, 2014. https://strandreleasing.com/films/cut/.

Akın, Fatih. "Keine Angst vor Islamismus in der Türkei." Interview by Andreas Kilb und Peter Körte. *Frankfurter Allgemeine Zeitung*, September 3, 2007. https:// www.faz.net/aktuell/feuilleton/kino/interview-mit-fatih-akin-keine-angst-vor -islamismus-in-der-tuerkei-1103163.html.

Akın, Fatih. "Mein Heimatgefühl hat sich ausgebreitet." Interview by Katharina Dockhorn. *epd Film*, no. 10 (2007). http://www.epd-film.de/33178_51923.php.

Akın, Fatih. "Mit Leibwächtern würde ich mich besser fühlen." Interview by Hanns-Georg Rodek und Peter Praschl. *Die Welt*, October 13, 2014.

Akın, Fatih. "Q&A: Fatih Akın Discusses His New Film *The Cut*." Interview by Stephen Heyman. *New York Times*, August 26, 2014.

Alanyalı, Iris. "Hier sehen Sie fünf türkische Jungfrauen." *Die Welt*, February 25, 2016.

Aldama, Frederick Luis, and Patrick Colm Hogan. "Puzzling Out the Self: Some Initial Reflections." *English Language Notes* 49, no. 2 (2011): 139–60.

Alexander, L. A. *Fictional Worlds: Traditions in Narrative and the Age of Visual Culture*. Charleston, SC: Createspace Independent Publishing Platform, 2013.

Alshater, Firas. *Ich komm auf Deutschland zu: Ein Syrer über seine neue Heimat*. Berlin: Ullstein extra, 2016.

Alshater, Firas. "It's Not My Dream Job, However, to Be a Refugee: An Interview with Firas Alshater." Interview by Ulla Brunner. Trans. Goethe-Institut Brüssel. Goethe-Institut, August 2016. https://www.goethe.de/en/kul/med/20819516.html.

Alter, Nora M., and Timothy Corrigan, eds. *Essays on the Essay Film*. New York: Columbia University Press, 2017.

Althusser, Louis. "Ideology and Ideological State Apparatuses." In *On Ideology*, trans. Ben Brewster, 1–60. London: Verso, 2008.

Alvaray, Luisela. "National, Regional, and Global: New Waves of Latin American Cinema." *Cinema Journal* 47, no. 3 (2008): 48–65.

Alworth, David. *Site Reading: Fiction, Art, Social Form.* Princeton, NJ: Princeton University Press, 2016.

Andrew, Dudley. "A Binocular Preface." In Andrew with Joubert-Laurencin, *Opening Bazin,* ix–xiii.

Andrew, Dudley, with Hervé Joubert-Laurencin, eds. *Opening Bazin: Postwar Film Theory and Its Afterlife.* New York: Oxford University Press, 2011.

Angerer, Marie-Luise. *Vom Begehren nach dem Affekt.* Zurich: Diaphanes, 2007.

Anker, Elizabeth. "Embodiment and Immigrant Rights in Alejandro González Iñárritu's Biutiful." In *Imagining Human Rights,* ed. Susanne Kaul and David Kim, 187–99. Berlin: de Gruyter, 2015.

Anker, Elizabeth S., and Rita Felski, eds. *Critique and Postcritique.* Durham, NC: Duke University Press, 2017.

Appadurai, Arjun. "Mediants, Materiality, Normativity." *Public Culture* 27, no. 2 (2015): 221–37.

Appadurai, Arjun. *Modernity at Large: Cultural Dimensions of Globalization.* Minneapolis: University of Minnesota Press, 1996.

Appiah, Kwame Anthony. *Cosmopolitanism: Ethics in a World of Strangers.* New York: Norton, 2007.

Arend, Ingo. "Wir trinken auf den Tod." *Der Freitag,* September 28, 2007. http://www.freitag .de/kultur/0739-rueckwaertsgang.

Arendt, Hannah. *The Human Condition.* Chicago: University of Chicago Press, 1958.

Article 16a. *Grundgesetz für die Bundesrepublik Deutschland.* Rev. pub. ed. in *Bundesgesetzblatt,* Teil III, Gliederungsnummer 100–1, July 19, 2017. http://www .gesetze-im-internet.de/gg/GG.pdf.

Badiou, Alain. "Alain Badiou: Reflections on the Recent Election." *Verso* (blog), November 15, 2016. https://www.versobooks.com/blogs/2940-alain-badiou -reflections-on-the-recent-election.

Badiou, Alain. *Ethics: An Essay on the Understanding of Evil.* Trans. Peter Hallward. New York: Verso, 2000.

Badiou, Alain. *St. Paul: The Foundation of Universalism.* Trans. Ray Brassier. Stanford, CA: Stanford University Press, 2003.

Badiou, Alain. "Twenty-Four Notes on the Uses of the Word 'People.'" In Alain Badiou, Pierre Bourdieu, Georges Didi-Huberman, Sadri Khiari, and Jacques Rancière, *What Is a People?* Trans. Jody Gladding, 21–31. New York: Columbia University Press, 2016.

Bagh, Peter von. "Common People: Aki Kaurismäki." *Film Comment* 47, no. 5 (September–October 2011): 38–42.

Baker, Lisa. "Storytelling and Democracy (in the Radical Sense): A Conversation with John Edgar Wideman." *African American Review* 34, no. 2 (2000): 263–72.

Bakhtin, Mikhail. *The Dialogic Imagination: Four Essays*. Trans. Caryl Emerson and Michael Holquist. Austin: University of Texas Press, 1981.

Balakian, Peter. *The Burning Tigris: The Armenian Genocide and America's Response*. New York: Perennial, 2003.

Balibar, Etienne. "The Borders of Europe." In Cheah and Robbins, *Cosmopolitics*, 216–29.

Ballesteros, Isolina. *Immigration Cinema in the New Europe*. Bristol: Intellect, 2015.

Baracco, Alberto. *Hermeneutics of the Film World: A Ricoeurian Method for Film Interpretation*. New York: Palgrave Macmillan, 2017.

Barad, Karen. *Meeting the Universe Halfway: Quantum Physics and the Entanglement of Matter and Meaning*. Durham, NC: Duke University Press, 2007.

Barkemeyer, Jörn. *Filmmusik bei Aki Kaurismäki: Eine Analyse der Musik und ihrer Verwendung als dramaturgisches Gestaltungsmittel*. Berlin: VDM, 2011.

Barker, Jennifer. *The Tactile Eye: Touch and the Cinematic Experience*. Berkeley: University of California Press, 2009.

Barnett, David. *Rainer Werner Fassbinder and the German Theatre*. Cambridge: Cambridge University Press, 2005.

Barthes, Roland. "Diderot, Brecht, Eisenstein." Trans. Stephen Heath. *Screen* 15, no. 2 (1974): 33–40.

Barthes, Roland. "The Reality Effect." In *The Rustle of Language*, 141–48. Trans. Richard Howard. New York: Hill and Wang, 1986.

Bath, Karin Luisa. "Festivals: Cannes 2009: Andrea Arnold's Fish Tank Makes the Most Waves." *Film Criticism* 33, no. 3 (2009): 68.

Baumbach, Nico. *Cinema/Politics/Philosophy*. New York: Columbia University Press, 2019.

Bazin, André. *What Is Cinema?* Trans. Hugh Gray. Vol. 1. Berkeley: University of California Press, 2005.

Becker, Ilka, Michael Cuntz, and Astrid Kusser, eds. *Unmenge: Wie verteilt sich Handlungsmacht?* Mediologie 16. Munich: Verlag Wilhelm Fink, 2008.

Begin, Paul. "Empathy and Sinophobia: Depicting Chinese Migration in *Biutiful* (Iñárritu, 2010)." *Transnational Cinemas* 6, no. 1 (2015): 1–16.

Beier, Lars-Olav, and Matthias Matussek. "Regisseur Fatih Akın: 'Erst mit zwei Frauen wurde die Geschichte sexy.' " *Der Spiegel*, September 26, 2007. http://www.spiegel.de/kultur/kino/regisseur-fatih-akin-erst-mit-zwei-frauen-wurde-die-geschichte-sexy-a-507996.html.

Bell, Alice, and Marie-Laure Ryan, eds. *Possible Worlds Theory and Contemporary Narratology*. Lincoln: University of Nebraska Press, 2019.

Bell, James. "Scenes from a Marriage." *Sight and Sound* 21, no. 7 (July 2011): 38–39.

Bennett, Jane. *Vibrant Matter: A Political Ecology of Things.* Durham, NC: Duke University Press, 2010.

Bergfelder, Tim. "Love Beyond the Nation: Cosmopolitanism and Transnational Desire in Cinema." In *Europe and Love in Cinema*, ed. Jo Labanyi, Luisa Passerini, and Karen Diehl, 61–83. New York: Intellect, 2012.

Berghahn, Daniela, and Claudia Sternberg, eds. *European Cinema in Motion: Migrant and Diasporic Film in Contemporary Europe.* New York: Palgrave Macmillan, 2010.

Bergson, Henri. *Laughter: An Essay on the Meaning of the Comic.* Trans. Cloudesley Brereton and Fred Rothwell. New York: Macmillan, 1914.

Berlant, Lauren. *Cruel Optimism.* Durham, NC: Duke University Press, 2011.

Berlant, Lauren. "Introduction: Compassion (and Withholding)." In *Compassion: The Culture and Politics of an Emotion*, ed. Lauren Berlant, 1–14. New York: Routledge, 2004.

Berlant, Lauren. "Starved." In Halley and Parker, *After Sex?*, 79–90.

Berlant, Lauren, and Lee Edelman. *Sex, or the Unbearable.* Durham, NC: Duke University Press, 2014.

Bersani, Leo. *Homos.* Cambridge, MA: Harvard University Press, 1996.

Best, Stephen, and Sharon Marcus. "Surface Reading: An Introduction." *Representations* 108, no. 1 (2009): 1–21. https://doi.org/10.1525/rep.2009.108.1.1.

Bhabha, Homi. *The Location of Culture.* New York: Routledge, 1994.

Bhabha, Homi. "Unsatisfied Notes on Vernacular Cosmopolitanism." In *Text and Narration*, ed. Peter C. Pfeiffer and Laura García-Moreno, 191–207. Columbia, SC: Camden House, 1996.

Blech, Norbert. "Der Anti-Gender Aufstand: Der neue gemeinsame Kampf von christlichen Aktivisten und Neurechten gegen Aufklärung und Emanzipation." Working paper for Deutsche Aidshilfe. *Magazin.hiv*, August 2016. https://magazin.hiv/wp-content/uploads/2016/08/2016-Homophobie-Grundlagenpapier-Norbert-Blech.pdf.

Blumenthal-Barby, Martin. "The Surveillant Gaze: Michael Haneke's *The White Ribbon*." *October* 147 (Winter 2014): 95–116.

Boni, Marta, ed. *World Building: Transmedia, Fans, Industries.* Amsterdam: Amsterdam University Press, 2017.

Bordwell, David. *Narration in the Fiction Film.* Madison: University of Wisconsin Press, 1985.

Bordwell, David. *Poetics of Cinema.* New York: Routledge, 2007.

Bordwell, David. *The Way Hollywood Tells It: Story and Style in Modern Movies.* Berkeley: University of California Press, 2006.

Bordwell, David. "Widescreen Aesthetics and Mise en Scene Criticism." *TheVelvet Light Trap* 21 (Summer 1985): 18–25.

Bordwell, David, and Noël Carroll, eds. *Post-theory: Reconstructing Film Studies.* Madison: University of Wisconsin Press, 1996.

Bradshaw, Peter. "Biutiful—Review." *The Guardian,* January 27, 2011.

Bradshaw, Peter. "*The Cut* Review: Fatih Akın's Armenian Genocide Epic Draws Blood." *The Guardian,* August 31, 2014.

Bradshaw, Peter. "Fire at Sea Review: Masterly and Moving Look at the Migrant Crisis." *The Guardian,* June 9, 2016.

Brady, Martin. "Brecht in Brechtian Cinema." In *"Verwisch die Spuren!" Bertolt Brecht's Work and Legacy: A Reassessment,* ed. Robert Gillett and Godela Weiss-Sussex, 295–308. Amsterdam: Rodopi, 2008.

Brecht, Bertolt. *Brecht on Film and Radio.* Trans. and ed. Marc Silberman. London: Methuen, 2000.

Brecht, Bertolt. *Brecht on Theatre.* Ed. Marc Silberman, Steve Giles, and Tom Kuhn. 3rd ed. London: Bloomsbury, 2015.

Brecht, Bertolt. "The German Drama: Pre-Hitler." In Brecht, *Brecht on Theatre,* 119–24.

Brecht, Bertolt. "Notes on *Pointed Heads and Round Heads.*" In Brecht, *Brecht on Theatre,* 162–66.

Brecht, Bertolt. "Notes on the Opera *Rise and Fall of the City of Mahagonny.*" In Brecht, *Brecht on Theatre,* 61–71.

Brecht, Bertolt. "Notes on *The Threepenny Opera.*" In Brecht, *Brecht on Theatre,* 71–80.

Brecht, Bertolt. "On Experimental Theatre." In Brecht, *Brecht on Theatre,* 133–46.

Brecht, Bertolt. "On Experiments in Epic Theatre." In Brecht, *Brecht on Theatre,* 117–19.

Brecht, Bertolt. "On Gestic Music." In Brecht, *Brecht on Theatre,* 167–70.

Brecht, Bertolt. "The Progressiveness of the Stanislavsky System." In Brecht, *Brecht on Theatre,* 132–33.

Brecht, Bertolt. "Short Description of a New Technique of Acting That Produces a *Verfremdung* Effect." In Brecht, *Brecht on Theatre,* 184–96.

Brecht, Bertolt. "A Short, Private Lecture for My Friend Max Gorelik." In Brecht, *Brecht on Theatre,* 146–48.

Brecht, Bertolt. "Theatre for Pleasure or Theatre for Instruction." In Brecht, *Brecht on Theatre,* 109–17.

Brecht, Bertolt. "Three Notes on *Verfremdung* and the Elder Breughel." In Brecht, *Brecht on Theatre,* 159–61.

Brecht, Bertolt. "The Threepenny Lawsuit." In Brecht, *Brecht on Film and Radio,* 147–202.

Brecht, Bertolt. "*Verfremdung* Effects in Chinese Acting." In Brecht, *Brecht on Theatre,* 151–59.

Breger, Claudia. *An Aesthetics of Narrative Performance: Transnational Theater, Literature and Film in Contemporary Germany*. Columbus: Ohio State University Press, 2012.

Breger, Claudia. "Affects in Configuration: A New Approach to Narrative Worldmaking." *Narrative* 25, no. 2 (May 2017): 227–51.

Breger, Claudia. "Cinematic Assemblies: Latour and Film Studies." In *Latour and the Humanities*, ed. Rita Felski and Stephen Muecke. Baltimore: Johns Hopkins University Press, forthcoming.

Breger, Claudia. "Configuring Affect: Complex Worldmaking in Fatih Akın's *Auf der anderen Seite (The Edge of Heaven)*." *Cinema Journal* 54, no. 1 (Fall 2014): 65–87.

Breger, Claudia. "Cruel Attachments, Tender Counterpoints: Configuring the Collective in Michael Haneke's *The White Ribbon*." *Discourse: Journal for Theoretical Studies in Media and Culture* 38, no. 2 (2016): 142–72.

Breger, Claudia. *Nach dem Sex? Sexualwissenschaft und Affect Studies*. Hirschfeld-Lectures no. 5. Göttingen: Wallstein, 2014.

Breger, Claudia. "Simple Truths, Complex Framings, and Crucial Specifications: Aki Kaurismäki's 'Le Havre.'" *Modern Language Notes* 130, no. 3 (April 2015): 506–27.

Breithaupt, Fritz. *Kulturen der Empathie*. Frankfurt am Main: Suhrkamp, 2009.

Brinkema, Eugenie. *The Forms of the Affects*. Durham, NC: Duke University Press, 2014.

Brinkema, Eugenie. "How to Do Things with Violences." In Grundmann, *A Companion*, 354–70.

Brown, Wendy. *Undoing the Demos: Neoliberalism's Stealth Revolution*. New York: Zone Books, 2015.

Bruns, John. *Loopholes: Reading Comically*. New Brunswick, NJ: Transaction, 2009.

Bruzzi, Stella. *New Documentary: A Critical Introduction*. London: Routledge, 2000.

Buckland, Warren. "Puzzle Plots." In *Puzzle Films: Complex Storytelling in Contemporary Cinema*, ed. Warren Buckland, 1–12. Malden, MA: Blackwell, 2009.

Burke, Hilsabeck. "The 'Is' in What Is Cinema? On André Bazin and Stanley Cavell." *Cinema Journal* 55, no. 2 (2016): 25–42.

Busche, Andreas. "Die Illusion vom Tod als Befreiung." *die tageszeitung*, September 19, 2001.

Busche, Andreas. "Tränen und majestätische Landschaften." *die tageszeitung*, October 15, 2014.

Buß, Christian. "Jedem seine eigene Heimat." *Der Spiegel*, September 25, 2007. http://www.spiegel.de/kultur/kino/0,1518,507815,00.html.

Butler, Judith. *Notes Towards a Performative Theory of Assembly*. Cambridge, MA: Harvard University Press, 2015.

Butler, Judith. *Precarious Life: The Power of Mourning and Violence*. London: Verso, 2004.

Campora, Matthew. *Subjective Realist Cinema: From Expressionism to Inception.* Oxford: Berghahn, 2014.

Canetti, Elias. *Crowds and Power.* Trans. Carol Stewart. New York: Continuum, 1978.

Cannon, Steve. " 'Not a Mere Question of Form': The Hybrid Realism of Godard's *Vivre sa vie.*" *French Cultural Studies* 7, no. 21 (1996): 283–94.

Cardullo, Bert. "Finnish Character: An Interview with Aki Kaurismäki." *Film Quarterly* 59, no. 4 (Summer 2006): 4–10. https://doi.org/10.1525/fq.2006.59.4.4.

Carroll, Noël. *The Philosophy of Motion Pictures.* Malden, MA: Blackwell, 2008.

Carroll, Noël. *Theorizing the Moving Image.* Cambridge: Cambridge University Press, 1996.

Cavell, Stanley. *The Claim of Reason: Wittgenstein, Skepticism, Morality, and Tragedy.* Oxford: Oxford University Press, 1999.

Cavell, Stanley. *The World Viewed.* Enl. ed. Cambridge, MA: Harvard University Press, 1979.

Chakrabarty, Dipesh. *Provincializing Europe: Postcolonial Thought and Historical Difference.* Princeton, NJ: Princeton University Press, 2000.

Chatman, Seymour. *Coming to Terms: The Rhetoric of Narrative in Fiction and Film.* Ithaca, NY: Cornell University Press, 1990.

Cheah, Pheng. "Introduction Part II: The Cosmopolitical Today." In Cheah and Robbins, *Cosmopolitics,* 20–41.

Cheah, Pheng. *What Is a World?* Durham, NC: Duke University Press, 2016.

Cheah, Pheng, and Bruce Robbins, eds. *Cosmopolitics: Thinking and Feeling Beyond the Nation.* Minneapolis: University of Minnesota Press, 1998.

Cheshire, Godfrey. "Iran's Cinematic Spring." *Dissent* 59, no. 2 (Spring 2012): 77–80.

Cheshire, Godfrey. "Scenes from a Marriage." *Film Comment* 48, no. 1 (2012): 60–63.

Citton, Yves. "Fictional Attachments and Literary Weavings in the Anthropocene." In Muecke and Felski, "Recomposing the Humanities—with Bruno Latour," 309–29.

"Clausnitz: Video zeigt rabiates Vorgehen der Polizei." *Zeit Online,* February 19, 2016, sec. Gesellschaft. https://www.zeit.de/politik/deutschland/2016-02/sachsen-clausnitz-fluechtlinge-markus-ulbig.

Clough, Patricia Ticineto, with Jean Halley, eds. *The Affective Turn: Theorizing the Social.* Durham, NC: Duke University Press, 2007.

Connolly, Kate. "Firas Alshater: The YouTube Star Who Became Germany's Most Hugged Refugee." *The Guardian,* March 20, 2016, sec. World News. https://www.theguardian.com/world/2016/mar/20/firas-alshater-interview-youtube-zukar-refugee.

Connolly, Kathleen Honora. "Spirits and Those Living in the Shadows: Migrants and a New National Family in 'Biutiful.' " *Revista Canadiense de Estudios Hispánicos* 39, no. 3 (2015): 545–63.

Connor, Steven. "Decomposing the Humanities." In Muecke and Felski, "Recomposing the Humanities—with Bruno Latour," 275–88.

Consumerfieldwork GmbH. "Meinungsumfrage zur Buchveröffentlichung von Thilo Sarrazin: Hohe Zustimmung für Sarrazin in der Bevölkerung." *openPR*, September 6, 2010. https://www.openpr.de/news/463082/Meinungsumfrage-zur-Buchveroeffentlichung-von-Thilo-Sarrazin-Hohe-Zustimmung-fuer-Sarrazin-in-der-Bevoelkerung.html.

Cook, Roger F. et al., eds. *Berlin School Glossary: An ABC of the New Wave in German Cinema* (Bristol: Intellect, 2013).

Cooke, Rachel. "Interview, Deniz Gamze Ergüven: 'For Women in Turkey It's Like the Middle Ages.'" *The Guardian*, May 15, 2016. https://www.theguardian.com/film/2016/may/15/deniz-gamze-erguven-mustang-turkey-interview-rachel-cooke.

Currie, Gregory. *Image and Mind: Film, Philosophy and Cognitive Science*. Cambridge: Cambridge University Press, 1995.

Cvetkovich, Ann. *Depression: A Public Feeling*. Durham, NC: Duke University Press, 2012.

Cvetkovich, Ann. "Public Feelings." In Halley and Parker, *After Sex?*, 169–79.

D., David. "Bruno Latour's Artistic Practices: Writing, Products and Influence." *Toronto Film Review* (blog), February 5, 2016. http://torontofilmreview.blogspot.com/2016/02/bruno-latours-artistic-practices.html.

Dalby, Alexa. "A Separation Wins Iran's First Oscar." *Middle East*, no. 431 (April 2012): 60–61.

Danks, Adrian. " 'People are waiting': Elia Kazan's *America America*." *Senses of Cinema* 62 (2012). http://sensesofcinema.com/2012/cteq/people-are-waiting-elia-kazan-and-america-america.

Dath, Dietmar. "Fatih Akın in Venedig: Dem Kranich folgen." *Frankfurter Allgemeine Zeitung*, August 31, 2014.

Dawson, Paul. *The Return of the Omniscient Narrator: Authorship and Authority in Twenty-First Century Fiction*. Columbus: Ohio State University Press, 2013.

Dawson, Paul. "Ten Theses Against Fictionality." *Narrative* 23, no. 1 (2015): 74–100.

Del Mar Azcona, María. " 'We Are All Uxbal': Narrative Complexity in the Urban Borderlands in Biutiful." *Journal of Film and Video* 67, no. 1 (2015): 3–13.

Del Río, Elena. *Deleuze and the Cinemas of Performance: Powers of Affection*. Edinburgh: Edinburgh University Press, 2012.

Deleuze, Gilles. *Cinema 1: The Movement-Image*. Trans. Hugh Tomlinson. London: Athlone Press, 1986.

Deleuze, Gilles. *Cinema 2: The Time-Image*. Trans. Hugh Tomlinson and Robert Galeta. Minneapolis: University of Minnesota Press, 1989.

Deleuze, Gilles. "Eight Years Later: 1980 Interview." In *Two Regimes of Madness: Texts and Interviews 1975–1995*, ed. David Lapoujade. Trans. Ames Hodges and Mike Taormina, 175-80. New York: Semiotext(e), 2006.

Deleuze, Gilles, and Félix Guattari. *A Thousand Plateaus: Capitalism and Schizophrenia*. Trans. Brian Massumi. Minneapolis: University of Minnesota Press, 1987.

Delgado, Maria. "Biutiful." *Sight and Sound* 21, no. 2 (2011): 48–49.

Delyto, Celestino, and María del Mar Azcona. *Alejandro Gonzáles Iñárritu*. Urbana: University of Illinois Press, 2010.

Denson, Shane, and Julia Leyda, eds. *Post-cinema: Theorizing 21st-Century Film*. Falmer: Reframe Books, 2016.

DiFrancesco, Maria. "Facing the Specter of Immigration in Biutiful." *Symposium* 69, no. 1 (2015): 25–37.

Doane, Mary Anne. "The Indexical and the Concept of Medium Specificity." *differences: A Journal of Feminist Cultural Studies* 18, no. 1 (2007): 128–52.

Doane, Mary Anne. "Indexicality: Trace and Sign: Introduction." *differences: A Journal of Feminist Cultural Studies* 18, no. 1 (2007): 1–6.

Donadio, Rachel. "Breaking Free of Cultural Confines." *New York Times*, November 22, 2015, AR 15.

Dort, Bernhard. "Towards a Brechtian Criticism of Cinema." In *Cahiers du Cinéma: 1960–1968: New Wave, New Cinema, Reevaluating Hollywood*, ed. Jim Hillier, 236–47. Cambridge, MA: Harvard University Press, 1986.

Duenschmann, Hermann. "Cinematograph and Crowd Psychology: A Sociopolitical Study." Trans. Eric Ames. In Kaes, Baer, and Cowan, *The Promise of Cinema*, 256–58.

Dufrenne, Mikel. *The Phenomenology of Aesthetic Experience*. Trans. Edward Casey. Chicago: Northwestern University Press, 1989.

Dyer, Richard. *Only Entertainment*. London: Routledge, 1992.

Ebert, Roger. "Review of *Le Havre*." *RogerEbert.com*, November 2, 2011. https://www.rogerebert.com/reviews/le-havre-2011.

Eleftheriotis, Dimitris. *Cinematic Journeys: Film and Movement*. Edinburgh: Edinburgh University Press, 2010.

Elsaesser, Thomas. "A Bazinian Half-Century." In Andrew with Joubert-Laurencin, *Opening Bazin*, 3–12.

Elsaesser, Thomas. "Ethical Calculus: The Cross-cultural Dilemmas and Moral Burdens of Fatih Akın." *Film Comment*, May–June 2008. http://www.filmcomment.com/article/the-edge-of-heaven-review/.

Elsaesser, Thomas. *European Cinema and Continental Philosophy: Film as Thought Experiment*. New York: Bloomsbury, 2018.

Elsaesser, Thomas. *Fassbinder's Germany: History, Identity, Subject*. Amsterdam: Amsterdam University Press, 1996.

Elsaesser, Thomas. "Performative Self-Contradictions: Michael Haneke's Mind Games." In Grundmann, *A Companion*, 53–74.

Emcke, Carolin. *Gegen den Hass*. Frankfurt am Main: Fischer, 2016.

Engell, Lorenz. "Eyes Wide Shut. Die Agentur des Lichts—Szenen kinematographischer verteilter Handlungsmacht." In Becker, Kuntz, and Kusser, *Unmenge: Wie verteilt sich Handlungsmacht?*, 75–92.

Engell, Lorenz, Joseph Vogl, and Bernhard Siegert, eds. *Agenten und Agenturen*. Weimar: Verlag der Bauhaus—Universität Weimar, 2008.

"Erdogan: Turkey Will 'Never Accept' Genocide Charges." Deutsche Presse-Agentur et al. *Deutsche Welle*, June 4, 2016. https://p.dw.com/p/1Jof5.

Ergüven, Deniz Gamze. "Interview with *Mustang* Director Deniz Gamze Ergüven." *Canım Istanbul* (blog), October 21, 2015. http://canimistanbul.com/blog/en/interview-deniz-gamze-erguven/.

Esfandiary, Shahab. *Iranian Cinema and Globalization: National, Transnational and Islamic Dimensions*. Bristol: Intellect, 2012.

Esslin, Martin. *Bertolt Brecht: The Man and His Work*. New York: Doubleday, 1960.

Eugenides, Jeffrey. *The Virgin Suicides*. New York: Farrar, Straus and Giroux, 1993.

Evans, Jennifer, and Elizabeth Heineman, eds. "Syllabus." *New Fascism Syllabus: Exploring the New Right Through Scholarship and Civic Engagement*, accessed March 16, 2019, http://www.thehistoryinquestion.com/syllabus/interrogating-the-past/the-syllabus/.

Ezli, Özkan. "Peripherien zwischen Repräsentation und Individuation: Die Körper der Minderheiten in Fassbinders *Katzelmacher* und *Angst Essen Seele auf*." In *Prekäre Obsession: Minoritäten im Werk von Rainer Werner Fassbinder*, ed. Nicole Colin, Franziska Schößler, and Nike Thurn, 93–123. Bielefeld: Transcript, 2012.

Fassbinder, Rainer Werner. "Alles Vernünftige interessiert mich nicht." Interview by Wolfgang Limmer and Fritz Rumler, 1980. In Fischer, *Fassbinder über Fassbinder*, 493–555.

Fassbinder, Rainer Werner. *The Anarchy of the Imagination: Interviews, Essays, Notes. Rainer Werner Fassbinder*. Ed. Michael Töteberg and Leo A. Lensing. Trans. Krishna Winston. Baltimore: Johns Hopkins University Press. 1992.

Fassbinder, Rainer Werner. "Die Gruppe, die trotzdem keine war." Interview by Corinna Brocher, 1973. In Fischer, *Fassbinder über Fassbinder*, 17–176.

Fassbinder, Rainer Werner. "Hollywoods Geschichten sind mir lieber als Kunstfilme." Interview by Christian Braad Thomsen. In Fischer, *Fassbinder über Fassbinder*, 233–41.

Fassbinder, Rainer Werner. " 'I've Changed Along with the Characters in My Films': A Discussion with Hella Schlumberger." In Fassbinder, *The Anarchy of the Imagination*, 16–30.

Fassbinder, Rainer Werner. *Katzelmacher/Preparadise Sorry Now*. Frankfurt am Main: Verlag der Autoren, 1982.

Fassbinder, Rainer Werner. "The Kind of Rage I Feel." In Fassbinder, *The Anarchy of the Imagination*, 3–10.

Fassbinder, Rainer Werner. "Meine Filme handeln von Abhängigkeit." Interview by Christian Braad Thomsen, 1971. In Fischer, *Fassbinder über Fassbinder*, 221–27.

Felski, Rita. *The Limits of Critique*. Chicago: University of Chicago Press, 2015.

Felski, Rita. *Uses of Literature*. Malden, MA: Wiley-Blackwell, 2008.

Feuer, Jane. *The Hollywood Musical*. 2nd ed. Basingstoke: Macmillan, 1993.

Fischer, Robert, ed. *Fassbinder über Fassbinder: Die ungekürzten Interviews*. Berlin: Verlag der Autoren, 2004.

Flatley, Jonathan. *Affective Mapping: Melancholia and the Politics of Modernism*. Cambridge, MA: Harvard University Press, 2008.

Fleming, Mike Jr. "OSCAR: Alejandro Gonzalez Iñárritu Q&A on 'Biutiful.' " *Deadline Hollywood*, December 19, 2010. http://deadline.com/2010/12/oscar-alejandro-gonzalez-inarritu-qa-on-biutiful-91880/.

Flesch, William. *Comeuppeance: Costly Signaling, Altruistic Punishment, and Other Biological Components of Fiction*. Cambridge, MA: Harvard University Press, 2009.

Fludernik, Monika. *Towards a "Natural" Narratology*. London: Routledge, 1996.

Foucault, Michel. *History of Sexuality*. Vol. 1, *An Introduction*. Trans. Robert Hurley. New York: Vintage, 1978.

Foucault, Michel. "On the Genealogy of Ethics: An Overview of Work in Progress." In *The Foucault Reader*, 340–72. Ed. Paul Rabinow. New York: Pantheon: 1984.

Freeman, Elizabeth. *Time Binds: Queer Temporalities, Queer Histories*. Durham, NC: Duke University Press, 2010.

Freud, Sigmund. "Beyond the Pleasure Principle." In *The Standard Edition of the Complete Psychological Works of Sigmund Freud*. Ed. James Strachey with Anna Freud, Alix Strachey, and Alan Tyson. Vol. 18 (1920–1922), *Beyond the Pleasure Principle, Group Psychology and Other Works*, 1–64. London: Hogarth, 1955.

Freud, Sigmund. "Der Witz und seine Beziehung zum Unbewussten." In *Studienausgabe IV: Psychologische Schriften*, 9–219. Frankfurt am Main: Fischer, 1970.

Freud, Sigmund. "Group Psychology and the Analysis of the Ego." In *The Standard Edition of the Complete Psychological Works of Sigmund Freud*. Ed. James Strachey with Anna Freud, Alix Strachey, and Alan Tyson. Vol. 18 (1920–1922), *Beyond the Pleasure Principle, Group Psychology and Other Works*, 65–144. London: Hogarth Press, 1955.

Freybourg, Anne Marie. *Bilder lesen: Visionen von Liebe und Politik bei Godard und Fassbinder*. Vienna: Passagen, 1996.

Frohne, Ursula. "Expanded Fassbinder—On the Aesthetic Legacy of Cinema in Contemporary Art." In *Fassbinder Now: Film and Video Art*, ed. Deutsches

Filminstitut and the Rainer Werner Fassbinder Foundation, 26–41. Frankfurt am Main: Deutsches Filminstitut, Filmmuseum, 2013.

Ganjavie, Amir. "Berlinale Dispatch #1: Gianfranco Rosi Talks About *Fire at Sea* (*Fuocoammare*, 2016)." *Bright Lights Film Journal*, March 28, 2016.

Gansera, Rainer. "Pflanzlich bewegt." *Süddeutsche Zeitung*, December 20, 2001.

Gemünden, Gerd. "Adding a New Dimension: The 61st International Film Festival Berlin." *Film Criticism* 36, no. 1 (2011): 85–93.

Gershon, Ilana, and Joshua Malitsky. "Actor-Network-Theory and Documentary Studies." *Studies in Documentary Film* 4, no. 1 (2010): 65–78.

Gilbey, Ryan. "Ocean's Heaven." *New Statesman* 141, no. 5100/5101 (April 9–22, 2012): 84.

Gilroy, Paul. *Postcolonial Melancholia*. New York: Columbia University Press, 2005.

Godard, Jean-Luc. "Interview, December 1962." In booklet included with *Vivre sa vie* Criterion Collection DVD, 28–31. New York: Criterion Collection, 2010.

Godard, Jean-Luc. "Jean-Luc Godard and *Vivre sa vie*: Interview with Tom Milne." In *Jean-Luc Godard: Interviews*. Ed. David Sterritt. Jackson: University Press of Mississippi, 1998. 3–8.

Godard, Jean-Luc. "*Vivre sa vie* Scenario." In booklet included with *Vivre sa vie* Criterion Collection DVD, 10–14. New York: Criterion Collection, 2010.

Göktürk, Deniz. "Mobilität und Stillstand im Weltkino digital." In *Kultur als Ereignis: Fatih Akıns Film 'Auf der anderen Seite' als transkulturelle Narration*, ed. Özkan Ezli, 15–45. Bielefeld: Transcript Verlag, 2010.

Göktürk, Deniz. "Turkish Women on German Streets: Closure and Exposure in Transnational Cinema." In *Spaces in European Cinema*, ed. Myrto Konstantarakos, 64–76. Exeter: Intellect, 2000.

Göktürk, Deniz, David Gramling, and Anton Kaes, eds. *Germany in Transit: Nation and Migration, 1955–2005*. Berkeley: University of California Press, 2007.

Goldberg, Peter. "Rough Seeing: Gianfranco Rosi's Fire at Sea." *Brooklyn Rail: Critical Perspectives on Arts, Politics, and Culture*, November 1, 2016. https://brooklynrail.org/2016/11/film/rough-seeing-gianfranco-rosis-fire-at-sea.

González-Enríquez, Carmen. "Irregularity as a Rule." *Irregular Migration in Europe: Myths and Realities*, ed. Anna Triandafyllidou, 247–66. London: Routledge, 2012.

Goodman, Nelson. *Ways of Worldmaking*. Indianapolis: Hackett, 1978.

Göttler, Fritz. "Im Dorf der Verdammten." *Süddeutsche Zeitung*, October 14, 2009. http://www.sueddeutsche.de/kultur/im-kino-das-weisse-band-im-dorf-der-verdammten-1.28208.

Gow, Christopher. *From Iran to Hollywood and Some Places In-Between: Reframing Post-revolutionary Iranian Cinema*. London: Tauris, 2011.

Gramling, David. "On the Other Side of Monolingualism: Fatih Akın's Linguistic Turn(s)." *German Quarterly* 83, no. 3 (2010): 353–72.

Green, André. *The Fabric of Affect in the Psychoanalytic Discourse*. Trans. Alan Sheridan. London: Routledge, 1999.

Gregg, Melissa, and Gregory J. Seigworth, eds. *The Affect Theory Reader*. Durham, NC: Duke University Press, 2010.

Groh, Thomas. "Es zählt der einzelne Mensch: Aki Kaurismäki's *Die andere Seite der Hoffnung* (Wettbewerb)." *Perlentaucher*, February 14, 2017.

Grundmann, Roy, ed. *A Companion to Michael Haneke*. Malden, MA: Wiley-Blackwell, 2010.

Grundmann, Roy. "Introduction: Haneke's Anachronism." In Grundmann, *A Companion*, 1–50.

Grundmann, Roy. "Unsentimental Education: An Interview with Michael Haneke." In Grundmann, *A Companion*, 591–606.

Gueneli, Berta. *Fatih Akın's Cinema and the New Sound of Europe*. Bloomington: Indiana University Press, 2019.

Hake, Sabine, and Barbara Mennel, eds. *Turkish German Cinema in the New Millennium: Sites, Sounds, and Screens*. Oxford: Berghahn, 2012.

Halle, Randall. *The Europeanization of Cinema: Interzones and Imaginative Communities*. Champaign: University of Illinois Press, 2014.

Halle, Randall. *German Film After Germany: Toward a Transnational Aesthetic*. Champaign: University of Illinois Press, 2008.

Halley, Janet, and Andrew Parker, eds. *After Sex? On Writing Since Queer Theory*. Durham, NC: Duke University Press, 2011.

Halsall, Francis. "Actor-Network Aesthetics: The Conceptual Rhymes of Bruno Latour and Contemporary Art." In Muecke and Felski, "Recomposing the Humanities—with Bruno Latour," 439–61.

Hamid, Rahul. "Freedom and Its Discontents: An Interview with Asghar Farhadi." *Cineaste* 37, no. 1 (Winter 2011): 40–42.

Haneke, Michael. "The Revenge of Children." Interview with Geoff Andrew. *Sight and Sound* 19, no. 2 (December 2009): 15–17.

Hansen, Mark B. N. *Feed-Forward: On the Future of Twenty-First Century Media*. Chicago: University of Chicago Press, 2015.

Hardt, Michael, and Antonio Negri. *Empire*. Cambridge, MA: Harvard University Press, 2001.

Haritaworn, Jin. *Queer Lovers and Hateful Others: Regenerating Violent Times and Places*. London: Pluto, 2015.

Harvey, Sylvia. "Whose Brecht? Memories for the Eighties. A Critical Recovery." *Screen* 23, no. 1 (1982): 45–59.

Hatavara, Mari, Matti Hyvärinen, Maria Mäkelä, and Frans Mäyrä, eds. *Narrative Theory, Literature, and New Media: Narrative Minds and Virtual Worlds*. New York: Routledge, 2016.

Hayot, Eric. *On Literary Worlds*. New York: Oxford University Press, 2012.

Heath, Stephen. "Lessons from Brecht." *Screen* 15, no. 2 (1974): 103–28.

Heidegger, Martin. *Der Ursprung des Kunstwerkes*. Stuttgart: Reclam, 1960.

Hennion, Antoine. "From ANT to Pragmatism: A Journey with Bruno Latour at the CSI." Trans. Stephen Muecke. In Muecke and Felski, "Recomposing the Humanities—with Bruno Latour," 289–308.

Herhuth, Eric. "The Politics of Animation and the Animation of Politics." *Animation: An Interdisciplinary Journal* 11, no. 1 (March 1, 2016): 4–22.

Herman, David. *Basic Elements of Narrative*. Oxford: Wiley-Blackwell, 2009.

Herman, David, ed. *Narrative Theory and the Cognitive Sciences*. Chicago: University of Chicago Press, 2003.

Herman, David. *Storytelling and the Sciences of Mind*. Cambridge, MA: MIT University Press, 2013.

Herman, David, James Phelan, Peter J. Rabinowitz, Brian Richardson, and Robyn Warhol. *Narrative Theory: Core Concepts and Critical Debates*. Columbus: Ohio State University Press, 2012.

Herzinger, Richard. "Intervention: Ergo totgeschlagen." *Perlentaucher* September 14, 2019. https://www.perlentaucher.de/intervention/der-ruf-wir-sind-das-volk-ist-in-einer-demokratie-eine-drohung.html.

Hogan, Patrick Colm. *Affective Narratology: The Emotional Structure of Stories*. Lincoln: University of Nebraska Press, 2011.

Holden, Stephen. "A Family Coming Apart at the Seams." *New York Times*, January 1, 2012.

Hong, Young-sun. "The Challenge of Transnational History." Forum post. *H-German Discussion Network*, H-Net, January 19, 2006. https://lists.h-net.org/cgi-bin/logbrowse.pl?trx=lm&list=H-German.

Horton, Andrew, ed. "Introduction." In *Comedy/Cinema/Theory*, 1–21. Berkeley: University of California Press, 1991.

Hosfeld, Rolf, and Christin Pschichholz, eds. *Das Deutsche Reich und der Völkermord an den Armeniern*. Göttingen: Wallstein, 2017.

Horwath, Alexander. "The Haneke Code: Talking Shop, Theory and Practice with the Director of *The White Ribbon*." *Film Comment* 45, no. 6 (November–December 2009): 26–31.

Huggan, Graham. "Perspectives on Postcolonial Europe." *Journal of Postcolonial Writing* 44, no. 3 (2008): 241–49.

Hull, Isabel V. "Deutsche Militärs und der Völkermord an den Armeniern." In Hosfeld and Pschichholz, *Das Deutsche Reich und der Völkermord an den Armeniern*, 182–214.

Huntington, Samuel P. "The Clash of Civilizations?" *Foreign Affairs* 72, no. 3 (1993): 22–49. https://doi.org/10.2307/20045621.

Hutcheon, Linda. *The Politics of Postmodernism*. New York: Routledge, 1989.

Institute of History, Armenian National Academy of Sciences. *Die armenische Frage und der Genozid an den Armeniern in der Türkei (1913–19): Dokumente des politischen Archivs des Auswärtigen Amts Deutschlands*. Ed. Wardges Mikaeljan. Yerevan: Armenian National Academy of Sciences, 2004. http://www.aga-online.org/german-records/attachments/deutscheAktenStuecke.pdf.

Isenberg, Noah. "Fatih Akın's Cinema of Intersections." *Film Quarterly* 64, no. 4 (2011): 58.

Itzkoff, Dave. "Ceremony in Iran for 'Separation' Director Is Canceled." *New York Times*, March 13, 2012.

Jacob, Christian. "Niemand dürfte dort festgehalten werden. Interview mit Arjan Hehenkamp." *die tageszeitung*, February 6, 2017.

Jagose, Annamarie. "Queer World Making: Annamarie Jagose Interviews Michael Warner." *Genders* 31 (2000). https://www.colorado.edu/gendersarchive1998-2013/2000/05/01/queer-world-making-annamarie-jagose-interviews-michael-warne.

James, Nick. "Shelter from the Storm." *Sight and Sound* 21, no. 7 (July 2011): 24–29.

Jansen, Peter W. "Der Griech aus Griechenland: Fassbinders zweiter Film 'Katzelmacher' läuft in Mannheim." *Frankfurter Rundschau*, October 4, 1969.

Jovanovic, Nenad. *Brechtian Cinemas: Montage and Theatricality in Jean-Marie Straub and Danièle Huillet, Peter Watkins, and Lars von Trier*. Albany: State University of New York Press, 2017.

J. S. "Die deutschen Kleinstädter: Fassbinder's 'Katzelmacher' ab Freitag im 'Cinema Paris.' " *Abend*, June 30, 1970.

Kaes, Anton, Nicholas Baer, and Michael Cowan, eds. *The Promise of Cinema: German Film Theory 1907–1933*. Berkeley: University of California Press, 2016.

Kaiser, Claire. "Exposed Bodies, Evacuated Identities." In Peucker, *Companion to Rainer Werner Fassbinder*, 101–17.

Kappelhoff, Herrmann. "Gestische Emblematik: Fassbinder's *Katzelmacher* und Brecht's 'sozialer Gestus.' " In *Schauspielen und Montage: Schauspielkunst im Film*, ed. Knut Hickethier, 193–221. St. Augustin: Gardez!, 1999.

Kappelhoff, Herrmann. *The Politics and Poetics of Cinematic Realism*. New York: Columbia University Press, 2015.

Karagiannis, Nathalie, and Peter Wagner. "Introduction: Globalization or Worldmaking?" In *Varieties of Worldmaking: Beyond Globalization*, ed. Nathalie Karagiannis and Peter Wagner, 1–14. Liverpool: Liverpool University Press, 2007.

Karnick, Kristine Brunovska, and Henry Jenkins. "Introduction: Funny Stories." In *Classical Hollywood Comedy*, ed. Kristine Brunovska Karnick and Henry Jenkins, 63–86. New York: Routledge, 1995.

Kaurismäki, Aki. "Aki Kaurismäki: 'Meine Filme sind nur Illusionen.' " Interview by Dominik Kamalzadeh. *Der Standard*, February 25, 2017.

Kaurismäki, Aki. Interview by Christine Masson, pressbook for *Le Havre*, Sputnik Oy, Pyramide International, and Pandora Film Produktion, 2011.

Keen, Suzanne. *Empathy and the Novel*. New York: Oxford University Press, 2007.

Keen, Suzanne. "Introduction: Narrative and the Emotions." *Poetics Today* 32, no. 1 (2011): 1–53.

Kemp, Philip. "A Separation." *Sight and Sound* 21, no. 7 (July 2011): 77.

Kenny, Glenn. "This Can't End Well: How We Live Now, or The New Humanism According to Alejandro Gonzalez Iñárritu." *Film Comment* 46, no. 6 (2010): 46–49.

Khatchadourian, Raffi. "Remembering the Armenian Genocide." *New Yorker*, April 21, 2015. https://www.newyorker.com/news/daily-comment/remembering-the -armenian-genocide.

King, Geoff. *Film Comedy*. London: Wallflower Press, 2002.

King, Geoff. *Spectacular Narratives: Hollywood in the Age of the Blockbuster*. London: Tauris, 2000.

Kirby, Emma Jane. "Why Tourists Are Shunning a Beautiful Italian Island." *BBC News Magazine*, February 13, 2016.

Kneer, Georg, Markus Schroer, and Erhard Schüttpelz, eds. *Bruno Latours Kollektive*. Frankfurt am Main: Suhrkamp, 2008.

Koepnick, Lutz. *The Long Take: Art Cinema and the Wondrous*. Minneapolis: University of Minnesota Press, 2017.

Koepnick, Lutz. *On Slowness Toward an Aesthetic of the Contemporary*. New York: Columbia University Press, 2014.

Korn, Karl. "Die Unbehausten: Eine filmische Bestandsaufnahme von R.W. Fassbinder." *Frankfurter Allgemeine Zeitung*, no. 282, December 5, 1969.

Kothenschulte, Daniel. "Berlinale: Auszeichnung für den Turbo-Dostojewski." *Frankfurter Rundschau*, February 21, 2011.

Kothenschulte, Daniel. "Die Logik des Traums." *Frankfurter Rundschau*, May 23, 2009.

Kothenschulte, Daniel. "Die schrecklichen Kinder." *Frankfurter Rundschau*, October 14, 2009. http://www.fr-online.de/kultur/goldene-palme-cannes-die-schrecklichen -kinder,1472786,3188608.html.

Kothenschulte, Daniel. "Der Tod fährt manchmal mit der deutschen Bahn." *Die Welt*, August 31, 2014.

Kothenschulte, Daniel. "Von Hoffnung und anderen Gefühlen." *Frankfurter Rundschau*, February 8, 2017, sec. TV & Kino. https://www.fr.de/kultur/tv-kino/hoffnung -anderen-gefuehlen-11645127.html.

Koutsourakis, Angelos. "The Ethics and Politics of Negation: The Postdramatic on Screen." *SubStance* 45, no. 3 (2016): 155–73.

Koutsourakis, Angelos. *Rethinking Brechtian Film Theory and Cinema*. Edinburgh: Edinburgh University Press, 2018.

Kozloff, Sarah. *Invisible Storytellers: Voice-Over Narration in American Fiction Film*. Berkeley: University of California Press, 1988.

Krekeler, Elmar. "Film: Der neue Kaurismäki. Was heißt Einwanderungsbehörde auf Finnisch?" *Die Welt*, March 30, 2017. https://www.welt.de/kultur/kino /article163258578/Was-heisst-Einwanderungsbehoerde-auf-Finnisch.html.

Krethlow, Carl-Alexander. "Deutsche Militärs und die Armenier 1835–1916: Demographische Konzepte, Sicherheitsmaßnahmen und Verstrickungen." In Hosfeld and Pschichholz, *Das Deutsche Reich und der Völkermord an den Armeniern*, 149–71.

Kuhn, Markus. *Film-Narratologie: Ein erzähltheoretisches Analysemodell*. Berlin: de Gruyter, 2013.

Kürten, Jochen, and Oliver Glasenapp. "Processing a Collective Trauma." *Quantara. de*, September 11, 2014. https://en.qantara.de/node/18318.

Ladi, Despina. "Wild at Heart." *Sight and Sound* 26, no. 6 (June 2016): 28–29.

Laine, Tarja. *Feeling Cinema: Emotional Dynamics in Film Studies*. New York: Continuum, 2011.

Laine, Tarja. "Haneke's 'Funny Games' with the Audience (Revisited)." In *On Michael Haneke*, ed. Brian Price and John David Rhodes, 51–60. Detroit: Wayne State University Press, 2010.

Landry, Olivia. *Movement and Performance in Berlin School Cinema*. Bloomington: Indiana University Press, 2019.

Landwehr, Margarete Johanna. "Voyeurism, Violence, and the Power of the Media: The Reader's/Spectator's Complicity in Jelinek's *The Piano Teacher* and Haneke's *Le Pianiste, Caché, The White Ribbon*." *International Journal of Applied Psychoanalytical Studies* 8, no. 2 (2011): 117–32.

Lane, Anthony. "Tehran Tales." *New Yorker* 87, no. 43 (2012): 78–79.

Latour, Bruno. *Down to Earth*. Trans. Catherine Porter. Cambridge: Polity, 2018.

Latour, Bruno. *An Inquiry Into Modes of Existence*. Cambridge, MA: Harvard University Press, 2013.

Latour, Bruno. "Life Among Conceptual Characters." In Muecke and Felski, "Recomposing the Humanities—with Bruno Latour," 463–76.

Latour, Bruno. *Pandora's Hope: Essays on the Reality of Science Studies*. Cambridge, MA: Harvard University Press, 1999.

Latour, Bruno. *Reassembling the Social: An Introduction to Actor-Network-Theory*. Oxford: Oxford University Press, 2005.

Latour, Bruno. "Why Has Critique Run Out of Steam?" *Critical Inquiry* 30, no. 2 (2004): 225–48.

Lellis, George. *Bertolt Brecht*, Cahiers du Cinéma *and Contemporary Film Theory*. Ann Arbor: University of Michigan Research Press, 1982.

Lenssen, Claudia. "Die Unmöglichkeit einer Insel." *die tageszeitung*, February 14, 2016.

Lentz, Michael. "Eine Ordnung muß wieder sein: Faßbinders Film 'Katzelmacher' uraufgeführt." *Handelsblatt*, November 24, 1969.

Levett, Anna. "Shouldn't Love Be the One True Thing? Godard and the Legacy of Surrealist Ethics." *Quarterly Review of Film and Video* 34, no. 8 (2017): 687–706.

Lewis, Malcom. "Le Havre." *New Internationalist* 451 (April 2012): 41.

Leys, Ruth. "The Turn to Affect: A Critique." *Critical Inquiry* 37, no. 3 (2011): 434–72.

Lilla, Mark. "The Liberal Crackup." *Wall Street Journal*, August 11, 2017, sec. Life. https://www.wsj.com/articles/the-liberal-crackup-1502456857.

Loeser, Clauss. "Der Weg nach unten." *Berliner Zeitung*, September 20, 2001.

Loshitzky, Yosefa. *Screening Strangers: Migration and Diaspora in Contemporary European Cinema*. Bloomington: Indiana University Press, 2010.

Love, Heather. "Close but Not Deep: Literary Ethics and the Descriptive Turn." *New Literary History* 41, no. 2 (2010): 371–91. http://doi.org/10.1353/nlh.2010.0007.

Love, Heather. "Close Reading and Thin Description." *Public Culture* 25, no. 3 (2013): 401–34.

Love, Heather. "The Temptations: Donna Haraway, Feminist Objectivity, and the Problem of Critique." In Anker and Felski, *Critique and Postcritique*, 50–72.

Ludewig, Alexandra. *Screening Nostalgia: 100 Years of German Heimat Film*. Berlin: Transcript, 2011.

MacCabe, Colin. *Godard: A Portrait of the Artist at Seventy*. New York: Farrar, Straus and Giroux, 2004.

Maland, Charles J. *Chaplin and American Culture: The Evolution of a Star Image*. Princeton, NJ: Princeton University Press, 1989.

Malitsky, Joshua. "A Certain Explicitness: Objectivity, History, and the Documentary Self." *Cinema Journal* 50, no. 3 (2011): 26–44.

Malitsky, Joshua. "Ideologies in Fact: Still and Moving-Image Documentary in the Soviet Union, 1927–1932." *Journal of Linguistic Anthropology* 20, no. 2 (2010): 352–71.

Manalansan, Martin F. "Servicing the World: Flexible Filipinos and the Unsecured Life." In *Political Emotions: New Agendas in Communication*, ed. Janet Staiger, Ann Cvetkovich, and Ann Reynolds, 215–28. New York: Routledge, 2010.

Marcus, Sharon, Heather Love, and Stephen Best. "Building a Better Description." *Representations* 135, no. 1 (2016): 1–21.

Marks, Laura U. *Hanan al-Cinema: Affections for the Moving Image*. Cambridge, MA: MIT Press, 2015.

Marks, Laura U. *The Skin of the Film: Intercultural Cinema, Embodiment, and the Senses*. Durham, NC: Duke University Press, 2000.

Massumi, Brian. *Parables for the Virtual: Movement, Affect, Sensation*. Durham, NC: Duke University Press, 2002.

Massumi, Brian. *Politics of Affect*. Malden, MA: Polity, 2015.

Massumi, Brian. *The Power at the End of the Economy*. Durham, NC: Duke University Press, 2015.

Massumi, Brian. *What Animals Teach Us About Politics*. Durham, NC: Duke University Press, 2014.

McBride, Patrizia. *The Chatter of the Visible: Montage and Narrative in Weimar Germany*. Ann Arbor: University of Michigan Press, 2016.

McElhaney, Joe. "A Nagging Physical Discomfort: Fassbinder and Martha." In Peucker, *Companion to Rainer Werner Fassbinder*, 204–25.

McMahon, Laura. "Imitation, Seriality, Cinema: Early Fassbinder and Godard." In Peucker, *Companion to Rainer Werner Fassbinder*, 79–96.

McNulty, Bridget. "Chekhov's Gun: What It Is and How to Use It." *Now Novel* (blog), January 28, 2014. https://www.nownovel.com/blog/use-chekhovs-gun/.

Mejia, Paula. "Two Questions with Deniz Gamze Ergüven." *Newsweek*, March 4, 2016.

Menne, Jeff. "A Mexican Nouvelle Vague: The Logic of New Waves Under Globalization." *Cinema Journal* 47, no. 1 (2007): 70–92.

Mennel, Barbara. "Criss-crossing in Global Space and Time: Fatih Akın's *The Edge of Heaven* (2007)." *Transit* 5, no. 1 (2009): 1–27. http://escholarship.org/uc/item/28x3x9r0.

Mercer, Kobena. "Diaspora Aesthetics and Visual Culture." In *Black Cultural Traffic: Crossroads in Global Performance and Popular Culture*, ed. Harry J. Elam Jr. and Kennell Jackson, 141–61. Ann Arbor: University of Michigan Press, 2005.

Merleau-Ponty, Maurice. *Phenomenology of Perception*. Trans. Donald A. Landes. London: Routledge, 2013.

Metelmann, Jörg. "Fighting the Melodramatic Condition: Haneke's Polemics." In Grundmann, *A Companion*, 168–86.

Metz, Markus, and Georg Seeßlen. *Der Rechtsruck: Skizzen zu einer Theorie des politischen Kulturwandels*. Berlin: Bertz + Fischer, 2018.

Mitchell, Stanley. "From Shklovsky to Brecht: Some Preliminary Remarks Towards a History of the Politicisation of Russian Formalism." *Screen* 15, no. 2 (1974): 74–81.

Möller, Barbara. "Flüchtling, kommst du nach Finnland." *Die Welt*, February 15, 2017.

Moretti, Franco. *Distant Reading*. London: Verso, 2013.

Morrey, Douglas. *Jean-Luc Godard*. Manchester: Manchester University Press, 2005.

Muecke, Stephen, and Rita Felski, eds. "Recomposing the Humanities—with Bruno Latour." Special issue, *New Literary History* 47, no. 2–3 (Spring/Summer 2016). https://muse.jhu.edu/issue/34275.

Mueller, Roswitha. "Brecht the Realist and New German Cinema." *Framework* 25 (1984): 42–51.

Mullins, Matthew. *Postmodernism in Pieces: Materializing the Social in U.S. Fiction.* Oxford: Oxford University Press, 2016.

Mulvey, Laura. "Visual Pleasure and Narrative Cinema." *Screen* 16, no. 3 (1975): 6–18.

Mulvey, Laura, and Colin MacCabe. "Images of Woman, Images of Sexuality." In *Godard: Images, Sounds, Politics,* ed. Colin MacCabe with Mick Eaton and Laura Mulvey, 79–101. Bloomington: Indiana University Press, 1980.

Muñoz, José Esteban. *Disidentifications: Queers of Color and the Performance of Politics.* Minneapolis: University of Minnesota Press, 1999.

Muñoz, José Esteban. "Introduction: From Surface to Depth, Between Psychoanalysis and Affect." *Women & Performance: A Journal of Feminist Theory* 19, no. 2 (2009): 123–29.

Naficy, Hamid. *A Social History of Iranian Cinema.* Vol. 4, *The Globalizing Era, 1984–2010.* Durham, NC: Duke University Press, 2012.

Nagib, Lúcia. *World Cinema and the Ethics of Realism.* New York: Continuum, 2011.

Nagib, Lúcia, Chris Perriam, and Rajinder Dudrah, eds. *Theorizing World Cinema.* London: Tauris, 2012.

Nancy, Jean-Luc. *The Inoperative Community.* Ed. Peter Connor. Trans. Peter Connor, Lisa Garbus, Michael Holland, and Simona Sawhney. Minneapolis: University of Minnesota Press, 1991.

Naqvi, Fatima. *Trügerische Vertrautheit: Filme von Michael Haneke.* Vienna: Synema, 2010.

Nestingen, Andrew. *The Cinema of Aki Kaurismäki: Contrarian Stories.* London: Wallflower Press, 2013.

Ngai, Sianne. *Our Aesthetic Categories: Zany, Cute, Interesting.* Cambridge, MA: Harvard University Press, 2012.

Ngai, Sianne. *Ugly Feelings.* Cambridge, MA: Harvard University Press, 2005.

Nicodemus, Katja. "Zwei Särge und die Liebe." *Die Zeit,* September 27, 2007. https://www.zeit.de/2007/40/Fatih-Akin-Film/.

Nielsen, Henrik Skov. "Fictionality as Rhetoric: A Response to Paul Dawson." *Narrative* 23, no. 1 (2015): 101–11.

Nielsen, Henrik Skov, James Phelan, and Richard Walsh. "Ten Theses About Fictionality." *Narrative* 23, no. 1 (2015): 61–73.

Nord, Christina. "Mit besten Grüßen nach Teheran." *die tageszeitung,* February 21, 2011.

Norris, Andrew, ed. *The Claim to Community: Essays on Stanley Cavell and Political Philosophy.* Stanford, CA: Stanford University Press, 2006.

Nussbaum, Martha C. "Patriotism and Cosmopolitanism." *Boston Review* 19, no. 5 (October 1, 1994): 3. http://bostonreview.net/martha-nussbaum-patriotism-and-cosmopolitanism.

Oliver, Kelly. *Earth and World: Philosophy After the Apollo Missions.* New York: Columbia University Press, 2015.

Olshansky, Dmitry. "The Birth of Structuralism from the Analysis of Fairy-Tales." *Toronto Slavic Quarterly* 25 (Summer 2008). http://sites.utoronto.ca/tsq/25/Olshansky25.shtml.

Ong, Aihwa. *Flexible Citizenship: The Cultural Logics of Transnationality.* Durham, NC: Duke University Press, 1999.

Ong, Aihwa. *Neoliberalism as Exception: Mutations in Citizenship and Sovereignty.* Durham, NC: Duke University Press, 2006.

Ostwald, Susanne. "Der Schmerz der Freiheit." *Neue Zürcher Zeitung*, February 14, 2016.

Ostwald, Susanne. "Fatih Akın scheitert mit 'The Cut.' " *Neue Zürcher Zeitung*, September 1, 2014. http://www.nzz.ch/feuilleton/kino/fatih-akin-scheitert-mit-the-cut-1.18374179.

Outinen, Kati. Interview by Peter von Bagh, in booklet included with *Le Havre* Criterion Collection DVD (New York: Criterion Collection, 2011).

Pahl, Katrin. "What a Mess." *Modern Language Notes* 130, no. 3 (2015): 528–53.

Parkinson, Anna. *An Emotional State: The Politics of Emotion in Postwar West German Culture.* Ann Arbor: University of Michigan Press, 2015.

Parr, Rolf. "Realismus—Marianne Wünschs Bestimmung einer Epoche." *kultuRRevolution* 54 (2008): 27–29.

Patalas, Enno. "Nana S. philosophiert." *Die Zeit*, October 12, 1962. https://www.zeit.de/1962/41/nana-s-philosophiert.

Paul, William. "Charles Chaplin and the Annals of Anality." In *Comedy/Cinema/Theory*, ed. Andrew Horton, 109–30. Berkeley: University of California Press, 1991.

Peirce, Charles Sanders. *Peirce on Signs: Writings on Semiotic by Charles Sanders Peirce.* Ed. James Hoopes. Chapel Hill: University of North Carolina Press, 1991.

Pethő, Ágnes, ed. *The Cinema of Sensations.* Newcastle: Cambridge Scholars, 2015.

Petrakis, John. "On Film: A Separation." *Christian Century*, April 18, 2012, 43.

Pettersson, Bo. *How Literary Worlds Are Shaped: A Comparative Poetics of Literary Imagination.* Berlin: de Gruyter, 2018.

Peucker, Brigitte, ed. *Companion to Rainer Werner Fassbinder.* Hoboken, NJ: Wiley-Blackwell, 2011.

Peucker, Brigitte. "Games Haneke Plays: Reality and Performance." In Grundmann, *A Companion*, 130–46.

Phelan, James. *Experiencing Fiction: Judgments, Progressions, and the Rhetorical Theory of Narrative.* Columbus: Ohio State University Press, 2007.

Phelan, James. *Living to Tell About It: A Rhetoric and Ethics of Character Narration.* Ithaca, NY: Cornell University Press, 2005.

Phillips, John. "Agencement/assemblage." *Theory, Culture and Society* 23, no. 2–3 (2006): 108–9.

Pilarczyk, Hannah. "Oscar-Kandidat *Mustang*: Fünf Mädchen für die Freiheit." *Der Spiegel*, February 23, 2016.

Pflegerl, Barbara. *Es war einmal, es war keinmal. Türkische Volksmärchen.* Vienna: Böhlau, 1992.

Plantinga, Carl. *Moving Viewers: American Film and the Spectator's Experience.* Berkeley: University of California Press, 2009.

Podalsky, Laura. *The Politics of Affect and Sensation in Contemporary Latin American Cinema: Argentina, Brazil, Cuba, and Mexico.* New York: Palgrave Macmillan, 2011.

Polan, Dana. "A Brechtian Cinema? Towards a Politics of Self-Reflexive Film." In *Movies and Methods*, ed. Bill Nichols, 661–72. Vol. 2. Berkeley: University of California Press, 1985.

Pollock, Sheldon, Homi K. Bhabha, Carol A. Breckenridge, and Dipesh Chakrabarty. "Cosmopolitanisms." In *Cosmopolitanism*, ed. Carol A. Breckenridge, Sheldon Pollock, Homi K. Bhabha, and Dipesh Chakrabarty, 1–14. Durham, NC: Duke University Press, 2002.

Potenza, Alessandra. "How Italy's Gianfranco Rosi Made the Stunning Oscar-Nominated Migrant Doc Fire at Sea." *The Verge*, January 24, 2017. https://www.theverge.com/2017/1/24/14371650/fire-at-sea-gianfranco-rosi-interview-academy-awards-documentary.

Propp, Vladimir. *Morphology of the Folktale.* 2nd rev. ed. Austin: University of Texas Press, 1968.

Puar, Jasbir. " 'I Would Rather Be a Cyborg Than a Goddess': Becoming-Intersectional in Assemblage Theory." *Philosophia: A Journal of Feminist Philosophy* 2, no. 1 (2012): 49–66.

Puar, Jasbir. "Queer Times, Queer Assemblages." *Social Text* 23, no. 3–4 (2005): 121–39.

Pye, Douglas. "The Western (Genre and Movies)." In *Film Genre Reader IV*, ed. Barry Keith Grant, 239–54. Austin: University of Texas Press, 2012.

Rabaté, Jean-Michel. *The Pathos of Distance: Affects of the Moderns.* New York: Bloomsbury, 2016.

Rancière, Jacques. *Dissensus: On Politics and Aesthetics.* Ed. and trans. Steven Corcoran. London: Continuum, 2010.

Rancière, Jacques. *The Intervals of Cinema.* Trans. John Howe. London: Verso, 2014.

Rangan, Pooja. *Immediations: The Humanitarian Impulse in Documentary.* Durham, NC: Duke University Press, 2017.

Rascaroli, Laura. "Becoming-Minor in a Sustainable Europe: The Contemporary European Art Film and Aki Kaurismäki's *Le Havre*." *Screen* 54, no. 3 (2013): 323–40.

Rawle, Steven. *Transnational Cinema: An Introduction.* London: Red Globe Press, 2018.

Rebhandl, Bert. "Ein schwebendes Verfahren." *die tageszeitung*, July 14, 2011.

Ricoeur, Paul. *The Rule of Metaphor: Multidisciplinary Studies of the Creation of Meaning in Language*. Toronto: University of Toronto Press, 1978.

Ricoeur, Paul. *Time and Narrative*. Trans. Kathleen McLaughlin and David Pellauer. 3 vols. Chicago: University of Chicago Press, 1984–1988.

Robbins, Bruce. "Comparative Cosmopolitanisms." In Cheah and Robbins, *Cosmopolitics*, 246–64.

Robbins, Bruce. "Introduction Part I: Actually Existing Cosmopolitanism." In Cheah and Robbins, *Cosmopolitics*, 1–19.

Robinson, Jeremy Mark. *Jean-Luc Godard: The Passion of Cinema*. Kent: Crescent Moon, 2009.

Roelvink, Gerda. *Building Dignified Worlds: Geographies of Collective Action*. Minneapolis: University of Minnesota Press, 2016.

Root, Colin. "Stretching the Screen: Horizontality, the CinemaScope Film, and the Cold War." *Quarterly Review of Film and Video* 32, no. 5 (2015): 456–68.

Rüb, Matthias. "Streit über Flüchtlinge: Wie Italien sich aus der Seenotrettung zurückzog." *Frankfurter Allgemeine Zeitung* 1 July 2019.

Ryan, Marie-Laure. *Narrative as Virtual Reality: Immersion and Interactivity in Literature and Electronic Media*. Baltimore: Johns Hopkins University Press, 2001.

Ryan, Marie-Laure. "Postmodernism and the Doctrine of Panfictionality." *Narrative* 5, no. 2 (1997): 165–87.

Ryan, Marie-Laure, and Jan-Noël Thon, eds. *Storyworlds Across Media: Towards a Media-Conscious Narratology*. Lincoln: University of Nebraska Press, 2014.

Said, Edward. *Orientalism*. New York: Pantheon, 1978.

Sarrazin, Thilo. *Deutschland schafft sich ab: Wie wir unser Land aufs Spiel setzen*. Munich: DVA, 2010.

Schaefer, Jerome P. *An Edgy Realism: Film Theoretical Encounters with Dogma 95, New French Extremity, and the Shaky-Cam Horror Film*. Cambridge: Cambridge Scholars Publishing, 2015.

Schiller, Nina Glick, and Andrew Irving, eds. *Whose Cosmopolitanism? Critical Perspectives, Relationalities and Discontents*. Oxford: Berghahn, 2014.

Schlegel, Friedrich. "Philosophische Lehrjahre 1796–1806 Erster Teil." In *Kritische Friedrich-Schlegel-Ausgabe*. Vol. 18. Ed. Ernst Behler. Munich: Schöningh, 1963.

Schneider, Peter. "The New Berlin Wall." *New York Times Magazine*, December 4, 2005, 66–71.

Schulz-Ojala, Jan. "Armenien-Drama von Fatih Akın *The Cut*: Der stumme Schrei." *Der Tagesspiegel*, October 15, 2015.

Scott, A. O. "Finding Solace, Oceans from Home." *New York Times*, October 20, 2011, sec. Movies. https://nyti.ms/2BuvdDn.

Scott, A. O. "*Fire at Sea* Is Not the Documentary You'd Expect About the Migrant Crisis. It's Better." *New York Times*, October 20, 2016. https://nyti.ms/2eqll31.

Scott, A. O. "The Mob Work Is Tough; Then He Has to Go Home." *New York Times*, December 28, 2010. https://nyti.ms/2Xn7Czh.

Sedgwick, Eve Kosofsky. "Melanie Klein and the Difference Affect Makes." In Halley and Parker, *After Sex?*, 283–301.

Sedgwick, Eve Kosofsky. *Tendencies*. London: Routledge, 1994.

Sedgwick, Eve Kosofsky. *Touching Feeling: Affect, Pedagogy, Performativity*. Durham, NC: Duke University Press, 2003.

Seeßlen, Georg. "*Die andere Seite der Hoffnung*: Erst einmal eins auf die Nase." *Die Zeit*, March 26, 2017.

Seeßlen, Georg. "Structures of Glaciation: Gaze, Perspective, and Gestus in the Films of Michael Haneke." In Grundmann, *A Companion*, 323–36.

Seidel, Eberhard. "Gesundes Volksempfinden 2006." *die tageszeitung*, October 7, 2006. http://www.taz.de/!368434/.

Seigworth, Gregory J., and Melissa Gregg. "An Inventory of Shimmers." In Gregg and Seigworth, *The Affect Theory Reader*, 1–25.

Şen, Faruk. "The Historical Situation of Turkish Migrants in Germany." *Immigrants & Minorities* 22, no. 2–3 (2003): 208–27.

Seppälä, Jaakko. "Doing a Lot with Little: The Camera's Minimalist Point of View in the Films of Aki Kaurismäki." *Journal of Scandinavian Cinema* 6, no. 1 (2016): 5–23.

Serner, Walter. "Cinema and Visual Pleasure." Trans. Don Reneau. In Kaes, Baer, and Cowan, *The Promise of Cinema*, 41–45.

Sharpe, Christina Elizabeth. *In the Wake: On Blackness and Being*. Durham, NC: Duke University Press, 2016.

Shaviro, Steven. *The Cinematic Body*. Minneapolis: University of Minnesota Press, 1993.

Shaviro, Steven. "The Cinematic Body Redux." *Parallax* 14, no. 1 (2008): 48–54.

Shaviro, Steven. *Post-cinematic Affect*. Washington, DC: Zero Books, 2010.

Shaviro, Steven. "Post-continuity: An Introduction." *Post-cinema: Theorizing 21st-Century Film*, ed. Shane Denson and Julia Leyda. Falmer: Reframe Books, 2016. http://reframe.sussex.ac.uk/post-cinema/.

Shaviro, Steven. *The Universe of Things: On Speculative Realism*. Minneapolis: University of Minnesota Press, 2015.

Silberman, Marc. "Exile Years: Introduction to Part Two." In Brecht, *Brecht on Theatre*, 101–8.

Silberman, Marc, Steve Giles, and Tom Kuhn. "General Introduction." In Brecht, *Brecht on Theatre*, 1–7.

Silverman, Kaja, and Harun Farocki. *Speaking About Godard*. New York: NYU Press, 1998.

Singer, Ben. *Melodrama and Modernity: Early Sensational Cinema and Its Contexts.* New York: Columbia University Press, 2001.

Sinnerbrink, Robert. *Cinematic Ethics: Exploring Ethical Experience Through Film.* New York: Routledge, 2016.

Sinnerbrink, Robert. "*Stimmung*: Exploring the Aesthetics of Mood." *Screen* 53, no. 2 (2012): 148–63.

Smith, Lawrence D. "Readymades, Rejects and the *Ready-to-Hand*: Found Objects in the Films of Aki Kaurismäki." *Scandinavian-Canadian Studies* 19 (2010): 230–60.

Smith, Murray. "Altered States: Character and Emotional Response in the Cinema." *Cinema Journal* 33, no. 4 (1994): 34–56.

Smith, Murray. "Film Spectatorship and the Institution of Fiction." *Journal of Aesthetics and Art Criticism* 5, no. 2 (1995): 113–27.

Smith, Murray. "The Logic and Legacy of Brechtianism." In *Post-theory: Reconstructing Film Studies*, ed. David Bordwell and Noël Carroll, 130–48. Madison: University of Wisconsin Press, 1996.

Sobchack, Vivian. *The Address of the Eye: A Phenomenology of Film Experience.* Princeton, NJ: Princeton University Press, 1992.

Sobchack, Vivian. *Carnal Thoughts: Embodiment and Moving Image Culture.* Berkeley: University of California Press, 2004.

Sontag, Susan. "Godard's *Vivre sa vie*." In *Against Interpretation: and Other Essays*, 196–208. New York: Picador, 2001.

Speck, Oliver C. *Funny Frames: The Filmic Concepts of Michael Haneke.* New York: Continuum, 2010.

Speight, Allen. "Friedrich Schlegel." In *The Stanford Encyclopedia of Philosophy*, ed. Edward N. Zalta. Stanford, CA: Stanford University, 1997–. Article published online March 19, 2007, and revised November 30, 2015. https://plato.stanford.edu/archives/win2016/entries/schlegel/.

Spellerberg, James. "CinemaScope and Ideology." *Velvet Light Trap* 21 (1985): 26–34.

Sperling, Nicole. "The Dark Is Just 'Biutiful' to Alejandro González Iñárritu and Javier Bardem." *Los Angeles Times*, December 30, 2010, https://www.latimes.com/archives/la-xpm-2010-dec-30-la-et-bardem-inarritu-20101230-story.html.

Spivak, Gayatri Chakravorty. "Can the Subaltern Speak?" *Marxism and the Interpretation of Culture*, ed. Cary Nelson and Larry Grossberg, 271–313. Chicago: University of Illinois Press, 1988.

Spivak, Gayatri Chakravorty. "Three Women's Texts and a Critique of Imperialism." *Critical Inquiry* 12, no. 1 (Autumn 1985): 243–61.

Stäheli, Alexandra. "Liebe ist stärker als der Tod." *Neue Zürcher Zeitung*, October 4, 2007.

States, Bert O. "The Phenomenological Attitude." In *Critical Theory and Performance*, ed. Janelle G. Reinelt and Joseph R. Roach, 26–36. Rev. ed. Ann Arbor: University of Michigan Press, 2007.

Stern, Lukas. "Die andere Seite der Hoffnung-Kritik." *critic.de*, February 14, 2017, https://www.critic.de/film/the-other-side-of-hope-10640/.

Sterritt, David. *The Films of Jean-Luc Godard: Seeing the Invisible*. Cambridge: Cambridge University Press, 1999.

Stevens, Dana. "Life Sucks: The Oscar-Nominated *Biutiful* Is Ready to Depress You." *Slate*, February 3, 2011.

Stewart, Garrett. "Pre-war Trauma: Haneke's *The White Ribbon*." *Film Quarterly* 63, no. 4 (2010): 40–47.

Stewart, Kathleen. "Afterword: Worlding Refrains." In Gregg and Seigworth, *The Affect Theory Reader*, 339–53.

Suchsland, Rüdiger. "Die 40 Tage des Fatih Akın. Venedig-Blog, 3.Folge." *Negativ* (blog), September 1, 2014. http://www.negativ-film.de/2014/09/die-40-tage-des -fatih-akin-venedig-blog-3-folge.

Suchsland, Rüdiger. "Langsames Leben, schöne Tage: Annäherungen an die 'Berliner Schule.'" *Film-Dienst* 58, no. 13 (2005): 6–9.

Svyatskaya, Svetlana. "The Overwhelming Moments of Misfortune: Jesper Just and Rainer Werner Fassbinder." In *Fassbinder Now: Film and Video Art*, ed. Deutsches Filminstitut and the Rainer Werner Fassbinder Foundation, 233–41. Frankfurt am Main: Deutsches Filminstitut, Filmmuseum, 2013.

Talu, Yonka. "Mustang." *Film Comment* 51, no. 6 (November–December 2015): 73.

Tierney, Dolores. "Alejandro Gonzáles Iñárritu: Director Without Borders." *New Cinemas: Journal of Contemporary Film* 7, no. 2 (2009): 101–17.

Töteberg, Michael. "Introduction." In Töteberg and Lensing, *The Anarchy of the Imagination*, xv–xvii.

Töteberg, Michael. *Rainer Werner Fassbinder*. Reinbek: Rowohlt, 2002.

Trier, Lars von. "Director's Statement: *Melancholia*." *Melancholia* press kit. TrustNordisk, April 13, 2011. http://www.trustnordisk.com/film/2010-melancholia.

Trier, Lars von, and Thomas Vintreberg, on behalf of Dogme 95. "The Vow of Chastity." *Dogme95.dk*, accessed May 18, 2019. http://www.dogme95.dk/the-vow-of -chastity/.

Trojanow, Ilija. "Verbale Umerziehung." *die tageszeitung*, August 23, 2017.

Turim, Maureen. "Three-Way Mirroring in *Vivre sa vie*." In *A Companion to Jean-Luc Godard*, ed. Tom Conley and T. Jefferson Kline, 89–107. Malden, MA: John Wiley, 2014.

Tuysuz, Gul. "7 Times Turkish President 'Mansplained' Womanhood." CNN, June 9, 2016. https://www.cnn.com/2016/06/09/europe/erdogan-turkey-mansplained -womanhood/index.html.

Vries, Hent de. "Introduction: Before, Around, and Beyond the Theologico-Political." In *Political Theologies: Public Religions in a Post-Secular World*, ed. Hent de Vries and Lawrence E. Sullivan, 1–88. New York: Fordham University Press, 2006.

Waldron, Travis. "The Awesome All-Women Crowd at Turkish Soccer Games." *Think Progress*, September 22, 2011. https://thinkprogress.org/the-awesome-all-women-crowd-at-turkish-soccer-games-59599735133/.

Wallraff, Günter. *Ganz unten*. Cologne: Kiepenheuer & Witsch, 1985.

Watson, Wallace Steadman. *Understanding Rainer Werner Fassbinder: Film as Private and Public Art*. Columbia: University of South Carolina Press, 1996.

Weber, Beverly. "Cloth on Her Head, Constitution in Hand: Germany's Headscarf Debates and the Cultural Politics of Difference." *German Politics and Society* 22, no. 3 (2004): 33–64.

Weber, Beverly. *Violence and Gender in the "New" Europe: Islam in German Culture*. New York: Palgrave, 2013.

Westphal, Anke. "Der Genozid und das Schweigen: Fatih Akıns *The Cut.*" *Berliner Zeitung*, September 1, 2014.

Wheatley, Catherine. *Michael Haneke's Cinema: The Ethic of the Image*. New York: Berghahn, 2009.

Wheatley, Catherine. "The Revenge of Children." *Sight and Sound* 19, no. 2 (2009): 14.

White, John. *Westerns*. New York: Routledge, 2011.

White, Patricia. *Women's Cinema, World Cinema: Projecting Contemporary Feminisms*. Durham, NC: Duke University Press, 2015.

White, Rob. "Editor's Notebook: Institutionalized." *Film Quarterly* 65, no. 3 (Spring 2012): 4–6.

White, Rob. "Three Types of Nothing." *Film Quarterly* 63, no. 4 (2010): 4–6.

Wikipedia, s.v. "Bülent Arınç," last modified May 25, 2018, 04:46. https://en.wikipedia.org/wiki/B%C3%BClent_Ar%C4%B1n%C3%A7.

Wikipedia, s.v. "Wir sind das Volk," last modified May 24, 2019. https://de.wikipedia.org/wiki/Wir_sind_das_Volk.

Williams, James S. "Aberrations of Beauty: Violence and Cinematic Resistance in Haneke's *The White Ribbon*." *Film Quarterly* 63, no. 4 (2010): 48–55.

Williams, Linda. "Melodrama Revised." In *Refiguring American Film Genres: History and Theory*, ed. Nick Browne, 42–88. Berkeley: University of California Press, 1998.

Williams, Raymond. *Marxism and Literature*. Oxford: Oxford University Press, 1977.

Wolf, Mark J. P., ed. *Revisiting Imaginary Worlds: A Subcreation Studies Anthology*. New York: Routledge, 2016.

Wollen, Peter. "Godard and Counter-cinema: Vent d'Est." In *Readings and Writings: Semiotic Counter-strategies*, 79–91. London: Verso, 1982.

Yacavone, Daniel. "Film and the Phenomenology of Art: Reappraising Merleau-Ponty on Cinema as Form, Medium, and Expression." *New Literary History* 47, no. 1 (Winter 2016): 159–85.

Yacavone, Daniel. *Film Worlds: A Philosophical Aesthetics of Cinema*. New York: Columbia University Press, 2015.

Zanetta, Julien. "Portrait of a Lady: Painting Emotion in Jean-Luc Godard's *Vivre sa vie*." In *Exploring Text and Emotions*, ed. Lars Saetre, 223–40. Aarhus: Aarhus University Press, 2014.

Zibula, Milan. "Chronik der Gefühle: Reduktion: In Aki Kaurismäki's trübseliger Retrowelt kommt mit der *Anderen Seite der Hoffnung* Realität an." *Freitag*, no. 12/2017 (March 23, 2017). https://www.freitag.de/autoren/der-freitag/chronik-der-gefuehle.

Zola, Émile. *Nana*. Trans. Douglas Parmée. Oxford: Oxford University Press, 2009.

Index

Academy Awards, 55, 176, 187

acting, 78–79, 83–84, 96, 98, 102, 141, 149–50, 251n55

activism, 2–4, 15, 22, 30, 43, 46, 135, 187, 200. *See also* politics; protest

actor-network theory (ANT): 12, 34; and posthumanism, 13; and realism, 155; and worldmaking, 15, 34

actor, film (conceptually), 10, 12, 34; and character, 37, 44, 61, 78–79, 84, 141, 147. *See also* "following the actors," as method

aesthetics: and collectivity, 6, 192; high-affect, 24, 31, 116, 129–30, 138, 157, 162, 187, 201, 207; and genre, 116, 139, 160, 191; modernist, 10, 20, 75–76, 95–96, 160, 230n83, 256n101; phenomenological, 11, 57, 61; political, 25–26, 116, 153, 161, 177, 186, 285n76; realist, 25, 55, 74, 82, 143–49. 159, 161, 178, 187; and visual beauty in cinema, 98, 102, 258n116

affect(s): as asignifying/asubjective, 8, 75, 85; and cinema, 83–84, 97, 120, 211 (*see also* worldmaking); and collectivity, 3, 24, 117, 120–21, 133–35, 198, 211; complexity of, 4, 10, 43–44, 51, 152–53; and contagion, 8, 120; cosmopolitan, 30; definitions of, 9, 96, 225n42; Deleuzian concepts of, 7, 25, 51, 75, 82, 96, 117, 224n29, 225n37; vs. distanciation, 22–23, 74, 95, 230n83; vs. emotions, 7, 47, 224n29, 225n42; and form, 10–11, 241n89; and hatred, 38; incongruity of, 98, 102, 150, 152–53, 160, 162, 164, 167, 208, 246n8 (*see also* complexity: of affects); and narration, 96–97, 173, 180; and nationalism, 3; negative, 2, 18, 44, 75, 77–79, 92, 137, 257n115; performance of, 100; and phenomenology, 82; politics of, 2–3, 133–35, 146, 186, 202–3, 224n33; positive, 75, 150; and racism, 3; and reason in politics, 3; and right-wing ideologies, 17; and sexuality, 78–79, 103; and spectatorship, 11, 35; transcultural, 521

affectscapes, 42–49, 92, 98–99

affect studies, 3, 6, 76, 96, 205, 220n7, 224n33, 226n44; anti-narrative criticism in, 96–97, 225n35; Deleuzian, 6–9, 82, 117, 224n29; and negativity, 96; and sexuality, 79, 103

affective turn: and collectivity debates, 3

affirmation, 26, 90–91, 131–32, 142, 159, 185, 205, 230n84

Agamben, Giorgio, 117, 126

agency: cinematic, 13, 178, 237n40; collective, 12, 13, 15, 34, 178; distributed, 13, 37, 49, 191, 227n56, 227n56, 238n45; divine, 189; human and nonhuman, 12, 13, 15, 33–34, 65, 71, 143, 177, 190–1, 227n55, 228n69, 241n85; nonsovereign, 10, 12–14, 33–34, 37, 71, 88–91, 106, 165, 167–68, 181, 187–88, 197, 199; and posthumanism, 13

Algerian War, 94

Ahmed, Sara, 9, 47, 49, 108, 261n152

Akın, Fatih: and Brechtian techniques, 42; *The Cut*, 24, 31, 113–31, 263n3, 265n34; *The Edge of Heaven* (*Auf der anderen Seite*), 16, 21–22, 29–54, 118, 263n3; *Head On* (*Gegen die Wand*), 30–31; and genre, 30–31, 113

alienation: affective, 29, 96; effect (*Verfremdung*), 32, 81–82, 85, 157

alignment, 39–40, 42, 45–46, 48, 53, 85–86, 99, 128, 162, 166, 173; acentral vs. central, 39, 66, 85–86; piecemeal, 99; spatial, 51–52, 56, 59, 65

allegory, 139–41, 169, 173, 196, 211

Alshater, Firas, 3–5, 7–8, 10, 12, 14, 17, 221n13, 230n90

Althusser, Louis, 76, 135

antimimeticism, 32

anti-Semitism in European politics, 27

apparatus theory, 12, 57, 88, 227n55

archive, 138–9, 147

Arendt, Hannah, 13–14, 228n66, 229n72, 267n52

Arslan, Thomas, 31; *Gold*, 113

Artaud, Antonin, 83, 86, 255n95

arthouse cinema, 5, 112, 115; vs. avant-garde and mainstream cinemas, 5; and genre, 31, 133, 138; and transnational European cinema, 20, 113, 138

artificiality, 98, 140

assemblage: affective, in cinema, 11, 85, 103, 110, 114, 148, 150, 169, 182, 211,

226n44; of collectives, 15, 21, 152, 177, 211, 227n56, 292n41; human-desert, 125–26, objectfull, 25, 159–60, 177, 206; worldmaking as, 10, 13, 32–33, 50-1, 75-76, 97, 148, 167, 193

asylum, 46, 136, 148–49, 152, 240n78

Ataman, Kutluğ: *Lola and Billy the Kid* (*Lola und Bilidikid*), 40

atmosphere, 8, 10, 11, 46, 71, 99

attachments, 3, 5, 29, 76, 95, 101, 104–5, 107, 117, 164–5, 171–72

attention, 67, 69, 79, 98, 105, 106, 129, 142, 157, 239n62, 248n23

audience: 7, 10, 37, 238n55; affect 16, 98, 109, 150; as collective, 120–21, 185; engagement, 30, 33, 35, 39, 48, 51, 55–56, 129, 142, 149, 160, 169 (*see also* alignment); experience 12, 81, 129, 154, 160, 173, 180, 187; feeling, 85, 98; response, 9, 16, 40, 51, 56, 99, 102, 171; as transnational/Western vs. local, 58, 60, 205, 209, 243n124.

auteur cinema, 13, 113–14, 138

authoritarianism, 59, 161, 163, 169–71, 173–74, 211, 220n8

authorship in cinema, 12–13, 37, 89, 94–95, 178, 258n116

autonomy, 11, 13–14, 34, 91, 125, 134, 284n59

Badiou, Alain, 117, 133–36, 143–44, 146, 175–76

Barthes, Roland, 76, 95, 281n20

Bazin, André, 23, 74, 76, 81–84, 116, 120, 158, 178, 249n37; and phenomenology, 75

becoming, 7, 9, 85, 136, 200

belonging: affective, in cinema, 5, 122, 128; as alternative framework to identity, 3; collective, 2–3, 75, 105, 108, 117, 120–22, 124, 130, 134, 167, 198–99, 202 (*see also* collectivity)

Bergfelder, Tim, 30

Berlant, Lauren: and cruel optimism, 165, 172, 253n80; and genre, 133–34; and phenomenology, 79; and sovereignty, 14; and worldmaking, 97–98

collectivity (*continued*)

national, 2, 42–46, 53–54, 86, 94–95, 99, 116; and political resistance, 26, 86, 117, 137, 153–54, 161, 171, 177, 199–212; reimagination of, 5, 21, 28, 92, 199; and religion, 116, 122, 161–62; and transnational cinema, 20, 201; and violence, 3, 5, 17, 76, 86, 95, 104, 107–8, 122–23, 125, 128–31, 136–37, 160, 189, 191–92; and worldmaking, 12–15, 34, 89, 107, 120, 123, 125, 147, 178

colonialism, legacy of, 45, 48, 144–46, 176

comedy, 25, 120, 132, 138, 152–54, 208 272n105, 272n112, 274n140

compassion, 39, 189

complexity: of affects, 4, 10, 47, 86, 134, 152–53; of narration, 31–33, 53, 55, 115, 170, 187; in transnational cinema, 31, 116; and worldmaking, 15, 117, 159, 189

conflict, 95, 102–3, 110, 127, 185–86

continuity, 32, 89, 91, 152, 171; intensified, 31, 156; post-, 121, 161

controversies, social, 15, 21, 25, 34; in cinema, 30, 55, 68, 72, 117, 141, 173–74, 190

conviviality, 21, 30, 93, 122, 131

Coppola, Sofia: *The Virgin Suicides*, 201

cosmopolitanism, 3, 21, 22, 27–29, 57, 62, 187; and collectivity, 28, 94; vernacular, 30; and worlding, 29

cosmopolitics, 29

Coutard, Raoul, 79

creatureliness, 13, 71, 116, 128–29, 146, 177, 181

crisis, refugee. *See* migration

critique, reconfigurative, 17, 21, 35, 211, 231n91; in cinema, 75, 79, 86, 95, 109, 164

crowd, 1, 4, 85, 107, 120–21, 128, 134, 152–53, 192, 199–200, 290n5

cruelty, 86, 109, 112, 167–68, 171–74, 187, 285n68

culturalism, 21, 26, 61–62, 204–6, 219n4, 234n7

curiosity, 33, 41, 42, 54, 62, 81, 85, 146, 248n23

Davrak, Baki, 40

deceleration. *See* rhythm

deconstruction, 115, 119, 155, 231n91

defamiliarization, 23, 75–76, 80–82, 95, 104–5, 109, 141–43, 145, 206, 245n4. *See also Verfremdung*, alienation (effect), distanciation.

Deleuze, Gilles: and affect studies, 7–9, 82, 224n29; and cinema, 9, 15, 82, 84, 153, 159, 271n97; and concepts of affect, 7, 25, 51, 75, 82; and worlding, 6, 8

democracy, 117, 175

desertion, 125–31, 267n48

desire, 78–80, 85, 88–89, 93–94, 98, 102, 107, 120

dialect, 101, 108

dialogue, 38, 104, 116, 152, 163, 192

dialogicity, 35, 238n47

difference: vs. commonality, 28, vs. identity, 3; vs. connection, 54

differences (smaller): 23, 143; and similarities, 37, 100, 106

director, 8, 12–14, 33–35, 55, 60–61, 78, 84, 89, 94, 238n45, 258n116. *See also* auteurs, film; authorship in cinema

disaffection, 42

disruption, 96–97, 98

dissimulation, 58, 68

distance: affective, 30, 35, 50–51, 75, 81, 85, 109, 113, 167, 169–70; of the camera/shot, 35, 38–39, 48, 50, 116, 122–31, 143, 162, 187, 247n13

distanciation: vs. affect, 22–23, 74, 95, 98, 230n83, 250n42; in cinema, 22–23, 32–33, 39, 74–76, 77, 79, 81, 86, 90–91, 93, 157, 167; vs. identification, 39, 81, 86; and narrative, 96, 169–70

documentary: and fiction, 11, 83–84, 148, 156, 156–58, 161–62, 279n8; and narrative cinema, 31, 43, 77, 115, 140–41, 147–50, 176, 281n21. *See also* realism

Dogme 95, 113, 156

Dort, Bernhard, 81–82, 86, 93

Dreyer, Carl: *La passion de Jeanne d'Arc*, 82–83, 86–87

Dyer, Richard, 138

East Germany: democratic reform and protest in, 1–2

Edelman, Lee, 96, 256n101

editing, 10, 32, 70, 102, 160, 169–70, 172, 183, 193, 201, 249n38

embodiment: and cinema, 16, 52, 56–57, 83, 166, 242n116, 288n118; and memory, 44; and movement, 26, 91, 106, 201; and perception, 56–57, 63, 66, 176

emotions: vs. affect, 7, 47, 224n29, 225n42; in cinema, 51–52, 76–77, 84–85, 105, 165, 186; normative, 44; and power, 101, 108, 171–72

empathy: and affective response, 16, 35, 39, 51, 75, 129, 251n55; and camera distance, 51, 127, 169; in cinema, 4, 39, 84–85, 99, 105, 127, 129, 160, 184, 187; cognitive notion of, 39, 51, 84–85, 244n144; critique of, 85; lack of, 44, 99

enfolding, 58–59, 66

epic, 114, 118–21, 123, 129–30

epic theater, 96, 246n8

epoché, 63

Ergüven, Deniz Gamze: *Mustang*, 26, 200–12, 291n15

ethics, 13, 15, 62, 68-69, 73, 90, 116, 127, 128, 160, 162, 177, 180, 187–90, 196

ethnicity, 2, 29, 95, 99, 122, 125–31, 266n42

Europe: concept of, 19; politics in, 54, 136–37, 145–46, 181–82, 195; religion in, 27; transnational cinema of, 19–21, 113, 199

European Union, and Turkey, 45–46, 291n19

event, 52, 133–35, 146, 270n79

fabula, 84, 97–98

face, 79, 83, 87, 92

fairy tale, 24, 114, 117–19, 131–38, 151, 153–54, 205–7, 273n119

Falconetti, Maria, 83–84

fantasy, 14, 38, 106–7

Farhadi, Asghar, 59, 243n124: *A Separation (Jodaí-e Nadér az Simín)*, 16, 21–22, 29, 54–73, 179

Farocki, Harun, 77, 78

fascism, 3, 8, 14, 17, 44, 85, 107, 117, 157, 164, 169, 220n8

Fassbinder, Rainer Werner, 31, 44, 113, 141, 164, 255n95; *Ali - Fear Eats the Soul (Angst essen Seele auf)*, 36–37, 151; and emotions, 101; *Katzelmacher*, 23, 42, 44, 75–76, 94–112, 164, 173; *The Marriage of Maria Braun (Die Ehe der Maria Braun)*, 44; and modernism, 95, 173;

feelings: vs. reason, 3, 76, 246n8; romantic, 101–2, 104, 259n128; sexual, 101–2, 259n128. *See also* affect; emotions

femininity: and melodrama, 127, 208; and objectification, 78–79, 88, 204; and sexuality, 78, 93, 204, 207–9; and solidarity, 70, 93; and victimhood, 36. *See also* gender

feminism, 40, 48, 70, 88–89, 93, 209

fetishization, 79, 92

fiction: and cinematic worlds, 11, 118, 137, 140–41, 148, 186; and documentary, 11, 83–84, 148, 156, 156, 161–62, 176, 279n8

film, vs. cinema, 221n14. *See also* cinema

film noir, 138–9

film theory: of the 1970s, 75–76, 77, 120; and affect, 16; in France, 77, 81

"following the actors," as method, 15–19, 34–35, 55, 62, 66, 72–73, 88–90, 95, 159, 167, 178

Ford, John: *The Searchers*, 119, 124

foreignness, 44, 95, 108

form, in cinema, 6, 8, 10–11, 30–32, 34, 39, 51, 88, 95, 97, 162, 205–6, 238n55, 241n89; genre as, 113, 118, 132, 138, 141–2, 148, 150, 152; realism as, 156-157, 160, 174

formalism, 11, 33, 82

Foucault, Michel, 78, 205, 267n52

France: cinema in, 81; and imperialism, 94; theater of, 81

Freeman, Elizabeth, 97

Freud, Sigmund, 79, 103, 120, 261n152, 274n140

futurity, 18, 96, 99, 100, 110, 111

ideology: 8, 16, 37, 189, 203; and
collectivity, 122, 125, 203; critique of
right-wing, 17, 220n8; and emotion,
76, 224n33; neoliberal 130–1, 189; and
narrative, 77, 132, 205–7
immediacy, 8–9, 25, 55, 74, 81, 85, 134–38,
149, 156–60, 179–80, 184
immigration, 1–2, 36: and collective
identity, 27, 136; collective resistance
to, 2, 234n4; and exile, 29; imaginaries,
41; irregular, 175, 189, 195, 288n119; and
labor, 188–91, 195–96 (*see also* guest
workers); undocumented, 132, 136,
144–45, 147–149, 156, 188–91. *See also*
migration
impasse, 106
imperialism: and cosmopolitanism, 28;
neo-, in Europe, 131; French, 94
Iñárritu, Alejandro González: *Biutiful*,
26, 156–62, 175, 186–98; and complex
narration, 31, 187; oeuvre of, 156, 187;
The Revenant, 113, 128
indexicality, 158–59, 186, 281n20, 281n22
individuality, 80, 86, 123, 126, 129, 146, 184
inequality, 5, 45, 54, 73
intensity: definition, 7, 9; in affect
studies, 7, 96, 202; as effect of
defamiliarization, 82, 95; and the
event, 134-35; in film, 35, 46, 75–76,
79, 86, 98, 100, 116, 120, 128-129, 161,
186, 195; in mediation, 142, 150-1, 179;
political 2; vs. empathy, 51
intention: and worldmaking, 7, 13, 205
interpretation, 5, 21, 67–68, 88, 90, 103–4
intersubjectivity, 57, 66, 85, 160, 192
intertextuality, 10, 34, 37, 86–88, 97, 106,
115, 119, 139, 141, 147
intimacy, 48, 52, 61–62, 104–5, 172, 201, 205
Iran: censorship in, 57, 60; cinema of,
22, 55, 58, 60, 243n124, 244n128;
government of, 59; protest in, 59;
society of, 56, 60
irony, 37, 44, 90, 110–11, 141–42, 256n101,
274n140.
Islam, 27, 36, 59; and gender, 58, 61, 203,
205, 209–210; media discourses on,
36; portrayals of, in film, 36–38, 52, 58,

122, 203, 210; stereotypes of, 36, 58,
205. *See also* Muslims
Islamophobia, 2, 36
Istanbul. *See* Turkey

joy, 3, 8, 26, 64, 121, 134, 137, 143, 150, 152,
164, 202–3
justice, 62, 68–69

Karina, Anna, 78, 83–84, 87, 93, 99,
252n65
Kaurismäki, Aki: and genre cinema, 114,
206. 209; *Le Havre*, 24, 114, 131–38,
138–43; *The Man Without a Past*, 139;
The Other Side of Hope, 24, 114,
136–38, 138–43; *La vie de bohème*, 139
Kazan, Elia: *America America*, 119, 123–24
Klausmann, Rainer, 31, 34, 38, 118, 268n58
Klein, Melanie, 103
Kurds, in Turkey, 43, 49
Kluge, Alexander, 95

Lacan, Jacques, 56, 79, 103
landscapes, 116, 123–26, 128–31, 168
Latour, Bruno: and agency, 12–13, 15, 34,
228n63; and collectivity, 14–15; and
film theory, 6, 30, 158–59; matters of
concern, 158–59, 169–70, 173, 206; and
phenomenology, 13, 228n63, 229n73;
and politics, 25, 117, 135; and realism
in film, 25, 155, 159, 174, 206; and
reference, 158–59, 161–62, 209, 281n22;
and worldmaking, 6, 9, 14, 25, 69, 90,
135, 158, 1 225n37. *See also* "following
the actors," as method
Lean, David, 114
Lee, Spike: *BlacKkKlansman*, 200
Leone, Sergio, 119, 124
lighting, 9, 64, 80, 98, 104, 126, 140, 144
life worlds. *See* worlds
linearity (of narrative; reading; time), 7,
9, 32, 86, 96, 103, 109, 207, 260n140,
261n152
localization, 19–21, 22, 25, 57–58, 61–62,
169–70, 173, 181, 231n93
love, 30, 47, 49, 78, 94, 99, 106, 150, 166,
167, 171, 193

MacCabe, Colin, 78
Makhmalbaf, Mohsen, 59
Malick, Terence: *Days of Heaven*, 119
Marks, Laura, 16, 56–58, 222n20
Marxism, 88, 133
masculinity: hegemonic, 38, 164, 220n8; and sovereignty, 88; and violence, 36, 170–72, 193. *See also* gender; patriarchy
Massumi, Brian, 7–8, 75, 85, 96, 104, 117, 133–36, 153–54, 202–3, 224n29 and n33, 291n16
matters of concern, 158–60, 162, 169–70, 173, 206
medium (specificity), 81–82, 158–59
mediation: foregrounded, 118–19, 141–43, 147, 178–79, 185; and worldmaking, 9, 34, 82, 138–43, 150, 158–59, 178–79, 225n34, 271n91, 274n129
melodrama, 95, 114, 127–28, 130, 138, 142, 187, 208, 268n56, 288n116.
memory, 24, 44, 58, 97
Mennel, Barbara, 30
Merleau-Ponty, Maurice, 56, 65
mess, 98–99, 103, 109, 258n118
methodology, 5–6, 15–19, 35, 55, 57–58, 79, 88, 103, 159, 204–5
migration: and cinema, 20, 60–61, 64, 125, 175–76, 177, 181–82, 184, 186–98; European "crisis" of, 20, 25, 28, 36, 136–37, 139, 145–46, 157, 161, 174–86, 195; irregular, 156, 175, 189, 195, 288n119; media discourses on, 36, 40, 287n102. *See also* immigration
mise-en-scène, 10, 55, 63, 65–66, 70, 98, 102, 106, 110, 116, 122, 139–41, 144-45, 149
modernism: aesthetics of, 75–76, 116, 157, 256n101; and cinema, 20, 22, 33, 35, 75, 77, 95–96, 138; and narration, 10, 96–97, 225n35
modernity, Euro-American, 2, 146, 205
modesty (prescriptions/standards), 60, 66
money, 101–2, 196
montage, 8, 92, 96–97, 116, 150, 160–61, 169–70, 186–88, 193-97, 226n44, 256n100

de Montaigne, Michel, 90
mood, 71, 92, 130, 137, 151, 152, 193, 195, 208, 245n149
movement, bodily, 31, 91, 98-100, 106, 129, 145, 150, 153, 156, 200, 202–3
multiculturalism, 27; death of, 28
multitude, 134, 200, 211, 251n52
multivectorality (narrative/worldmaking), 10, 33, 37, 86, 97-99, 104, 114, 205, 207
Mulvey, Laura, 77–78, 79–80, 86, 96, 120
music, 32, 53, 94, 98, 106, 110–11, 129–30, 139, 150–54, 183
musical, 25, 137–38, 150–54
Muslims: and bare life, 127; hatred against, 28, 35–36; integration of, 40. *See also* Islam

narration: as assemblage, 10, 51, 148, 150, 178, 192; classical forms of, 32, 33, 54, 114, 118, 237n36, 237n38; and cognition, 32, 239n59; elliptical, 188, 193, 195; foregrounded, 22, 30, 31, 33–35, 36–37, 42, 46–47, 49, 53, 73–74, 118, 179–80, 185; linear, 32, 207; multivectoral, 10, 33, 37, 86, 97, 104, 109, 114, 148, 205; nonsovereign, 22, 33–35, 160, 168; and temporality, 95, 99
narrative: and complexity, 31–33, 53, 114, 164, 170, 187, 192; critical opposition to, 8, 96–97; definition of, 9; and ideology, 77, 132, 205; and simplicity, 114, 132; worldmaking, 6–7, 9–10, 29, 31, 171, 192–93, 229n78
narrator, 37, 160, 67–69, 171–72, 206
nation, 18, 20, 49, 53, 86, 94–95, 116, 134, 136, 220n8; and affect, 44
nationalism: 2; and affect, 3, 109, 211; and collective closures, 7, 19, 108, 117, 174, 176, 211
negative affect, 2, 18, 44, 75, 77–79, 92, 137, 257n115
negativity: and affect studies, 96; and cinema, 77, 79, 132, 274n140; and modern politics, 2, 44
neoliberalism: 2, 27, 134, 211; in education, 18; ideology of, 130–31; and precarity, 26, 187–89,

neorealism, 55, 74, 82, 245, 157, 245n2

neuroscience, 84, 103, 132, 134

Nuevo Cine Mexicano, 156

New German Cinema, 44, 257n110

new materialisms, 155

New Wave (*Nouvelle Vague*), French, 81

nonhuman agency, and cinema, 13, 15, 33–34, 49, 63, 177, 208241n85

nonsovereignty: of actors/agency, 10, 12–16, 37, 71, 88–91, 127, 181-84, 187–190, 192, 197, 199; in cinema, 14, 16–17, 54, 57, 64–65, 147, 207; of narration, 22, 25, 33–34, 160, 167–70, 284n59; of perception: 22, 55, 57, 65, 179. *See also* perception

objectfullness, 25, 159–60, 171, 173–74, 192, 197–98

objectification, 88, 90, 162

Ong, Aihwa, 28

ontology, 9, 14, 82, 122, 125, 134, 155–56, 159, 225n37, 280n14; film/media 81, 158–59; ontological pluralism, 190

openness, affective, 4, 44, 49; structural, 6, 140

optimism, 97, 111, 131–32, 137, 150, 154, 160, 253n80

Orientalism, 58, 204–5

orientation, affective, 17, 39–40, 42, 44, 66, 72, 87, 97, 129, 153, 268n61

Other, the, 62, 90, 116

Pabst, G.W.: *Pandora's Box*, 87, 92

pain, 91, 104, 106, 136, 154, 173, 177, 191

Panahi, Jafar, 59, 203

Parain, Brice, 93

paranoia, 16, 56, 79, 230n83

parody, 37, 41, 142

patriarchy, 23, 38, 40, 61, 76, 79, 88–89, 94–95, 99, 166, 210

"people, the": in cinema, 24–25, 117, 136, 153, 175, 199, 271n97, 292n42; as a political slogan, 1, 219n2

perception: as embodied, 66, 72; and film, 10, 16, 57–59, 61–62, 66, 71, 224n34; multisensory, 56, 174; nonsovereign,

22, 55, 57, 65, 179; partial, 66–68; poetics of, 61, 63; as social, 58; and vision, 65–66, 193

performance, 39, 44–45, 77, 84, 91–92, 100, 138, 141, 150–51, 166, 184, 283n45; of affect, 100, 166

performativity, 9, 100, 164, 292n41

Petzold, Christian, 31

phenomenological close-up (poetics of), 16, 55

phenomenological realism, 31, 74, 113, 245n2

phenomenology: and affect, 9, 82, 222n19; and cinema, 22, 56–57, 73, 75–76, 79, 129, 156, 244n144; and nonsovereign agency, 13–14; and reading, 79; and temporality, 95; and worldmaking, 6, 9, 12

physicality, 6, 26, 106, 166, 201–2; and collectivity, 153, 183, 200

pity, 39, 117, 129

planetary humanism, 22, 49

pleasure, 16, 37, 47, 91, 97, 98, 107, 120, 136, 142, 146, 150, 165, 246n8, 248n21.

Poe, Edgar Allen, 87–88

point of view, 39, 42, 53, 65, 89, 91, 178

politics: and activism, 30, 43, 46, 135, 210; and aesthetics, 25–26, 116, 153, 161, 174, 186, 285n76; of affect, 2–3, 133–35, 146, 186, 202–3, 224n33; and cosmopolitanism, 29, 72; and identity, 18, 29, 52, 78, 136, 235n16; and sexuality, 78–79, 204

positionality, 48, 53, 63, 72

positive affect, 75, 150. *See also* joy; optimism

post-Brechtianism, 22, 42, 164, 206

postcolonialism, 27, 40; and nationalism, 28

postcritique, 16, 17, 35, 204

posthumanism: and agency, 13, 37, 127, 234; and collectivity, 3, 125

postmodernism: and narration, 54, 173–74; and representation, 155, 159

postsecularism, 27–28, 233n3

Propp, Vladimir, 132

protest: Black Lives Matter movement, 200; in film, 37–38, 43, 200; Gezi Park, 26, 200, 210; in Iran, 59; Occupy movement, 135, 200

proximity: aesthetics of, 35, 156; affective, 39, 89; critical 231n91

psychoanalysis: and affect, 103, 225n42; and film theory, 16, 56, 78–79, 96, 120, 239n62, 244n144; and nonsovereign agency, 12

psychology, 83, 85, 120

puzzle plots, 32, 68

queerness, 47, 98, 151, 195, 257n114, 277n170

queer studies, 47, 96–97, 248n21

racialization, 27, 47, 144, 181

racism: and affect, 3, 8, 10, 18, 152, 219n3; and cosmopolitanism, 29; in film, 53, 152–54, 187–88, 195–96, 273n119, 275n148; in Germany, 10, 233n2. *See also* foreignness; xenophobia

Rancière, Jacques: and democracy, 117, 175; and political aesthetics, 25–26, 161, 174, 250n42, 285n76; and the sensible, 5, 24, 26, 54, 72, 116, 174–75, 197

reading: and affect, 16, 230n83; close, 5, 11, 97, 252n69; literal, 90; modes of, 57–58, 77; multisensorial, 10, 16, 18; multivectoral, 97, 205, 260n140; postcritical, 16–17, 35, 204, 230n83, phenomenological, 79; psychological, 84; symptomatic, 96, 103; thick, 104. *See also* reconfiguration; suspicion

realism: in cinema, 74, 82–83, 117, 127, 137, 144–47, 155–98, 201, 249n37, 388n116; documentary, 25, 140, 147, 158, 161–62, 175–77, 186, 281n20; phenomenological, 31, 74, 113, 245n2; (re)turns to, 155; speculative, 155; subjective, 129, 156, 189–90, 192

reason vs. feeling, 3, 76, 246n8

reception: of Brecht, 23, 76; in cinema, 5, 10, 12, 16, 58, 114, 160, 205, 207, 221n14, 238n45. *See also* audience

reconfiguration: critique as, 17–18, 21, 23, 35, 205; cinematic worldmaking/narration as, 10–11, 52, 54, 55, 97, 161, 188, 198

reference: and cinematic worlds, 12, 34, 141, 161–62, 206, 209, 227n50, 227n52, 281n22; and indexicality, 158–59

reflexivity, 76, 86, 89, 91, 115, 118–19, 122, 138, 155, 173

refugees: in cinema, 119, 125–31, 136–37, 139–49, 157, 179–80, 287n102; and "crisis" (*see* migration); reception of, in Germany, 1, 14, 45, 234n4; status of, 46, 136

religion: in America, 201; and collectivity, 116–17, 122, 161–62, 169, 176, 189–90, 195; in Europe, 27; in film, 36–38, 52, 58, 67, 86, 146–47, 161, 210; persecution based on, 58; and secularism in society, 62, 233n3; and worldmaking, 72

Renoir, Jean, 87

resistance, 5, 18, 26, 36, 43, 52, 86, 106, 117, 161, 171, 198–212

revolution, 43, 52, 117, 133–35, 141, 146, 199–212

rhythm, in cinema, 98–100, 104, 109, 141

Rimbaud, Arthur, 90

romance, 47, 101–102, 106–7, 150, 259n130

Romanian "new wave," 113

Rosi, Gianfranco: *Fire at Sea* (*Fuocoammare*), 25, 156–61, 175–86, 191

Rude, Jadu: *Bravo!*, 113

rupture, 24, 51, 95–96, 116–17, 131, 135, 169, 225n35

Sacotte, Marcel, 92

Schanelec, Angela, 31

Schubert, Franz, 110

Schygulla, Hanna, 44, 99, 110, 111

scientific paradigms: in the humanities, 18

Scorsese, Martin, 119

secularism: 22, 27, 40, 58, 62, 204, 209, 233n3

Sedgwick, Eve, 103, 142, 230n83
Seigworth, Gregory J., 9
sensation: in cinema, 8–11, 13, 16, 31, 82, 178, 186, 192, 198, 201, 207
September 11, 2001, 28, 36
Serner, Walter: *Kino und Schaulust*, 120
sex: in cinema, 46–47, 79, 90, 99, 101, 171; and money, 101–102; work, 36–37, 74–75, 78, 88–92, 102, 104, 108, 251n59, 252n80, 259n130
sexuality: and affect, 47, 78–79; and cinema, 46–47, 74, 78, 88, 120; and identity, 78–79; and violence, 76, 123, 171–72, 193, 277n174; and women, 78, 88, 107, 204, 209
Shaviro, Steven, 7–8, 16, 224n34
shame, 38
Shklovsky, Viktor, 82
shock, 102, 160, 191, 193, 256n101
shot: -countershot, 66, 93, 149, 160, 174, 188, 284n54; frontal, 95, 107, 144, 184–85; length, 89. *See also* camera; cinematography; mise-en-scène
de Sica, Vittorio: *Bicycle Thieves*, 157; *Miracle in Milan*, 139, 147, 153
Silverman, Kaja, 77–78, 80, 88
simplicity, 114–15, 128, 132
situation, 97, 99
Smith, Murray, 39, 76, 85
Sobchack, Vivian, 9, 16, 56–58, 62, 66, 242n116
solidarity, 5, 70, 72, 93, 117, 130–31, 135–37, 141, 151–54, 188–89, 197; translocal, 20, 30
sovereignty: 13–14; and cosmopolitanism, 28; and masculinity, 88; and narration, 33–35
Spain, immigration politics in, 189
speculative realism, 155
spectacle, 41, 78, 81, 97, 127–29, 144
spectatorship, 6, 7, 10–11, 15–16, 35, 40, 56, 58, 77, 81, 85, 205
story-telling. *See* narration; worldmaking
story world, 6
Straub, Jean-Marie, 95
subjection, 77–79, 91, 239n62

suspicion, 35, 56–58, 62, 67, 79, 81, 204–5, 231n91
sympathy: concept(s), 3, 7, 39, 85; in film, 16, 39, 99, 109, 142-7, 176, 184, 195, 230n89, 239n64, 245n144

Tarantino, Quentin: *The Hateful Eight*, 128
temporality: and historical period, 139–40; and narration, 95–97, 118, 281n21
theater: Brecht and, 76, 81–82; and emotions, 76
theatricality, 75, 104 140–41, 142, 144; charges of, 83, 88; realism vs., 155, 157, 160, 178
thick description, 59, 260n140;
tragedy, 51, 190, 191
transnational cinema, 5, 19–21, 58–59, 139, 232n101, 243n124; as localized, 19, 53; and narrative complexity, 31, 115
transnationalism: definition of, 20, 232n101; and movement, 54
Trump, Donald, 2, 18, 28, 219n3, 229n74
truth, 68–69, 93–94, 117, 157, 159–60, 168, 171
Turkey: and the European Union, 45–46, 291n19; in film, 30, 41, 42–43, 50, 201, 203; and historical narration, 119; leftist activism in, 30; and the Ottoman Empire, 119, 122, 265n26, 265n34; political resistance in, 36, 43, 115, 204, 209; relationship with Germany, 41, 47, 119, 233n2; secularism in, 27, 209, 233n2;

universalism, 3, 21, 22, 28, 45, 49, 62–63, 85

Verfremdung, 81–82, 85, 206. *See also* Brecht, Bertolt; alienation; defamiliarization; distanciation.
violence: and collectivity, 2–3, 28, 76, 86, 95, 107–9, 116, 122–124, 129, 160, 169-173; exposure to systemic, 177, 181, 188–89; in film, 38, 52, 68, 78, 98–104, 127–29, 191–195, 197, 211; and sexual desire, 103, 106, 123, 171–72

vision: cinematic, 16, 56–57; and
perception, 62–63, 65–66, 175,
178–79
voice-over, 25, 157, 160, 163, 167–68, 178,
201, 210
voyeurism, 66, 128, 178

War on Terror, 27, 36, 177, 185
West, the, 27, 176, 181, 205
West Germany. *See* Germany
western (genre), 24, 113–14, 124–25,
129
White, Rob, 57
white supremacy: in American politics,
2, 18, 200
widescreen format, 24, 31, 114, 116, 123,
128–29, 267n45
women: in cinema, 77–78, 86, 87, 166,
202–3; and sexuality, 78, 204. *See also*
femininity; gender
world cinema, 19
worlds: in cinema, 11, 19, 99, 115, 125,
140, 167, 172 (*see also* worldmaking);
fictional vs. real, 11, 34, 140, 148, 159;
and multiplicity, 14, 87; as shared, 53,
62, 76, 93, 125, 143, 159, 161, 173–74,
187, 197, 229n74; terminology, 6; vs.
"the world," 21, 34

worlding, 6, 8, 125, 134, 228n68,
228n69,256n103
worldmaking: affective cinematic, 9–11,
13, 37, 39, 75, 84–86, 140–41, 212; and
affect studies, 6; assemblages, 10–11,
13, 18, 32–33, 75, 85–86, 97, 103, 114,
119, 205; cognitive models of, 6–7;
collective, 12–13, 34, 89, 154, 178, 184,
201, 204; and complexity, 15, 55, 59,
114, 117, 159–60, 189; and conflict,
95; in contemporary cinema, 32,
141, 212; definition of, 10; and genre,
24, 148, 160; and intertextuality, 10,
34, 119–20, 139; methodology of, 18,
225n37; narrative, 9, 97, 118–19, 173;
nonsovereign, 16, 54–55, 57, 64–65,
68, 90, 115, 117, 160, 207; notions of,
6; realist, 157–58, 161, 164, 195, 197;
and religion, 72; rhythm, 104, 109;
and transnational cinema, 21, 32
World War I, 119, 157, 168
World War II, 140

xenophobia, 75–76, 103

Yacavone, David, 6, 11, 12

Zola, Émile, 87